MODERN SHIP DESIGN

MODERN SHIP DESIGN

by

Thomas C. Gillmer

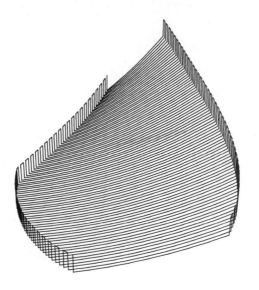

Second Edition

Naval Institute Press
Annapolis, Maryland

Library of Congress Card No. 74-25031

ISBN 0-87021-388-1

Endpaper photograph courtesy of Litton Industries.

All photographs not otherwise credited are official U. S. Navy.

MANUFACTURED IN THE UNITED STATES OF AMERICA

Foreword

Strong naval and merchant fleets are essential for a nation's survival, as the history of the United States bears out. Without skilled and knowledgeable men to design and construct our ships, however, there would be neither a navy nor a merchant marine.

Naval architecture and marine engineering, by definition and application, encompass both the merchant and naval fleets. The progress and development of these sciences have been directly affected by the needs of the times. For instance, in a period of international emergency or trade expansion, there has always been an acceleration of the training of ship designers and the adoption of new design and construction techniques. During the Civil War, steam replaced sail, and wood gave way to iron and steel. During both world wars the concepts of mass production were successfully applied to the shipyards. Even now, the naval and merchant fleets are undergoing change in response to contemporary events.

The modern merchant vessel is not as complicated or sophisticated as today's naval vessel. However, the design and construction of both have the structure of the ship in common. Both require a hull that will float and that is compatible with the power plant required to propel the ship at the speed and with the stability desired. After this has been determined, naval and merchant vessels begin to differ markedly. Just as the needs of national defense determine the design and construction of naval vessels, so do the needs of merchants and consumers dictate commercial design. The commercial design must result in a vessel that will carry the maximum amount of cargo and will efficiently and safely house the crew. The naval design must provide a ship with the weapons and communications systems that will best serve her mission.

This treatise on ship design is responsive to present needs and is extremely timely. It relates the physical laws and principles of ship architecture and construction to the newest possibilities of hull design and propulsion. The author evaluates the feasibility and utilization of gas turbines, nuclear power, and automation. He recognizes that the use of lightweight metals and modern materials results in more speed and a more versatile ship than complete reliance on older materials would permit. Likewise, he explores the contributions of the hydrofoil and the air cushion concepts.

As the naval architects and marine engineers of this generation proceed to their drawing boards, laboratories, model basins, and shipyards, they will be equipped with some of the finest tools and techniques ever conceived by man. The United States Navy and our merchant marine can only profit from their efforts.

Chairman
Federal Maritime Commission

HELEN DELICH BENTLEY

Preface to the Second Edition

Since publication of the first edition of this book, many changes have occurred, especially in the field of computer-aided design and in the areas of ship research, which have prompted additions to this second edition of *Modern Ship Design*.

The use of computers in ship design and construction had not yet produced a great impact in the United States five or six years ago. At that time, a large share of this type of material for the first edition was obtained only by travel to and study at European shipbuilding centers. While the United States has always been a world leader in computer technology, the specific application of it to ship construction had not, by 1969, expanded in this country as it had in countries more oriented to the shipbuilding industry.

Now, however, it is most gratifying that the United States is assuming a role of leadership in computer-aided design and that one of the leading centers is located here in Annapolis. Dr. John C. Gebhardt, of CADCOM, Inc., has obligingly contributed the major portion of the new Chapter 14, and this treatment may well be the best statement on the use of computers in naval architecture and shipbuilding yet expressed anywhere.

The remaining chapters have undergone intensive scrutiny and in some cases considerable revision. They have also been reordered in a new sequence that is believed better adapted to logical and developing study. New illustrations and diagrams have been added or substituted. The ship's hydrostatic curves have been enlarged for easier reading and example use and inserted in a back pocket. Also, the appendixes have been enlarged with additional material which it is hoped will be useful reference.

The success of the first edition of *Modern Ship Design* encourages me to say that I think this new edition promises to be equally useful. It will provide a sustained source of modern ship design practice.

THOMAS C. GILLMER

Annapolis, Maryland
January, 1975

Preface to the First Edition

Throughout the preparation of this book, the author has been aware of the formidable scope of the field of modern ship design and of the difficulty of placing the various elements in proper and realistic perspective. Such a task has become compounded in the past decade, primarily because of the great increase in new ship tonnage and the additional complexities of ships produced in an era of space-age technology. It is of some interest, therefore, in this expanding and important profession to provide an introductory review of the current state of the art.

Such an introduction as this must contain not only discussions of the new techniques but also the basic theories and foundations of the art and science of naval architecture. These elements are everlasting and consist of the physical theories of buoyancy, stability, fluid resistance, and mechanics as they apply to ships. They are presented on the following pages in a rather fundamental sense for a beginning student who, in acquiring these principles, will have the basis for both specialized applications and for more comprehensive courses to follow.

There is no pretense that this book is to be a textbook of naval architecture. There are other books that have had this distinction, and when they were written, perhaps twenty to forty or more years ago, it was possible to encompass the theories and methods of designing a ship in a single volume. It would be impossible in today's technology to do this. It is indeed becoming difficult, because of the complexities of modern ships and their advancing configurations and systems, to even circumscribe the areas of knowledge expected of a naval architect.

At any rate, it is not the intention here to provide this professional knowledge in all specific areas of required competency. It *is* the intention however, to introduce to the serious student of ship design the general scope of these areas and to provide some perspective to the various tasks of the ship designer.

Because this book will probably find its greatest use at the U.S. Naval Academy, the emphasis is primarily upon the procedures and interests surrounding the design of naval vessels. This accounts somewhat for the more extensive notations on stability, vulnerability, submarine statics, research, etc., and the inconsiderable notice of American Bureau of Shipping Rules, for example. This is not, however, to deny the significance of other than naval vessels or to subordinate the position of merchant ships in any way. It is indeed difficult to distinguish between some naval vessels and merchant vessels. The logistics required by the modern Navy, the varied theaters of operation, the research and development of new and bizarre types of craft—all this seems to remove any categorical classification of *naval* ships.

There are in operation in today's Navy, in addition to the warcraft types and the traditional and ubiquitous supply vessels, high-speed logistics ships, large bulk carriers of oil, trawler-like research vessels, small deep-submergence vessels, high-speed, seagoing hydrofoil craft, air cushion craft, multi-hulled vessels, and prosaic types too numerous to mention. With this multiplicity of watercraft, it is quite natural that the Navy may be considered the great showcase for all types of ships, and a *naval ship* is representative of all ships and the best of ships. The theories and principles of resistance, powering, ship control, buoyancy, stability, ship motions, and ship strength are those principles applying to all ships alike. These are the basis for understanding the ways of ships and the means for their design.

It has become rather common to regard a naval ship as a *weapon*. While this may be only another controversy of semantics, it would seem worthwhile for our purpose here to emphasize that a ship is a ship most fundamentally. It may be thought of, as indeed it is, a system; a ship system if you will, but it is far more than a weapon, or a weapon system. Take away its offensive power, striking capability, or whatever makes a weapon, and you still will have a ship—a ship no less capable of moving in a sea, of being self-sufficient on the seas, a secure, seaworthy habitat of transport across the oceans—this is the identity of a ship. It is an historic concept.

Annapolis, Maryland   THOMAS C. GILLMER

Acknowledgments

For the invaluable assistance and cooperation given the author during the research for and preparation of the manuscript, the following people are especially to be mentioned: Rear Admiral Jamie Adair, U.S. Navy, Director, Ship Acquisitions, Naval Ship Systems Command, U.S. Navy Department; Rear Admiral Randolph W. King, U.S. Navy, Deputy Commander for Research and Development, Naval Ship Systems Command; Captain W. L. Pryor, U.S. Navy (retired), General Dynamics Corp., Electric Boat Division; Mr. J. S. Petersen, Senior Naval Architect, Burmeister and Wain; Dr. J. H. Van Riet, Managing Director, Blohm and Voss, A.G.; Dr. Ake Jacobsson, Director, Swedish Shipbuilder's Computing Center; Mr. W. Vollert, Director and Chairman, Swedish Shipbuilder's Association; Dr. Masao Kinoshita, Director and Manager, Research Laboratory, Hitachi Shipbuilding and Engineering Company; Dr. Y. Yamanouchi, Director, Ship Dynamics Division, Ship Research Institute of Japan.

The author is also indebted to the following corporations and institutions for their generosity in providing illustrative and descriptive material relating to their activities: General Dynamics Corp.; Maryland Shipbuilding and Drydock Co.; Avondale Shipyards, Inc.; Newport News Shipbuilding and Drydock Co.; Litton Industries (Ingalls Shipyard); North American Rockwell Corp.; General Dynamics (Quincy Shipyard); American Stern Trawler's Association; Stal-Laval Turbin AB; British Hovercraft Corp. Ltd.; Blohm and Voss, A.G.; Swedish Shipbuilder's Computing Centre; Ship Research Institute, Ministry of Transport, Japan.

In the preparation of the second edition the author found that there were several critical areas in the world of ship design which in the context of this book would be more enhanced through the helpful advice and suggestions from several of the new generation of practitioners in the profession.

The very valuable contribution by Dr. John Gebhardt in the discussions of computerization in Chapter 14 has already been noted in the Preface. In the areas of ship research and the progressing knowledge of ship motion the material has been updated through the helpful interest and information provided by Dr. Roger C. Compton, of the Naval Academy faculty.

Dr. Bruce Johnson of the Naval Engineering Department has most helpfully kept the author up to date on the progress of, and supplied with illustrations of the magnificent new towing tank facility which is nearing completion in the new engineering building and which was but an embrionic plan and hope during my last faculty years.

All of my former colleagues in the faculty of Naval Engineering have most helpfully supported the effort which was needed to keep this publication continued and to justify the terminology of its title.

Contents

MODERN SHIP DESIGN

A Water-jet Propelled Navy Hydrofoil

The Boeing Company

CHAPTER 1

The Modern Ship Concept

There is a statement in the original preface of this book concerning the historic concept and identity of a "ship." This is a valid idea and, perhaps, since readers or users of books so seldom read the preface it is worth briefly repeating. Broadly stated, it describes a ship as a habitat of transport capable of moving in a sea and across the oceans and being self-sufficient, secure and seaworthy. This statement is recognizable as being most general and surrounded by elements of conditional relativity. Yet it is a fundamental idea and a good basis upon which to build the subsequent discussions, not only in this chapter but throughout the entire book.

The ship concept in a conventional sense is a matter of an inner image of those who regard it or reflect upon it and the image may be fuzzy or clear or disproportionate in one characteristic or another, all depending upon the individual's interests. In this discussion and in the involvement of this book a serious and concerned attempt will be made to see this ship as a whole and integrated concept, recognizing in it the developments and growth of modern technology and at the same time giving little credence or attention to the fads and the novelties often passing in the name of "modern progress."

There are many varied and confusing ship configurations (one is tempted here to refer to them as "seagoing systems" but this sort of reference will be delayed to later in the chapter), but when the purpose and employment of these shape-identities are understood, hopefully the confusion will clear. It is first perhaps a matter to be categorized, logically, according to the fundamental force systems by which the hull is supported in or on the water.

Ships Typed According to Physical Support

We will assume that the mode of support by which the vessels are categorized embodies this support when the vessel is operating in its designed functional manner. Using the most basic reference datum, the surface of the sea, ships are designed to operate above, on, and or below this datum. Because of the very diverse physical phenomena in these various spheres of operation, the consequent physical characters and configurations of the ships are similarly diversified.

AEROSTATIC SUPPORT

Beginning just above the sea's surface datum, there are vessels designed to move and cruise smoothly slightly above it, supported by a self-induced cushion of air. Remarkably, these are called *air cushion vehicles* (or vessels) and in a limited sense they are amphibious (figure 1–1).

Resolving the categories to a degree of greater association with the sea and its surface effect we can next identify a type supported also by a self-induced air cushion but whose air cushion is contained and directed by the configuration of the vessel's hull. This is a *captured air bubble vessel,* or CAB. The cushion of low pressure air is here allowed to build up in the underbody chamber by the vessel's forward advance and is contained along the sides by the hull's rigid side "curtains," or thin downward-projecting hull edges. These types of air cushion vehicles are not amphibious (figure 1–2).

Bell Aero Space Co., Division of Textron

Figure 1–1. A One-hundred Ton Surface Effect Ship, an *Air Cushion Vehicle* (ACV), Making a Test Run. These vessels are supported on a cushion of relatively low pressure air supplied by ducted internal fans. They are propelled at potential speeds up to 80 knots by turbine-driven water jets.

Figure 1–2. Another Type of Surface Effect Ship, a Captured Air-Bubble Vehicle (CAB), is supported on a cushion of air which is screened at the sides by the rigid side structure of the vessel.

In the two types of air cushion craft identified above the support is by the self-induced, low pressure cushion of air below and acting upon the broad structure of the vessel. They basically are *air buoyant* and the pressure acting upward on the bottom of the craft results in a net lifting force which separates the hull from water. This separation allows the vehicle to move horizontally in the desired direction, using either aircraft type propulsion or water jets and thus avoiding the restrictive drag through the water. This elimination of water drag is essentially the basis of reasoning which justifies these air-supported types of watercraft. The technological theory and detailed descriptions of these vessels, as well as the theories of water resistance, will be explored at some length in one of the chapters to follow.

HYDRODYNAMIC SUPPORT

Continuing to type basic ship categories according to the nature of their support upon the water,

we must next recognize the idea of *dynamic support* generated by relatively rapid forward motion of particular rigid shapes on the water's surface or penetrating the surface. Like an airplane wing cuts through the air as an airfoil, a similar foil cutting through water produces a considerable upward lift. Struts or supports attached to these foils are the "legs" that hold the vessel's hull above the water and the identity of this system naturally and commonly is regarded as a *hydrofoil* (figure 1–3).

The next and less efficient means of dynamic support is that which is most common among small craft. These dynamically supported waterborne craft are recognized, again, by a particular hull configuration. They are known as *planing hulls*. The bottoms are of flat dihedral (shallow *V* section) surfaces which give vertical lift and at the same time provide directional tendency. Planing craft are generally restricted in size because of the enormous power plants and structural stresses

Figure 1–3. The USS Plainview, a large (320-ton) Hydrofoil-Supported Vessel. These craft are the fastest and have the best seakeeping potential of the various hydrodynamically supported vessels.

Figure 1–4. The HMS Tenacity, a Fast Fisheries Patrol Vessel, is essentially a planing hull. A large example of this type, she is 142 feet long, powered by gas turbines, and capable of 40-knot speeds. She was originally intended as a fast surface-to-surface missile carrier.

involved in the larger hulls. Their operation is also restricted to a reasonably flat water surface (figure 1–4).

HYDROSTATIC SUPPORT

Finally, slowing down the speed of the types of vessels and noting the ultimate type of support, the oldest and most reliable, we can identify ships of *hydrostatic support*. All ships and boats and primitive watercraft up until the twentieth century have depended upon the easily attained buoyant force of water for their operation.

This hydrostatic support, which is commonly recognized as *flotation,* is based on a fundamental physical law that was clearly defined by the ancient philosopher-mathematician Archimedes, in the second century B.C. Paraphrasing his statement (which is known generally as *Archimedes' Principle*), it is said that a body immersed in a liquid is buoyed up (or acted upon) by a force which is equal to the weight of the liquid displaced. This principle, then, applies to all vessels which float (or submerge) in water, salt or otherwise. And from this statement the name of the ship type or category identity is derived, being generally called *displacement* types or *displacement* hulls.

The type is so common and familiar that it would seem to need no further discussion; however, it will be most appropriate if we examine displacement ships more closely beyond a simple introduction.

There are subcategories which are of sufficient diversion of type and standardization of configuration to warrant special discussion. For example, there are some vessels in which the desirability of reasonably high speed be combined with the ability to move more comfortably in rough water than a planing hull, or carry light cargo, armament or other reasonable payloads. High-speed planing hull characteristics can be modified to produce a semidisplacement hull or semiplaning hull (figure 1–5). Such compromise craft will of course not be as fast as full planing hulls but will be faster than conventional displacement hulls, but must carry more power and less weight than the latter. Such types are obviously the result of "trade-offs" and it might be said that this is the rationale that produces any variation from the design norm.

The example cited above is an obvious "compromise" or a transitory category between clear-cut physically defined categories—it is not a good example of a variation of a true displacement type ship. Such variations must be recognized as primarily displacement vessels, and the variations depend primarily on the distribution of buoyant volume—the extent of the depth and breadth of the hull below the water.

Beginning with the most ubiquitous type of ship in the displacement category, it can be generally classified as the *common carrier*—a *seagoing vessel*. It may be employed in passenger service, light general cargo carrying, fishing by trawling, or hundreds of other tasks which do not require exceptional capacity, speed, submergence or other special performance (figure 1–6). It is simply the most common and easily recognizable type of ship; moderate displacement, moderate speeds, moderate to large lengths, and moderate capacities. It generally but not necessarily embodies the maximum in cruising range and seaworthiness. It is the "ship for all seasons." It is the standard to which all other ship classifications in the displacement category may be referred (figure 1–7).

The nearest relative to the above standard is nearly as common and in the "modern" context has attained the status of a product of critical importance not only to world commerce but to the survival of the industrial world. It is of course the

Figure 1–5. USS Welsh, a Fast Navy Gunboat, is capable of planing speeds but has a combination power plant more economical for cruising at lower speeds. She thus operates as a semi-planing hull.

Swan-Hunter Shipbuilders, Ltd.

Figure 1–6. The Handsome and Conventional Displacement Ship Vistafjord. She is an excellent example of a modern luxury ship designed as a passenger cruise ship, one of the last examples of a disappearing type, the seagoing passenger ship.

Swan-Hunter Shipbuilders, Ltd.

Figure 1–7. The Hard-Working and Valuable Displacement Ship SS Remura, currently the **fastest cargo ship in the world, is capable of sustained cruising speeds of 25 knots.**

Figure 1–8. The Heaviest and Largest of All Displacement Ships, the Crude Oil Tanker. Sometimes referred to as Large Crude Carriers and Very Large Crude Carriers, such ships are built as large as one-half-million tons capacity.

bulk oil carrier, the tanker or supertanker (figure 1–8). These terminologies are common but unspecific and in this discussion they are inadequate, for what was called a supertanker four to five years ago is today not a supertanker. The industry itself has created a far more explicit nomenclature. Based upon the index of 100,000 tons oil cargo capacity, the size categories are LCC, VLCC and ULCC; meaning consecutively Large Crude Carrier, Very Large Crude Carrier, and Ultra Large Crude Carrier. Any greater than 100,000 tons but less than 200,000 is a LCC, those between 200,000 and 400,000 are VLCC's and those over 400,000 are ULCC's. The current necessity for these designations becomes clearly significant when we realize that before 1956 there were no tankers larger than 50,000 tons, and not until the early sixties were any ships built larger than 100,000 tons. 1968 saw the first ship over 300,000 tons. The designation (which was once popular) the "largest ship in the world," becomes nearly meaningless today as these ever-enlarging characterless, anonymous ships keep rolling off their sub-assembly staging in

Japanese and European shipyards. With all of their bulk and enormous capacity (*four* football fields can be placed end to end on the decks of one of these), these ships are cheap, the cheapest of all in many ways, but most simply in dollars per ton of cost to build. And rightly they should be, designed and built as profit makers, enormously long and wide and deep, carrying the optimum (perhaps maximum) quantity of crude oil per voyage at the least expenditure. It is perhaps only marginally appropriate here to note that these ships are built so cheaply that many, unlike their smaller but higher quality sisters, have but one boiler. The dependability on boiler performance is paramount in ship operation; the venerable old *Queen Mary* had twenty-four, the modern *Queen Elizabeth II,* twelve (apparently, judging by her recent embarrassment, not enough). Few of these elephantine tankers have more than one propeller shaft, or a single rudder. While their navigation bridges are nearly one quarter of a mile from their bows, they move at a top service speed which is so low that a normal voyage from the Arabian oil ports to their European destination requires two months.

Yet with these excesses both large and small these ships belong to a category of displacement ships which we must recognize for its great range of buoyant support. Ships such as these are characterized basically by the very large and disproportionate hull volume below the surface when fully loaded. Indeed, the cargo weight far exceeds the weight of the ship itself exclusive of the cargo. The drafts or depth of water required for a fully loaded VLCC runs to 50 or 60 feet and the ULCC may be 80 feet. This great depth, together with the boxlike underbody, represents an enormous underwater bulk. Such ships belong in a separate and exclusive category of displacement vessels. They are truly *deep displacement* ships.

Experimentally there exists another type and form of displacement hull. It is also of very deep hull with extreme draft. However, its similarity to the crude oil carrier of the preceding discussion goes no farther than that. This type of vessel is called (for want of a better name) the SWATH, meaning Small Waterplane Area Twin Hull. Briefly, this experimental and rather rare breed of ship is designed for relatively high speed, stable platform in reasonably rough water. Its future is problematical, but the theory of placing the bulk of the displacement well below the surface and extending the support to the above-water platform

Figure 1–9. The Deep-draft Types are Still largely Experimental Concepts. They are categorized as Small Waterplane Area Twin-Hull designation, or SWATH. Potentially fast for displacement ships, they are very stable with minimum motion in a seaway.

or deck through the narrow waterline fins or struts is sound. The necessity of twin hulls connected by an upper platform is primarily to provide the necessary operating stability. As a matter of fact, the Navy's first SWATH vessel is named *Stable* (figure 1–9).

The most significant class of displacement hull for special application is the submarine, a vessel for completely submerged operation. The nature of the submarine and a description of all its various operational attitudes, both static and dynamic, is covered in subsequent chapters, where such operational theory can be related to that of more conventional displacement vessels. It is only necessary here to emphasize that submersible vessels are specifically displacement vessels applying the theory of Archimedes' law and all that it implies (figure 1–10).

MULTIHULL VESSELS

There is one other type of hull in common use which has not yet been mentioned, primarily because it fits into none of the categories described but rather can exist comfortably in any. More than just the transitory character of a semi-displacement hull it can in its variations fall in or between the various support systems. This craft is the so-called *multihull vessel*—the catamaran and the trimaran. These vessels are most frequently displacement hulls in their larger sizes, such as the SWATH mentioned above, or more conventionally, the types of ocean research vessels requiring stable platforms and protected areas for launching equipment (figure 1–11). There are also the twin-hulled air-cushion vessels mentioned earlier, and high-speed planing catamarans. Actually, the multihull ship is an adaptation of any of the basic hull categories to a special application which requires exceptional stability and/or inter-hull working area thus provided.

Figure 1–12 indicates the body profiles (with no relative scale) that have just been described and relates them to the means of physical support so briefly introduced above. It may be noticed that from left to right they are arranged basically from high speed to low speed, except for the multihull types which may be either, depending upon purpose.

There are other criteria and parameters beyond speed capability which justify the design of ships of widely varied configurations, and these standards no doubt account for the specific categories of configuration, based upon the nature of the supporting forces, already described.

These other criteria should be briefly explored and related. There is no question that operating environment and required employment are powerful modifying factors. But if environment and required employment were the only preconditions which contributed to the nearly infinite variety of configurations of ships which we have tried in the preceding pages to categorize in a rational way, then there would be very few categories.

To briefly consider the motivating conditions we must certainly first examine the economic factor. The cost of the ship per ton together with its payload and earnings is perhaps the most powerful consideration that has influenced the greatest number of seagoing ships both today and in recent history.

Our technology enables us to build fast ships, big ships, luxurious ships for passenger travel, excessively equipped ships for war or for research; but for all these and other special purposes there is a price tag. A warship or a research vessel has no concern with gross earnings or profits, and hence for its own purpose it most often requires emphasis on speed and technical function. For these the cost factor is high.

Perhaps a more orderly examination would be a comparative listing of significant requirement factors compared with ship type. The ship types are those described previously and pictured in figure 1–12. The requirements (which are by no means complete—but typical) could be listed as follows:

- Speed (propulsive power and ship form)
- First cost (cost per ton)
- Economy (operating cost)
- Earning capacity (profit per ton)
- Cruising range (fuel capacity)
- Sea-keeping capability (all-weather sea worthiness and endurance)
- Carrying capacity (deadweight tonnage)
- Comfort and livability
- Reliability
- Ecological compatibility

The graphical comparisons in figure 1–13 convey the great variations of some of these qualities among the type categories more effectively than any discussion.

Figure 1–10. The Modern Navy Attack Submarine—the best example of an advanced submersible vessel. Nuclear-powered, they are designed for optimum performance entirely below the surface.

Figure 1–11. The Oceanographic Research Vessel USNS Hayes, one of the best examples of a multihull vessel, generally a costly, controversial type.

Finally, it is necessary in such general comparisons and categorizations as this to come back to the perspective of practicality. It is all very well to arrange type categories and fit together these vastly different seacraft with respect to the common denominator of supporting force but the questions of relative significance in harder terms must ultimately be answered. How many ships of each of these categories can justify themselves in terms of economic support; environmental capabilities; how many are purely experimental; what can be expected of their future? These and other appropriate questions can well be asked and where they apply to the problems and estimates of the ship designer, an attempt has been made in the following chapters to provide the background to adequately evaluate these things.

A more detailed and viable discussion of these comparative factors can only be made after the technical presentations of this book have been absorbed. Thus we must defer until Chapter 15 the more complete comparative summary.

But it must be emphasized here, that the pre-dominent portion of this book will deal with the physical nature of *displacement* ships simply because almost all of the ships on the world's oceans are and will be, as far as can be seen, displacement ships. They carry the raw materials of world commerce, and without them the civilized industrialized world would quickly collapse.

The new ships of recent years have presented noticeably progressive features in their external configuration. The old-type stacks or funnels have been replaced by raked, streamlined stacks, *macks* (combined mast and stack), or transverse pairs of slim diesel funnels. Superstructures have become crisp and uncluttered. Hulls of tankers and bulk carriers have become monsters in volume; fast cargo carriers and naval vessels have taken on new grace in their sheer and flare. Below the waterline, hydrodynamic knowledge has added bulbous forefoot extensions and improved rudder configurations. There are a multitude of internal developments provided by a modern technology, including the less visible changes in strength and performance allowed by improved metals and other materials.

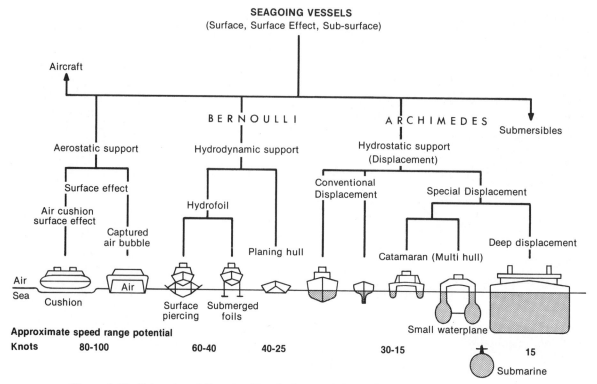

Figure 1–12. Categories of Seagoing Vessels Arranged According to their mode of support on or in the sea

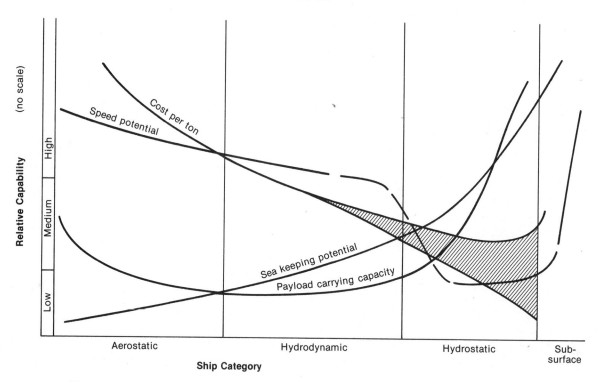

Figure 1–13. The Relative Performance and Associated Capabilities of the ship categories of Figure 1–12

The Systems Approach

However, the greatest and perhaps most important change in new ships and their design is not in itself very evident in their structure or configuration. This factor is the recognition by designers, planners and operators that a ship is an extensively complex but integrated total *system*.

It is possible (but increasingly more difficult) to design and build a ship with no regard for the systems engineering approach. It is even possible to be unaware that it is a system. Whether one is aware or not or to whatever degree the designer integrates its subsystems, the ship will be a system, and its functional success is, to a great extent, predicated on its design as a functioning system.

Because of the rapidly mushrooming technology of this century, there has been an increasing natural tendency toward specialization within the engineering professions. This is simply the result of the enormous amount of technical knowledge required and the inability of any individual engineer to be completely knowledgeable in all ranges even within his own profession. Such specialization has led to the need, and indeed demand, for a methodology to deal with complexes of assemblies made up of many components of specialized engineering. In order that such complex assemblies of technology as the Polaris submarines or nuclear aircraft carriers, for example, are capable of their optimum performance, they must be designed in an orderly and integrated manner. This approach is ordinarily referred to as *systems engineering*.

Systems engineering is employed in the design of all naval vessels and most commercial craft today, and it is important that the student of ship design becomes aware of and familiar with its nature early in his engineering education. We might define this approach as a process for *achieving significant objectives, allocating resources, organizing information,* and *providing coordination* so that all major aspects of a problem can be precisely determined and coordinated with the subprocesses according to a predetermined plan. Systems engineering supplies the bridge between what is needed and what is technically feasible and practical.

Systems in Ships

Systems engineering when applied to a ship, whether it is a large ocean transport or warship or whether it is a very small vessel, implies total integration of all subsystems to provide a functional unit that achieves the basic mission or objective of the ship. This means that ship control must function through the internal and external communications system, and the machinery and propulsion systems must function in response to control, signaling their response on display instruments at the central control station. The weapons systems of a warship must function on order with simultaneous execution and respond to all safety and protective systems. Systems engineering includes all automatic control systems; ventilating, heating, and air-conditioning systems; as well as a multitude of engineering and electronic subsystems that maintain order and perform daily living functions as well as emergency functions. In other words, the ship has grown in its century or more of successful mechanical propulsion from a large floating vessel containing a relatively isolated power plant, isolated cargo holds, isolated living quarters, and lonely navigation bridge with its crude mechanical or sound signaling device to the engine room. In a sense, the ship of a century ago was a system too, but a relatively simple one. However, its design concept lacked the systematic, integrated approach demanded today for the successful modern ship.

In the design of a modern warship, the shipbuilders and naval architects involved recognize essentially the following major subsystems in terms of functional groupings:

- Hull
- Machinery and Propulsion
- Ship Control
- Weapons
- Sensors
- Navigation
- Central Computer
- Communications
- Damage Control
- Hotel (provisions and services)
- Rigging and Mooring

The interfaces and interplay among these must be identified and defined. The secondary subsystems in each must then be defined by more detailed functional blocks. All components must be designed for optimum functionality, recognizing their interrelationships with other subsystems and their multiple functions where they exist. Emergency operation and casualty procedures must be provided, and, in the design stages particularly, prime consideration must be given to volume relationships, payload capacity, habitability, ship motion effects, and acoustic influences. These multiple, integrated considerations are generally resolved before the actual preliminary design has begun and always before it has proceeded beyond the initial stages.

It has been suggested, and sometimes with apprehension, that an integrated, "whole" ship has a tendency to become an inflexible black box, with no capacity for growth. If such a concept were true, it could contain components that would perhaps be incompatible with logistics plans that must support other ships. If the validity of this critical corollary were recognized, the defects in such resulting ships could certainly be resolved and eliminated in the design process. Actually the integrated ship can be made *more* rather than less compatible with logistics by using the maximum of standardized components and adapters for special applications in the subsystem design. The command control subsystem, for example, would require multi-purpose, interchangeable displays tied together at the central computer subsystem that are properly programmed to achieve the required compatibility and flexibility. It must be recognized also, in the "whole" ship design, that proper systems engineering provides for standardization, interchangeability, and central procurement of parts and unitized components.

The Effective Ship's System

In the preceding section, one might receive the impression that nowadays all modern ships or new ships are designed and built as completely integrated systems that provide a whole and unitized ship. This impression is not completely true; rather systems integration is a goal or direction to be achieved in as great a degree as economics allow, demands require, and skills of the designers and builders enable. To state this differently, all ships are systems, but the integration of their subsystems varies within wide limits. Their usefulness in achieving their objectives or fulfilling their mission depends upon the percentage or degree of integration. The measure of this degree is found in the science of *systems effectiveness*. While it is not the purpose of this text to mount even a small excursion into the realms of this science (most engineering students encounter the study of systems effec-

tiveness early in their engineering curriculum), it will be helpful to touch on the necessity for the designer to expose his ship's system design to this orderly *evaluation procedure*.

In the evaluation of a ship's system or any subsystem's design in this discussion, it is necessary to generalize. Because of the great number of types and sizes of ships, the varying complexities of their designs, and the nearly infinite range requirements, it is not possible to standardize an approach to effective system design that will apply to every ship. A brief example of several prevalent procedures in an abstract way may be of help.

Simply stated, *systems effectiveness* is defined as the probability that the system will operate successfully when required under specific conditions throughout a given time cycle or period. This definition is most general and can be applied to any system including the ship.

While actual operational systems effectiveness extends beyond the designer's control and contains at least two other factors (human decisions and responses) that are external to design, the designer is initially the creator of the system and its effectiveness.

Citing some situations in terms of engineering integration, we may illustrate what is *not* an effective system. A whole system comprised of determinate subsystems cannot be effective where there are overlapping requirements, incompatibility, mechanical deficiencies, lack of adaptability to environment, etc. As a very simple and obvious example, the propulsion unit of a high-speed planing hull must be, if it is a marine propeller, of comparatively small diameter, of high pitch, and of rapid revolutions per minute to be compatible with the hull system. To be compatible with its environment, it must be of a suitable metal which will not form a terminal of an electrolytic system in order to protect against electrolysis. The designer must ask himself such questions as: Does subsystem A have a material reliability of 50 percent while subsystem B (which is dependent on subsystem A) has a reliability of 95 percent when the total system requirement is to be 90 percent reliable? Further, are associated subsystems, such as fuel requirements, compatible? Are there gasoline-fueled auxiliary generators in a system where the primary fuel is diesel oil?

From these very simple examples of systems effectiveness, it is but a short step to realize the

Figure 1–14. USS Enterprise (CVAN-65)—The Largest of All Ship Systems

necessity for full evaluation of the many systems existing in a modern, complex ship. Such evaluation responsibilities lie with the Design Analysis Section of the Naval Ship Systems Command and the design offices of shipbuilding centers.

There are on board any ship essentially three basic types of systems: (1) The familiar and traditionally understood *mechanical systems* or hardware systems, (2) the *man-machine systems* or, as they are often called, man-machine interfaces, and (3) the *organizational systems* or *concept systems* sometimes called software.

The elements of these three categories do not perform their functions separately but must be completely integrated and interdependent allowing, of course, for failures by the inclusion of manual overrides, stand-by and emergency equipment. There is, as in any integrated whole, no sharp division be-

tween the categorical groupings, but there is a necessary degree of overlap where, for example, it is difficult to say where an essentially mechanical system becomes one with a man-machine interface. It will not be necessary to attempt to catalogue all of the mechanical systems common to all ships. This would be of questionable use or validity because of the variation in ship types and mission. However, figures 1–15 and 1–16 will provide the student with an excellent view of some of the "hardware" systems the designer is dealing with in a destroyer.

In order to bring the mechanical systems into meaningful and useful articulation, the most important systems that must be considered are the man-machine type, and of these the most significant is the command control center. Of secondary, but hardly less significant, importance are the navigation and the communications systems. These two

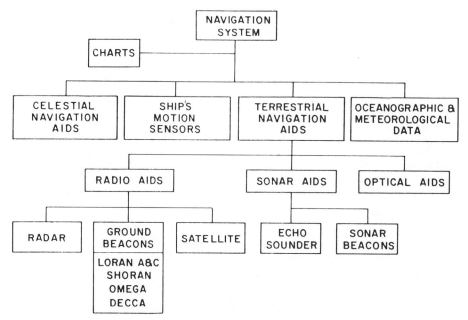

Figure 1–15. Navigation System

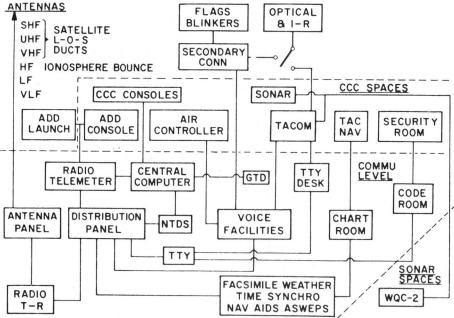

Figure 1–16. Communication Systems

systems are both fundamental and key systems, both essentially man-machine oriented. Examples of these systems for a destroyer type vessel with a predominantly anti-submarine mission in preliminary block diagrams are shown in figures 1–15 and 1–16. Notice that in the subsystems arrangements shown, certain elements and components appear common to all. Radio, sonar, radar, and weather aids are essential components in navigation, communications, and command control that are subject to integration and dependent interface design.

The organizational or concept type systems are less obvious as design problems and actually in many ship types are not considered to be of importance. The applications and systems engineering of this abstract system type are extensively varied. The organization of sequential functions, crew berthing and manning level considerations, stability, flooding effects, maneuvering and mooring procedures; all of these, as well as the planning of relative locations for the Captain's and the Commodore's cabins, can be systematized and integrated with the ship's essential systems and subsystems. Like computer programs, they represent software, and their effectiveness can be analyzed and optimized accordingly.

Systematized Design Philosophy

In the early stages of design planning, concurrent with the feasibility study, it becomes necessary to evolve an organized and systematized concept of the ship. At this stage the concept is dim, without configuration or dimensions; it is seriously out of focus. As the planning time progresses and preliminary design begins, the delineation improves, and at the same time, the systems design continues toward optimization. In a real sense, the ship concept as a *whole system* with a federation of subsystems has become the guiding pattern to which all of the components are cut. Chapter 13 thoroughly discusses the integration of the systems philosophy with the real work of the ship designer, that is, the development and refinement of concept into plans. This is the process of design.

The knife-edged Bow of the Destroyer Spruance (DD-963) Shows She is Built for Speed

CHAPTER 2

Dimension, Form, and Flotation

Considering all the complexities of the many systems and subsystems within a ship, with their important and critical designs, there is no feature as important to a ship as its geometric configuration.

Ship Geometry

The shape of a ship's hull, whether it is slim and graceful or full and bulky, is the very essence of its character. This form determines the power required to drive it; it reflects directly the ship's speed; it determines the quantity of payload and the comfort and habitability within the ship; more important, it largely establishes the limits of safety and stability as well as the motion of the ship among waves. All of these factors are basic and, as was seen in the previous chapter, form the critical substance of the ship system. It is essential that, before proceeding further with the methods and theory of design, we must establish some familiarity with the ship's geometry.

LINES

To delineate a three dimensional complex form such as a ship's hull and present it in a two dimensional medium, such as scaled drawings, we must resort to a direct application of descriptive geometry. In the case of the ship, the three basic projections become the *sheer plan*, the *half-breadth plan*, and the *body plan*.

For those whose memory of descriptive geometry is unreliable or lacking altogether, we can begin with the following analogous description. Suppose we place a ship's basic hull shape in an imaginary rectangular box whose bottom and sides just touch the ship's surface. The bottom of this box may be used as a reference base and called simply the *base plane*. Now, if we might also imagine planes parallel to this base plane slicing through the ship's hull form at regularly spaced vertical intervals, we have the familiarly known *waterlines*. It does not matter whether the ship will float at any of these levels; these intersections or traces are only used for references and delineate the horizontal segments of the hull from the bottom to the upper deck levels.

The waterlines are generally spaced every one or two feet and numbered from the keel or *base line*, the centered line of the base plane where it touches the ship. One of the specially designated waterlines is the *designed waterline (DWL)*, where the ship is designed to float at a predetermined load.

Now imagine that there are planes which slice down through the hull parallel to the ends of the box and cut the hull like bread slices. These intersections are called simply *sections*. They are located at regular intervals; the locations are called *stations* and are numbered from forward aft. The first section is called the *forward perpendicular,* and the aftermost one, the *after perpendicular.* (The abbreviations are logically *FP* and *AP* respectively.) The exact location of these perpendiculars is of some importance because the *length between perpendiculars* (*LBP* or L_{pp}) is significant. In Naval design practice, the length between perpendiculars is customarily coincident with the designed waterline length or *DWL.* For merchant ship practice, the location of the after perpendicular most frequently is coincident with the vertical rudder post. In all cases, the forward perpendicular is coincident with the forward extremity of the *DWL.* This is also called the zero station.

Normally there are ten station spaces numbered from zero through ten, making, in all, eleven basic sections. In larger ships, the number of station spaces is frequently doubled or at a greater multiple of ten. The section halfway between the first and last section is referred to as the *midship section* and designated by the symbol ⊠. In many large commercial and some naval ships, the actual shape of this section does not vary for some distance forward and aft of the

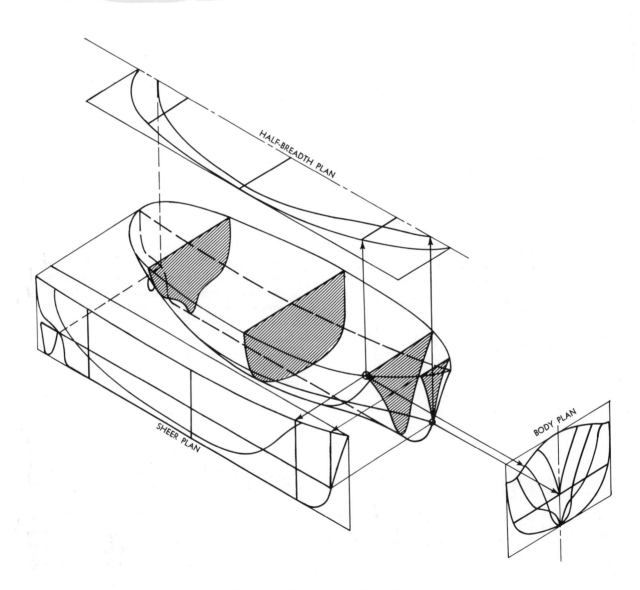

Figure 2–1. Projection of Ship's Lines

midship section location. This extent, in such ships, is called the *parallel middle body*.

A third series of planes is referred to the central plane of symmetry of the ship. A longitudinal plane splitting the ship equally and vertically from stem to stern is the *centerline plane*. This plane must contain the vertical profile of the ship including the external stem contour and stern and keel contours, showing the rudder and appendage profiles as well as the main deck at center. Parallel to this centerline plane are regularly spaced reference planes cutting the ship's hull along lines called *bow and buttock lines* or *buttock lines* or simply *butts*. The spacing interval of the buttock lines is up to the designer but usually is a basic unit dimension of one foot, two feet or four feet. It is useful to space the buttock lines so that one falls near a distance equal to one-half of the half-breadth of the ship from the center plane. This is referred to as the *quarter beam buttock* and is useful in relating the ship's curvature to similarly located reference lines on other ships.

Returning to the imaginary circumscribing box referred to at the outset, we can now visualize more simply three basic projections of the ship's form. The side of the box can be used as a screen on which to project the ship's profile showing all of the profile shapes and buttock lines. If the ship's surface were transparent and the lines of intersection of the reference planes were opaque, with a projecting lamp like the sun at an infinite distance, the shadow outline on the screen would form the *sheer plan*. Likewise, the shadow form on the bottom of the box would be the *half-breadth plan* (being symmetrical, only one-half is needed, and so it is named).

On the end of the box, the projection is basically the *body plan*. However, to avoid confusing intersections of the many section shapes, the forward sections are shown to the right and the after sections to the left of the center line. In the above manner, it is possible to describe the systematized *lines drawing* of a ship which is remarkably universal in its application. At the present time with our computerized technology, there is as yet no acceptable substitute for, or alternate means of, delineating the huge surfaces of a ship's form in a more satisfactory way than the lines drawing.

After the ship has been designed and its hull form determined and graphically described as above, it is customary to set up a matrix system with which a digital computer can cope. This matrix arranged in tabular form and called a *table of offsets*, is taken from the scaled lines drawing, expressed in full-size dimensions, and faired by computer. (See chapter 14.) *Fairing* is nothing more than the refining and smoothing of the minor lumps, inconsistencies, and inaccuracies in the drawing.

The fairing process is necessary, particularly in large vessels where the original design work may have been done at a scale whose ratio to full size was 1:100. Small discrepancies, such as the width of a pencil line in the design process, take on significant magnitude when blown up to full size.

MATHEMATICAL LINES

There have been, in the recent history of naval architecture, frequent and various proposals and ideas toward the development of a mathematical means of describing a ship's hull form assuming given criteria. One of the original methods, which was proposed and for a while used in a limited way, was put forth by Admiral David Taylor. His objective was, as has been generally the objective of other advocates of mathematical lines since, to produce a ship's lines or form description mathematically, without fairing, lifting offsets, or planimetering areas as in conventional graphical methods. By doing so successfully, the designer could select certain parameters and determine selected form characteristics including transverse sections and waterline shapes. The shapes of the curves, however, were restricted to hyperbolic sections and fifth-degree parabolic curves of areas and waterline. Some sections were fourth-degree parabolic where finer, sharper sections were required.

While the mathematical formulae involved the use of a great variety of initial parameters, there was some flexibility available to the designer. However the method, because of the parameters required, was restricted to the underwater body. Consequently, conventional drafting methods were required for the upper portions of the hull amounting, in all, to a limited saving in labor as well as restrictions to the hull shape.

Until the recent sophistication of the electronic computer, very little further interest was given to mathematical methods. Several means have been successfully developed for rapid fairing of lines after basic or "skeletal" lines have been drawn conventionally and offset tables have been made for use in the computer. Such methods simplify the work but do not eliminate the designer-draftsman from the process.

At present there are basically two sources for mathematical lines: (a) those using formulations for the hulls' surfaces (as indicated above), and (b) the procedures using lines fairing. Recently improved formulations have been proposed using high-order polynomials. These describe a hull's shape very well for calculations but produce an unfair hull because of the inherent "waviness" of polynomials. The fairing procedures do not, on the other hand, describe the entire hull—only the underbody. The two approaches will most likely be combined in using input from the unfaired skeletal table of offsets and/or from a graphical description provided by an electronic graphics display terminal.

With the designer using the computer as a rapid tool to perform the tedious and laborious mathematical analysis of configurations and a graphics display terminal to visualize, compare, and record the alternatives of configurations, the ultimate interactive computer-aided design is envisioned—a process where the designer remains the creator of the design and fully retains his initiative.

It is not difficult to imagine the many advantages of using true, mathematical lines. Such methods, successfully applied, would eliminate the time-consuming and costly process of originating and drawing lines by hand. Calculations for the various hydrostatic characteristics would be simplified and quickly provided. Such characteristics as resistance, speed, and power as well as seakeeping ability could be quickly and properly optimized.

Further discussion of the computer's application in ship design will be presented in chapter 14, but it should be said here that while no easily adaptable means have been found for the original delineation of the ship by the computer, it is firmly established in nearly every other design process.

THE MEASURE OF A SHIP

Before proceeding further in the technology of ship design, some of the language and terminology applying both to geometry and floatation properties must be resolved.

The first of these definitions most properly should concern size or three-dimensional magnitude. The popular layman's description of a ship's size is simply a statement of its length. Such a description is not only grossly inadequate, it is inaccurate. It is necessary to recognize that a linear dimension, such as length, is one-dimensional. An eight-oared rowing shell is actually longer than the average harbor tug boat, yet no one would dispute which vessel is larger.

There are several notations for the size of ships, and some can be confusing. Nevertheless, these denominations concern themselves with three dimensions. The two categories of size are weight and volume, and in our normal understanding, the terms may seem of opposing meaning. *Displacement* of a ship is a statement of its weight; *tonnage* is a measure of its volume or capacity.

Displacement. The weight of the water (salt water at 64 pounds per cubic foot) that the ship displaces when floating freely is called *displacement*. The waterline or drafts must be designated to indicate its loading condition, and therefore the weight of the ship is established equivalently for a given loading or condition of floatation as shown in discussions of *Archimedes' Principle* elsewhere in this book. The symbol Δ is used for displacement.

Tonnage. The capacity of a ship, either gross or net, is described in *cubic feet,* divided by 100 and is known as *tonnage.* Historically, a very important and standard cargo for European sailing vessels was wine, stored and shipped in casks called *tuns.* These tuns of wine, because of their uniform size and their universal demand, became a standard by which a ship's capacity could be measured. A tun of wine weighed approximately 2,240 pounds, and occupied nearly 60 cubic feet. Port dues and fees were levied on the basis of this standard, but it quickly became evident that a more equitable basis of measurement was needed to compare vessels of different construction and styles. The first standard measurement rules were established in England in the seventeenth century and consisted simply of the length of keel multiplied by the inside breadth and depth of the hold divided by a factor of 94. This formula became law and was considered a fair and uniform average indicating the number of tuns of wine that vessels of the period could carry. The language had evolved at this time, also, to the present spelling, "ton" and "tonnage", and the standard weight of the so-called English long ton became 2,240 pounds. The long ton is the same today and is the ship designer's standard of weight.

The subject of tonnage and measurement rules, which to a large extent are responsible for ship's harbor dues, fees, canal revenues, etc., are most complex and involved. Further knowledge in this area should be sought in such sources as *Principles of Naval Architecture,* SNAME 1967 or in various government shipping regulations.

There is one usage of the term *tonnage* to be noted before proceeding to other terms. The increasing size of large bulk cargo carriers has, since World War II, made the term *deadweight* tonnage most common. In this instance, tonnage does refer to weight and indicates the difference in displacement between the loaded and unloaded condition. A very simple description of deadweight tonnage is that of the cargo-carrying ability of a ship, expressed as total weight. With this in mind, the term becomes most graphic when applied to the great tankers being built and conceived in magnitude of several *hundred thousand* deadweight tons. The deadweight tonnage of ships of the World War II era seldom exceeded 20,000 tons.

In the category of dimensions, it is necessary to define some terms used frequently in ship design. The following terms are therefore categorized, and their definitions considered precise and unbending:

Molded hull form. The molded hull form is the surface of the ship's hull inside the planking, plating, or skin fabric. It is considered to be a smooth, faired form not subject to structural irregularities caused by plate laps, butt straps, appendages, etc.

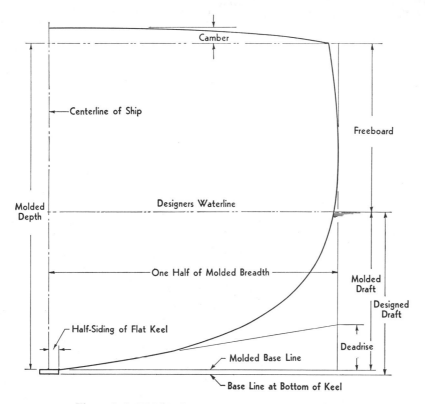

Figure 2–2. Midship Section Molded Form Definitions

Drafts. The *forward draft* and *after draft* are those vertical distances from the base line to the waterline of reference measured at the forward and after perpendiculars respectively. The *molded draft* is measured from the molded base line. The *keel drafts* are measured from the bottom of the keel. *Draft scales* for keel drafts are placed on both sides of the ship as close as possible to the perpendiculars referenced. The *mean draft* is the arithmetical mean of the drafts forward and aft. The *designed draft* is the height of the designed waterline above the base line.

Freeboard. The freeboard is the vertical distance from the water or designated waterline to the weather deck edge at any given location along the ship.

Sheer. The sheer is the difference between the freeboard at any point and that of the midship section. The *sheer line* is the line of intersection of the main or weather deck with the side of the ship.

Trim. When a ship is not floating at the designed waterline or at a waterline parallel to it, then it is *out of trim.* The amount of trim is the difference between the drafts forward and aft. There are some ships where the above definitions of trim must be modified, in that they are designed with a keel that is not horizontal but sloped down aft. Such ships are said to have a designed *drag;* the amount of drag is the greater designed draft aft minus the designed draft forward. So the trim of a ship with drag is the difference between the drafts forward and aft in excess of the drag. In such cases, it is practical to assign positive and negative values to trim and indicate trim (down) by the stern or trim (down) by the bow respectively.

FORM COEFFICIENTS

In order to refer to certain proportions of ships; to compare them in form with no regard to their actual dimensions or difference in dimensions; to be able to describe their shapes more precisely than "fat" or "thin", "full" or "fine"; there are certain geometric qualities that can be related as ratios or dimensionless coefficients. These coefficients of form are exceptionally useful in comparing certain performance characteristics associated with hydrodynamic phenomena.

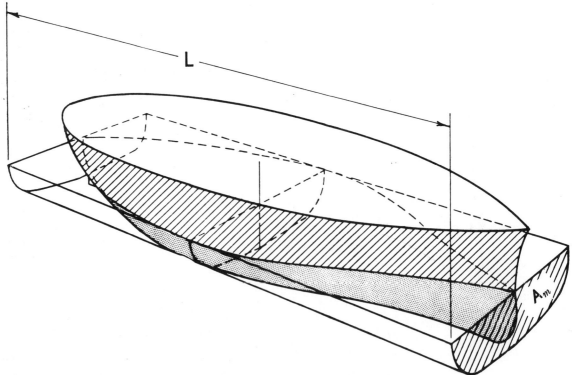

Figure 2–3. Prismatic Coefficient Relationships

In the following relationships, the symbols used are defined as follows:

L_{pp}—length between perpendiculars or designed waterline length

T—draft to the waterline, or draft, molded, of the ship

B—beam or breadth molded or breadth at waterline in following equations

∇—displacement volume at draft T

A_m—area of midsection at draft T

A_w—area of waterplane at draft T

Please note that the above dimensions may be either molded dimensions or non-molded (where molded dimensions are not used, as with wood, fiberglass, ferrocement or other structural materials) assuming, of course, constant dimensional systems.

The coefficients most commonly used by naval architects are as follows:

Midship section coefficient

$$C_m = \frac{A_m}{B\,T}$$

Block coefficient

$$C_b = \frac{\nabla}{L_{pp}\,B\,T}$$

Prismatic coefficient (see figure 3–3)

$$C_p = \frac{\nabla}{A_m\,L_{pp}} = \frac{\nabla}{C_m\,B\,T\,L_{pp}} = C_b/C_m$$

Waterline coefficient

$$C_{wp} = \frac{A_w}{B\,L_{pp}}$$

There are also certain commonly used ratios of dimensions, and these with their approximate range of values are:

Length—beam ratio

L_{pp}/B range, 3 to 12

Length—draft ratio

L_{pp}/T range, 7 to 30

(except on specific types of hulls, such as deep fin or keel sailboats)

Beam—draft ratio

B/T range, 1.8 to 4

Volumetric coefficient

$$\nabla/L_{pp}^3$$

(L is cubed in the expression to maintain a dimensionless relationship.)

Displacement—length ratio

$$\frac{\Delta}{(L_{pp}/100)^3}$$ range, 50 to 500

(The above ratio was devised by D. W. Taylor and differs from the preceding ratio only in its dimension. The number 100 is present merely to keep the values to convenient numbers.)

LOCI AND CENTERS OF THE SHIP

Center of Buoyancy. The center of buoyancy is the line of action of all the buoyant forces on the immersed portion of the ship's hull. It passes through the geometric center of the underwater form, at which point it is called the center of buoyancy. The force of buoyancy acts vertically at this point, and, for a ship floating at rest, the weight of the ship acts downward vertically through or in the vertical line containing the center of buoyancy. It is generally identified by the letter B. Its vertical position is designated VCB and longitudinal position LCB.

Center of Gravity. The center of gravity is the locus of all of the gravitational forces of the entire ship. This center has the conventional meaning used in mechanics when used with reference to the whole ship; i.e., it is the point at which the sum of the moments of all the weights in the ship with reference to any axis through this point is equal to zero.

On ships of usual form, the center of gravity is near the waterline and the midship section. The weight of the ship may be considered to be concentrated here with the total gravitational force acting downward through it. For a ship floating at rest, the center of gravity lies in the same vertical line as the center of buoyancy. This is an important consideration in design calculations for trim and equilibrium. The center of gravity is generally indicated by the letter G. Its vertical position is with reference to the bottom of the keel amidships and is designated $\overline{KG}$.

Center of Floatation. The center of floatation is the geometric center of the waterplane at which the ship is floating and which is circumscribed by the waterline. It should not be confused with the center of buoyancy with which it has no direct relation. It is the location of the axis about which the ship trims.

The Metacenter. When the ship rolls, heels, or is inclined from its condition of equilibrium, the center of buoyancy moves accordingly to conform with the changing shape of the immersed form. When the ship is inclined transversely (i.e., directly to one side), the center of buoyancy moves out in a pseudo-eliptical path. The instantaneous center of this curved path, as soon as the center of buoyancy begins to move, is the *metacenter*. A more easily visualized location of this point is its description as the intersection of the new line of buoyant force when the ship is inclined to a very small angle with the original line of buoyant force during the upright equilibrium position. The metacenter is used as a convenient reference point and indicates, when referred to the center of gravity, the degree of initial stability. (See chapter 11.)

The metacenter is designated by the letter *M*

and is correctly named the *transverse metacenter* when it conforms to the above definition stipulating *transverse* inclination. When the inclination is longitudinal (i.e., change of trim), the reference point generated as above is the *longitudinal metacenter* and is designated *M'*. However, the longitudinal metacenter has very little use in ship design and is of value primarily when investigating damaged conditions and loss of buoyant volume forward and aft.

In subsequent discussions, the use of the term *metacenter* will assume the *transverse* metacenter.

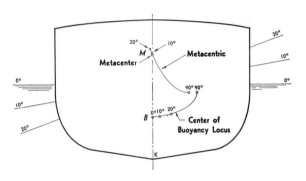

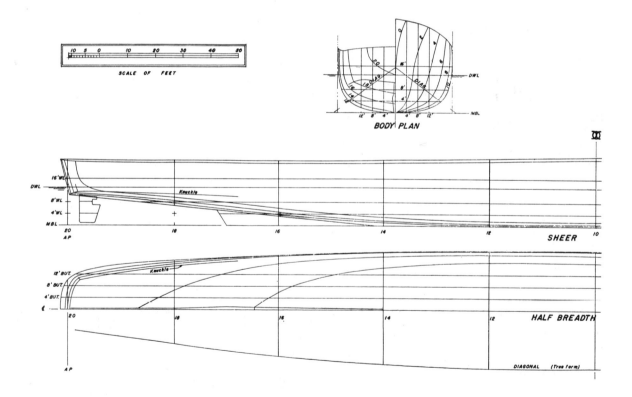

SCALE OF FEET

BODY PLAN

SHEER

HALF BREADTH

DIAGONAL (True form)

The *longitudinal metacenter* will be specifically stated where it is referred to.

Metacentric Height. The metacentric height is the *vertical* distance measured on the ship's vertical center line between the metacenter and the center of gravity. It is designated $\overline{GM}$.

Metacentric Radius. The metacentric radius is the distance between the center of buoyancy B and the metacenter M (where M is the center of the locus of centers of buoyancy for small angles of inclination). It is designated $\overline{BM}$.

RELATIVE LOCATION OF CENTERS

The following notations are used by naval architects when locating the various centers in relation to the ship's structure:

$\overline{KM}$—height of the metacenter above the keel

$\overline{KB}$—height of the center of buoyancy above the keel

$\overline{KG}$—height of the center of gravity above the keel

LCB—longitudinal location of the center of buoyancy, usually measured from the forward perpendicular.

Ship Forms

The potential variety of ship hull forms is infinite; it is as infinite as the possible variety of ships, the imaginations of their designers, and the requirements of their owners. Because of the requirements of the sea, however, and the natural limitations of hydromechanics together with general functions that tend to categorize themselves, there are hull forms exhibiting similarities that tend toward optimization. The following discussion will attempt to restrict itself to these more common and characteristic shapes.

The most simple and basic description of a common ship or boat form is that of an opened envelope. Such a description is inadequate, but it serves as an object of reference. If this opened envelope, with its vertical ends (the stem and stern) and bulging sides, was slit open at the bottom, it would have a foil shape with regular sections. Let us assume a symetrical foil shape as a second state of development such as in figure 2–8. With a top and bottom on the foil (deck and hull bottom), it would be evident when

Figure 2–5. Lines Drawing

PRINCIPAL DIMENSIONS		
LENGTH BETWEEN PERPENDICULARS	383'	0"
LENGTH, OVERALL (MOLDED)	390'	6"
BREADTH, EXTREME (MOLDED)	40'	10 7/16"
DEPTH AT CENTER (MOLDED)	23'	10"
DRAFT, DESIGNED WATERLINE (MOLDED)	13'	0"
DISPLACEMENT (MOLDED, SALT WATER)	3010	TONS

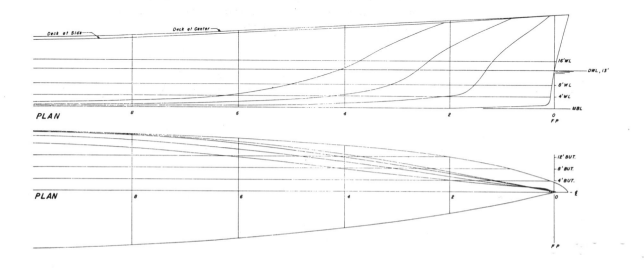

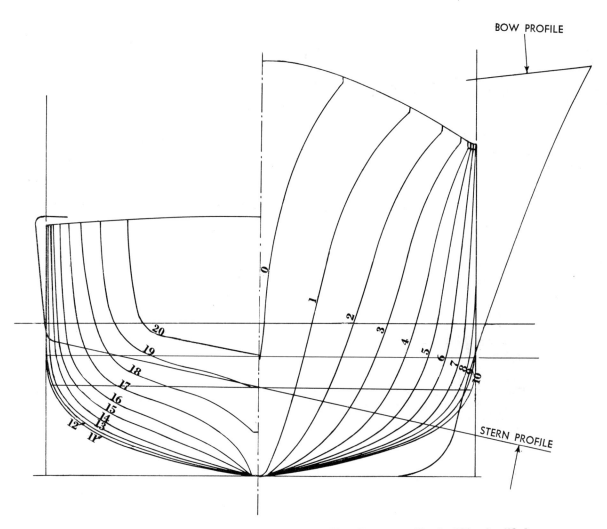

Figure 2–6. Typical Body Plan and Fore-Aft Profiles (Destroyer Type). This simplified graphical expression of hull shape is frequently used as a substitute for the lines drawing in technical reports relating to ships.

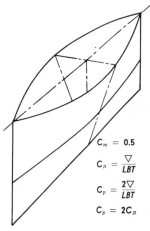

$C_m = 0.5$

$C_B = \dfrac{\nabla}{LBT}$

$C_p = \dfrac{2\nabla}{LBT}$

$C_p = 2C_B$

Figure 2–7. Simple Envelope Hull

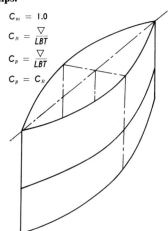

$C_m = 1.0$

$C_B = \dfrac{\nabla}{LBT}$

$C_p = \dfrac{\nabla}{LBT}$

$C_p = C_B$

Figure 2–8. Foil Hull

the form is pushed through water that the edges between the sides and bottom should be rounded or cut away to allow an easier flow of water past and under the bottom. This, then, becomes basically the ship form, and the extent of rounding and fairing of the vertical surfaces into the flatness of the bottom becomes one of degree and compromise.

Further modifications of this simple and basic form are found to be desirable, necessary, and almost always more expensive. It is axiomatic that the most economically built ships in the bulk cargo service, with their low power and speed, are similar in character to the simple and basic shape described above.

For greater seaworthiness, better speeds, drier decks, and better motion in a sea, various changes are made in the basic form. The stem is angled or raked forward with a corresponding extension of deck space. The deck area also becomes widened when the bow sections are flared out with the resultant concavity typical of flared bows. Farther aft, the flatness of the bottom is given a gentle rise and transverse slope bending into a broader stern.

The extent of the fairing, rounding, and hollowing frequently produces ship forms that seem to have very little similarity to the basic shape described above. This is so apparent that some designers refer to another geometrical reference shape. This is the *double wedge* form where the vertical, sharp edge of the wedge is forward (the

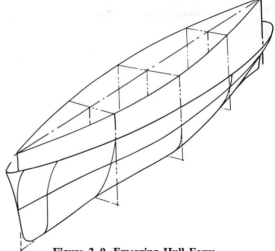

Figure 2–9. Emerging Hull Form

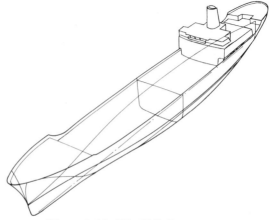

Figure 2–10. Ship Hull Form— Basic Modern Cargo Liner

Official U.S. Navy Photograph

Figure 2–11. USS Severn (AO-61), a Typical Hard-Working Fleet Oiler. This is an ubiquitous form of hull found in most of the bulk carriers and cargo vessels of the world. Vessels of this type have extensive parallel middle bodies.

bow), and the horizontal or 90-degree turned wedge is aft and is truncated, becoming the flat stern found in many vessels. This basic shape is perhaps more adaptable to smaller higher-speed vessels. However, the double wedge is also recognizable in many large warships and in more modern auxiliary and naval support vessels.

There are two portions of the ship's below-water hull form that are of more concern than others to the designer in his search for speed and economy through efficient hydrodynamics. These are the *entrance* and the *run*. The entrance is that portion of the hull from the leading edge of the stem aft to the section of greatest breadth (not necessarily midships). This entrance should very gradually widen with little or no noticeable change in curvature. Hollow waterlines are sometimes evident in this portion of the ship but become particularly difficult and often disadvantageous because they create "shoulders" that cause secondary wave-making disturbances.

In slow speed, full-bowed ships with high block coefficients (C_b), the entrance becomes even more difficult. A most promising and evident solution to this problem on such ships in recent years is a forward extension of the stem below the water in a bulbous form. (See chapter 5.) This form,

evolving from the ancient ram bow to the "Taylor Bulbous Bow" and to its present elongated form as the "Inui Bow", has become a common characteristic in supertankers, other cargo vessels, and warships.

The second concern in below-water hull design is the *run*. The run is that portion of the bottom aft from the widest section to the trailing edges of the stern. Like the entrance, the run should have no quick changes of curvature. The curvature, where it exists, should be gradual and, in the final quarter of the hull, should be nearly flat.

There is a tendency, because of diminishing pressure and expansion of the potential flow lines, for the flow of water along the run to peel away from the surface of the ship. In fact, this hydrodynamic flow characteristic of *separation* must exist someplace along the run. While it is desirable to prevent separation or delay it along the hull's surface, neither can be effectively done. The magnitude of the eddy currents produced by separation are an indication of the seriousness of the problem in any particular ship form.

Between the entrance and the run in most large commercial ships is a region where the transverse sections below the waterline are constant and identical in shape. This is called the *parallel*

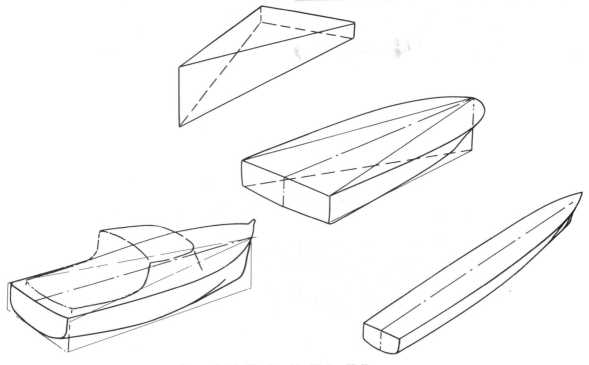

Figure 2–12. The Double Wedge Hull

Figure 2–13. Soviet Helicopter Ship Moskva, a Further Example of the Application of the Double Wedge to the Requirement of Both Deck Space and Speed

middle body. Ships with large parallel middle bodies and high prismatic coefficients (C_p) are those of relatively high cargo capacities. Ships of very high or extreme block, prismatic, and midsection coefficients are the ore carriers, supertankers, and other bulk-cargo carriers. Ships of lower form coefficients are generally the smaller vessels: working vessels, fishing trawlers, tugs, naval destroyers, and sailing yachts.

Most naval vessels do not have a parallel middle body. Naval combatant ships such as frigates, destroyers, cruisers, and aircraft carriers are characterized by smooth, gentle curvatures and sweeping lines from a sharp or fine entrance through a well-rounded and an easy run, terminating generally with a transom stern.

Some typical form coefficients of specific vessel types are given in table 2-1 for comparison.

Table 2–1. Typical Form Coefficients

Coeffi-cients	Destroyer	Cargo Liner	Harbor Tug	Great Lakes Bulk Freighter	Passenger Liner
C_b	0.521	0.643	0.585	0.874	0.597
C_m	0.833	0.967	0.892	0.990	0.956
C_p	0.625	0.664	0.655	0.883	0.625
C_w	0.740	0.768	0.800	0.918	0.725
Ratios					
L/B	9.82	6.92	4.18	9.67	8.38
L/T	32.75	16.82	9.33	29.00	26.25
B/T	3.33	2.43	2.23	3.00	3.14

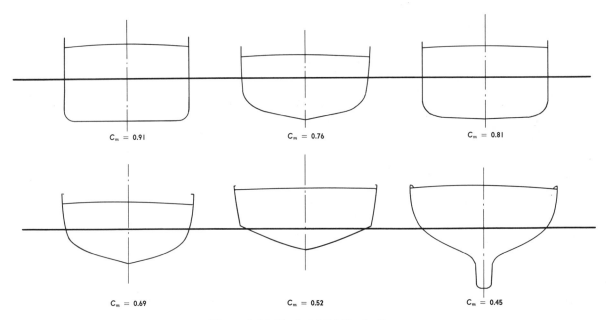

$C_m = 0.91$ $C_m = 0.76$ $C_m = 0.81$

$C_m = 0.69$ $C_m = 0.52$ $C_m = 0.45$

Figure 2–14. Typical Midship Sections

The shape of the midsection is characteristic of size and form as well as function. Several such typical sectional forms are shown in figure 2–14. The midsection coefficients indicated are also typical.

Notice that one midsection features a noticeable corner. This is typical of many small craft capable of higher speeds. The corner or edge is the *chine* and hulls with this characteristic are called chine form. Meant for light displacement and planing operation, a chine form hull is essentially a multi-surfaced hull, the bottom being distinct from the sides and separated from each by the chine. The bottom of chine form hulls is essentially a **V** section; the angle of the **V** is very acute forward and gradually widens and flattens toward the after sections. The aftermost sections are essentially flat. However, an exception is in a better chine form for rough water. This is one of nearly constant **V** from midship, aft maintaining a fairly high chine and in many designs, an above-waterline chine.

The L/B ratio of most high-speed chine hulls is generally lower than the lowest figure given in table 2–1 for larger deepwater displacement vessels. It can be as low as two.

Origin and Design of Ship Form

With few exceptions, the process of originating or generating the hull form of a new ship remains

a unique function for genuine, creative, engineering design. There are many procedures in modern engineering referred to as design. It appears that the number of such procedures has multiplied proportionately with the growth of the computerized analysis and the popular systems concepts. It is possible to arrange, with the help of a computer and available machinery components, an efficient, optimized mechanical system. Computers are able to provide, with a great supply of input data banking their memory, very useful design information. Mathematical analysis and lengthy computations are accomplished easily by computers. Stability problems are solved as well as powering and seakeeping analyses. All of this is part of the designer's information toward optimization, but none of it is, in itself, original design. There are misnamed design courses in engineering schools that are actually no more than problem analysis courses in which students become equipped to select combinations of ready-made hardware to perform given functions. In this modern world, there are certainly many demands for these talents, but fulfilling them should not be confused with creative design.

Ship design has been described often as an art, sometimes in a derogatory way by engineers whose creativity and vision are limited. It is certainly true, as was pointed out in this chapter, that it is not presently practical to create genuine ships lines mathematically, and this consequently limits the computer in originating ship forms. However, the successful naval architect who designs a ship's hull must be first an engineer, educated in the various engineering sciences and fully familiar and current with hydromechanics as well as structural theories. Beyond this professional knowledge, it must be recognized that, to design a new ship form, there is an additional capability that has often been neglected in his training. This is the capacity to visualize forms three dimensionally and translate the object to a communicable graphic medium.

The ship designer's first encounter with this problem comes very early in the design process. Because the ship's hull form is the limiting boundary and resticting shape that must contain the mechanisms for propulsion, living accommodations, cargo holds, and all of the functional media of ship operation, it must be determined very early. The following general notes on this procedure may be helpful to a young designer in his beginnings with this part of ship design. The development of his capacity to cope with the process and to thoroughly understand it will most certainly provide him with confidence. His will be the satisfaction of knowing how to function and produce in the most fundamental and important phase of ship design.

THE LINES AND THEIR DRAFTING

In the beginning of the delineation process, it can be assumed that certain dimensional characteristics are already closely established. These are the length, breadth, depth, draft, and volume of displacement.

A competent designer moves by experience and, like a computer (but better), he is a memory bank of the do's and don'ts and co-related dimensions and coefficients.

The form coefficients are helpful in the beginning and, having some knowledge of ship type and speed, the designer is able to choose an approximate prismatic coefficient. He is also able at this point to plot a curve of areas which represents, as described below, the shape of the prismatic coefficient.

CURVE OF AREAS

After selecting a suitable prismatic coefficient, it is possible to compute a corresponding midship

section area. On coordinates with suitable and convenient scales and with section area as ordinate and length-on-waterline as abcissa, the midsection area is plotted. Through this point, a fair curve of slightly bell-shape form is sketched. The area under this sketched curve, when divided by the area of the circumscribing rectangle, should be the ratio equal to the prismatic coefficient. Such an equality is achieved by reworking the curve and maintaining its fairness until it is satisfactory. Such a curve is never actually symmetrical, since the greater proportion of its area is aft of the midsection. The total area under this curve represents volume of displacement, and its distribution accounts for the characteristic prismatic coefficient. Comparisons should be made at this stage of the process with sectional area curves for existing or prior ship designs of the same type.

When this preliminary sectional area curve has been satisfactorily determined, it is possible to obtain the below-water areas for any section throughout the ship's length. Such areas should be used as guides and approximations but should not be too restrictive in the following processes of fairing out the lines.

THE GRID

With the dimensional features of the ship to be designed known and the above areas and coefficients prepared, the first step in the graphic delineation of the hull is the establishment of the reference grid.

This basic layout of the *waterline, section* and *buttock lines* in their *straight line* projection with the proper spacing in the sheer plan and half-breadth plan as well as body plan must be very precisely done. Any small dimensional error or lack of parallelism at this point dooms the ultimate fairness of the drawing and agreement between views. Some designers place this grid on the reverse side of the drawing vellum on which they are drawing the ship's lines. This will preserve its integrity during the very many routine erasures that must occur while fairing the lines.

The profile of the ship showing the contours of the stem and stern as well as the sheer line or weather deck at edge should first be drawn in the sheer plan. This is the first evidence of the emerging ship's hull form, and, to the designer, it becomes his first look at the ship's image. At this stage, the shape and contours of this plan are arbitrary and independent of other views, and the designer is able to work freely within the limits of the overall criteria.

The next lines or curves should be drawn in the half-breadth plan, and they should be the shape of the designed waterline and the weather deck edge (sheer in half-breadth). These lines are again fairly arbitrary and freely established. They, too, should reflect the designer's experience and the criteria requirements of the vessel.

The designer next moves to the body plan and, projecting the governing points from the other two views, draws in the midship section. At this point, he must give some regard to the sectional area previously estimated and the midship section coefficient. When he is satisfied with the midsection shape, he returns to the sheer plan. Using the limiting points of intersection, he runs-in a bow and buttock line at approximately the quarter-beam distance from the centerline. (This is the quarter-beam buttock.) When this line is faired and its intersections check out in all views, he returns to the body plan and puts in two more sections, preferably numbers two and eight. These must check out in all views before proceeding.

It becomes obvious at this stage that each additional line produces an accumulating number of additional intersections that must agree in all views for fairness. The process of working-in a sequence of views and reference planes rather than attempting to draw all or several waterlines, all the buttock lines, or all sections is most important. The shape is being developed by gradually "caging" it in; by building an integrated structure of limits of cross-referenced intersecting planes.

The sequence should continue, with buttock line, waterline, and section until all of the lines are completed. Because the buttock lines are involved with only half the ship (from the center plane of symmetry), there are less of these than the sections and waterlines. Hence, the sequential procedure concentrates primarily on waterlines and sections, interspersing buttock lines when necessary.

Finally, as a check on fairness when the lines are nearly completed, a fourth reference cutting plane called a *diagonal* is established. Depending upon the designer's requirements and the size and shape of the ship, one or several diagonals may be used. Larger vessels often need but one. The diagonal plane's position is established in the body plan as an edge-viewed plane at an angle to the centerline plane passing downward through the hull near the bilge in an attempt to intersect the hull surface as nearly perpendicularly as possible.

The projection of this intersection after rotating it parallel to a basic reference view, generally the half-breadth plan, is called the *development of the diagonal* and is shown as such in figure 2–5.

TABLE OF OFFSETS

When the lines are completed and faired (all intersections in agreement in three views) and the designer is satisfied with the hull form, a rectilinear tabulation of the reference plane intersections is made. The intersections are tabulated, normally according to the section or station numbers and include the heights above the base line of each section where it is crossed by a bow and buttock line as well as the deck edge and stem and stern contour. Also tabulated are the half-breadths at each section where they are crossed by the waterlines. The referenced distances are recorded in feet, inches and eighths of inches (such

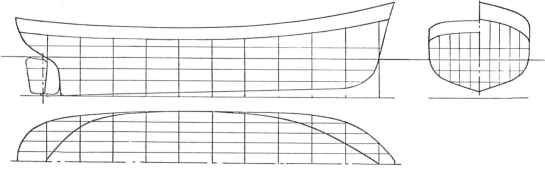

Figure 2–15. Basic Grid and Profiles—Lines Development

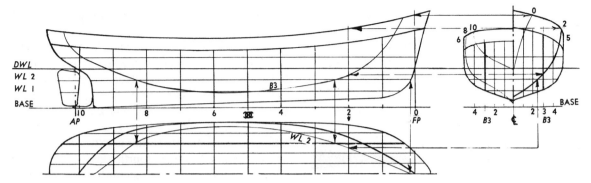

Figure 2–16. Development of Lines

as 6–4–3, meaning 6 feet 4⅜ inches) full ship scale.

This first table of offsets is often referred to as *uncorrected offsets* and is sent along to the builder with the ship's plans. In the past the loftsmen in the shipyard's mold loft laid down the lines from the offsets on a large wooden floor (loft) where the enlargement revealed small discrepancies undetectable in the designer's scale drawing. The offset table was corrected to this larger fairing process, and a corrected or lofted offset table was made. This process is largely obsolete except in small shipyards, and the fairing process is now accomplished by computers.

Further use is made of the offset table as computer input, not only in the fairing process but also in the many tedious calculations made for hydrostatic characteristics and stability. In modern ship design, it becomes the basis of the ship's configuration for further computer modification and refinement toward the preliminary and contract design stages.

Hydrostatic Parameters

The ship designer, in order to facilitate his computations and articulate his expressions of ship characteristics, has developed over the years a number of classic parameters. The basis of these expressions, as well as their method of application, must be understood by the student of this profession. Before developing these significant expressions, it will be useful to restate *Archimedes' Principle* as it applies to ships, for it is from this expression that the hydrostatic parameters have grown: *The total weight of the floating vessel, including all that it contains or that is attached, must equal the weight of the water it displaces.*

A further and more general statement of this law says that a body immersed in a fluid will experience an upward force due to hydrostatic pressure equal and opposite to the weight of the fluid displaced by the body. From this statement, we have the ultimate substantiation for the phenomenon which applies, regardless of the "floatability" of the vessel, to submersible craft, submerged objects, or appendages. It is a basic statement of buoyant force.

WATER DENSITY AND DISPLACEMENT

The displacement of a ship at any draft is obtained by dividing the submerged volume at that draft expressed in cubic feet by the appropriate density factor (35 cubic feet per ton of salt water, or 36 cubic feet per ton of fresh water). Using the submerged volume at the designer's load waterline, the *designed displacement* may be computed. From these calculations, a curve of displacement versus draft can be drawn and is referred to as the *displacement curve*. It will be discussed further.

TONS PER INCH IMMERSION

When a ship undergoes a change in displacement, it is extremely useful at times to make a quick computation of the change in draft. The most convenient and rapid method is to divide the change in displacement (in tons) by the *tons per inch immersion*. This latter factor is exactly what its name implies; i.e., the number of tons required to produce a change in mean draft of one inch in salt water.

The sides of a ship over a vertical distance of one inch are nearly vertical at most operating drafts. This means that there will be no noticeable change in the area of the water planes in a change of draft of one inch. If we can make this assumption, then it is apparent that the additional volume displaced by the ship in sinking one inch will be the product of the water plane area in square feet and the thickness of the layer in feet ($\frac{1}{12}$). The weight in tons of the increased volume is $\frac{1}{35}$ of the volume. Hence:

$$\frac{\text{area of waterline}}{35} \times \frac{1}{12} = \text{tons per inch immersion}$$

or simplified

$$TPI \text{ (tons per inch immersion)} = \frac{A_w}{420}$$

Recapitulating, the above equation indicates that the weight of a layer of displaced water is equal to the area of the water plane times a thickness of one inch divided by 35, the volume in cubic feet of one ton of sea water. This change in displacement, according to Archimedes' Principle, must be exactly equal to the change in weight which causes it.

The ship's curves of form, which include displacement and other curves, give the value of tons per inch immersion in salt water for the complete range of drafts. Unless otherwise specified tons per inch immersion is *always* given for *salt water*.

In using the value of tons per inch immersion, the student must remember the original assumption that the sides of the ship are nearly vertical throughout the change of drafts for which tons per inch immersion is used. This means simply that for large changes in drafts the value may be considerably in error. In such case, a draft somewhere midway between the original and the final drafts would give a more correct value for *TPI* when *TPI* is obtained from the curves. In any case, common sense must be the guide in working with tons per inch immersion, keeping in mind the form of the ship and the range between the initial and final drafts. If it becomes necessary to use tons per inch immersion in fresh water, the following equation applies:

$$TPI_{fw} = \frac{35}{36} TPI$$

DRAFT VERSUS DENSITY RELATIONS

Because of the variable densities between salt and fresh water, a ship of a given weight or displacement will have different drafts in the two liquids.

It is useful to predict the change in draft when moving from salt water to fresh water, or from fresh to salt. It has been found in this connection that many students are inclined to make the hasty generalization that if the ratio of densities of fresh and salt water is $\frac{35}{36}$, then they have merely to multiply the draft in fresh water by this ratio to obtain the draft in salt water. This is not correct in the case of ships, for a moment's inspection will reveal that the density ratio is a function of volumes, whereas the draft is only a single linear dimension of three variable dimensions making up the volume of the ship. Consider for a moment two ships of equal displacement at the *same drafts*. One ship is wide and full with a flat bottom, while the other is sharp-ended and narrow with considerable deadrise. Consider both of these ships passing from fresh water to salt water simultaneously. The change in draft caused by the change in water density reflects the change in buoyant layer. Recalling Archimedes' Principle, the ships are buoyed up by water of a greater density than the original and hence will rise in the water until the weight of the volume of water displaced equals their own weight. In the case of the wide, full ship, the displacement volume is more a function of her fullness in sides and ends and hence requires less change in draft to make up the change in buoyant volume. In the case of the ship with a sharper, narrower hull a greater change in draft must result to compensate for the lack of fullness in the hull.

The correct approach to this situation may be developed as follows:

A ship is passing from water of specific gravity, δ, to water of specific gravity, δ_1. The displacement, Δ, is the same in both cases but the volume of displacement changes.

$$\nabla = \text{volume before change} = \frac{36\Delta}{\delta}$$

$$\nabla_1 = \text{volume after change} = \frac{36\Delta}{\delta_1}$$

The change in volume, $\nabla_1 - \nabla$, can be considered as a layer of uniform thickness of volume $A_w \frac{d}{12}$ in cubic feet, where

A_w = waterplane area in square feet
d = thickness of layer in inches.

The distance, d, is the change in draft in passing from water of one density to another, assuming A_w remains constant throughout the distance, d, which is a close approximation.

Therefore

$$A_w \frac{d}{12} = \nabla_1 - \nabla$$

$$\frac{d}{12} = \frac{1}{A_w}(\nabla_1 - \nabla).$$

In terms of the displacement from above,

$$\frac{d}{12} = \frac{36\Delta}{A_w}\left[\frac{1}{\delta_1} - \frac{1}{\delta}\right]$$

The above equation expressed in terms of *TPI*, the tons per inch immersion,
where

$$A_w = 35(12TPI)$$

is

$$d = \frac{36\Delta}{35TPI}\left[\frac{1}{\delta_1} - \frac{1}{\delta}\right]$$

Note that the sign of the numerical value of d indicates whether change is an increase or decrease in draft. In the case of a ship passing from salt to fresh water, the formula reduces to

$$d = \frac{36\Delta}{35TPI}\left(1 - \frac{1}{\frac{36}{35}}\right)$$

$$d = \frac{\Delta}{35TPI}.$$

In the case of a ship passing from fresh to salt water, the formula becomes

$$d = -\frac{\Delta}{35TPI}.$$

HYDROSTATIC CURVES (DISPLACEMENT AND OTHER CURVES)

The large folded print in the pocket in the back of the book is an exact copy of the original *curves of form,* prepared by the designers, for the destroyer USS *Gearing.* (It is typical of all other ships of similar size and seagoing purpose and will be used henceforth for examples throughout this book.) These curves are typical and represent the standard presentation of hull characteristics which are functions of form. The most convenient way of recording these characteristics graphically is on coordinates of mean drafts vs. displacements. Because the basic variation in underwater hull form is the result of varying drafts, the ordinate scale is in *feet of mean draft*. The abscissa is in *tons of displacement*. For functions of drafts other than displacements, suitable scale factors are provided to convert the reading in tons to the proper dimensions.

The following description of the individual curves will serve as a guide to their use and preparation.

Curve (1)—Displacement in Salt Water. The draft scale used for this and all subsequent curves is the mean draft to the bottom of the keel. This is below the molded base line, a distance of the thickness of the keel. It is sometimes referred to as the *base line at the bottom of the keel amidships.*

The salt water displacement curve is probably the most frequently used of all the curves, because it is generally the starting point for the use of the other curves in obtaining other data.

The method of using this curve is practically self-explanatory. If the displacement is desired, enter the ordinate scale with the mean draft, note the intersection of the horizontal line corresponding to the given mean draft with curve (1), and read the corresponding displacement in tons on the horizontal scale vertically above. If the displacement is given and the mean draft is desired, the procedure is simply reversed.

Curve (2)—Displacement in Fresh Water. For the same mean draft, the ship's displacement will be less in fresh water than in salt water or, conversely, for the same displacement or weight, (which is the more logical case) the ship will float at a lesser draft in salt water than in fresh water. The horizontal separation of curves (1) and (2) is proportional to $^{35}/_{36}$, the density ratio of pure, fresh water and standard, sea water. Curve (2) is used in the same manner as curve (1).

Curve (3)—Center of Buoyancy above Bottom of Keel Amidships. The use of this curve involves translating a displacement or draft reference into a linear value of *KB*. This is done, as in the case of most of the subsequent curves, by the use of a scale factor. For this curve, as on other curves, the scale factor is printed on the curve itself. For *KB*, it is 100 tons = 1 foot. The value is read by entering with the mean draft, reading horizontally to curve (3) and thence vertically to the displacement value above. The reading is converted to feet by the scale factor given above.

Curve (4)—Center of Buoyancy Aft of Station 10 (Longitudinal Position of the Center of Buoyancy). This curve gives the longitudinal location of the center of buoyancy, *B*, with reference to the midship section, in this case Section 10. (This section is sometimes called the midship perpendicular, *M.P.*). Enter with the given mean draft and read to the displacement scale vertically above. This reading, as above, is divided by the scale factor (100 tons = 2 feet) which gives the longitudinal distance of *B* from section 10 in feet.

Curve (5)—Area of Waterlines. This curve provides the area in square feet of any waterplane parallel to the base plane at a given mean draft. Entry and reading are made in the same way as curves (3) and (4) above. The scale factor in this case is 100 tons = 1000 square feet.

Curve (6)—Center of Gravity of Waterplane Aft of Section 10. This curve provides the longitudinal location of the *center of floatation* with reference to the midship section. By definition, the center of flotation is the centroid or geometric center of the waterplane. The distance of this point, as given from section 10, may be reoriented for convenience in trim problems to the forward perpendicular by simply adding half of the length between perpendiculars. Entry and reading are made as before using the scale factor, 100 tons = 2 feet.

Curve (7)—Tons per Inch Immersion. This curve provides a source for values of tons per inch immersion at any mean draft without recourse to the computation described in the foregoing section. The values, as defined for this characteristic, are given for *salt water only.* If fresh water values are desired, the plotted values must be multiplied by $^{35}\!/_{36}$. Entry and reading are made as before using a scale factor of 100 tons = 2 tons.

Curve (8)—Area of Station 10 (Midship Section). This curve gives the value of the area of Section 10 up to any given mean draft. It is one of the more important hull characteristics and is provided on all typical curves of form. The values are obtained similarly to those for curve (7) using the scale factory of 100 tons = 50 square feet.

Curve (9)—Station 10 with Plating (Outline of the Midship Section). This curve provides essentially what its name implies. Its coordinates are to the same scale as is the draft scale in feet. It shows the actual shape of the midship section to the outside of the plating for the half-breadth of the ship (scale is 100 tons = 1 foot).

Curve (10)—Transverse Metacenter above Bottom of Keel Amidships. This curve provides the frequently used value of $\overline{KM}$ for the complete ranges of mean drafts encountered. Entry and reading is made in the usual manner. Scale factor is 100 tons = 2 feet.

Curve (11)—Longitudinal Metacentric Radius. The longitudinal metacentric radius must not be confused with the transverse metacentric radius (the value which is more frequently used). Values are obtained as before using the scale factor 100 tons = 200 feet.

Curve (12)—Approximate Moment to Alter Trim One Inch. The values given here are the moments to change trim one inch for any of the various mean drafts involved. The values are labeled *approximate*, inasmuch as they are obtained from the approximate relationship $\dfrac{\Delta \times \overline{BM'}}{12L}$ rather than the exact relationship $\dfrac{\Delta \times \overline{GM}}{12L}$. The values are obtained in the usual manner using a scale factor of 100 tons = 100 foot tons.

Curve (13)—Addition to Displacement due to One Foot Change of Trim by Stern. A vessel which is trimmed by the stern at any given mean draft generally has a greater displacement than the same untrimmed ship at the same mean draft. This is the result of the conventional ship forms which have increasingly fuller waterlines aft as draft increases. The converse is true when the ship is trimmed by the bow.

Although the correction to the untrimmed displacement is small unless the trim is excessive, it is a factor that must be applied for an accurate value of displacement.

When a ship is trimmed by the stern, it generally has a greater immersed volume than when floating on an even keel at the same mean draft as given by curves (1) or (2). The correction to be added to the displacement for one foot of trim by the stern is taken from curve (13) using the scale factor (100 tons = 2 tons). For a trim of other than one foot, correct the value obtained in proportion to the amount of trim. When the ship is trimmed by the bow, the correction is subtracted.

HYDROSTATICS OF SUBMERSIBLES—
WEIGHT AND BUOYANCY

In expanding the study of the basic laws of floatation to include the submarine, let us review some basic definitions.

Displacement is the weight of water displaced by a body immersed or partly immersed in water. The buoyant force acts normally to the surface of the water and is always numerically equal to the displacement. Weight is equal to the actual weight of the body. Note that if the body is floating freely, weight and displacement or buoyancy always are numerically equal. Under some submerged conditions, the weight and displacement or buoyancy are equal. This will be explained later. *Displaced volume* is equal to the volume of water displaced by the immersed portion of the body. In a fully submerged submarine, the displaced volume can be changed only by altering the shape of the submarine.

Consider the simplified profile of a submarine (figure 2–17) to be loaded until it floats with a zero angle (no trim) at a certain waterline specifically designated as a diving trim waterline. Then, the volume above the waterline (shaded area) is equal to the reserve buoyancy.

If it is desired to completely submerge the submarine, we must complete the flooding of the tanks (heavy outline), thus taking on a volume of water exactly equal to the reserve buoyancy. The main ballast tanks provide this volume. (See figure 2–18.)

In order to submerge without changing the trim or list, the centers of volume of the ballast tanks and the reserve buoyant volume must act in the same vertical line.

Submarine on the Surface Floating at Diving Trim. The submarine on the surface is, of course, like any surface ship. The total weight, W, equals the total buoyant forces, B, and is acting in the same vertical line. The center of gravity is assumed to be above the center of buoyancy.

Submarine Submerged. Refer to figure 2–19. Vectors W and B represent the original lines of action of the weight and buoyant force. Submergence has been accomplished by completely flooding the ballast tanks, thereby adding a weight w to the submarine. The weight, w, acts on the tank's combined center of volume. To compensate for the additional weight, the submarine has submerged until the additional buoyant force, b, derived from the reserve buoyancy, is equal to w. Note that w and b are equal and opposite forces acting in the same line; thus no trimming or listing moment is introduced. The resultant

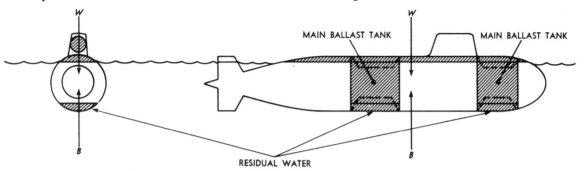

Figure 2–17. Simplified Diving Trim

forces of weight, W_s, and buoyancy, B_s, are moved longitudinally by the same amount. In this condition, the submarine is said to be in a state of neutral buoyancy, that is, the total weight of the submerged submarine, W_s, is equal to the weight of the total volume of water it displaces, B_s. In this state, the submarine would remain suspended, neither rising nor sinking, unless acted on by some additional force. The center of gravity is now assumed to be below the center of buoyancy. The reason for this location will be considered later in the study of stability.

Surfacing the Submarine. This operation merely necessitates forcing the water out of the tank, thereby eliminating w, thus causing the submarine to gain positive buoyancy, that is, B_s is greater than W_s. The unbalance between weight and

buoyant forces causes the vessel to rise to the surface and float as before submergence so that B and W are equal.

Conversely, if, while the submarine is submerged and in a state of neutral buoyancy, some weight is added to the submarine, the W_s is greater than B_s, and the submarine will sink until it rests on the bottom or some external dynamic force is provided to overcome the inequality of forces. (The external dynamic force is provided by the diving planes. In practice, W_s and B_s are seldom exactly equal, and the diving planes are used to overcome this unbalance of static forces.)

Note that the preceding discussion is based on an equality of volume, not weight, and therefore diving trim for a particular unflooded volume of the ballast tank will be the same *regardless of the density* of water in which the boat is floating.

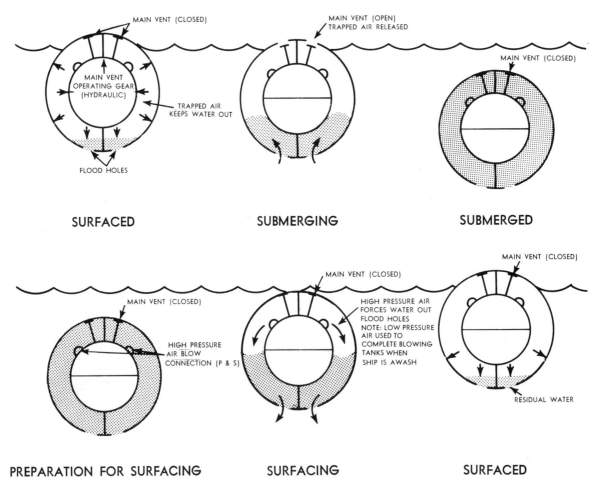

Figure 2–18. Use of the Main Ballast in Diving and Surfacing

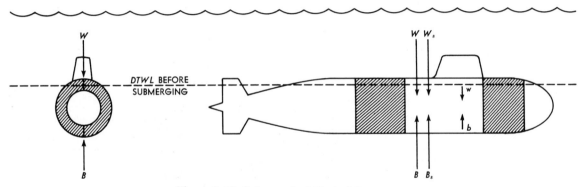

Figure 2–19. Submerged at Neutral Buoyancy

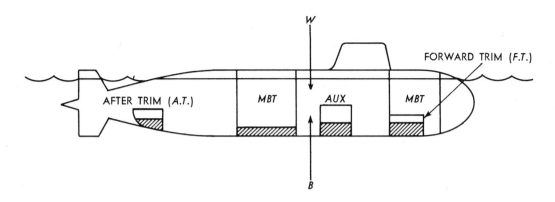

Figure 2–20. Submarine on Surface in Diving Trim

For simplicity, a profile of a submarine showing two general groups of ballast tanks, auxiliaries, and forward and after trim tank (located inside the pressure hull) will be used in the following discussion. It is assumed that the submarine has no way on and that control of the submerged submarine can be maintained by shifting, adding, or removing weight. The most convenient form of weight to use is seawater, because of the facility with which it can be moved by means of pumps or air pressure and directed through a trimming manifold to the desired location.

It is the purpose of this section to discuss submarine statics by introducing various tanks as they are required to maintain satisfactory control of the submarine while diving and when submerged. For each condition, a simple force analysis is made and a corresponding trim analysis is made in terms consistent with accepted submarine phraseology. The following notations are used:

Dotted line vector—individual weight and buoyant forces
Solid line vector—force resultant
W—weight of submarine
W_s—weight submerged at neutral buoyancy
W_1, W_2, W_3—resultant weight for specific condition
w—weight added or removed
w (with subscript)—weight of sea water in a particular tank
B—buoyant force on surface in diving trim
B_s—buoyant force submerged
b—buoyant force of reserve buoyancy

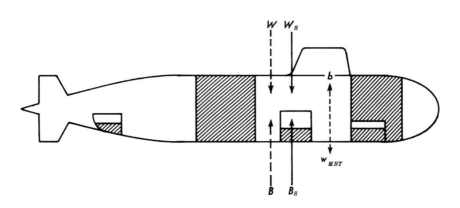

Figure 2–21. Submerged—Neutral Buoyancy and Zero Angle

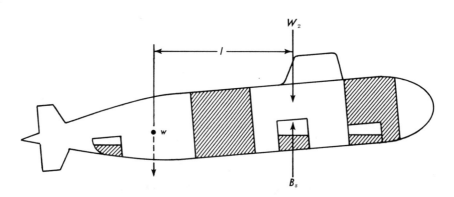

Figure 2–22. Submerged—Weight Added Aft

Figure 2–20.—The submarine is floating in diving trim with residual water in the ballast tanks. Auxiliary and trim tanks are partially filled.

Figure 2–21.—As seen above, if the ballast tanks are flooded, the submarine will submerge with neutral buoyancy and no change of trim and zero angle. Note that when the submarine is sub-

merged the center of buoyancy is located longitudinally at the auxiliary tanks.

Figure 2–22.—Let us add some weight, w, aft of the center of buoyancy. The addition of weight could be caused by sea water replacing fuel oil in a tank aft. The resultant force, W_2, is greater than B_s and is initially moved out of the line of action of B_s. This movement causes the boat to trim by the stern until W_2 and B_s are again in the same vertical line as shown above. Since W_2 is greater than B_s, the boat has negative buoyancy or sinks. The condition is referred to as "heavy overall, heavy aft."

Figure 2–23.—To correct the above condition, three additional tanks are installed in the boat: forward trim, *FT*; auxiliary, *AUX*; and after trim, *AT*. These tanks contain a variable amount of water, the weight of this water being included in the weight of submarine, W_s. They are interconnected by means of the trim system. Appropriately, they are called *variable ballast tanks* and perform two functions:

1. *Compensation for trimming moment change.* This compensating moment change causes the vessel to trim until the lines of action of W_s and B_s are normal to the keel (zero angle on the submarine).

2. *Compensation for overall weight addition or removal.* In order to compensate for the condition of "heavy overall, heavy aft," we must accomplish two things:

    a. Remove the after trimming moment.
    b. Decrease the weight of the ship so that $W_s = B_s$.

To compensate for the moment wl, we may pump water overboard from *AT* until the following equation is satisfied:

$$w_{AT} \, l_1 = w \, l$$
$$\text{but} \quad l_1 > l$$
$$\therefore \quad w_{AT} < w.$$

Next, the overall weight addition must be compensated. Since w_{AT} is less than w, the remainder can be taken out of the auxiliary tank so that the following equation is satisfied:

$$w_{AT} + w_{AUX} = w.$$

The geometric center of the auxiliary tank is assumed to be in the same vertical line with B_s when the submarine is submerged, and hence no trimming moment is introduced by removing water from the auxiliary tank. Performing the indicated procedure brings the boat back to a condition of neutral buoyancy and zero angle. The procedure described is the fastest method of returning the boat to a "final trim" condition. However, the student should remember that there are other solutions, i.e., pump from *AT* to *FT* to remove the trimming moment and then pump from the auxiliary tank to the sea to remove the excess weight, w.

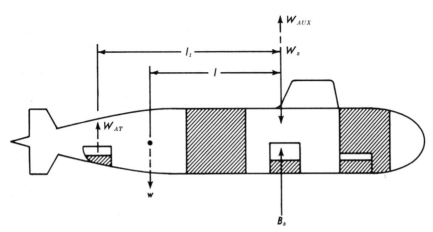

Figure 2–23. Submerged—Neutral Buoyancy and Zero Angle

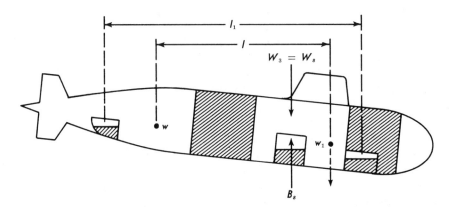

Figure 2–24. Submerged—Weight on Board Shifted Forward

Figure 2–24.—This condition involves a shift of weight already on board. This movement of w causes a trimming moment but does not alter the overall weight, $w_3 = w_s = B_s$. The boat trims by the bow but maintains neutral buoyancy. This condition is known as "all right overall, heavy forward" or "all right overall, light aft."

To correct this condition requires a shift of water only—none of it being discharged overboard. The shift could be made in three ways:

   1. From *FT* to *AT*
   2. From *FT* to *AUX*
   3. From *AUX* to *AT*

If we correct by shifting from *FT* to *AT,* the following equation must be satisfied:

$$w_{FT}l_1 = wl.$$

Figure 2–25.—This condition represents a case in which the weight is removed whose center of gravity is vertically in line with B_s. The situation might arise in submarine operation where miscellaneous weights are removed throughout the vessel, and the assumption is made that they are equivalent to a single weight removed from a position in the vertical line containing B_s. The condition involves overall weight compensation only, no trimming moment being introduced. The boat remains on an even keel, but gains positive buoyancy, $B_s > W_4$, and begins to rise.

To correct this condition, we must take on sea water in the auxiliary tank from the sea in an amount equal to the weight removed, w. The positive buoyancy of the boat is destroyed, and neutral buoyancy is re-established.

In surfacing, as water is blown from the *MBTs,* the boat attains positive buoyancy and rises to the surface until a state of equilibrium is reached, $W = B$. The submarine is now floating at a *DTWL.*

The foregoing illustrations are merely to call the student's attention to the manner in which the tanks are used. An almost endless number of weight alterations can be envisioned for an operating submarine, but all can be analyzed in a manner similar to the above.

FACTORS AFFECTING PRACTICAL SUBMARINE STATICS.

Before leaving the subject of submarine statics, it would be well to call the student's attention to the following, which complicate the operations of a submerged submarine. Consider the equations:

Weight submerged (W_s) =

        buoyant force submerged (B_s)

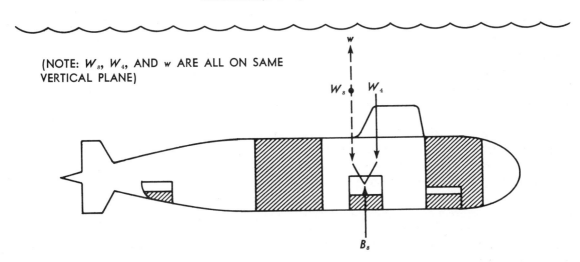

(NOTE: W_s, W_4, AND w ARE ALL ON SAME VERTICAL PLANE)

Figure 2–25. Submerged—Weight Removed From Amidships

This equation must be satisfied if the submerged submarine is to remain in neutral buoyancy.

Buoyant force submerged (B_s) = volume of water displaced times the density of water

The two factors on the right side of the equation are not constant and are best studied separately.

Volume of Water Displaced.—As a submarine submerges, the hydrostatic pressure increases, and, at greater operating depth, an appreciable amount of the volume of displacement is lost due to the compression of the hull. Thus, holding the density constant, B_s is decreased as the ship goes deeper, and a "heavy overall" condition will exist. Since the operating personnel have control over weight primarily, W can be decreased by pumping out variable ballast water until W_s again equals B_s. The volume of water displaced (and hence B_s) can be altered to a very small degree by raising or lowering the periscopes and various masts. Often the minute change in B_s thus effected will be sufficient to keep the submarine in a state of neutral buoyancy without changing the weight of the ship.

Density of Water.—The density of seawater depends primarily on two factors: temperature and salinity. As the temperature decreases, the density increases. Conversely, as the salinity decreases, the density increases. In the open ocean the salinity varies but little and can be considered constant. The temperature, however, is a variable, usually decreasing at different rates as the depth increases—depending on the location. Submarines carry instruments which trace the temperature gradient with changes in depth, such records being of invaluable assistance in planning future operations. Suffice to say that because of the temperature decrease, the density of the seawater will increase as the submarine goes to greater depths. If, in the above equation, the volume of water displaced is held constant, the effect of increasing depth would be to increase the buoyant force. Therefore, B_s would exceed W, and the vessel would become "light overall." Weight must be added in the form of variable ballast water to make $W_s = B_s$. Considering both factors of the right side of the above equation to be variables, it will be seen that they tend to counteract each other. Although the vessel's hull is compressed as it goes deeper (decrease in B_s), the smaller amount of water displaced may weigh more than the larger amount of water displaced near the surface. The combined effect would cause the submarine to become light, and variable ballast water would have to be taken aboard. In the vicinity of mouths of freshwater rivers and in various other parts of the ocean, the salinity is far from constant. This presents a second variable in density determination and further complicates correct ballasting.

These actualities in no way invalidate the basic concepts developed in this section. To be in a state of neutral buoyancy, the total weight of the submarine must equal the weight of the water it displaces.

That the ocean is, in effect, divided into *layers* of water of varying densities, due mainly to temperature differences, is an aid to the submariner, as well as serving to complicate the life of a diving officer. Ships can actually rest on layers with very little or no headway on, an advantage when rigged for silent running. *Layers* also offer protection from detection by surface craft in that they deflect the stream of impulses from sonar gear.

The Equilibrium Polygon

As indicated in the foregoing it is necessary on submarines operating below the surface to compensate for variations in longitudinal moments and weight by making adjustments in the variable ballast. This ongoing daily problem can be some-

what simplified or mechanized by a graphical plotting method called the *equilibrium polygon*.

Referring to figure 2–26, which is a typical example of this graphical method of accounting, we can note that the horizontal dimension represents variable ballast *moment* about the trim axis of the submerged submarine. (The axis location is here designated *0*.) The vertical dimension or scale represents the *weight* of variable ballast. Thus each side of the polygon represents the effect of filling one of the variable ballast tanks. These tanks are identified along the appropriate side of the polygon here shown for a typical submarine.

For example, referring to figure 2–26 the line *OA* shows the development of the weight of ballast together with its moment as the *forward trim tank* is filled. Proceeding and adding to this weight and moment summation as the *forward variable fuel oil tank* is filled, point *B* is reached. Next, proceeding with filling the *auxiliaries* which are located very near the submerged center of buoyancy (trimming axis) the moment change is negligible and the direction of *BC* is therefore

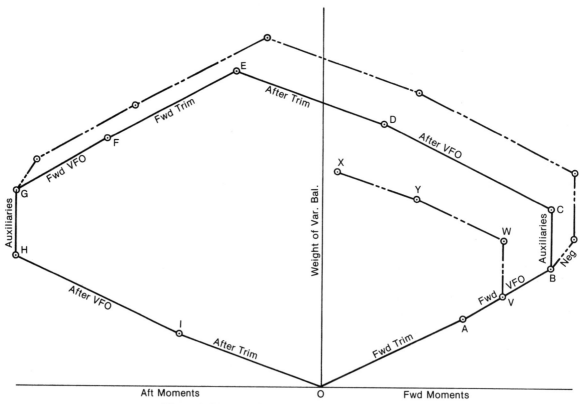

Figure 2–26. Equilibrium Polygon for Submarines.

vertical. The *after variable fuel oil tank* when filled reverses the direction of the moment and the line of the developing polygon moves left from C to D. Finally, with the filling of *after trim,* point E is reached, which is the top of the polygon. It thus represents the total summation of added ballast weight and the net moment produced, either forward or aft of point 0. (In this case slightly aft). Point E could have been reached by plotting from after trim tank to forward instead of from forward aft as described above. If this direction is plotted also as shown in figure 2–26 then the polygon is completed and closed. In this form it makes a useful tool. It should be noted that the tanks when plotted from aft, forward will show up as parallel to the polygon sides, showing these same tanks plotted from forward aft. Thus side FE is parallel and equal in length to side OA etc.

In using the equilibrium polygon (which we must note here, is an operational tool and not a design procedure), it can be seen that any desired submerged condition may be reached by adjusting the variable ballast according to the method of plotting the polygon. It is only necessary to *stay within the figure.* For example, if it is wished to reach point X it can be determined on the plot which would indicate filling FWD Trim, partially filling (as indicated), FWD, VFO, the Auxiliaries, AFT, VFO and AFT Trim.

It should be noted in the use of the equilibrium polygon that the ballast weights of water taken on (added) are computed on the basis of the capacity of the tanks at the rate of 35 cu. ft. per ton.

The broken line in figure 2–26 external to the polygon indicates the additional side used when the submarine is of the type equipped with a negative tank and it is considered part of the variable ballast system. The negative tank as used produces a total submerged weight which exceeds the neutral submerged buoyancy, and thus the condition must be assumed as "heavy over all" and the submarine will sink.

USS Long Beach—a Stable Guided-Missile Platform

CHAPTER 3

The Ship at Rest — Static Stability

In addition to being buoyant in the sea, a ship must also possess the equally important characteristic of positive stability. This characteristic must prevail continually, both at rest and in motion, in still water and among waves.

The concepts of stability for ships are derived essentially from the basic theories of mechanics, and every ship designer must be thoroughly conversant with them. To provide a complete and thorough understanding of these theories as they are applied to ships, this chapter will deal with them in a definitive and derivative way. Since it is most important that these fundamental concepts be very clear, it is necessary to begin with a basic reference to equilibrium.

Equilibrium—A Concept

Because the following study is one of static forces, we will deal with *static equilibrium*. While in the broader sense *equilibrium* refers to an overall balance of forces, which involves no acceleration or deceleration, we will narrowly define static equilibrium as follows: *A body at rest is said to be in equilibrium.*

If this body is disturbed by an outside force and returns to its original position when the force is removed, it is said to be in *stable equilibrium.* Thus, a ship that is inclined from its normal upright position and tends to return or right itself is said to be *stable.*

On the other hand, a body that continues to move in the same direction after it is originally set in motion is said to be in *unstable equilibrium.* A ship is said to be unstable when, after being inclined by a slight force, it continues to incline, possibly until it capsizes. An initially unstable ship may sometimes incline until it reaches a point of stable equilibrium because of the change in its underwater hull form.

A body is said to be in *neutral equilibrium* if it comes to rest at any position to which it is moved or displaced. A cylindrical, homogeneous log floating in water would be in neutral equilibrium.

Thus, we have three states of equilibrium: *stable, unstable,* and *neutral.*

A body in stable equilibrium exhibits a tendency to right itself when its aspect to the horizontal plane is changed. This tendency is called *static stability* and is a measurable quantity as will be outlined below.

51

THE BASIS FOR SHIP EQUILIBRIUM

Consider a ship floating upright on the surface of motionless water. In order to be at rest or in equilibrium, there must be no unbalanced forces or moments acting on it. There are two forces that maintain this equilibrium: (1) the force of gravity, and (2) the force of buoyancy. When the ship is at rest, these two forces are acting in the same perpendicular line, and, in order for the ship to float in equilibrium, they must be exactly equal numerically as well as opposite in direction.

The *force of gravity* acts at a point or center where all of the weights of the ship may be said to be concentrated; i.e., the *center of gravity*. Gravity always acts vertically downward.

The *force of buoyancy* acts through the center of buoyancy, where the resultant of all of the buoyant forces is considered to be acting. This force always acts vertically upward. When the ship is heeled, the shape of the underwater body is changed, thus moving the position of the center of buoyancy.

Now, when the ship is heeled by an external inclining force and the center of buoyancy has been moved from the centerline plane of the ship, there will usually be a separation between the lines of action of the force of gravity and the force of buoyancy. This separation of the lines of action of the two equal forces, which act in opposite directions, forms a couple whose magnitude is equal to the product of one of these forces (i.e., displacement) and the distance separating them. In figure 3–1 (a), where this moment tends to restore the ship to the upright position, the moment is called the *righting moment,* and the perpendicular distance between the two lines of action is the *righting arm* ($\overline{GZ}$).

Suppose now that the center of gravity is moved upward to such a position that when the ship is heeled slightly, the buoyant force acts in a line through the center of gravity. In the new position, there are no unbalanced forces, or, in other words, a zero moment arm and a zero moment. In figure 3–1 (b), the ship is in neutral equilibrium, and further inclination would eventually bring about a *change of the state of equilibrium.*

If we move the center of gravity still higher, as in figure 3–1 (c), the separation between the

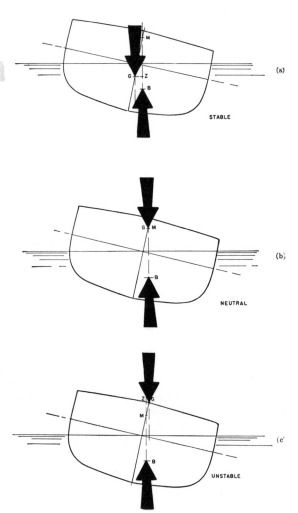

Figure 3–1. Stable (a), Neutral (b), and Unstable (c) Equilibrium in the Upright Position. The hull is shown inclined by an outside force to demonstrate the tendency in each case.

lines of action of the two forces as the ship is inclined slightly is in the opposite direction from that of figure 3–1 (a). In this case, the moment does not act in the direction that will restore the ship to the upright but will cause it to incline further. In such a situation, the ship has a negative righting moment or an *upsetting moment.* The arm is an *upsetting arm,* or *negative* righting arm ($\overline{GZ}$).

These three cases illustrate the forces and relative position of their lines of action in the three fundamental states of equilibrium.

THE POSITION OF THE METACENTER AND EQUILIBRIUM

The *metacenter, M,* may also be defined as the limiting intersection which is approached by the lines of action of the buoyant force and the original vertical line through the center of buoyancy. This intersection then lies on both the line of action of the center of gravity when the ship is upright and the line of the buoyant force.

Consequently, it can be readily seen from the previous section that when the metacenter is above the center of gravity, as in figure 3–1 (a), there is a positive righting couple formed when the ship is inclined, and the ship is in stable equilibrium.

When the metacenter and the center of gravity coincide, as in figure 3–1 (b), no couple is formed, and the ship is in neutral equilibrium.

When the metacenter is below the center of gravity, as in figure 3–1 (c), a negative or upsetting couple is formed, and the ship is in unstable equilibrium.

In considering this relation between the metacenter and the ship's state of equilibrium, it is necessary to remember that the definition of the metacenter is actually valid only for angles of inclination from zero degrees up to the range of seven to ten degrees. Beyond this, the intersection of the lines of action of the center of buoyancy and the vertical centerplane of the ship has no significance. Therefore, in using the relative positions of the metacenter and the center of gravity as a criterion of stability, we must limit ourselves to *small* angles of inclination. Obviously stability itself cannot be limited to such a restricted range. Consequently, we must differentiate between *overall stability* and *initial stability* (the stability related to the metacenter and the center of gravity).

METACENTRIC HEIGHT, MEASURE OF INITIAL STABILITY

The distance between the center of gravity, when it is in the vertical centerline plane, and the metacenter is the *metacentric height*. However, when the center of gravity is not in the vertical centerline plane, the metacentric height is measured as the distance between the point projected perpendicularly from the center of gravity to the vertical centerline plane and the metacenter. In figure 3–2, the metacentric height is $\overline{GM}$ with the ship's center of gravity at either G or G_1. Unless otherwise specified, the metacenter and metacentric height refer to the *transverse metacentric height*. If the longitudinal metacenter is being discussed, the associated metacentric height is designated $\overline{GM'}$ and spoken of, therefore, as the *longitudinal metacentric height*.

If M is above G, the metacentric height is positive. If M is below G, $\overline{GM}$ is negative.

$\overline{GM}$ is the measure of the *initial stability* or the ability of the ship to resist initial heel from the upright position. A ship with a positive $\overline{GM}$ will tend to float upright and will resist initial inclining forces. A ship with a negative $\overline{GM}$ will cease to float upright when disturbed by the most minute

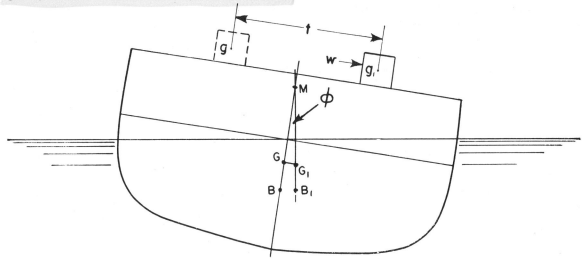

Figure 3–2. Inclined Equilibrium

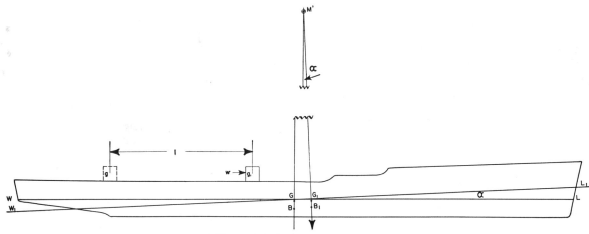

Figure 3–3. Longitudinal Stability

outside force. Such a ship may be said to be initially unstable, but to say that her condition of equilibrium is unstable may be incorrect. She may list at some angle and resist further inclination and be, therefore, in a state of stable equilibrium from this angle of list on.

LONGITUDINAL STABILITY

In the foregoing discussion, we have generally assumed transverse inclinations, such as heel or list, but the principles involved are equally applicable to longitudinal inclinations, i.e., changes of trim. There is no difference in principle between longitudinal and transverse inclinations. The location of M', the longitudinal metacenter, is always so high that we can safely predict that we will never have a negative longitudinal metacentric height $(\overline{GM'})$. See figure 3–3.

RIGHTING ARM

The couple formed by the forces of buoyancy and gravity in the above discussion is, quantitatively, the product of the weight of the ship and the distance between the two forces. The perpendicular distance between the lines of action of the two forces is commonly called the *righting arm* or $\overline{GZ}$. When the weight or displacement of the ship is constant, we can use the value of $\overline{GZ}$ as a measure of the static stability through all angles of inclination.

For small angles of inclination (i.e., where the line of action of the buoyant force when inclined intersects the vertical centerline, substantially at M), $\overline{GZ}$ is equal to $\overline{GM} \sin \phi$, where ϕ is the transverse angle of inclination in degrees.

Therefore, the value of $\overline{GM}$ may be used in comparing the initial stability of ships of the same type and size.

RANGE OF STABILITY

Range of stability is defined as that range of inclination in degrees either to port or starboard, from the position of equilibrium, through which the ship is statically stable.

The magnitude of this range is primarily dependent upon the relation of freeboard and beam and the location of the center of gravity. The definition of this range implies safety of heel throughout without capsizing. This meaning is not to be accepted literally, however. It simply indicates an angle to which the ship may be inclined without capsizing if inclined gradually in calm, motionless water by inclining moments not exceeding the righting moment at any angle. The more important practical consideration, however, is the angle at which the righting arm is maximum. The importance of this angle will be brought out later in discussions and applications of stability curves.

It is sufficient here to point out that beyond the *angle of maximum righting arm* under actual inclining forces, the ship is in serious danger of capsizing and, in general, will capsize upon reaching that angle.

Initial Stability

THE SHIFT OF CENTER OF GRAVITY WITHIN A SYSTEM (WEIGHT SHIFT)

Consider a system consisting of a body of

weight, W (figure 3–4), with the center of gravity located at G and containing a small weight, w, which is available for shifting within this system originally located at g. If we shift w from g to g_1, taking moments about G, we have

$$W\overline{GG_1} = w\overline{gg_1}$$

or,

$$\overline{GG_1} = \frac{w\overline{gg_1}}{W}.$$

Note that $\overline{GG_1}$ and $\overline{gg_1}$ are parallel and in the same direction, regardless of the direction of shift.

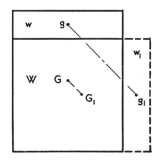

Figure 3–4. Shift of Center of Gravity

To facilitate the determination of the effect of a weight shift on the draft forward and aft and on the list, it is helpful to determine the components of the shift in the ship's center of gravity parallel to the three basic planes of the ship; that is, the vertical, transverse, and longitudinal components of the shift in the center of gravity. This is accomplished by considering the weight shift to be reduced to component movements which are vertical, longitudinal, and transverse.

Consider a weight to be moved from the second deck, port side, and aft to the main deck, starboard side, and forward.

First, assume the weight to be moved vertically from the second deck, point g to g_1, at the same height that the weight will occupy on the main deck when in its final position. The ship's center of gravity will move vertically as follows:

$$\overline{GG_1} \text{ (vert.)} = \frac{wv}{\Delta}$$

where

v = vertical distance which the weight, w, is shifted.

Δ = displacement of the ship.

Secondly, assume the weight to be moved longitudinally from point g_1 to its final longitudinal position, g_2. The ship's center of gravity will move longitudinally as follows:

$$\overline{G_1G_2} \text{ (long.)} = \frac{wl}{\Delta}$$

l = longitudinal distance which the weight, w, is shifted.

Lastly, assume the weight to be moved transversely from ·point g_2 to its final transverse position, g_3. The ship's center of gravity will move transversely as follows:

$$\overline{G_2G_3} \text{ (trans.)} = \frac{wt}{\Delta}$$

t = transverse distance which the weight, w, is shifted.

The numerical subscripts assigned to G and to g have no significance other than denoting successive positions of the centers of gravity of the ship and the weight. As examples, note that in figures 3–2 and 3–3, the ship's center of gravity is denoted by G. The center of gravity moves to G_1 in each case in response to weight shifts which are longitudinal and/or transverse respectively.

CONDITIONS OF EQUILIBRIUM IN AN
INCLINED POSITION

A ship in equilibrium in an inclined position, as in figure 3–2, must have the center of gravity directly in a vertical line with the center of buoyancy. Referring to the diagram, if the ship is floating in equilibrium at some angle of list, ϕ, the center of gravity is off the vertical centerplane axis of the ship at some position, G_1.

When the ship was upright, the center of gravity was located on the vertical centerline plane at a position, G.

In order to move the center of gravity from G to G_1, a weight, w, within the system was shifted transversely from point g to g_1.

Then,

$$\overline{GG_1} \text{ (trans.)} = \frac{wt}{\Delta}.$$

If the shift occurs perpendicularly to the vertical centerline plane, it can be seen from figure 3–2 that

$$\overline{GG_1} \text{ (trans.)} = \overline{GM} \tan \phi.$$

Then,

$$wt = \Delta \, \overline{GM} \tan \phi$$

where ϕ = angle of inclination (less than seven to ten degrees).

For longitudinal inclinations, the same principles are applicable. Using the longitudinal metacenter M' and the equation, $\overline{G_1G_2} \text{ (long.)} = \frac{wl}{W}$, the following relation can be derived from figure 3–3:

$$\Delta \overline{GM'} \tan \theta = wl$$

where θ = angle of longitudinal inclination.

A useful relation in this case is

$$\tan \theta = \frac{\text{change in trim}}{\text{length between draft marks}}.$$

COMPUTATION OF THE METACENTRIC RADIUS AND THE LOCATION OF M

Initial stability is discussed before overall stability, because it logically follows the discussion of equilibrium. The metacentric height, the measure of initial stability, is an important tool in buoyancy and stability calculations, but the overall stability (to be discussed subsequently) is the complete measure of the ability of the ship to resist inclining moments.

In order to numerically fix the value for metacentric height, either transverse or longitudinal, we must actually locate the metacenter and the center of gravity in relation to some fixed datum plane, preferably a horizontal plane through the bottom of the flat keel amidships. These values are normally called $\overline{KM}$, $\overline{KM'}$ and $\overline{KG}$, respectively. The methods of computing these values will be given in the discussions immediately following.

Figure 3–5 shows diagrammatically the cross section of a ship and her water plane shape. The ship is heeled to a small angle of inclination by an external moment so that she floats at the waterline,

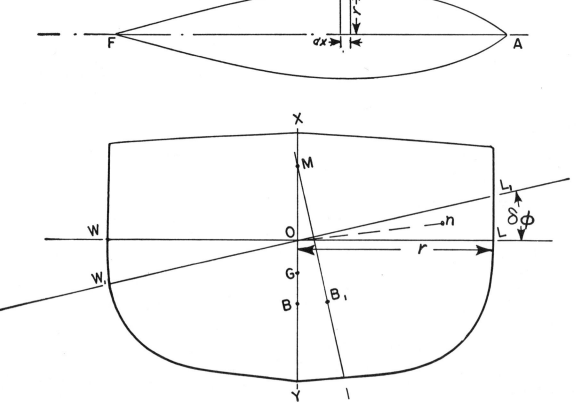

Figure 3–5. Computation of Metacentric Radius

W_1L_1, instead of WL. The location of the center of buoyancy shifts from B to B_1 as previously discussed.

Let r = half-breadth of the ship
    $\delta\phi$ = small angle of inclination in radians
    n = center of gravity of triangle LOL_1
    dx = increment of length, L
    ∇ = volume of displacement
    ρ = density of water

Now, the area of triangle LOL_1 is $1/2r\,r\delta\phi$. The distance from the apex (O) to the center of gravity (n) equals $2/3r$ for a small angle ($\delta\phi$). The moment of area of triangle LOL_1 about the longitudinal centerline plane is

$$\frac{1}{2}r\ r\delta\phi\ \ On$$

$$\frac{1}{2}r\ r\delta\phi\ \frac{2}{3}r.$$

The moment of wedge (having triangle LOL_1 as its section and dx as its thickness) is

$$\frac{1}{2}r\ r\delta\phi\ \frac{2}{3}r\ dx$$

or for the entire ship, we have by integration,

$$\int_O^L \frac{1}{2}r\ r\delta\phi\ \frac{2}{3}r\ dx.$$

Because the volume of the emerged wedge WOW_1 is equal to the immersed wedge LOL_1, the added buoyancy due to LOL_1 is exactly equal to the lost buoyancy due to WOW_1. Hence, there are two equal moments acting in the same direction about the centerline plane.

Therefore, the total moment is:

$$\int_O^L 2\cdot\frac{1}{2}r\cdot r\delta\phi\cdot\frac{2}{3}r\cdot dx$$

or,

$$\int_O^L \frac{2}{3}r^3\delta\phi dx.$$

This total moment or moment of both wedges is equal to the change in the moment of the buoyant volume of the ship. By mechanics, the total change in moment of the buoyant volume of the ship is

$$\rho\nabla\ \overline{BB_1}.$$

Therefore,

$$\rho\nabla\overline{BB_1} = \int_O^L \rho\frac{2}{3}r^3\delta\phi dx.$$

For small angles, $\overline{BB_1} = \overline{BM}\sin\phi = \overline{BM}\ \delta\phi$

$$\nabla\ \overline{BB_1} = \nabla\ \overline{BM}\delta\phi = \delta\phi\int_O^L \frac{2}{3}r^3 dx$$

$$\overline{BM} = \frac{\int_O^L \frac{2}{3}r^3 dx}{\nabla}.$$

Since $\int_O^L \frac{2}{3}r^3 dx$ is the expression for moment of inertia of the waterline plane about the longitudinal centerline, which we will designate by I, then

$$\overline{BM} = \frac{I}{\nabla}.$$

Similarly, it may be shown that

$$\overline{BM'} = \frac{I'}{\nabla}$$

where $\overline{BM'}$ is the longitudinal metacentric radius, and I' is the moment inertia of the waterplane about a transverse axis through the center flotation.

An example of the evaluation of the metacentric radius is given in table 3–1. (The approximate integration here is by the Trapezoidal Rule.)

Table 3–1

Half Ordinate	Cube of Half Ordinate	Multiplier	Function of Cubes $f(I)$
.5	0.125	1/2	0
2.5	15.6	1	16
6.6	287.5	1	288
10.1	1030	1	1030
12.5	1953	1	1953
13.7	2571	1	2571
14.0	2744	1	2744
13.9	2686	1	2686
13.0	2197	1	2197
10.8	1260	1	1260
6.6	287.5	1	288
2.1	9.26	1	9
0.5	0.125	1/2	0

$$\Sigma f(I) = 15042$$

$$I = \int_o^L \frac{2}{3} r^3 dx = \frac{2}{3} h \quad f(I) = \frac{2}{3} \cdot 20 \cdot 15042$$

if

$$\Delta = 400 \text{ tons}, \nabla = 400 \cdot 35 \text{ ft.}^3 \text{ in salt water.}$$

$$\therefore \overline{BM} = \frac{I}{\nabla} = \frac{\frac{2}{3} \cdot 20 \cdot 15042}{400 \cdot 35} = 14.3 \text{ feet.}$$

The computation for $\overline{BM'}$ is similar to the foregoing, using for r the half length of the ship at the waterline. This computed moment of inertia about the midship section must be later corrected for the distance between the midsection and the center of flotation, so that the moment of inertia about the center of flotation is obtained before dividing by the volume to get $\overline{BM'}$. The value of the longitudinal metacentric radius, $\overline{BM'}$, is generally well in excess of the waterline length.

Values of $\overline{KB}$ are also computed for various drafts and after addition to corresponding values of $\overline{BM}$ are plotted as $\overline{KM}$ on the ship's hydrostatic curves. Values of $\overline{BM'}$ are plotted directly as are those of $\overline{KB}$.

THE INCLINING EXPERIMENT AND THE METACENTRIC HEIGHT

In preceding discussions, the importance of the location of the center of gravity was discussed in its relation to the metacenter and the center of buoyancy. Inasmuch as the locations of the center of buoyancy and the metacenter are given in relation to the keel, we must, similarly, locate the center of gravity in relation to the keel.

In the preliminary stages of design, the center of gravity is estimated from its actual position on similar ships. Later on in the design, the position is calculated by the long and tedious process of summing up all of the weights and moments of each item in the entire ship. This calculation is made not only to estimate the position of the center of gravity, but also to insure that the total weight of the ship will be equal to the desired displacement.

The nature of the center of gravity should be kept in mind when thinking of its actual position. Remember that its location is *not* a function of ship's form as are the locations of the metacenter and center of buoyancy. The position of G is a function of the distribution of the weights on board the ship and of the ship itself. Therefore, it is not possible to plot a curve showing the positions of the center of gravity for a range of drafts or displacements.

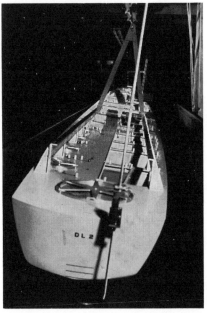

Official U.S. Navy Photograph

Figure 3–6. Stability Model Rigged for Inclining Experiment in Laboratory Test

For large ships where the readily movable weights are a relatively small proportion of the total weight, the exact location of the center of gravity is determined for certain standard conditions of loading.

To determine accurately the vertical location of the center of gravity for the standard conditions of loading, an *inclining experiment* is performed. The results are fully tabulated and calculated in forms set down in the *Inclining Experiment Booklet*. They are corrected to show all data to the standard conditions of loading and finally made available aboard ship in the *Stability and Loading Data Booklet*.

THE INCLINING EXPERIMENT

The theory of the inclining experiment is based on the conditions requisite for equilibrium in an inclined position as given by the equation:

$$\Delta \overline{GM} \tan \phi = wt.$$

Before actually performing the inclining experiment, the values of w and t are determined. Knowing the athwartship distance, t, on deck available for the weight movement, an approximation of the size of the inclining weight, *w,* to produce an angle of inclination of a few degrees can be made by estimating $\overline{GM}$ from previous experiments with the same type of ship in a similar condition.

The inclining weights are generally ingots or pigs of iron and are accurately weighed with the location of their centers of gravity plainly marked on them. They are placed known distances off the centerline. The total inclining weight, *w,* is generally made up in three or four lots and distributed at predetermined positions longitudinally along the deck. This makes possible several angles of inclination and also avoids concentration of too great a load on the deck structure.

Several plumb bobs are suspended in positions, such as hatch openings, to afford a sufficient length of pendulum for accurate readings. The lengths of the plumb bobs must be such that the inclinations will produce deflections of at least two inches. The length is accurately measured just before the experiment.

The actual procedure is as follows:

- The ship must be floating freely.
- All dock lines should be slackened; all liquid tankage and boilers must be either full or empty insofar as possible, and the bilges dry so that there is a minimum of loose liquid.
- The experiment should be performed at slack tide and when there is minimum wind. A preferable location is in a flooded graving dock with the caisson in position.
- All weights aboard should be secure so they will not shift. Checks should be made on the contents of all storerooms.
- The crew should be sent ashore, or if aboard, should be restricted to some convenient location that is made a matter of record.
- After the inclining weights have been put aboard, and immediately prior to commencing the inclining, the following data are recorded:
  a. Drafts forward and aft
  b. Temperature of water
  c. Density of water by hydrometer

From these data and the displacement and other curves, the displacement, Δ, may be determined accurately.

- When all is ready, one or more of the inclining weights is moved according to the previously arranged program, and upon signal after movement is completed, observers read and record:
  a. Deflection of pendulums
  b. Amount of inclining weight and distance moved

The deflection of the pendulum measures the angle of inclination, ϕ. From the values of *w* and *t,* and the foregoing, the metacentric height, $\overline{GM}$, is calculated. Usually several inclinations are made to both port and starboard with intermediate checks at zero. In such cases, the tangents of the angles of inclination from the initial position are plotted against the moment (both port and starboard) of the inclining weights from their initial position. Theoretically, the plot of tangents of small angles of inclination against the corresponding inclining moments will be a straight line. Variation of the resulting plot from a straight line indicates that conditions for the experiment are not favorable, or that an error has been made. The slope of the straight line fitted to these points is datum to solve for the metacentric height, $\overline{GM}$. The straight line plot is only a means of averaging the data graphically.

From the plot, the slope of this straight line is $\dfrac{\tan \phi}{\text{inclining moment}}$. In this case, tan ϕ is a selected magnitude of tangent of angle of inclination, and the moment is the corresponding total inclining moment.

$$\overline{GM} = \frac{wt}{\Delta \tan \phi} = \frac{1}{\Delta \text{slope}}$$

Now, from the displacement and other curves, we may take the value for the height of the metacenter above the keel, $\overline{KM}$, and subtract the value of $\overline{GM}$ obtained from the inclining experiment, and *the final result is the height of the center of gravity above the keel,* $\overline{KG}$, *for the particular loading.*

COMPUTATION OF MOMENT TO CHANGE TRIM

Any longitudinal weight movement in the ship results in the relationship for longitudinal equilibrium given by the equation

$$\Delta \overline{GM}' \tan \theta = wl.$$

The angle, θ, is normally small and usually less than 1°. Suppose the change in trim is one inch, or, in other words, the longitudinal inclination is the angle whose tangent is $1/12 \div L$, where L is the waterline length. Remember that change in trim is the algebraic difference of the changes in draft forward and aft.

Consequently, the above equilibrium relationship may be written

$$\Delta\overline{GM'}\;\frac{1}{12L} = wl$$

$$\frac{\Delta\overline{GM'}}{12L} = wl.$$

Since θ in this case is the angle subtended by a change in trim of one inch, then wl is the *moment to change trim one inch*. This moment will be designated as C henceforth.

$$C = \frac{\Delta\overline{GM'}}{12L}.$$

In actual use, very close approximations may be made by using values of $\overline{BM'}$ instead of $\overline{GM'}$, there being comparatively little difference in the positions of B and G relative to M'. This is only true for longitudinal stability.

Overall Stability

The most satisfactory means of presenting a complete picture of stability is a plot of the righting moments or righting arms with their angles of inclination for several displacements, each of which is called a *static stability curve*. Such a curve may be used to determine several important characteristics for each displacement, among which are (1) the righting arm at any inclination, (2) the $\overline{GM}$, (3) the angle of maximum righting moment, (4) the range of stability, and (5) the dynamic stability.

It is possible to compute the righting arms, $\overline{GZ}$, for a range of angles of inclination, but this involves a tedious process of locating the many positions of B over the range of inclination. There are several methods of determining $\overline{GZ}$ by calculation or mechanical integration. One method, which is the basis of the procedure used by naval ship designers, provides the fundamental source of all static stability curves. A brief description of this method follows.

DEVELOPMENT OF CROSS CURVES OF STABILITY

A double body plan showing the shape of both sides of each section of the ship is drawn. Figure

3–7 is a double body plan in which the even numbered sections have been omitted in the interest of clarity. An integrator, which is an instrument for measuring areas and moments of areas simultaneously, is now adapted to the following procedure (see figure 3–8).

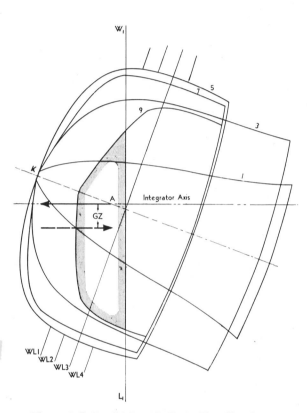

Figure 3–7. Partial Double Body Plan Showing Use of Integrator for Calculating $\overline{GZ}$

This double body plan is placed under an integrator in such a way that the axis of the instrument is perpendicular to the inclined waterline for which the righting arm is to be determined (W_1L_1 in this case) and passes through a selected point on the vertical centerline, point A in figure 3–7. The tracing point of the instrument is then run successively over the underwater portion of each section and the area and moment of area of each section about the integrator axis is recorded. The underwater portion of section 9 below the inclined waterline W_1L_1 is indicated by the shaded outline of figure 3–7. The areas and

Figure 3–8. Using an Integrator to Determine Data for Cross Curves of Stability of a Ship's Hull Form

moment of areas are summed up for the water-line length by the Trapezoidal Rule. The summa-tion of areas is the underwater volume beneath the inclined waterline. This volume, when divided by the density factor (35 ft³/ton) gives the dis-placement beneath the inclined waterline. The summation of moment of area is the moment of volume about a plane through the instrument axis and perpendicular to the sections. The moment of volume divided by the volume gives the dis-tance of the center of buoyancy from the inte-grator axis. Note that the force of buoyancy acts in a line parallel to the instrument axis inasmuch as the latter was set up perpendicular to the in-clined waterline. The buoyant force is shown by the dashed arrow in figure 3–7.

If we assume that the ship's center of gravity is located at the intersection of the vertical center-line and the instrument axis (i.e., point *A* in

figure 3–7), then the line of action of the gravita-tional force will coincide with the integrator axis, as shown by the full arrow of figure 3–7. The distance between the line of action of the center of buoyancy and the integrator axis is the righting arm, $\overline{GZ}$. This is, of course, for the determined angle of inclination at the displacement as cal-culated and for the assumed position of the center of gravity.

This calculation is made for angles of inclina-tion from zero through 90 degrees at 10-degree increments. The process is repeated for the same inclinations about other upright waterlines, such as WL_1, WL_2, and WL_4 of figure 3–7. Note that this requires thirty-six calculations, nine for vary-ing angles about each of four upright waterlines. Note further that considering any upright water-line, such as WL_3, the underwater volume will vary with the angle of inclination. It should be

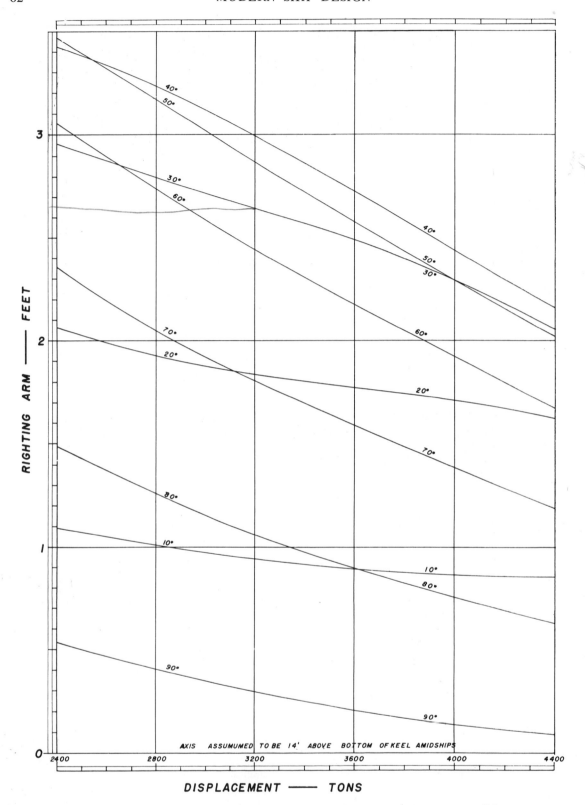

Figure 3–9. Cross Curves of Stability for a typical United States Destroyer-type Ship.

understood that the displacement of a ship will not change simply because we incline the ship. However, for the purpose of computation, it is far simpler to maintain the same set of waterlines, realizing and taking into account that there will be a different displacement below waterline WL_3 when the drawing is inclined to 10 degrees than when inclined to 20 degrees. The result of each calculation is a righting arm for a specified angle of inclination and at a calculated displacement.

The results of the multitudinous calculations obtained from the procedure as described above are the righting arms of the ship for every specified angle of inclination (at 10 degree increments through 90 degrees) at various displacements.

These values are plotted as curves with righting arms as ordinates and displacements as abscissae with an individual curve for each angle of inclination considered. These curves are called the *cross curves of stability,* a typical example of which is shown in figure 3–9. Figure 3–9 bears the note "axis assumed to be 14 feet above bottom of keel amidships." This indicates that the bottom of the keel amidships was the zero reference for the height of the assumed center of gravity and that the axis of the integrator used to develop the cross curves intersected the centerline 14 feet above the bottom of the keel. Hence, *the assumed $\overline{KG}$ for these curves is 14 feet* for this particular ship.

CURVES OF STATIC STABILITY

If we may consider for a moment the *cross curves* in three dimensions instead of two with the angle of inclination as the third coordinate, we would have a three dimensional figure, such as figure 3–10. Now, selecting a particular displacement, we may take a section through this figure, and the resulting curve is a plot of the righting arm as ordinate and the angle of inclination as abscissa. In other words, this sectional curve is a *curve of static stability*. This curve shows the righting arm at any angle of inclination for the original *assumed position* of the *center of gravity* and the displacement selected.

The value of the cross curves is particularly emphasized in view of the variation in displacement in everyday operation. The cross curves, therefore, are the source for the static stability curve at any operating displacement.

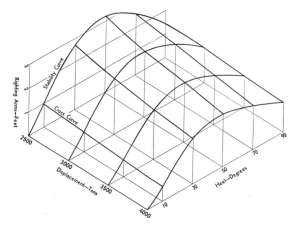

Figure 3–10. Cross Curves and Stability Curves

If it is desired to plot a static stability curve for any specified displacement, the values of the righting arms are taken from the cross curves for each angle of inclination directly above the desired displacement on the abscissae of the cross curves. These values are plotted on the static stability coordinates. Figure 3–11 gives the static stability curve for a ship at 3300 tons displacement.

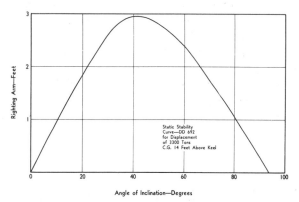

Figure 3–11. Uncorrected Static Stability Curve

VERTICAL CORRECTION FOR POSITION OF G.

It will be remembered that the position of the center of gravity was assumed in the original computation of righting arms for the cross curves. After the exact location of the center of gravity and the displacement corresponding to each of the standard conditions of loading have been determined by the inclining experiment, final static stability curves are drawn for the standard conditions. The plotting of these curves involves a correction for the distance between the actual and assumed positions of the center of gravity.

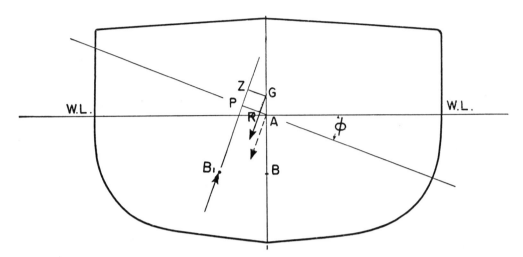

Figure 3–12. Correction for Exact Vertical Location of *G*

For example, suppose the assumed position of the center of gravity had been placed on the designer's waterline (at *A*) in figure 3–12. Now, for this displacement and actual condition of loading, suppose the true position of the center of gravity is at *G*, above the assumed position by the distance, $\overline{AG}$.

If we were to incline the ship to some finite angle, ϕ, the actual righting arm will be $\overline{GZ}$ instead of $\overline{AP}$, as it would have been if the center of gravity had been at *A* as was originally assumed.

From the figure,

$$\overline{GZ} = \overline{AP} - \overline{AR}$$

but

$$\overline{AR} = \overline{AG} \sin \phi$$

$$\therefore \overline{GZ} = \overline{AP} - \overline{AG} \sin \phi.$$

This means that any righting arm for the final corrected curve is equal to the righting arm for the uncorrected curve *minus* the distance between the real and assumed centers of gravity multiplied by the sine of the angle of inclination when the real center of gravity is above the assumed position.

If the actual position of *G* is below the assumed position, *A*, it will be found by similar reasoning that the correction ($\overline{AG} \sin \phi$) is additive. It is necessary to actually apply such a correction to the original stability curve to obtain the final corrected stability curve for any selected displacement.

$\overline{AG} \sin \phi$ may be plotted as a sine curve with the maximum ordinate, $\overline{AG}$, at 90 degrees to the same scale as the original stability curve. A convenient practice is to plot $\overline{AG} \sin \phi$ above the abscissa axis when *G* is above *A* and below the abscissa axis when *G* is below *A*. The sine curve may be thought of then as a new axis for the stability curve, and the final stability curve is always that portion of the original curve above the sine correction curve. Note that the corrected righting arm for any angle of inclination is measured by the *vertical* distance between the uncorrected curve and the sine curve. (See figures 3–13 and 3–14. Note that these figures, with figure 3–11, constitute a complete correction sequence.

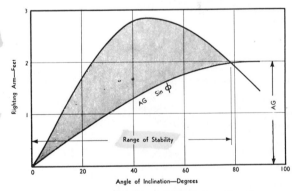

Figure 3–13. Correction to Static Stability Curve for Rise in *G*

While the above procedure is a simple way of plotting and obtaining the final corrected curve, it should be kept in mind that we are actually subtracting from or adding to the original stability curve the correction, $\overline{AG} \sin \phi$ through the range of angles of inclination.

The sine correction is applicable for all vertical movements of the position of the center of gravity from any assumed or uncorrected position.

It is a convenient convention to utilize the quadrants as set form in analytical geometry and plot the stability curves through 90 degrees on each side of the upright axis when stability both

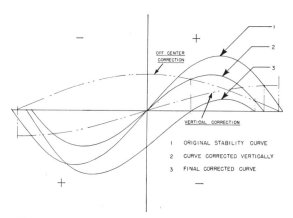

Figure 3–14. Static Stability Curve Showing Vertical and Transverse Corrections Port and Starboard

to port and starboard is desired. The flexibility of such a diagram will be more fully realized in later discussions. It is sufficient here to note that stability to starboard is taken to the right of the ordinate axis and is positive above the abscissa axis. Stability to port is taken to the left on the diagram and is positive below the axis. The signs of the quadrants, then, are as given in figure 3–14. When the stability curve is desired for only one side, either port or starboard, it is customary to plot the curve in the first quadrant.

TRANSVERSE CORRECTION FOR POSITION OF G

The consideration of an athwartship shift in *G,* while not applicable to the intact, symmetrically loaded ship, nevertheless follows logically any discussion of the vertically corrected stability curve.

We may apply similar reasoning to the transverse relocation of *G* as we applied to the vertical correction.

The actual position of the center of gravity is at some position, *G,* which is on a line perpendicular to the vertical centerline plane passing through the original center of gravity, *A*. In other words, it is off-center by the amount, $\overline{AG}$.

From figure 3–15, the correct righting arm is $\overline{GZ}$

$$\overline{GZ} = \overline{AP} - \overline{AR}$$
$$\overline{AR} = \overline{AG} \cos \phi$$
$$\overline{GZ} = \overline{AP} - \overline{AG} \cos \phi$$

where *AP* is the original or uncorrected righting arm.

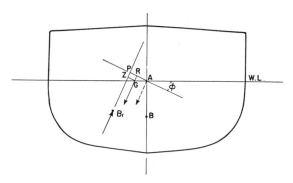

Figure 3–15. Correction for Transverse Shift of *G*

This means, in effect, that the original righting arm ($\overline{AP}$ in this case) has been reduced due to a horizontal weight shift by the same amount that the center of gravity of the ship has moved transversely from the centerline times the cosine of the angle of inclination. This loss in righting arm, $\overline{AG} \cos \phi$, is referred to as the ship's *inclining arm* and when multiplied by the displacement, Δ, is equal to the *inclining moment*.

To establish equilibrium conditions, any inclining moment existing on the ship must be exactly balanced by a righting moment at some finite angle of list on the side where the inclining arm exists. In addition to the list, the overall stability characteristics suffer a definite deterioration on the side where the list exists. These two primary effects may be shown most effectively on the plot of static stability in figure 3–16. In this plot, the original curve of static stability indicates an upright ship with positive righting arms as shown through a range of 105 degrees. The figure further indicates that a transverse weight shift has resulted in a starboard inclining arm, $\overline{AG} \cos \phi$, plotted in the amount of the cosine curve shown.

It should be noted that, when the stability

curve both to port and starboard is being investigated, this correction curve is conventionally plotted above the axis when G is on the starboard side, and below the axis when G is on the port side. If, on the other hand, the stability curve for only one side is being constructed, the stability curve is customarily constructed in the first quadrant. In this case, the cosine correction curve is drawn above the horizontal axis when the ship's center of gravity is off-center on that side of the ship for which the stability curve is being constructed. Where the center of gravity is off-center to the other side, the cosine correction curve is drawn below the horizontal axis.

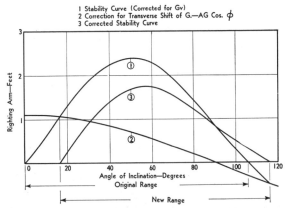

Figure 3–16. Correction to Static Stability Curve for Transverse Shift of G

Where the inclining arm curve intersects the righting arm curve, the point of equilibrium is established. This also establishes the angle of list at the value ϕ_1. The ordinates of the final or corrected overall stability curve are obtained by subtracting the ordinate of the inclining arm curve from the original stability curve. These ordinates are plotted on the axis of the original curve. The reduction in overall stability may be readily seen by comparing the original and corrected stability curve.

The transverse weight shift resulting in the shift of G has done nothing to alter the vertical height of G nor the displacement, Δ. It is, therefore, correct to say that the vertical distance between G and M has not changed, since the position of M depends upon the displacement. Consequently, *the original value of the metacentric height, $\overline{GM}$, remains unchanged due to a horizontal weight shift.* The effect on the range of stability must be considered on the basis of the

individual changes of the two limits bounding the new, positive righting arm curve. The lower limit, of course, is at the angle of permanent list, while the upper limit of static stability may be increased or decreased depending upon whether the original range was greater or less than 90 degrees.

On the side opposite to the angle of list caused by the off-center location of G, the magnitude of the righting arms is correspondingly increased in the amount $\overline{AG} \cos \phi$. This is of less importance to the damage control officer because he is obviously more concerned with the residual stability on the side where it has been reduced and where the list exists. Where the center of gravity is off the centerline and the resulting stability curve is unsymmetrical, a plot of the stability curve for 90 degrees each side of the upright gives a complete picture of the stability situation. Figure 3–14 shows the corrections for both an upward and starboard movement of G leading to such a plot. The algebraic sum of the corrections applied successively to the static stability curve result in the final stability curve shown.

METACENTRIC HEIGHT AND STABILITY CURVE

Recalling that $\overline{GM}$ is the distance in the ship's centerline plane from the center of gravity, G, to the metacenter, M, and that the metacenter, M, was located as the angle of heel approached zero, we have then a means of obtaining the slope of the stability curve at or near the origin, the slope being $\overline{GZ}/\phi$ or $\overline{GZ}/\sin \phi$ for small angles. For small angles, $\overline{GZ} = \overline{GM} \sin \phi$ or $\overline{GZ}/\sin \phi = \overline{GM}$. But we know that the left-hand expression is equal to the slope, $\overline{GZ}/\phi$. Then $\overline{GZ}/\phi = \overline{GM}/1$, or, in other words

$$\frac{\overline{GZ}}{\phi \text{ radians}} = \frac{\overline{GM}}{\text{angle whose circular measure is one}}.$$

This means that if we erect a perpendicular on the stability curve of figure 3–17 at the angle of inclination of 57.3 degrees (1 radian) and draw a tangent to the curve at the origin, the height of the intersection of this tangent with the perpendicular will be equal to the $\overline{GM}$ on the righting arm scale.

When the ship's center of gravity is not on the centerline, $\overline{GM}$ cannot be determined by measuring the slope of the static stability curve, which has been corrected for the off-center position of the center of gravity. $\overline{GM}$ remains unchanged due to a horizontal weight shift. Hence, to determine $\overline{GM}$ graphically, it is necessary to measure the slope at the origin of the static stability curve drawn for the ship's center of gravity on the centerline but at its final, vertical height. In other words, in figure 3–16, $\overline{GM}$ must be determined by the slope at the origin of the curve labeled 1. (Corrected for G_v rather than by the slope of the curve labeled 3, *Corrected Stability Curve*.)

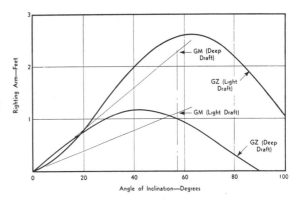

Figure 3–18. Comparison of Stability Curves of a Ship in Two Extreme Displacement Conditions (same $\overline{KG}$)

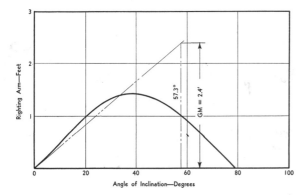

Figure 3–17. Metacentric Height

COMMON STABILITY CHARACTERISTICS

It should be emphasized that there is little or no relationship between $\overline{GM}$ and $\overline{GZ}$. However, (without generalizing) there is a common characteristic for certain vessels of destroyer-type form and larger vessels with fine ends. This similarity is such that there is a consistent variation of $\overline{GM}$ and $\overline{GZ}$ where the magnitude of one varies inversely to the other between deep and light draft. This characteristic is illustrated in figure 3–18.

Many ships have this characteristic of a gentle initial slope in the stability curve, which is indicative of a moderate or low $\overline{GM}$ value. Such a curve is shown in figure 3–18 (light draft). The slope of this curve increases sharply as the angle increases.

Relating such a curve to a cast where the center of gravity is corrected for a higher position, it can be seen from figure 3–18 that this initial "dip" in the curve may create a condition where the $\overline{GM}$ becomes negative. Such a condition will result in a symmetrical list as shown. In this condition, the ship will not remain upright but will heel to one side or the other, depending upon the direction of any initial inclining force, until

the changing underwater shape restores positive stability at an angle of list. The situation is generally described as "lolling." The most ordinary example of this situation is an unloaded cargo vessel where, in the light condition, the center of gravity has risen to a level where the sine correction curve intersects the stability curve at the low angle of list shown in figure 3–19. In a cargo vessel, this situation is not serious because the stability characteristics are designed for a wide range of vertical locations of centers of gravity, and, even though the $\overline{GM}$ may be negative, there will be sufficient positive stability to maintain a satisfactory range and maximum righting arm. Furthermore, this condition can readily be corrected by reloading or ballasting. However, no naval vessels are so designed, and any symmetrical list *indicative of a negative $\overline{GM}$* should be viewed with considerable concern.

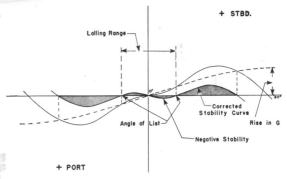

Figure 3–19. Static Stability Curve Showing Range of Instability

In summary, a ship can assume a list because of two fundamental reasons: an off-center weight causing the center of gravity to move out of the vertical centerline plane, thus causing an inclining moment; and a high center of gravity in ships whose corrected stability curves show a negative righting arm in the initial stages of inclination. The former case will, of course, result in a list on the side toward which the center of gravity moves and an overall unsymmetrical condition of stability. The latter case will result in a list on either side with an overall-symmetrical condition of stability.

Weight Effects on Stability

WEIGHT ADDITION

In order that we may take into account all of the changes in characteristics that affect the stability of a ship, it is useful to use a standard procedure to be followed in calculating such changes. Also, because the characteristics that are changed by weight addition are of an individual nature, it is best to isolate the considerations into separate processes.

INCREASED DISPLACEMENT

We know, first, that adding a weight will increase the displacement, so that the final displacement is equal to the original displacement plus the added weight. Also, it must be apparent that this additional displacement involves an increased draft. This increase in draft may be applied to the original mean draft to obtain a draft that may be used as an entering argument to obtain the characteristics for the final condition from the hydrostatic curves.

VERTICAL SHIFT OF G AND M

Secondly, when a weight is added, there will be some change in the vertical location of the center of gravity, G. This new location of G may be determined by using the appropriate moment equation. At this point, also, a new or altered metacentric height may be determined combining the new $\overline{KG}$ and a new $\overline{KM}$ (determined for the new displacement).

CHANGE IN TRIM AND CHANGE IN DRAFTS

With the weight aboard at its designated location, there very likely will be a trimming moment introduced. This trimming moment is the direct result of two newly introduced forces: the added downward force of gravity through the center of gravity of the added weight and the added upward force of buoyancy through the center of the added buoyant layer.* These forces must, of course, be exactly equal in magnitude in order to establish a final, overall equilibrium between the weight of the ship and its supporting buoyancy. Also, because the forces are acting vertically in opposite directions and are separated longitudinally, the couple thus formed is equal to the distance between the forces multiplied by either of the two forces. The couple is more conveniently expressed, for the purpose here, as a moment taken with reference to the center of the added buoyant layer. In this case, it would be equal to lw where l is the longitudinal distance between the two centers, and w is the added weight.

Now, with the moment that is introduced by the couple described above, a change in trim results. This change in trim occurs about the trimming axis, which is in the waterplane at which the ship is floating with the weights aboard. This axis is located perpendicular to the longitudinal centerplane at the final center of flotation. The final drafts forward and aft, then, may be determined by adding first, to the original drafts, forward and aft, the change in drafts due to the additional displacement; and secondly, the algebraic addition of the change in drafts forward and aft due to the change in trim illustrated in chapter 2.

List. The determination of the list that may result from any introduced inclining moment may finally be computed by using, in the equation for inclined equilibrium, the final displacement, the final $\overline{GM}$, and the inclining moment introduced.

---

*The center of the added buoyant layer is sometimes referred to as the *mean center of flotation* or the *center of immersion*. The curves of form indicate the longitudinal position of the centers of flotation as centers of gravity of waterplanes aft of ⊠. An arithmetical mean of the locations of the centers of flotation of the original and final waterlines will be considered as the *center of the added buoyant layer,* even though the variation of the center of flotation with draft is not one of constant rate. In many cases, the actual difference in longitudinal position between the centers of flotation of two relatively close waterlines is so small that it may be neglected. However, this is a matter that must be determined in each individual problem depending upon the limits of accuracy required, the range of drafts involved, etc.

Illustration of Procedure. The above description of the procedure involved in determining the effects of adding a weight might be further clarified by the following illustrations that point out the numerical relationships step by step. See figures 3–20 (a); (b); (c); (d).

Given: $\overline{KG}$, w, T_f, T_a, and location for w.

1. Determine: T_m and Δ (corrected for trim).

2. Determine:

$$\overline{KG_1} = \frac{\Delta \, \overline{KG} + w\overline{Kg}}{\Delta_1}, \quad \Delta_1 = \Delta + w,$$

$$Tm_1 = T_m + \delta T_m,$$

$$\delta T_m = \frac{w}{TPI} = \text{parallel sinkage},$$

$\overline{KM_1}$ (determine from curves at T_{m1}),
$\overline{G_1 M_1} = \overline{KM_1} - \overline{KG_1}$.

For the location of b, mean center of flotation, see the preceding footnote.

Trimming arm (longitudinal distance from b to g) $= l$

3. Determine:

Moment to change trim one inch $= C$ (from curves)

Trimming Moment $= w$ [Trimming Arm (l)]

$$\text{Change of trim} = \frac{\text{Trimming Moment}}{C}$$

$$= \delta \, Trim$$

Location of trimming axis
    $=$ distance of CF_1 from stem.

Forward trim change, d_f
$$= \frac{\delta \, Trim \, (\text{Distance from stem to } CF_1)}{L}$$

Aft trim change, $d_a = \delta \, Trim - d_f$
Final draft forward $= T_f + \delta \, T_m + d_f$
Final draft aft $= T_a + \delta \, T_m - d_a$.

4. Determine: Angle of list, ϕ

$$\tan \phi = \frac{wt}{\Delta_1 \overline{G_1 M_1}}.$$

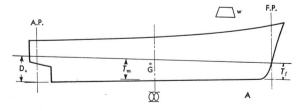

Figure 3–20(a). Original Condition

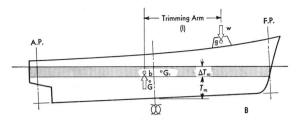

Figure 3–20(b). Weight Added—Parallel Sinkage

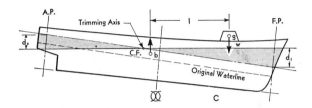

Figure 3–20(c). Weight Added—Trim

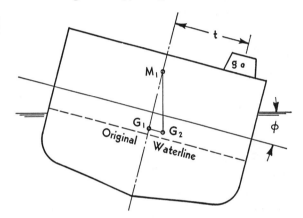

Figure 3–20(d). Weight Added—List

WEIGHT REMOVAL

Change in Drafts and Trim. Insofar as the removal of a weight affects changes in trim and drafts, the procedure in calculating such effects is handled in exactly the same way as the addition of weight. The steps will be:

1. The determination of the change in draft due to the decreased displacement because of the removed weight, with the consequent change in $\overline{KG}$ and $\overline{KM}$.

2. The determination of change in trim and, subsequently, the final drafts in a manner similar to that used in weight addition. The trimming axis is the axis through the final center of flotation (after weight removal), at the waterline through Tm_1. It is the mean draft with the weight removed.

Changes in List—Analysis of Moments. In determining list caused by weight removal, specific consideration must be given to the cause of list. When a list exists and is due solely to the weight that is to be removed, then the act of removing the weight results in an upright ship with G on the centerline. In this case, the procedure of determining change in list is a simple reversal again of the weight addition procedure.

However, in practice, weight removal does not normally involve the simple situation described above. We must expect that the ship in the original condition is either upright or has a list and that the removal of a weight will cause a change in list resulting in a final or residual list. This situation is often encountered in everyday problems of weight removal such as the consumption of fuel and stores, unloading deck cargo, landing craft, boats, planes, vehicles, etc., or in problems of grounding and jettisoning. Such weight removal generally results in residual inclining moments, and any discussion of weight removal must be approached with these practical considerations in mind. A problem of weight removal resulting in a residual list may be solved as follows:

1. Determine the original off-center location of G.

2. Determine the transverse shift in G caused by removing the weight.

3. By combining the two values determined above, find the final off-center location of G and the resulting list.

Residual List by Moment Equation. The above analysis may be resolved into an equation for the residual angle of list caused by the weight removal. In considering the amount of residual list, it should be kept in mind that the change in list is the result of the moment of the removed weight. Taking this moment relative to the centerplane, it is wt, where w is the removed weight and t is its transverse distance to the centerline. It is actually the difference between the original and final transverse moments of the ship. These moments are respectively, $\Delta \overline{GM} \tan \phi$ and $\Delta_1 \overline{G_1M_1} \tan \phi_1$, so therefore we may write

$$\Delta \overline{GM} \tan \phi - \Delta_1 \overline{G_1M_1} \tan \phi_1 = wt$$

$$\tan \phi_1 = \frac{\Delta \overline{GM} \tan \phi - wt}{\Delta_1 \overline{G_1M_1}} \qquad *$$

where
Δ = original displacement of ship with weight on board
w = weight removed from ship
Δ_1 = final displacement with w off ship
$\overline{GM}$ = original metacentric height with w on board
$\overline{G_1M_1}$ = final metacentric height with w off ship
t = distance from w to centerline of ship
ϕ = original angle of list
ϕ_1 = final angle of list with w off ship.

Applications of the above equation are unlimited insofar as the location of weight or the original and final list is concerned (within the range of the application of $\overline{GM}$). For example, if an off-center weight is removed when the ship is originally upright, the residual list is simply

$$\tan \phi = \frac{-wt}{\Delta_1 \overline{G_1M_1}}$$

The minus sign indicates that the list is on the opposite side from the removed weight.

---

*If the numerator is minus, the final list will be on the opposite side from the original.

CHAPTER 4

Ship Hazards and Vulnerability

For a ship that is designed to go to sea, to expose herself to the frequently inhospitable and often hostile environment of the oceans, the hazards are many but her degree of vulnerability can generally be reduced to only two, or possibly three, categories. Ships are lost at sea through an ultimate loss of buoyancy, when they sink. The events and circumstances leading up to this catastrophic finality can be of a considerable variety and combination. The most serious contributive factors from the designer's point of view are either structural failure, causing loss of stability or buoyancy or both through flooding, or other loss of stability resulting in capsizing or plunging. The elements of structural adequacy will be discussed in chapter 11, and this chapter will consequently be primarily devoted to hazardous and deteriorated buoyancy and stability situations.

There are, of course, other hazards that will be noted, some of which are not particularly related to the ultimate failures cited above. A ship may be reduced to a useless, uninhabitable hulk by extensive fire or by grounding. A warship may, because of an underwater explosion, be also rendered mechanically useless or, because of nuclear fallout and resulting radiation, become untenable. These hazards and others must be considered by the planners and designers.

Before covering design, however, we must first consider the more common and often frequently encountered situations that can reduce and impair buoyancy and stability.

Watertight Subdivision

From the earliest times in man's experience with shipbuilding, he has been concerned with the flooding and sinking of his ship. It may come as a surprise to many beginning the study of ships that in the days of wooden ship construction, or indeed today when buoyant, floatable material is used in the basic construction of the hull, there was no assurance and little likelihood that the vessel would remain afloat when flooded completely or even partially. We need only recall *Archimedes' Principle* to think clearly on that point. However, flooding became a matter of increasing concern as ships became larger and were constructed of iron in the nineteenth century. As they continued to grow and as disasters occurred, such as the tragic sinking of the *Titanic* in 1912, ship designers began to formulate rigorous criteria for watertight internal subdivision for the restriction of flooding when the hull was penetrated. These criteria for modern ships are resolved by specific flooding calculations and the concept of floodable length. In introducing these concepts, it is necessary to establish certain basic definitions. The most important and relevant of these are

Bulkhead Deck. The bulkhead deck is the uppermost deck to which the transverse watertight bulkheads extend (usually the main deck).

Margin Line. The margin line is a line drawn parallel to, and three inches below, the bulkhead deck at the side.

Permeability (volume). Permeability is the percentage of volume in a space which can be flooded and is expressed as

$$\mu = \frac{\text{available volume}}{\text{total volume}}.$$

Floodable Length. Floodable length is the maximum length of a compartment which can be flooded to cause a damaged ship to float at a waterline tangent to the margin line.

Curve of Floodable Length. The curve of floodable length is a curve that at every point in its length has an ordinate representing the length of ship which may be flooded with the center of length at that point and without the margin line being submerged.

The floodable length curve is a most valuable tool in assessing the ship's vulnerability and designing for the proper or desired degree of invulnerability. A brief description of this curve and example will be helpful.

Assume that the floodable length curve, shown in figure 4–1, has already been determined and drawn on the profile of the ship. Take a point, such as A on the curve, which may be at any distance, X, from the midship section, $\bigotimes$. The point, A, then is at a distance, l, above the base line of the plot, its ordinate distance, as the length of the compartment whose center is at X and which, when flooded, would trim the ship to a new waterline WL_1 tangent to the margin line.

Any further increase in the length of a compartment at this point would indicate a point of intersection above A with flooding to a waterline deeper than the margin line and consequent sinkage.

The process of calculating the values for plotting the floodable length curve is a lengthy and tedious one but can be greatly facilitated by proper use of a digital computer. The method and theory can be quickly indicated, however.

In order to determine the extent and position of flooding which will bring the ship from its operating waterline, WL in figure 4–1, to the waterline, WL_1, tangent to the margin line, we must write an equation of moments about the original center of buoyancy.

Thus

$$\Delta_1 \overline{BB_1} = wx$$

and

$$x = \frac{\Delta_1 \overline{BB_1}}{w}$$

where Δ = original displacement
  Δ_1 = final displacement
  $w = \Delta_1 - \Delta$, weight of flooding water
  B = original center of buoyancy
  B_1 = final center of buoyancy
  x = distance from B to center of flooded compartment.

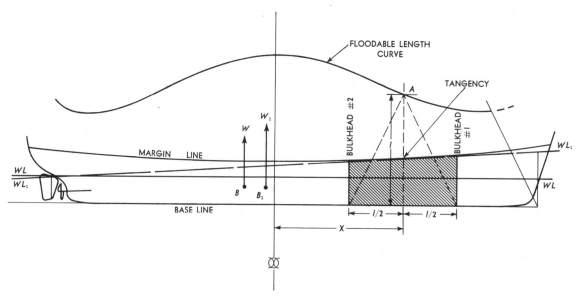

Figure 4–1. Curve of Floodable Length

The volume of water admitted is 35w, and the total volume of the compartment is therefore

$$v = \frac{35w}{\mu}.$$

The calculations for volumes of the ship's hull at various trimmed waterlines are made less tedious by using previously prepared curves called *Bonjean's Curves*. These are a series of curves along the ship's profile that show, at each station, the sectional area of that section up to the main deck or above. It is possible, therefore, to plot any inclined or trimmed waterline on Bonjean's Curves and then pick off the necessary sectional areas for computing the displacement at that waterline. An example of a Bonjean Curve is indicated in figure 4–2.

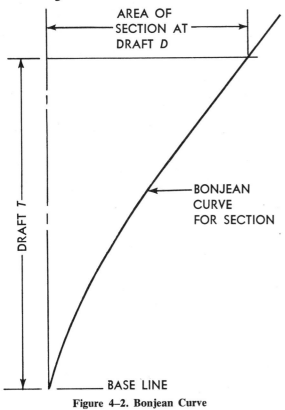

Figure 4–2. Bonjean Curve

For our purpose, it will not be necessary to examine further the methods of plotting the floodable length curve beyond that which is required to provide the student with some appreciation of its application. It must be pointed out, however, that, as presented here, the floodable length curve represents only the concept of its basic use. In actual design work and practice, it must be real-ized that full cognizance is taken of structural variations in individual designs, of double bottom voids, and of permeable variations between machinery spaces, cargo spaces, living spaces, etc.

Before leaving the concept of floodable length, it should be further pointed out that, in such flooding calculations, the basic assumptions include that of symmetrical flooding which, of course, allows for no transverse moment or resulting list. This assumption can be, and is, ultimately modified by superimposing upon the floodable length curve another curve for floodable length for transverse stability which does deteriorate even under symmetrical conditions. The reasons for this deterioration will be discussed in subsequent sections. A modified floodable length curve is shown in figure 4–3.

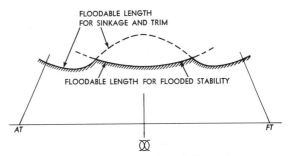

Figure 4–3. Floodable Length Restraints

LOOSE WATER

In preceding chapters, static stability curves have been introduced, and the effects of weight shifts and weight changes on the static stability curves have been discussed. It was implied that the center of gravity of the shifted or added weight remains fixed in the ship irrespective of the motion of the ship. In the case of solids, this is true if the material is properly secured to prevent shifting. In the case of liquids, this is true only if the liquid completely fills its container. If the tank or compartment is only partially filled, the liquid is unimpeded from moving from side to side as the ship rolls, because the surface of the liquid tends to remain horizontal. Water in such a compartment is called *loose water*. Some spaces in the ship usually contain loose water or other liquids, such as fuel oil. In addition, the ship is susceptible to receiving additional loose water because of damage. The presence of loose water produces a deleterious effect on both the initial and overall stability.

FREE SURFACE

Liquid which only partially fills a compartment is said to have a *free surface* which will tend to remain horizontal. The effect is that when the ship is heeled, the liquid will flow to the low side (i.e., in the direction of inclination) and add to the inclining moment.

Actually, the movement of the liquid is an athwartship shift of weight which varies with the angle of inclination. However, in considering the effect of free surface, it is more convenient to consider the effect of the movement of the liquid as changing the apparent height of the center of gravity.

To consider the effect on initial and overall stability, we must assume first a very small angle of inclination such that the liquid in the tank to be considered does not touch the top of the tank nor expose the bottom of the tank. Figure 4–4 shows a compartment partially filled with liquid which has a free surface, wl, with the ship upright. When the ship is heeled to the small angle, $\delta\phi$, the free surface shifts to w_1l_1, remaining horizontal.

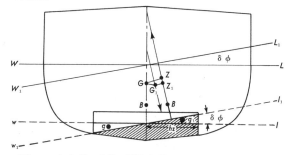

Figure 4–4. Partially Filled Compartment with a Free Surface Liquid

In referring to figure 4–4, let

g = centroid of liquid to shift the triangle wsw_1

g_1 = centroid of the shifted liquid in triangle lsl_1

h_z = half-breadth of the tank at the waterline

$\delta\phi$ = small angle of inclination

dz = increment of the length of the tank

v = volume of the liquid in the tank

i = moment of inertia of the free surface area about the longitudinal axes through the centroid of the free surface area

γ = specific gravity of the free surface liquid

w = weight of the liquid = $v\gamma/36$

∇ = volume of displacement of the ship; 35Δ for salt water.

Consider a tank of width $2h_z$ and length L. As the ship is heeled to a very small angle, $\delta\phi$, the liquid in the tank must adjust so that its surface remains horizontal. This adjustment results in a transverse shift in the center of gravity of the ship due to the shifted liquid volume, v_o. This shift can be expressed in an equation of moments taken about the centerplane of the ship:

$$\overline{gg_1}\,\gamma_t\,v_o \cong \overline{GG_1}\,\Delta$$

$$Now, \overline{gg_1}\,v_o = \int_o^L \frac{1}{2}\,h_z\,\tan\delta\phi\,\frac{4}{3}\,h_z\,h_z\,dz$$

$$= \left[\frac{2}{3}\int_o^L h^3(z)\,dz\right]\tan\delta\phi.$$

The integral, $i = \frac{2}{3}\int_o^L h^3(z)\,dz$, is defined as the moment of inertia of the free surface area about the centerline of the tank. Thus we can write

$$\overline{GG_1} = \frac{\gamma_t\,i}{\gamma_w\,\nabla}\tan\delta\phi.$$

When the ship heels to the angle, $\delta\phi$, the center of buoyancy, B, moves to a new position, B_1. The righting arm acting on the ship is $\overline{G_1Z_1}$. From the diagram we can see that

$$\overline{G_1Z_1} = \overline{GZ} - \overline{GG_1}\cos\delta\phi$$

or,

$$\overline{G_1Z_1} = \overline{GZ} - \frac{\gamma_t\,i}{\gamma_w\,\nabla}\sin\delta\phi.$$

Recalling that for small angles $\overline{GZ} = \overline{GM}\sin\phi$,

$$\overline{G_1Z_1} = \left(\overline{GM} - \frac{\gamma_t\,i}{\gamma_w\,\nabla}\right)\sin\delta\phi.$$

The term, $\frac{\gamma_t\,i}{\gamma_w\,\nabla}$, can be thought of as a negative correction to the metacentric height, *and, in particular, as a virtual rise in the center of gravity of the ship since M does not change.*

In this case, $\overline{GG_v} = \frac{\gamma_t\,i}{\gamma_w\,\nabla}$ is the *virtual rise* of the center of gravity and is called the *free surface effect.* This relationship will hold regardless of what liquid is contained in the tank, the location of the tank, and whether the ship is in fresh or salt water.

In the operational situations involving flooding damage, the tank or compartment may be considered flooded with water of the same density as that in which the ship floats. The relationship may then be simplified to

$$\overline{GG_1} = \frac{i}{\nabla}.$$

Note that ∇ is the volume of displacement of the *ship* and not the volume of the loose water.

The foregoing derivation was made upon the assumption of small angles of inclination, and the relationship thus derived may be considered as the reduction in $\overline{GM}$ due to free surface. *While the development of the free surface effect was predicated on small angles of inclination, the equation above may be considered to give reasonably accurate predictions of the virtual movement of the ship's center of gravity for normal angles of inclination.* For this reason, the free surface effect may be considered to cause a reduction in the ship's static stability curve in the amount of $i/V \sin \phi$. This correction is applied to the stability curve in the same manner as any vertical rise in the center of gravity as shown in figure 4–5. Bear in mind that there are certain specific tanks where, for the larger angles of inclination, the

value of $i/V \sin \phi$ is materially in error due to the great increase in free surface areas. This is specifically true in the case of deep, narrow tanks approximately half-full. In addition to liquid stowage, remember that any loose, bulk cargo such as coal, grain, etc., may shift position, and the ship will experience a loss of stability according to the principles set forth above.

POCKETING

The effect of $\overline{GG_1} \sin \phi$, due to free surface, is always modified to some extent by *pocketing*. Such a modifying effect is basically the contact of the liquid with the top of the tank or the exposure of the bottom surface of the tank, either of which generally takes place at some finite inclination and pockets the liquid in one side of the tank and reduces the breadth of the free surface area. Depending upon the size and shape of the tank and the amount of liquid contained, this becomes an extremely variable factor and one not subject to a simple solution. However, because pocketing always reduces the increasing area of free surface, its effect is to prohibit the

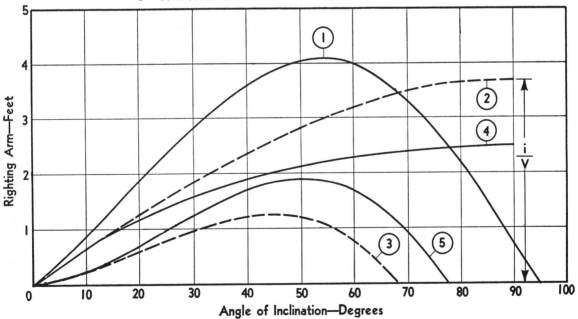

1 Uncorrected for Free Surface
2 Free Surface Effect not corrected for Pocketing
3 Corrected for Unrestricted Free Surface
4 Free Surface Effect corrected for Pocketing
5 Corrected for Pocketed Free Surface

Figure 4–5. Effect of Free Surface on Overall Stability

realization of unrestricted free surface throughout the complete range of stability. In the case of deep, narrow tanks mentioned in the previous section, the effect of the increasing free surface area and the ultimate effect of pocketing is one of modifying the unrestricted effect of increased free surface area. Hence, if it is neglected, we may consider pocketing as an indeterminate *factor of safety,* knowing that if we allow for the full free surface effect, we have described the extreme conditions. This is demonstrated in figure 4–5.

The practice of carrying fuel oil tanks 95 percent full instead of pressed full permits a free surface which pockets at small angles of inclination. Although $\overline{GM}$ and initial righting arms may be slightly reduced by the free surface effect, the pocketing prevents an appreciable loss of overall stability. The remaining five percent of the tank space is necessary to allow for expansion of oil.

SURFACE PERMEABILITY

In any compartment in a ship, there are generally some solid objects that will project through the surface of any flooding water or contained liquid in the compartment. If these solid objects are made fast so that they will not float and are not permeable themselves, the free surface effect of the liquid in the compartment will be diminished in proportion to the amount of free surface so reduced by the objects. It should be realized that in many ships' compartments, the amount of surface so reduced will depend upon the depth of the liquid in the compartment. Because of the nonuniformity in shape of the many and varied objects in shipboard compartments and their various heights, the amount of surface suppressed will vary.

The *surface permeability factor* is the ratio of the moment of inertia of an actual free surface to the moment of inertia of the same surface with no objects projecting through the surface. It is indicated by the symbol, μ_s.

This factor is multiplied by the unrestricted free surface moment of inertia, i, to obtain the actual free surface moment of inertia. The factor used must be a matter of judgment since its value changes with angle of heel, depth of water, contents of compartment, etc. As in pocketing, when surface permeability is neglected, the calculated results indicate less stability than the ship actually possesses.

Controlled Flooding and Submarine Stability

SURFACE STABILITY

From the standpoint of stability, a submarine operating on the surface can be considered as a surface vessel. However, its stability characteristics are different from those of a surface ship of comparable displacement, and thought should be given to factors causing this departure. Figure 4–6 shows a comparison of righting moments for a surfaced submarine and a typical destroyer, both having approximately the same displacement.

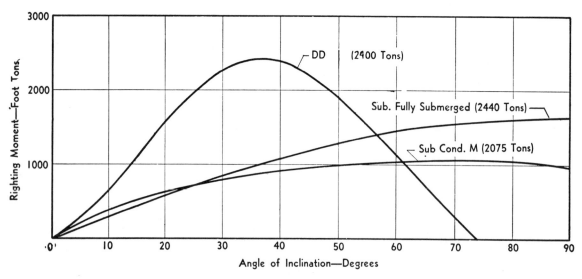

Figure 4–6. Curves of Static Stability for DD and Typical Submarine

It will be recalled that stability characteristics of all surface ships depend on two things:

1. The underwater form and the positions of B *and* M. Surface ships of normal form have comparatively high freeboard and straight sides with some flare, particularly near the bow. For a favorable position of *G*, large righting arms and a good range of stability are obtained. This is because the waterplane area will increase through a fairly wide range of angles of inclination (until the deck edge is immersed), thereby causing *B* to shift outwards a greater amount than if the waterplane area was relatively constant. A correspondingly greater development of righting arm is realized.

Conversely, the submarine has a low freeboard and is nearly circular in section. There is no appreciable increase in the waterplane area as the angle of inclination is increased.

2. The vertical distribution of weights. As was observed previously, that many heavy weights of the submarine are low enables *G* to be located lower than it is in a comparable surface vessel. A low *G* is the principal factor in overcoming the adverse effects of the submarine's form on stabil-

ity. To insure a low *G*, lead ballast is usually placed in the bottom of the main ballast tanks (MBTs), its weight being about three percent of the submerged displacement. For a given *B* and *M*, the effect of lowering *G* is to improve the overall stability by realizing a very good stability range, although the righting arms are still relatively small. In figure 4–6, note that the submarine's poor stability form and low center of gravity combine to produce a low, flat curve having a much greater range than the surface ship.

TRANSITION STABILITY

During diving and surfacing operations, *B*, *M* and *G* are not fixed, but vary systematically. It is extremely important to know how the locations of these points vary with respect to each other in order that the *minimum metacentric height* during this transition period can be determined. To facilitate this study, an adequate number of intermediate conditions between "surface, diving trim" and "fully submerged" are calculated to permit the plotting of the curves shown in figure 4–7.

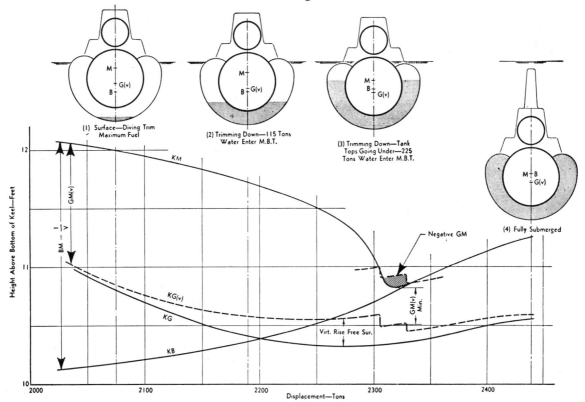

Figure 4–7. Trimming Down Curves for Condition *M*

1. Surface, diving trim with maximum fuel. It has been seen that the submarine in this condition behaves like a surface ship as far as stability is concerned. Elaborate weight studies are made to locate *G*. Knowing the displacement, *B* and *M* can be found from the "Displacement and Other Curves."

2. Trimming down. As a result of the vessel's sinking to a higher waterline, a chain of events occurs. The waterplane area decreases; $\overline{BM}$ decreases; *B* moves upward but at a slower rate than $\overline{BM}$ is decreasing; therefore, *M* moves downward. *G* moves downward as the result of flooding the lower portion of the *MBTs*. However, the large amount of free-surface present in the partially flooded *MBTs* and elsewhere causes a virtual rise of *G* to $G_{(v)}$. The locus of $G_{(v)}$, plotted as the dotted line, is the effective curve in making this stability study.

3. Trimming down. The tank tops are in the process of being submerged, and the reduction of waterplane area is proceeding at an increasing rate as the process of trimming down proceeds. Consequently, $\overline{BM}$ is being reduced at a greater rate, this being reflected by the increasing negative slope of the $\overline{KM}$ curve. *B* continues to rise and *G* (actual) is now below *B*. In this condition, it is assumed that the position of *G* and the amount of free surface are such that $G_{(v)}$ is also below *B*. The minimum value of $\overline{GM}$ occurs shortly after condition three, figure 4–7.

Modern U.S. Navy submarines are designed to have a positive minimum $\overline{GM}$. However, it is possible to shift the $\overline{KG_{(v)}}$ curve upwards until it intersects the $\overline{KM}$ curve. This could be done by a vertical redistribution of weights to raise the $\overline{KG}$ curve, an excessive amount of free surface in the vessel in addition to that in the *MBTs*, or a combination of these two undesirable conditions. The shaded area in figure 4–7 represents the existence of negative stability.

The value of $\overline{GM}$ is always minimum immediately upon surfacing. If the submarine surfaces with a strong beam wind or sea, she will often assume a list. List control valves are placed in the low-pressure blow lines so that the boat can be righted by reducing the blowing of main ballast tanks on the side opposite the list. As water is blown from *MBTs* reducing free surface, $\overline{GM}$ increases and stability improves.

4. Fully submerged. This condition forms the end-points for the curves.

It is assumed that the *MBTs* are completely flooded. Note that the $\overline{KG_{(v)}}$ and $\overline{KG}$ curves are not coincident in this condition. The free surface in the *MBTs* is now zero, but free surface present in the vessel will continue to be effective in causing a departure of the two curves.

With reference to the $\overline{KM}$ and $\overline{KB}$ curves in the vicinity of this condition, it should be noted that they are actually separate curves. Although this separation is too minute to indicate, it will exist as long as there is any structure of the submarine above the surface to provide a waterplane. Actual coincidence of the curves can occur only when the vessel is fully submerged, and $\overline{BM}$ is reduced to zero.

SUBMERGED STABILITY

As implied above, a fully submerged vessel has no waterplane area. Thus *I*, and consequently $\overline{BM}$, become zero. *B* and *M* are now coincident points, and $G_{(v)}$ must be below *B*. The magnitude of $\overline{BG_{(v)}}$ becomes the criterion of submerged stability, and the equation of the submerged static stability curve is

$$\text{Righting arm } (\overline{GZ}) = \overline{BG_{(v)}} \sin \phi.$$

The equation for righting moment is

$$\text{Righting moment} = W_s \overline{BG_{(v)}} \sin \phi.$$

A comparison of righting moments of the submarine on the surface and submerged is made in figure 4–6. Note that the submerged range of stability is 180 degrees.

LONGITUDINAL STABILITY (*Submerged*).

As in the case of surface ships, the longitudinal stability of a surfaced submarine is of little concern because of the very large values of the longitudinal metacentric height, $\overline{GM'}$. However, as the waterplane vanishes when the vessel submerges, $\overline{BM'}$ is reduced to zero, and *M'* becomes coincident with *B* and *M*. In other words, the actual transverse and longitudinal metacentric heights are equal; $\overline{GM} = \overline{GM'} = \overline{BG}$. But recall that stability considerations are based on the virtual height of the center of gravity, $G_{(v)}$. $\overline{G_{(VT)}M}$ is greater than $\overline{G_{(VL)}M'}$, where the subscript *VT* and *VL* denote transverse and longitudinal locations of the virtual center of gravity.

As in transverse stability, the magnitude of $\overline{BG}_{(VL)}$ becomes the criterion of longitudinal stability. Hence $\overline{BG}_{(VT)} > \overline{BG}_{(VL)}$. As may be suspected, the reason for this inequality is that the effect of free surface in decreasing transverse stability is less than the effect of free surface in reducing longitudinal stability. The longitudinal dimension of most tanks and bilges in a submarine is greater than the transverse dimension. Calculation of longitudinal free surface correction requires calculating the moments of inertia of tanks and bilges about their athwartship axis and necessitates cubing the larger of their two dimensions. It is possible for a free surface having only a small effect on transverse stability to make the vessel unstable longitudinally. In the interest of submerged control of the vessel, it should be evident that free surface must be reduced to a minimum. Particular attention should be given to the *MBTs*. It is possible for air bubbles to form at the top of the tanks, due to leaky blow valves, causing the introduction of free surface as well as a loss of main ballast weight causing the ship to become light. The *MBT* vents are usually opened periodically (cycled) to allow any air bubbles to escape. An effort should also be made to keep the bilges reasonably dry.

Free Communication with the Sea

When one or more of the exterior boundaries of a ship are ruptured so that the sea may flow freely into and out of the damaged compartment with a minimum of restrictions as the ship rolls, the condition is described as partial flooding with *free communication with the sea.* Under this condition, both $\overline{GZ}$ and $\overline{GM}$ are usually initially increased in an equal amount to the lowering in G due to the added weight of flooding water (since flooding is due to gravity, the floodwater is below the waterline, and, in the normal forms, the center of gravity of the flooded water is below the ship's center of gravity). They are reduced subsequently because of the virtual rise in G due to the free surface effect of the flooding water and the virtual rise in G due to the so-called free communication effect. This latter effect, which may be visualized by reference to figure 4–8, occurs only when the partially flooded compartment is not on the centerline of the ship.

In the case illustrated, the off-center compartment shown is flooded through a hole in the exterior boundary of the ship. (Note that the compartment is vented above.) Because of the added weight of the flooding water, the ship will sink to the new waterline, W_1L_1. This will cause a change in the position of G and, because of the increased displacement, will relocate M, establishing a new static stability curve which must be corrected for the final position of G.

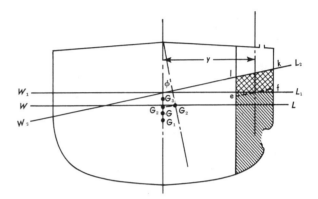

Figure 4–8. The Principle of Moments and Lost Buoyancy Volume

With the off-center compartment flooded, the ship will assume a list which is further aggravated by the free surface effect of the flooding water. As the ship lists, additional water will flow into the compartment, tending to level off at the height of the external waterline. The list will increase because of this tendency, causing still more water to enter, in turn causing greater list in decreasing increments until a final list corresponding to the waterline, W_2L_2, is reached.

This last cause of list, beyond that caused by the effect of the initial off-center flooding water and its free surface effect, is due to the increasing amount of loose water flowing into the off-center compartment and is called the *free communication effect.* It always results in a further deterioration in stability and can be shown to be equivilant to a virtual rise in the center of gravity. In the case of a centerline compartment, there will be no additional ingress of flooding water from the sea and hence no free communication effect, because the shift of water within the compartment due to free surface effect will maintain the inside water level at the same height as the outside water level.

It should be appreciated that an exact evaluation of the free communication effect by the method studied thus far is virtually impossible due to the fluctuation in the amount of flooding water, and hence the ship's displacement, with the angle of list. Since the method studied (the added weight method) is best suited to all investigations of stability except the case of partial flooding in free communication with the sea, it is preferable to use an approximate formula for the free communication effect with the added weight method than to adopt a separate method for handling such problems.

The effect of the initial and overall stability of a ship, when free communication with the sea occurs, may be considered to take place in the following steps (see figure 4–8):

1. A mass of water is admitted and causes the ship to sink parallel to its original waterline, WL, to W_1L_1. The amount of this water (w) is determined by the volume of the flooded compartment below W_1L_1. There is a vertical shift of the ship's center of gravity from G to G_1 due to this added weight (usually downward).

$$\overline{KG_1} = \frac{\Delta \overline{KG} + w \overline{Kg}}{\Delta_1},$$

where

Δ = original displacement (at waterline WL)

w = weight of flooding water up to waterline W_1L_1

$\Delta_1 = \Delta + w$ = displacement of the ship at waterline W_1L_1

$\overline{KG}$ = original vertical height of the ship's center of gravity

$\overline{KG_1}$ = vertical height of the ship's center of gravity when displacing Δ_1 tons

$\overline{Kg}$ = vertical height of the center of gravity of the floodwater, w.

2. A free surface is created which causes a virtual rise in the center of gravity from G_1 to G_2.

$$\overline{G_1G_2} \text{ (vert.)} = i/\nabla_1,$$

where

∇_1 = volume of displacement at waterline W_1L_1

i = moment of inertia of the free surface area about a longitudinal axis through its centroid.

3. The ship lists due to the off-center weight, w, and causes an additional quantity of water to flow in. Note that if the shell opening did not exist, the ship would list to the dotted waterline and the surface of the floodwater would parallel the dotted waterline along line ef. The additional flooding water, w_1, represented by the area, $efkl$, is dependent upon the horizontal cross sectional area of the bilged compartment, the angle of list, and the distance from the center of gravity of the compartment to the ship's centerline.

The effect of free communication on stability is best *approximated* by the theory of moments. Prior to the entry of the additional water represented by the area, $efkl$, the transverse moment introduced at an angle, ϕ, was $\Delta_1 \overline{G_2M_1} \tan \phi$, where M_1 is the location of the metacenter when the ship is floating at waterline W_1L_1. After the additional water, w_1, represented by the area $efkl$, flows in, it causes an additional transverse moment, w_1y, where y is the transverse distance from the center of gravity of the floodwater to the centerline. This additional water causes a further virtual rise in the ship's center of gravity from G_2 to G_3. As in the discussion of the free surface effect earlier in this chapter, consider a horizontal weight shift due to flooding the section indicated in the diagram by the area, $efkl$:

$$\Delta_1 \overline{G_2G_2'} = w_1 y,$$

where G_2' = actual position of CG after a horizontal shift due to the flooding of $efkl$,

but, $$w_1 = \frac{a\, y \tan \phi}{35} \text{ (for salt water)},$$

$$\therefore\ \overline{G_2G_2'} = \frac{a\, y^2 \tan \phi}{35\, \Delta_1} = \frac{a\, y^2 \tan \phi}{\nabla_1}.$$

But relating a horizontal shift to a virtual vertical shift, it can be seen that

$$\overline{G_2G_2'} = \overline{G_2G_3} \tan \phi$$

$$\therefore\ \overline{G_2G_3} = \frac{a\, y^2}{\nabla_1} = \textit{free communication correction.}$$

$\overline{G_2G_3}$ (vert.), a virtual rise in the ship's center of gravity over and above the free surface effect, is the free communication effect. Similar to the free surface effect, it reduces the initial stability by reducing the metacentric height in the amount of $\overline{G_2G_3}$ (vert.) and reduces the overall stability by reducing the righting arms at all angles of inclination in the amount of $\overline{G_2G_3}$ (vert.) sin ϕ.

Consequently, in a damaged ship where partial flooding exists in free communication with the sea, the static stability curve for the increased displacement must be corrected by three sine curve values as follows:

1. $\overline{GG_1}$ (vert.) sin ϕ, for added weight (this will probably be an additive correction)

2. $\dfrac{i}{\nabla_1}$ sin ϕ, for free surface effect

3. $\dfrac{ay^2}{\nabla_1}$ sin ϕ, for free communication effect.

To simplify the correction, instead of plotting the three individual sine curves mentioned above, it is better to lump the entire result together as an overall virtual rise in G which is

$$\overline{GG_3} \text{ (vert.)} = \pm\overline{GG_1} \text{ (vert.)} + \frac{i}{\nabla_1} + \frac{ay^2}{\nabla_1},$$

and the overall sine correction is $\overline{GG_3}$ (vert.) sin θ.

It should be noted that there is a further reduction to the static stability curve due to the initial off-center weight, w. This correction is

$$\overline{G_3G_4} \text{ (trans.)} \cos \phi = \frac{wy}{\Delta_1} \cos \phi.$$

Added Weight vs. Lost Buoyancy

In the foregoing discussion, it has been assumed that when a ship undergoes flooding, either partial or solid, with or without free communication with the sea, the weight or displacement has been increased by the weight of the flooding water. This method may be called the *added weight method* and carries with it the assumption that none of the hull surface exposed to the buoyant forces of the water is lost.

The *lost buoyancy method* assumes that flooding water in free communication remains part of the sea, and therefore, the part of the hull that has been flooded no longer contributes buoyancy to the ship. In other words, the vertical pressure-forces about the flooded compartment act upon the sea rather than the ship. Thereby comes the name, *lost buoyancy*. Consider an empty box-shaped lighter, whose weight is entirely due to its structure, divided longitudinally into three compartments. The center compartment is then flooded in free communication. By the lost buoy-

ancy method, this flooding water remains part of the sea, and the middle section of the lighter possesses no buoyancy. However, the structural weight of the lighter remains the same whether flooded or not and must be supported by a buoyant force equal to this weight. Since we have lost buoyancy amidships, it must be made up at the buoyant end sections by increasing the draft such that the water displaced by the end sections equals the structural weight of the lighter. To sum up the foregoing, let us say the added weight method deals with a change in weight, whereas the lost buoyancy method deals with a change in shape.

We can itemize the effects of each method as follows:

- *Added Weight* causes:
  a. Change in tons displacement
  b. Change in volume of displacement
  c. Change in draft
  d. Change in the location of the center of gravity
  e. Change in the location of the center of buoyancy
  f. Change in the location of the transverse and longitudinal metacenters.

- *Lost Buoyancy* causes:
  a. Displacement that remains unchanged
  b. Displacement volume that remains unchanged in magnitude but not in form
  c. Change in draft
  d. No change in the center of gravity location
  e. Change in the center of buoyancy
  f. Change in the locations of the transverse and longitudinal metacenters.

Application of Lost Buoyancy Method to Free Communication

Any discussion of the lost buoyancy method would not be complete without noting its application to flooding with free communication with the sea.

To analyze the effect of flooding with free communication on the initial stability, or more simply, the final effective $\overline{GM}$, we need consider only the movement of M, since application of the lost buoyancy principle calls for no shift in location of G. The location of M is determined by the location of B and the length of $\overline{BM}$, the metacentric radius. If either factor changes, the location of M must change. Remember that statements herein are made with the lost buoyancy principle in mind.

1. The buoyant forces acting on the hull remain the same after damage, but the points of application shift. Hence, the center of buoyancy, B, moves.

2. Since an increase in draft is required to provide the necessary displacement to replace the damaged volume considered lost, the area of the waterplane area may change, thereby changing $\overline{BM}$.

Therefore

$$\overline{KM} = \overline{KB} + \overline{BM}$$
$$\overline{KM_1} = \overline{KM} + \delta M = \overline{KB} + \delta B + \overline{BM} + \overline{\delta BM}$$

where

δB = change in location of the center of buoyancy

$\overline{\delta BM}$ = change in length of the metacentric radius.

It follows that $\delta M = \delta B + \overline{\delta BM}$.

By the principle of moments, the change in position of the center of buoyancy multiplied by the volume of the ship must equal the distance between the center of volume of the lost buoyant volume and the center of volume of the added buoyant layer, multiplied by the magnitude of lost buoyancy volume. (See figure 7–9.)

$$\delta B \, \nabla = v \frac{T - X}{2} + \frac{\delta T}{2} = v \frac{T + \delta T - X}{2}.$$

The above expression assumes that the center of the lost buoyant volume is located at the midpoint in the distance from the bottom of the damaged compartment to the undamaged waterline.

$$\therefore \; \delta B = \frac{v}{2\nabla} (T + \delta T - X)$$

where ∇ = displacement volume of the ship

v = lost buoyancy volume

T = original draft of the ship

X = Height of the bottom of the damaged compartment above the keel

δT = Change in draft.

It also may be proved that

$$\overline{\delta BM} = -\frac{i}{\nabla} - \frac{y^2 Aa}{\nabla(A - a)} \qquad *$$

where i = moment of inertia of the free surface about its neutral axis

y = horizontal transverse distance from CG of the bilged compartment to the centerline of the ship

---

* Original $\overline{BM} = \dfrac{I}{\nabla}$ (at draft T).

$\overline{BM}$ after bilging $= \overline{B_1 M_1} = \dfrac{I_1}{\nabla_1}$ (at draft $T + \delta T$).

But, $\nabla_1 = \nabla$,

therefore, $\overline{B_1 M_1} = \dfrac{I_1}{\nabla}$,

$I_1 = I - (i + ay^2) - (A - a)d^2.$

(This assumes that the ship is wall-sided, i.e., I at draft T is equal to the moment of inertia of the waterplane at draft $T + \delta T$ before the lost buoyant portion is removed.)

Where I_1 = transverse moment of inertia of remaining waterplane about its center of gravity.

d = transverse distance from centerline to c.g. of remaining waterplane,

and by moments, $d = \dfrac{ay}{A - a}$,

$$I_1 = I - (i + ay^2) - \frac{(A - a)(ay)^2}{(A - a)^2} = I - i - ay^2 - \frac{a^2 y^2}{(A - a)}.$$

Therefore,

$$\delta \overline{BM} = \frac{I_1 - I}{\nabla} = \frac{I - i - ay^2 - \dfrac{a^2 y^2}{(A - a)} - I}{\nabla}$$

$$= -\frac{i}{\nabla} - \frac{ay^2}{\nabla} - \frac{a^2 y^2}{(A - a)\nabla} = -\frac{i}{\nabla} - \frac{A \times ay^2}{\nabla(A - a)}.$$

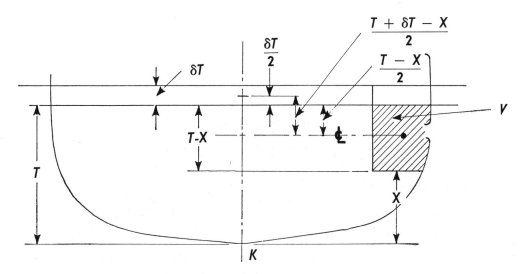

Figure 4–9. Free Communication Effect by Lost Buoyancy Method

A = area of the original intact waterline plane of the ship

a = area of flooding surface in the bilged compartment.

Consequently, we may write

$$\delta M = \frac{v}{2\nabla}(T + \delta T - X) - \frac{i}{\nabla} - \frac{y^2 Aa}{\nabla(A - a)}.$$

Therefore,

$$\overline{GM_3} = \overline{GM} + \frac{v}{2\nabla}(T + \delta T - X) - \frac{i}{\nabla} - \frac{y^2 Aa}{\nabla(A - a)}.$$

The lost buoyancy method is not always convenient to use in practice and frequently is more adapted to studies made in the design stage. It is considered by some designers to be considerably more useful under some circumstances than the added weight method.

The added weight method, on the other hand, while theoretically less accurate, is more practical from the standpoint of applying corrections to the stability curves where lost buoyancy is involved. There is no necessity, nor would it be practical, to correct the shape of the uncorrected stability curve for change in the shape of the underwater body due to damage when using the added weight method. It is primarily for simplicity and utility that the added weight method is recommended when dealing with deterioration of stability due to flooding. The lost buoyancy method is discussed here, however, to familiarize the student with the method and, secondly, to indicate an alternate means of solution.

Stability Criteria

In chapter 3, there was some discussion of general stability characteristics relating to metacentric height and the righting arm curve. It should be properly pointed out now that the primary criteria for the safety of a ship are neither the $\overline{GM}$ nor the extent of the righting arm curve but rather the maximum righting arm and the angle at which it occurs. But also to say that these values are unrelated to $\overline{GM}$ and range of stability would not be wholly true. Most frequently, the stability characteristics of a ship are such that a large $\overline{GM}$ indicates a large maximum righting arm, and a large angle of maximum righting arm indicates a large range of stability.

There have been, over the years, a number of rather arbitrary criteria set forth regarding quantitative aspects of righting arm versus heeling arm by ship design agencies. One particular study is worth citing, and it is basically a part of the stability design procedure as well as operational criteria followed by the U.S. Navy. These heeling arms originate, for the intact ship, from external or operational sources, such as strong wind or centrifugal force in a high-speed turn. *Beam winds and rolling* often combine to make a hazardous situation. A ship heeled in still water by an external force requires only sufficient

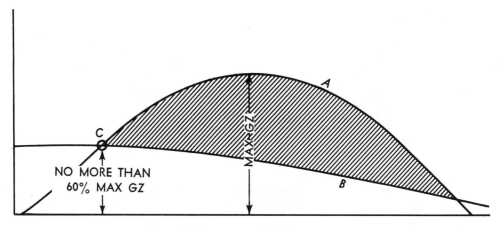

Figure 4–10. Damaged Stability Limitations

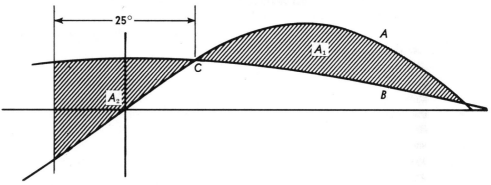

Figure 4–11. Damaged Stability Limitation

righting moment to overcome the heeling moment. However, when rolling action by wave motion is introduced, an additional allowance of dynamic stability is required to absorb the energy imparted to the ship by the rolling action. In computing the allowable heeling moments, wind velocities of from 50 to 100 knots are used, depending upon the type and size of the ship. For vessels which are intended to keep the sea in all weather, 100 knot winds are used.

The heeling arm produced by the wind is calculated from the equation:

$$M_w = \frac{.0035\ V_w{}^2\ Ah\ \cos^2\phi}{2240\ \Delta},$$

where V_w = wind velocity

h = height of the ship's lateral resistance above 1/2 draft

A = projected lateral area above WL

ϕ = angle of heel

Δ = ship displacement.

After plotting the wind's heeling arm curve (B in figure 4–10) superimposed on the ship's static stability curve for the existing condition of displacement and KG, the arbitrary criteria for adequate stability under these circumstances must show that: (a) the righting arm at the angle of heel (point C in figure 4–10) is not greater than 60 percent of the maximum righting arm, and (b) the area of residual righting energy or dynamic stability (A_1 in figure 4–11) is not less than 140 percent of area A_2, where this area represents the ship's rolling energy and is limited to a 25-degree angle.

Stability in a turn may sometimes be critical (see chapter 11), particularly in high-freeboard ships when making high-speed turns. The heeling moment produced under such circumstance is the result of the centrifugal force. This expression is developed in chapter 8 and is stated as $\dfrac{\Delta\, v^2}{g\, r}\, \overline{GL} \cos \phi$, and therefore the heeling arm is $\dfrac{v^2\, \overline{GL}}{g\, r} \cos \phi$

where v = ship velocity

$\overline{GL}$ = distance between the center of gravity and the underwater center of lateral resistance

g = gravity acceleration

r = radius of the turning circle.

This heeling moment, as all others, varies as the cosine of the heeling angle, and also, for practical purposes, r may be considered as half of the tactical diameter.

Under these circumstances, the criteria for adequate stability is again based on the superposition of the heeling arm curve on the applicable static stability curve. The stability is considered satisfactory if:

- The angle of steady heel (point C in figure 4–11) does not exceed 10 degrees in the case of a new design or 15 degrees for ships in service.
- The heeling arm at point C is not more than 60 percent of the maximum righting arm.
- The residual righting energy or dynamic stability (shaded area in figure 4–11) is not less than 40 percent of the total area (intact or upright dynamic stability) under the ship's stability curve.

It is interesting to note that these same criteria are used for conditions on passenger vessels when a heeling moment develops because crowds of passengers move to one side of the ship.

Criteria for Subdivision of Naval Vessels

Numerous considerations are involved in determining the optimum arrangement of subdivisions for a naval vessel, but the principal factors are

- Ability to survive underwater attack
- Protection of vital spaces against flooding
- Interference of subdivision with arrangements
- Interference of subdivision with access and systems
- Provision for carrying liquids

- Possibility of collision damage
- Possibility of stranding

There are always conflicts among these various factors. Where conflicts occur, the relative importance of the conflicting factors must be determined.

ABILITY TO SURVIVE UNDERWATER ATTACK

Transverse bulkheads are the most effective form of internal subdivision from the standpoint of developing the ship's overall resistance to the type of damage which usually results from underwater attack. Longitudinal bulkheads generally have an unfavorable effect on resistance to underwater damage, because they introduce the danger of unsymmetrical flooding unless the off-center spaces formed by these bulkheads are cross-connected to insure rapid cross-flooding or unless these spaces are kept full of liquids. Decks and platforms other than the weather deck may have either favorable or an unfavorable effect. If damage occurs below a watertight deck and the space below the deck floods completely, the effect is definitely favorable because high flooding is prevented and free surface of flooding water is eliminated. On the other hand, if damage occurs above a watertight deck and flooding of spaces below is prevented, the effect of the watertight deck is unfavorable since the ballasting effect of the low flooding will not be obtained. Because of the uncertainty as to the location of the damage relative to the deck and the probability that all decks will be ruptured except on the largest ships, no reliance can be placed on watertight decks and platforms below the weather deck in evaluating a ship's resistance to underwater attack. A watertight weather deck throughout the ship's length is desirable to prevent flooding from the sea into undamaged spaces in the event of underwater damage which involves sufficient heel to submerge this deck.

PROTECTION OF VITAL SPACES AGAINST FLOODING

Vital spaces are defined as those spaces that are manned at general quarters and those unmanned spaces that contain equipment essential to the primary mission of the ship. It is obviously desirable to surround each of these spaces within the hull by a completely watertight envelope, since

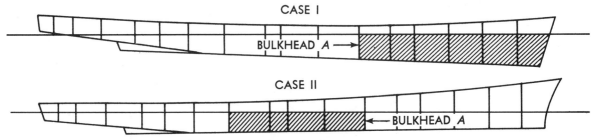

Figure 4–12. Limitations to Compartmentation

such protection might prevent flooding of the space in the event of damage in the vicinity and thereby preserve the function which the space accommodates.

It is possible that a subdivision fitted as protection for vital spaces because it involves longitudinal bulkheads may reduce the overall resistance of the ship to underwater attack by establishing unsymmetrical spaces. This disadvantage must be accepted. The disadvantage should, of course, be minimized in preparing arrangement plans by locating vital spaces, insofar as possible, to avoid the possibility of unsymmetrical flooding.

INTERFERENCE OF SUBDIVISION WITH ARRANGEMENTS

The provision of a series of transverse watertight bulkheads which is necessary to develop resistance to underwater attack will often interfere with obtaining the most favorable arrangement of spaces. Since all of the main transverse bulkheads extend continuously from the keel up, all compartments on the various levels between two main transverse bulkheads will be of the same length, whereas the optimum arrangement might require compartments of different lengths. The most favorable location of bulkheads, from the standpoint of resistance to underwater attack, may make it impossible to obtain the desired length of main compartments from the arrangement standpoint because of the floodable length. Generally, the desired locations for the machinery spaces and magazines establish the approximate location of the adjacent main transverse bulkheads.

INTERFERENCE OF SUBDIVISION WITH ACCESS AND SYSTEMS

Penetration of watertight subdivisions by piping, electric cables, ventilation ducts, and access openings involves considerable weight and expense since watertight fittings must be provided. Additional disadvantages are that the access and ventilation closures must be set, throughout the life of the ship, in accordance with the various damage control doctrines, and rapid access is hindered by the necessity for opening and securing doors in the process of passing through the subdivisions.

The bulkheads which have the greatest number of penetrations, and through which rapid access is most often required, are those between the main and second decks in the midship region. If these bulkheads are not watertight, it must be assumed that for cases of damage in the region of the non-tight bulkheads, flooding will occur fore and aft along the second deck until watertight bulkheads are reached. This is equivalent to disregarding the buoyant effects of the portion of the ship above the second deck between the watertight bulkheads. On some ships having a relatively high freeboard, the damaged stability investigations may show that the damaged stability and reserve buoyancy will be adequate, with some of the main transverse bulkheads considered non-tight above the second deck. In such a case, it is essential to make the second deck watertight, at least in the outboard areas which may be submerged after damage, to avoid progressive flooding into the spaces below.

In cases where it is necessary to take full advantage of all buoyant volume below the weather deck to meet the criteria for resistance to underwater damage, it will usually be possible to accept some non-tight penetrations of the main transverse bulkheads without introducing any appreciable danger of progressive flooding into intact spaces. The procedure for establishing the areas in which non-tight penetrations are acceptable is described below and illustrated by figures 4–12 and 4–13.

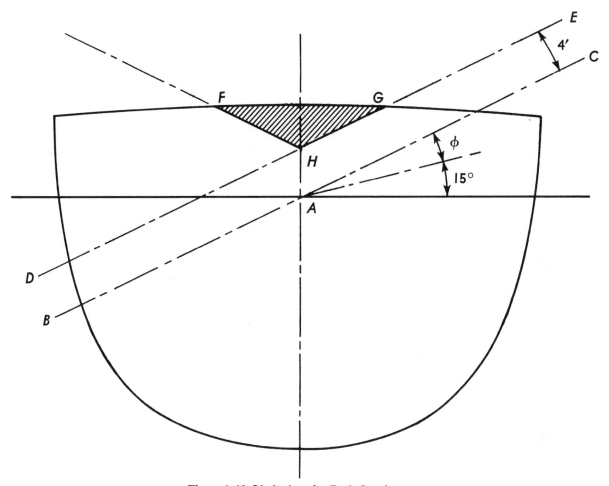

Figure 4–13. Limitations for Deck Openings

For any bulkhead, such as bulkhead *A* in figure 4–12, the designer determines the maximum extent of flooding of the adjacent compartments that can occur both immediately forward and immediately aft of bulkhead *A* without causing the ship to capsize or founder. These extents of flooding are represented by the cross-hatched portions of the ship in figure 4–12.

The designer will next calculate the drafts forward and aft for each of these two cases of flooding and draw the trimmed waterlines at which the ship will float in each case.

He now determines which of the two cases of flooding will produce the deeper immersion of bulkhead *A*. This establishes the maximum height to which the water will rise on bulkhead *A,* assuming the ship settles without heeling in still water, for the two most extensive cases of flooding of adjacent compartments which the ship can

survive and which could involve danger of progressive flooding through bulkhead *A*.

Allowances for heel due to unsymmetrical flooding, roll, and wave action are applied in the manner illustrated by figure 4–13. This illustration represents bulkhead *A* of figure 4–12, and point *A* corresponds to the intersection of the deeper trimmed waterline of figure 4–12 (case 1) with bulkhead *A*.

It is assumed that the ship is subject to an angle of heel of 15 degrees. It is also assumed that the ship is rolling to an angle, ϕ, of the magnitude given by figure 4–13. Waterline *BC* is drawn through point *A* to represent the condition with the ship inclined to an angle equal to 15 degrees plus ϕ. To allow for wave action, line *DE* is drawn four feet above waterline *BC*. Line *DE* and the corresponding line on the opposite side of the ship, which are designated as the **V** *line* for bulkhead *A,* outline the area *FGH* through which non-tight penetrations are acceptable.

The weather deck should, of course, be watertight to prevent flooding from the sea when the ship is heeled over as the result of underwater damage, and similar tightness of the second deck should be provided in regions where transverse bulkheads between the second and main decks are non-tight. As indicated above in the case of the transverse bulkheads, there may be an area near the ship's centerline in which non-watertight penetrations are acceptable. The extent of this area is determined in a manner which is similar to that caused in establishing the **V** lines for the transverse bulkheads. Where ventilation penetrations occur outboard of the **V** lines for the deck, the penetration may be made watertight either by installing a watertight closure at the deck or by making the ventilation duct watertight up to its intersection with the **V** line.

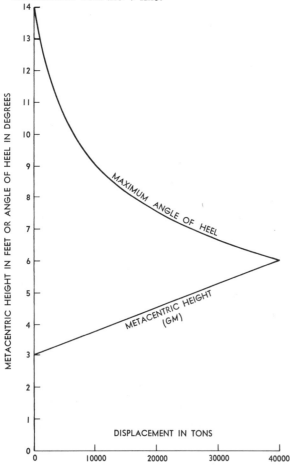

Figure 4–14. Standards of Initial Stability

PROVISION FOR CARRYING LIQUIDS AND SUBDIVISION

In naval vessels the location of liquid loading has traditionally been most important, probably more so prior to our era of missiles and atomic weapons. However, deep side tanks are still most effective protection from underwater side attack. To the extent that this is important to the mission of the particular ship, tanks should be used. It must be appreciated that because of their large transverse moment and ever-present free surface, deep side tanks will have a deleterious effect on stability. This disadvantage can be reduced and controlled by the installation of cross-connecting pipelines with control valves. Double or single bottom tanks are generally preferable and are more universally used in both warships and merchant ships. They not only provide protection from underwater damage but form an integral part of the ballasting system and center of gravity control both vertically and longitudinally. Their effect in grounding and stranding will be discussed later.

COLLISION DAMAGE AND SUBDIVISION

Because ships are vulnerable to collision primarily at the bow, a watertight, transverse bulkhead is located at least five percent of the ship's waterline length shaft abaft the forward perpendicular. This is generally used in merchant ships and small craft as well. It is frequently referred to as the *collision bulkhead.*

STRANDING SUBDIVISION AND STABILITY

The most effective subdivision for protection against the hazard of stranding consists of a complete inner bottom. (Where, in smaller vessels, it is impractical to fit an inner bottom, it is frequently possible to make the lowest platform deck watertight.) Because of stability considerations, the double-bottom spaces should be subdivided as extensively as possible. This increases the flexibility of their usage in the ballasting systems and generally does not interfere or conflict with the other subdivision criteria.

From the stability standpoint, when stranding does occur, there are several interesting problems involving the center of gravity, one of which is pointed out subsequently under *docking.* The other involves the frequently desirable action of removing weight from the ship in order to refloat her. The process is called *jettisoning,* and should be considered when necessary.

JETTISONING WHEN AGROUND

In a ship floating freely, jettisoning is merely a problem of weight removal. With the grounded ship, jettisoning introduces several considerations worthy of emphasis. It should be noted first, however, that from the standpoint of good seamanship and the overall success of refloating a grounded ship, jettisoning is *not* considered good practice where it is not possible to prevent the lightened ship from going further aground closer

inshore. The decision to jettison, of course, should be made by the commanding officer, depending upon the circumstances. Where the danger of further grounding does not exist or is remote, such as a case of grounding on a mud flat in protected waters, there is often no reason why jettisoning should not be a practical course of action.

In originating an equation for jettisoning a weight or weights when aground (assuming the ship does not refloat), one approach is to consider the problem on the basis of two separate situations of which it is a composite, i.e., *weight removal* and *grounding.*

Figure 4–15. SS Ellin Aground off Point Arguello, California

Let us establish that a ship aground having jettisoned a weight is in the same condition from the stability strandpoint as the same ship which jettisoned the same weight from the same place while afloat and then grounded to the same draft.

With the second condition in mind:

Let Δ = original displacement afloat
$\overline{KG}$ = original height of G afloat
w = weight jettisoned from Kg
Δ_1 = grounded displacement (by draft)
$\overline{KG_2}$ = final virtual height of G
$\overline{KG_A}$ = height of G afloat after weight removal
Δ_A = displacement after weight removal.

Then

$$\overline{KG_A} = \frac{\Delta\overline{KG} - w\overline{Kg}}{\Delta - w}.$$

Now the ship goes aground and, from the "docking" equation,

$$\text{virtual } \overline{KG}_{(\text{aground})} = \frac{\Delta_A\overline{KG_A}}{\Delta_1},$$

we may substitute the terms above so that

$$\overline{KG_2} = \frac{(\Delta - w)\dfrac{\Delta\overline{KG} - w\overline{Kg}}{(\Delta - w)}}{\Delta_1}$$

or

$$\overline{KG_2} = \frac{\Delta\overline{KG} - w\overline{Kg}}{\Delta_1},$$

where G_2 is the virtual position of the center of gravity of a grounded ship, considering the jettisoned weight. Here, Δ_1 is still the original displacement minus the upward ground force, or simply, the final displacement or buoyant force after the tide has fallen. It is the same as before jettisoning because both the original displacement and the upward force due to grounding are reduced by the amount of the jettisoned weight.

For practical considerations of safety to the ship, exclusive of stability, the addition of low weights within the ship is more often the best approach. When aground on an unprotected reef, beach or lee shore, the best action to take is to flood low compartments and wait for assistance.

The circumstances involving stranding are generally so varied that there is little in the way of specific design criteria or doctrine that can be set forth. The notations of the virtual center of gravity when jettisoning have little to do with subdivision except where they apply to the con-

siderations of ballasting and de-ballasting protective bottom compartments.

Generally, the above discussion involving subdivision criteria is that which guides naval ship designers in the Naval Ship Systems Command, and it is restated here as intactly as possible for the benefit of students aspiring to such design.

DOCKING

The conditions surrounding cases of dry-docking are basically weight removal situations. Essentially, the ship is only partially waterborne. The remaining portion of the ship's weight rests upon the bottom of the dock.

The problem may be most readily explained by treating it as a *weight removal problem*. When the ship comes to rest along her keel and is no longer a freely floating body, she cannot maintain her original displacement. The reduction in displacement resulting from her diminishing draft is entirely accounted for by the upward force acting on the ship's bottom. The ship can be considered as if it were still a floating body of reduced displacement; the reduced displacement being due to the upward force at the bottom (which is considered as a removed weight). If we assume, as is normally the case, that this force acts at the first point of contact, the keel, we have the point at which our imaginary weight has been removed. An evaluation of this condition will account for the emerged layer and a new position of M and G. Combining the changes in G and M, we have a new transverse metacentric height, and, if desired, we may plot a corrected theoretical static stability curve. Because the point of application of the bottom force would actually move when the ship is heeled, a complete static stability curve taken from the upright characteristics would be of questionable accuracy. We are most immediately concerned, in grounding and docking, with the modified *initial* stability characteristics, that is, the new $\overline{GM}$. The value of this $\overline{GM}$ will be useful in determining the tendency of the ship to stay upright on the keel blocks; or when aground, the value will indicate any danger of falling down on her side, endangering the ship further and tremendously complicating the problem of refloating her.

Recalling our equation for moments about the keel in finding a new $\overline{KG}$ when a weight is removed, we have

$$\overline{KG_1} = \frac{\overline{KG}\Delta - w\overline{Kg}}{\Delta_1}, \text{ where } \Delta_1 = \Delta + w.$$

Now, in grounding or docking where we have deduced that the weight removed is at the keel, then the moment, $w\overline{Kg} = 0$, and our equation reduces to

$$\overline{KG_1} = \frac{\overline{KG}\Delta}{\Delta_1}.$$

$\overline{KG}$ is the original height of the center of gravity, and $\overline{KG_1}$ is the final or effective height of the center of gravity for the reduced draft corresponding to the displacement, Δ_1. The change from G to G_1 is known as a *virtual* shift.

We must speak of $\overline{KG_1}$ as an effective height of the center of gravity, because we have removed no real weight, and the actual center of gravity of the weight distribution of the ship is unchanged. However, for the stability condition of the ship, the virtual location of G is $\overline{KG_1}$, and the vessel will act as though the actual location of G is at that height. (See figure 4–16.)

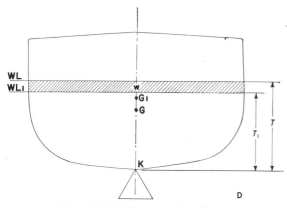

Figure 4–16. Forces in Docking

The student must be aware that in problems of docking where the force on the keel causes a virtual rise in G, there is also a corresponding change in M, the metacenter, due to the lowering waterline. The location of G will invariably move upward, and, generally, as the draft decreases, the value of $\overline{KM}$ increases. In some cases, the value of $\overline{KM}$ may decrease. In most ships, G goes up more rapidly than M, and there will be some point where the $\overline{KM}$ and $\overline{KG}$ curves cross, and $\overline{GM}$ becomes negative. There are some cases, however, where the rate of increase of $\overline{KM}$ de-

velops so rapidly that the value of $\overline{KG}$ never reaches it, and the ship will be stable throughout as long as it is partially waterborne. This is the case with most flat-bottomed vessels. It is conceivable that there may be situations where the $\overline{KG}$ curve and the $\overline{KM}$ curve cross twice, making the value of $\overline{GM}$ go from positive to negative and back to positive. This, however, would be an abnormal ship form.

Structural Impairment and Shock Phenomena

Aside from damage which penetrates a ship's hull and invades its watertight integrity, there are other considerations (particularly for naval vessels) of underwater, noncontact damage that must be anticipated and considered in the design. Where damage anticipated from contact invasions of the hull is of a localized nature and the design action is toward containment, the shocks produced by underwater explosions will generally extend the damage. Structural failure will be observed over a wide area, machinery and other heavy equipment will be displaced from their foundations, and a general reduction in longitudinal strength may take place. It is important to be aware of the nature and origin of this type of hazard.

When a shock motion is introduced by the action of underwater explosion, a wide variety of motions may result at various parts of the ship as shown in figure 4–17. From this diagram, it can be seen that the accelerations reach their peak at the lowest frequency for the upper decks but build up more gradually to a higher value for the low decks nearest the explosion. These shock characteristics transmit themselves through the ship in a vibration wave. The characteristic frequencies of underwater shocks should be studied by the designer of ships seeking protective qualities from the extensive literature and test data available from the Naval Ship Research and Development Center. These data should then be compared with the ship's natural vibration characteristics.

Design for shock resistance can take two different approaches. The first is to "harden up" or increase the ruggedness of components and systems intended to resist shock motions. Components can actually be tested on medium weight shock machines to evaluate their ability to resist

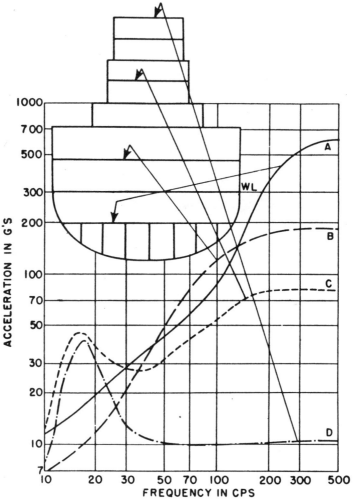

Figure 4–17. Typical Shock Spectra at Different Levels in a Ship

Courtesy of Harry L. Rich

shock. The second approach is to attenuate the shock wave by spreading it out as indicated in the paragraph above.

PLASTICITY IN SHIP STRUCTURES

The student must understand that dynamic loads imposed by explosions as described above will result in either elastic or plastic deformation. There is, of course, little concern regarding the structure of the ship where the deformation is elastic, and the yield point has not been reached in the main structural members. There are, of course, other dynamic loads that hazard any ship, such as the repetitive slamming in head sea conditions whose result is similar underwater shock. The nature of such action is difficult and complex to describe analytically. The most effective analysis has been through the scale testing of structural models.

In any case, the designer must be cognizant of the existence of these types of problems, and, for his purpose, they might first be described in two categories: (a) those dynamic loads that are recurrent or produce impact of a more or less regular frequency, such as slamming, and (b) those of an isolated impact as in the case of explosions under water.

In the first case, the design should be optimized toward restricting local recurrent plastic deformation and allowing for no such deformation in the structural members that provide continuous longitudinal strength to the ship's girder. Secondly, the

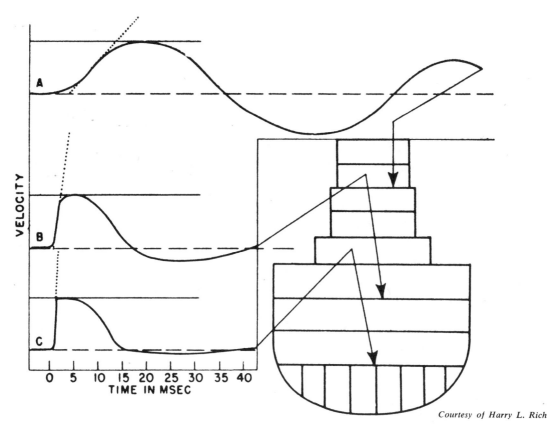

Figure 4–18. Characteristic Shock Motions at Different Levels in a Ship Resulting from an Underwater Explosion

designer must not attempt to avoid fatigue failure by allowing yield stress to be reached in any essential strength member.

In the case of explosive loads, hull damage must be distinguished from equipment and installation damage. The latter's preventive design measures have been mentioned above where "hardening" methods were recommended. Further, of course, to this end are the many methods of shock mounting available and the considerations of the location of machinery elements away from bulkheads or such spatial arrangements allowing excursions of fixed equipment.

The hull requires another concept. One possibility is to develop arrangements which will defeat possible underwater shock by permitting and accepting local destruction in outboard portions of the structure without catastrophic collapse of critical interior bulkheads. Simultaneously, an attempt may be made to restrict with these designs the longitudinal extent of damage and to assure that the ship's girder strength is affected as little as possible by the localized damage. This type of

protection system is employed in capital ships and aircraft carriers. Portions of the ship's structures are thus designed to withstand a required severity of attack. This is accomplished by maximum energy absorption in plastic deformation of those structural elements which finally are destroyed, so that correspondingly less energy has to be absorbed by the holding part of the structure.

The above doctrines are essentially very general in nature, and the designer must consider the particular mission of his ship in designing for these dynamic loads.

It is not amiss, in ending any such discussion, to emphasize once more the importance of maintaining the structural continuity of the hull girder, which must allow only elastic deformation below the stress limit. Any plastic deformation in this continuous girder results, frequently, in stress concentrations and sometimes failure. Although alternating plastic deformation will lead to failure, nonrecurrent plastic deformation may occasionally relieve stress concentrations.

A Workman Checks One of the Controllable Pitch Propeller Blades of the Destroyer Spruance (DD-963)

CHAPTER 5

Forces Opposed to Propulsion

In the many hundreds of years of ship design as well as for the thousands of years of ship development and construction, there had been, until the past century, little curiosity concerning the nature of energy required by a ship to sustain its forward velocity. This, perhaps, was natural enough when we consider the primary propulsion source of vessels prior to the mid-nineteenth century. For sailing vessels, there is no determinate control of propulsive power or, for that matter, no quantitative rationalization for it.

It was not until the advent of steam power and the construction of the *Great Eastern* in the middle 1850s (she required six years to build and three months to launch) that it became clear to shipowners and shipbuilders that a more rigorous approach to ship design was needed. The ship, *Great Eastern,* in many ways advanced in concept and certainly ambitious in scope, contributed more to the art of ship design, perhaps, than was realized at the time. With all of her faults— her disastrous financial loss, her technical experiments and failures; all of it, bitter experience— the greatest benefit was the experience and vision acquired by a young engineer who had been associated in a minor way with her construction. William Froude, a discerning engineer-designer whose ability was keenest when turned toward scientific inquiry, recognized the great necessity

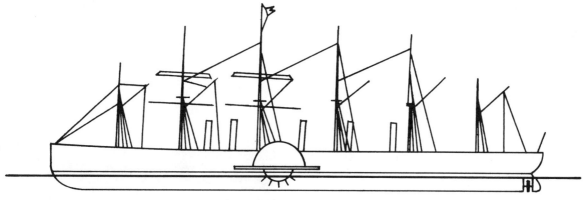

Figure 5–1. The Great Eastern

95

of determining, in the design process, the power required to propel a ship of a specific size and hull form. The *Great Eastern* had been hopelessly underpowered (about 2600 horsepower for her 25,000 tons) and propelled with half her power driving inefficient side paddle wheels and the remainder driving an awkward, inadequate screw propeller. The energy loss through these devices had to be enormous. It was possible neither for her to earn enough to buy the fuel to drive her nor for her propulsive system to force her through the water at a reasonable speed.

Froude's Experiments

From these unhappy origins in experience grew William Froude's determination to learn the true and natural relationship of power to the speed of a ship. It was ultimately out of his determined and brilliant experiments with models and parent ship forms together with his invaluable literature and papers that *Froude's Law of Comparison* evolved.

It will be helpful in understanding this most fundamental principle to review very briefly the approach taken by Froude in his original thinking and investigations.

Upon testing similar models of various sizes in a sheltered stream, Froude soon concluded what he had probably strongly suspected all along— that there was *no* proportional or mathematically describable relationship of water resistance between two models as a function of size alone. He also advanced his knowledge of associated wave patterns sufficiently to obtain a grant of £2000 from the British Admiralty to continue his work. With these funds, he built a towing tank of about 300 feet with a small carriage placed on an overhead rail and powered by a steam winch. He was now able to control his models' speed more precisely and measure their drag or resistance on a scale. Actually, he had built the prototype of all present-day, modern towing tanks. This first essential, but rather primitively instrumented tool soon began to open many of the previously locked-up secrets of hydrodynamic knowledge.

During this period of emerging knowledge and industrial revolution, scientists throughout Europe were becoming more appreciative of the *scientific method*. Froude and scientists like him were able to reason constructively by separating the components of problems and precisely scrutinizing them.

One of the components of the ship-powering problem was the apparent wave disturbance made by the model or the ship moving through the water. These self-created waves obviously represented an energy loss. A rigid object moving through water must move that water aside, and this displacement creates a system or pattern of normal forces not existing when the object is at rest. Froude also observed that the pattern of the waves was a function of the model's speed— small, closely spaced wavelets developed when moving slowly with widening, larger waves as speed increased. Most importantly, these patterns were similar, regardless of model size. It became apparent that there must be a relationship between wave-making resistance and velocity, and this might very well be associated with the velocity of a free wave, where the speed of the wave is proportional to the square root of its wave length ($v \propto \sqrt{L}$). So, what of the forces involved? How much of the total energy is consumed in making waves? Unfortunately, in a towing tank, the dynamometer, or force measuring instrument, can only measure the total resistance (or drag) of the model—it cannot measure wave resistance separately.

A resistance component that was also recognizable was the *frictional* resistance of the molecules of water being dragged along next to the hull. If the amount of this friction could be separately evaluated and if there were no more major components of the total resisting forces, then it might be possible to relate the model and parent ship characteristics.

FROUDE'S HYPOTHESIS

Froude's experiments, because of this or similar reasoning, took another turn. Instead of models in ship forms, he conducted tests on flat surfaced, comparatively thin planks towed on edge just below the water's surface. In such tests, there were negligible waves formed. Using planks with varieties of surface finishes (from smooth varnish to sand, cotton, paraffin, etc.), he soon discovered that there were several variables affecting friction. Important among them were velocity, area of surface, smoothness of surface, and viscosity and density of the water. Froude finally accounted for these variables. He sorted them out in the following workable expression:

$$R_f = fSV^n$$

where R_f = frictional resistance of the fluid
S = wetted surface
V = velocity
f and n are constants that depend on the length and nature of the surface.

At this point, Froude had evolved his theory:
1. That geometrically similar hull forms moving at corresponding speeds (i.e. their wave patterns were the same) had wave-making resistances proportional to their size or displacements.
2. That the frictional resistance could be separately computed for both model and parent ship, and thus by subtracting it from the model's total resistance, scaling up the wave resistance, and adding the ship's computed frictional resistance, the total ship's resistance could be obtained.

The Division of Resistance

The theory required substantiation with full-scale ships because the experiments had been concerned only with models of small difference in size. Froude was also unaware of the more subtle elements of the problem involving turbulent and laminar flow. Notable also, his fellow countryman, Sir Osborne Reynolds, had yet to make his significant studies in fluid flow.

However, William Froude proceeded to test the model of a specific ship whose full-scale counterpart, HMS *Greyhound,* was to be made available by the Admiralty for towing tests.

After testing both model and ship, it was apparent that their total resistance values when plotted against speed had much the same shapes.

To compare logically the ship's and model's characteristics graphically on the same coordinates, it is necessary to reduce the quantitative data to common ratios that are essentially dimensionless. Thus, the common ordinate for resistance is better expressed as resistance per ton displacement, R/Δ, and the speed coordinate as the speed-length ratio, $V/\sqrt{L}$. This latter expression, sometimes referred to as *Taylor's Quotient,* deserves greater explanation at this point. It is a well-known and commonly used factor in naval architecture and associated professions. It is a most valuable and natural expression, one of the ship designer's and ship operator's most useful tools. The speed-length ratio is obviously not a dimensionless ratio, yet it is related very closely

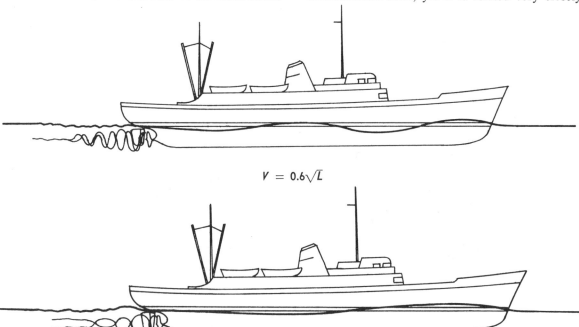

$$V = 0.6\sqrt{L}$$

$$V = 1.3\sqrt{L}$$

Figure 5–2. Surface Displacement Ship Wave-making Signatures at Various Speeds

No Class You

to Froude's Number, which is dimensionless. It is perhaps best to start the explanation with this other significant number.

FROUDE'S NUMBER

During his investigations of models of varying sizes and varying speeds, Froude observed, in addition to the similarity of wave patterns, the growth of wavelength with speed. For example, a model of 10 feet moving at approximately one knot would have nearly eight waves along its waterline; at 1.5 knots there would be about four waves; and at three knots, *one* wave. Also, in models of proportionately larger or smaller lengths, the waves were the same in number along their hulls when their ratios of speed to square root of length were equal. This speed of the wave, which is coupled to the speed of the ship and must be identical because it is generated by the moving ship, can be then expressed in relation to the *ship's length*. Froude recognized it first simply as

$$v \propto \sqrt{L} \quad \text{or} \quad v = C\sqrt{L}.$$

It was soon more rigorously advanced by dimensional analysis to the universally recognized form now called *Froude's Number*:

$$F_n = \frac{v}{\sqrt{gL}}.$$

Common usage by naval architects for many years has found it simpler and more practical to omit the gravitational constant (invariably the applications were at constant g) and to express v in *knots* and L in *feet*—Froude's Number has become a dimensional expression.

Thus, speed-length ratio,

$$V/\sqrt{L}$$

is a modification of Froude's Number,

$$v/\sqrt{gL}$$

in a more simple, workable form for English and American designers. In other countries, the Froude Number is used consistently in its dimensionless form.

Best form of Froude's #

COMPONENTS OF RESISTANCE

Returning to Froude's experiments and the *Greyhound* tests, the model resistances were plotted together with the ship's resistances, both *total* and frictional, on the coordinates as noted above, and their frictional resistances were subtracted from the total. These differences, which were to be called the *residual resistance,* compared nearly identically. The residual resistance, although it contains such other factors as air resistance and eddy-making resistance, is substantially and significantly *wave-making resistance.** Thus were Froude's theories accepted.

In light of the accumulated and related knowledge since Froude's experiments, it is possible to incorporate his theories in a more rigorous and universally applicable development. An expression for total resistance of a partially immersed body was known to Froude, as it is also known today, to be

$$R_t = \rho S v^2 C_t.$$

The coefficient C in this expression was reasoned to be a function of the various components of resistance, such as fluid friction, wave-making, eddy, etc., and it was Froude's reasoning that friction and wave-making must be separated since they behaved and related differently. By separating frictional resistance, the rest is logically called residual resistance but consists primarily of wave-making resistance. The coefficient C now depends on Froude's Number or $V/\sqrt{L}$.

Therefore $\quad R_t = R_r + R_f$
where $\quad\quad R_f = \rho S v^2 (\phi_1\, R_n)$
$\quad\quad\quad\quad R_r = \rho S v^2 (\phi_2\, F_n).$

It should be noted here that the total resistance, R_t, may be converted to an expression of power when it is multiplied by its corresponding velocity. Thus, converting to familiar horsepower units, $\dfrac{R_t\, v}{550}$, we may define a common and important parameter called *total effective horsepower, EHP_t.* This expression, frequently modified to simply *effective horsepower, EHP,* is frequently used in ship's powering discussions and will be more thoroughly explored in the following chapters.

Continuing only with resistance and dealing only

---

*Very recent pressure and frictional resistance surveys show that much of the residual resistance includes less identifiable wave-making resistance at speed-length ratios below 1.0, and that a greater proportion's origin is primarily viscous.

with wave-making or residual resistances between the ship and its model, we find that at corresponding speeds (i.e., model and ship at same speed-length ratio)

$$\phi_2 \, F_n = \frac{R_{rm}}{\rho_m \, S_m \, v_m^2} = \frac{R_{rs}}{\rho_s \, S_s \, v_s^2}$$

$$R_{rs} = R_{rm} \left(\frac{\rho_s \, S_s \, v_s^2}{\rho_m \, S_m \, v_m^2} \right)$$

$$R_{rs} = R_{rm} \frac{\Delta_s}{\Delta_m}.$$

Note that in this expression, both $\rho_s \, S_s \, v_s^2$ and $\rho_m \, S_m \, v_m^2$ can be reduced dimensionally to the weight of the ship and the weight of the model respectively.

The relationship developed here between R_{rs} and R_{rm} (the residual resistance of the ship and its model respectively) is known as *Froude's Law of Comparison*—viz., the residual resistances of geometrically similar ships are in the same ratio as that of their displacements, when both ships are at the same speed-length ratio.

Official U.S. Navy Photograph

Figure 5–3. Transverse Waves of the Wave-making Portion of R_t Are Clearly Visible in this Bow Photograph of the USS Reeves (DLG-24)

The experiments of William Froude leading to his discoveries and his theories separating the *two* major resistance components have been introduced here because of their critical importance to naval architecture; both now and in the past, they have pointed up the limitations of surface ships. Much effort and expense are devoted to the studies of *frictional resistance* and *wave-making* resistance phenomena. While much has been learned, there is still much to be known of their individual natures. It is difficult to say which is least or most understood. No attempt will be made in this discussion to clarify the more obscure details or even to point out the many complexities. Scientific literature in ship hydrodynamics is voluminous on these topics and is being increased daily. We will look briefly into some ramifications of frictional and wave-making resistance and note those areas of interest that are considered of most significance.

Wave-Making Resistance

Were it not for *wave-making* resistance, the speeds of ships would not be as embarrassingly slow as they are. They have improved over the centuries only by a small amount; sailing vessels can go no faster today than was possible a century ago; steam, diesel, or nuclear powered surface vessels are held to speeds that were possible long ago.

The practical limiting speed for displacement surface vessels is basically that of wavelength to ship length, where one wavelength, created by the ship, is equal to the ship's waterline length. This, expressed quantitatively, is $V/\sqrt{L} \approx 1.3$, and V is sometimes called the *hull speed*. When a surface ship attempts to exceed this speed, it finds itself literally climbing a hill that it is creating. In exceptional cases of slim, highly powered ships such as destroyers, it is possible to exceed this speed, but it is seldom profitable.

Courtesy of Hitachi Zosen

Figure 5–4. Bow Waves at Point of Origin, Generated by the Full Bow of a Japanese 120,000 Ton Supertanker

In the search for higher speeds, some watercraft have been designed to remove themselves from the surface and its limitations. Hydrofoil vessels lift off the surface, planing craft skim on it, surface effect craft are supported on a cushion of air above it, and new high-speed submersibles operate continuously below it.

The fact remains, however, that the surface is still the most practical, economical, and pleasant place to be. Its disadvantages must be dealt with as best we can or at least be accepted. Let us deal with the disadvantages of the surface by examining some characteristics of the natural behavior of a water surface.

The surface of the sea is, of course, a surface of discontinuity between two fluids, water and air. It is held in place loosely by gravity, and, for most practical purposes, we can largely ignore the lighter air. A heavy fluid acted upon by gravity and other forces has an undulating surface, and, when the force system is a simple or disciplined one, it tends to oscillate in an essentially regular pattern of three-dimensional waves. A ship moving through the otherwise undisturbed water's surface sets up a very characteristic pattern of waves. In this pattern, there are essentially two primary points of origin of waves that are, logically enough, at the bow and at the stern.

The bow wave train is more significant, first, in that the waves generated here persist along the ship's hull, affecting the pressure distribution in the water where the ship is acting, and secondly, because the bow wave train is the larger and more predominant one. In observing the characteristic and familiar pattern, a series of diagonal or oblique crests are first apparent. These are simply the diverging crests moving outwardly from the point of disturbance. (See figure 5–5). The system's basic wave train, of which the diverging crests are only a part, advances with the ship, and the line of crests and troughs are perpendicular to its course vector. It is these transverse waves, advancing with the ship and seemingly locked to it, that must be noted in relation to the ship's speed limitations and resistance characteristics. The length of these waves (the distance between crests in the direction of their movement) is, of course, a function of their velocity ($L_w = .557V^2$) which is also the ship's velocity. Their amplitude, on the other hand, is independent of both velocity and wave-

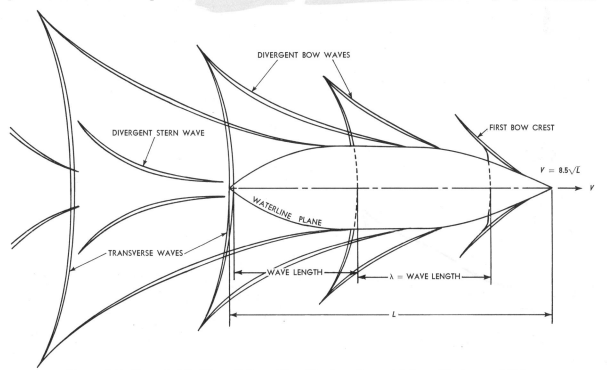

Figure 5–5. Characteristic Wave Pattern (Plan View) as Generated by a Displacement Ship at a Sub-Hull Speed, $V = .85\sqrt{L}$

length and is a function of the energy expended in generating them. This is apparent in observing the profile of these waves along or near the side of a moving ship.

A tugboat, which often moves at or near her hull speed when proceeding alone, generates a very deep-troughed wave along her side. This reflects her full, deep hull and the amount of water that she must displace in relation to her length. All full, deep ships such as tankers, tugs, trawlers, submarines on the surface, bulk cargo carriers, etc. generate wave patterns of pronounced, deep amplitude waves if moving in the higher speed-length ratios. On the other hand, the shallower, narrower hulls with slim, sharp forward waterlines generate comparatively shallow transverse wave trains. It is particularly difficult at times to even discern those of a naval destroyer-type vessel, and some craft move so easily and have so *little displacement* that overriding

the quasi-limiting speed ($V/\sqrt{L} = 1.3$) is no problem. When such craft are designed with flat surfaces and straight buttocks and their sections resolve the pressure vectors down and away laterally from the hull, they are able to rise dynamically and *plane*; they are essentially free from wave-making resistance. Such craft are of limited economical value because of their inability to haul significant payloads or to negotiate sea conditions less than ideal.

BULBOUS BOWS

The search for means to reduce wave-making resistance has turned and probed in many directions. Some solutions are fanciful and impractical, others are of significant and far-reaching importance. Perhaps the most significant of these is the result of the development of a characteristic appendage or shape that extends back to warships of antiquity. As early as the classic period of the

Courtesy of Stevens Institute of Technology

Figure 5–6. Full Hull Model (12 Meter Sailboat, Upright Test) Showing Wave Development at Hull Speed, $V/\sqrt{L} \approx 1.3$

ancient Greeks and the seasoned Phoenicians, perhaps as early as 700 or 800 BC, there is evidence of a protuberance at the lower forefoot of a ship extending substantially ahead of the main structure of the hull. This distinctive feature was obviously, because of its metal-clad sharpness, a ram. This ram was so successfully used that it was carried on war galleys for centuries and was used by Greek, Roman, Genoese, and Venetian galleys. It was less successful when war vessels propelled by oars were largely abandoned in favor of the vertically structured fortresses that carried hundreds of cannons and were propelled by sails.

With the advent of mechanical propulsion in the nineteenth century, the ram bow soon reappeared and, with other developments in the warship design revolution, became a distinctive feature of the emerging "dreadnought" type of ship at the advent of the twentieth century. It was on hulls of this type that David W. Taylor had experimented in the old Navy model basin in Washington, and in which he discerned a reduction of wave resistance and a hydrodynamic superiority in higher speed ranges. Taylor was convinced that a bulbous nose located deeply at the forefoot and of rounded, faired-in form would produce less wave drag because of a newly created pressure pattern in the vicinity of the bow wave. Such a bow was designed and built specifically with this feature on the USS *Delaware* in 1907. The performance of the ship fully justified this odd shape, and from that date large American-built ships of reasonably high power were built with bulbous bows. Many large foreign-built ships likewise adopted this distinctive form, but it is oddly significant that the two great ocean queens of the past thirty years, the *Queen Elizabeth* and the *Queen Mary,* totally rejected the bulb in their design (as did many other large British ships).

Courtesy of International Public Relations Co., Ltd.

Figure 5–7. Bulbous Bow Characteristic of the Inui Type. This projecting bulb is on a relatively high-speed cargo ship with a sharp waterline entrance. Higher block coefficient tankers use a less projecting bulb, which is faired into the hull.

This conception of the bulbous bow as conceived by Taylor and applied to large ships subsequently was understood and designed to augment speed in the higher values of $V/\sqrt{L}$. These ranges were determined to be from $V/\sqrt{L} = 0.9$ to 1.9 by various contemporary studies. However on some ship forms, it was noted that the advantages became evident at lower speeds. Most merchant ships and cargo carriers are economically powered to cruise at speeds no higher than $V/\sqrt{L} = 0.8$. Consequently, with the prevailing theories surrounding the bulbous bow as well as the added cost in their construction, many ships did not have them and so were excluded from whatever advantages might have ensued.

In 1962, Dr. Takao Inui of the University of Tokyo presented a paper at the annual meeting of the Society of Naval Architects and Marine Engineers in New York City in which he advanced some remarkable theories and test results of his studies of wave-making resistance. These theories were the result of a number of years of research in the model basin at the University of Tokyo where Inui had developed new and ingenius techniques of analysis. His studies have led him through various configurations of bulb forms not only at the bow but at the stern, where the extensions concentrated on wave cancellation and speed augmentation in the moderate to low Froude Number values.

Dr. Inui's experiments, with his associated techniques and theoretical support, have shown substantial and in many cases remarkable reductions in resistance when his bulbous bows have been used. In fact, his work has been so enthusiastically accepted that not only are these bulb shapes incorporated in most new cargo and tanker constructions, but also many older ships have undergone conversion to take advantage of the shape. The bulbous bow is often and sometimes erroneously referred to as the *Inui Bow*.

It is of interest to compare this Inui Bow with the previous bulbous bow introduced by David W. Taylor.

The *Taylor Bow* was conceived and is still used to augment speed characteristics in speed-length ratios of 1.0 and higher. The Inui Bow was developed for ships of greater range in speed, and its advantageous effects in some instances overlap the ranges of the former. In the lower speed categories, a curious and not entirely understood

Courtesy of Hitachi Zosen

Figure 5–8. Molded Bulbous Bow on a Moderate-Sized Bulk Carrier (Launching Day—Japan)

phenomenon exists with the new-type bulbs. While it has been emphasized that these bulbous bows are forms applied to the forward extremities of the ship for the prime purpose of altering and, in a sense, neutralizing the pressure field there to reduce wave-making resistance, it would then seem natural that the advantages would diminish with lower speeds as the percentage of wave-making resistance diminishes. At speed-length ratios of 0.6 in large, full tankers and ore-carrying ships, tests have shown reductions in *total* resistance up to 15 percent with the new-type bulbs. At such a speed, this approaches nearly total elimination of wave-making resistance. Also, these greater resistance reductions appear to occur on ships of full shapes (block coefficients of 0.8 or more) and pronounced **U** sections forward where the shape includes flat-bottomed sections well forward. The reductions also are greater when the ship is light or higher in the water, rather than at full load. This means that bulbs on these ships are more effective nearer the surface. Such phenomena, when considering the added wetted area of the bulbous form with consequent additional frictional resistance, leads to speculation that there is more than a simple reduction of wave-making resistance. It has been suggested by investigators with this type of form at the University of Michigan towing tank that an alteration in flow characteristics around the bow and along the bottom of the bulbous form is perhaps the source of the reduction. Without the bulb, there exists a separation in the flow near and under the bow. With the bulb, this flow is improved, and its average velocity over the entire underbody is slowed so that a reduction in viscous resistance occurs.

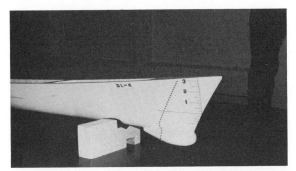

Figure 5–9. Bow of Towing Tank Model and an Actual Ship Showing a Typical Sonar Bulb of a Destroyer Type Ship. This form of bulb is not primarily for hydrodynamic augmentation and offers a challenge to researchers to improve its drag characteristics. (Note the STUD-type turbulence stimulators on the model for inducing full turbulent flow.)

This same phenomenon has been observed independently and with similar conclusions by Dr. Kinoshita, formerly of the University of Tokyo (and formerly the teacher of Dr. Inui). As Technical Director and Manager of Product Development of the Hitachi Shipbuilding Company, leaders in the development and building of supertankers, Dr. Kinoshita has devoted considerable study in his company's research laboratory to the action of the bulbous bow.

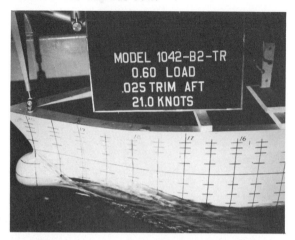

Figure 5–10. Towing Tank Test of a Model with Slow-Speed Bulbous Bow Near Optimum Speed

Dr. Kinoshita points out that, in addition to the probable separation phenomenon (which might not always exist), there is, with the large bulbous bow extension, a rather gradual and uniform pressure reduction from the bow, aft. Without the bulb, this uniformity does not exist, but rather the pressure drops off rather quickly from positive to negative. Such sudden pressure reduction produces an increased velocity with accompanying higher frictional resistance and generally unstable flow characteristics. Such reasoning is convincing.

However, Dr. Inui pursues the research road requiring more rigorous analysis and recently observed that, with slower, high form coefficient ships with considerable parallel middle body, the problem is of great complexity. It is quite possible that, with his *photogram-metrical* analysis, he will ultimately show the limits of the reduction of wave-making resistance in hulls of various forms. He promises that analytical treatment of the bulb on fuller, low-speed tankers of parallel middle body will be forthcoming.

At least at this writing, and in summary, it is evident that, while wave generation is a large component of the ship's expended power, it is possible by the incorporation and placement of proper form to greatly reduce the expended power and in specific situations to effectively cancel it. It remains, however, a difficult and awkward natural phenomenon with which the ship designer must deal and of which he must be aware.

Frictional Resistance

The nature of *frictional* or *skin resistance* had been, to some extent, more evident and familiar than wave-making resistance to scientists before Froude's revealing studies. It had been known, for example, that frictional resistance was a function of the surface roughness, the area of the surface, the velocity of the fluid over the surface, and the density of the fluid. There was some confusion concerning the nature of the flow of the fluid, and consequently no meaningful quantitative analysis had been made. Froude was obliged to develop his own means to evaluate frictional resistance, and while these means were workable, they were also awkward and based largely on experimental data where reproducibility was sometimes doubtful. Ultimately, a fuller understanding of frictional resistance emerged with the investigations of Sir Osborne Reynolds about 1888.

In his experiments with fluid flow in pipes and conduits, Reynolds was able to discern a retardation of the fluid where it moved along the conduit's surface. It was possible to isolate and describe this portion of the fluid (or water) flow as a *boundary layer,* where the particles of fluid in contact with the solid surface adhere to it and the velocity of the fluid varies with its distance out into the free stream. This indicated, of course, a shearing effect between adjacent layers of the fluid near the sides of the vessel, and this became understood, then, as the locus of concentration for study of the nature of fluid friction. It soon became evident, also, that within this boundary layer the amount of retardation of the free flow or measurable resistance was a function of several variables that arranged themselves into a usable relationship. These variable factors were

L—the length or extent of the surface over which the fluid flowed

v—the velocity of the fluid

ν—a viscosity-density characteristic of the fluid.

There were other distracting factors and some suggestive but puzzling phenomena. However the above factors were so evidently persistent that they were arranged into their recurring relationship and given the name, *Reynolds' Number*.

So, $R_n = \dfrac{vL}{v}$

where the unit value of the properties is such as to make the relationship dimensionless, such as,

v = velocity of the fluid in feet/sec

L = characteristic length of the body along the fluid flow in feet

v = kinematic viscosity in ft²/sec.

Courtesy of General Dynamics

Figure 5–11. The Boundary Layer Shows as a White Band Adjacent to this Ship's Hull. The waves angle out in oblique crests at $V = 0.6\sqrt{L}$.

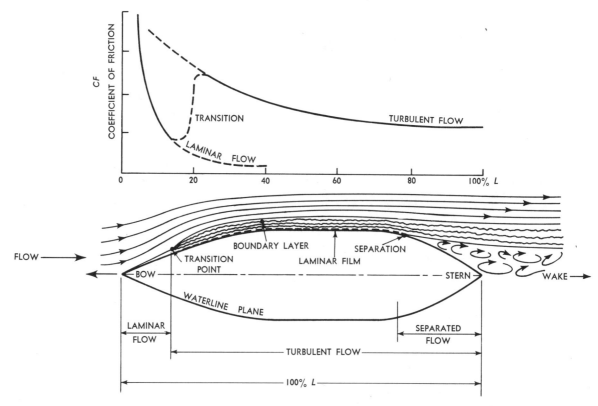

Figure 5–12. Transitional Flow of Water About a Ship at LWL. The extent of laminar flow and transition to turbulent flow depends on the size of the ship, its speed, the smoothness of the hull, etc. There may be no laminar flow at all in larger vessels.

Reynolds, in the course of his experiments, observed also that the nature of the flow of a liquid through a glass tube when a stream of dye was injected changed the nature of this dye stream quite remarkably when the R_n was increased beyond a fixed value. The stream was noticed to waver and then to become confused and dispersed. This phenomenon today is referred to as a transition between a flow of *laminar* type and one of *turbulent* type. It is a most significant observation because, for any expression by which frictional resistance is computed, the nature of the flow must be consistently either turbulent or laminar, and the expression used is only applicable to one or the other.

BOUNDARY LAYER PHENOMENA

Anyone who has traveled by ship and has looked down over the side at the passing water has surely noticed the white, foamy region next to the hull. This is the visible portion of the *boundary layer* at the surface, and it is convincingly *turbulent*. Because of the ship's speed, the

length and comparative roughness of its surface, this boundary layer is essentially always turbulent. Hence all calculations for frictional resistance must recognize this flow regime. In relating model tests to parent ships, the flow around the model must be artificially triggered into a turbulent condition to maintain a rational comparison.

To describe the flow pattern about an ideal hull form of smooth surface when towed through calm water will be helpful in understanding better the nature and occurrence of fluid friction.

At a slow and steady speed, a ship's hull-form model in a towing tank in many situations has nearly 100 percent laminar flow about its hull with perhaps only a small area of turbulence near the stern. If the speed or length (R_n) or both are increased, the transition point from laminar to turbulent flow moves forward. It will continue to move forward with increasing R_n until essentially the entire flow is turbulent. However, the transition point does not change or move proportionately with increased Reynolds Number, and this suggests that frictional resistance is also, in some

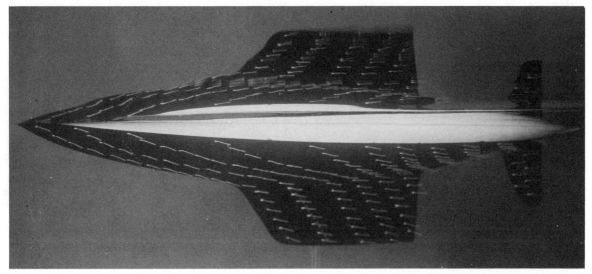

Courtesy of Halsey C. Herreshoff

Figure 5–13. Underwater View of a Sailing Yacht Model Undergoing Tests at the Ship Model Towing Tank at M.I.T. The mirror image of the hull is visible as it is reflected onto the water-air interface. The yarn tufts attached to the hull indicate hydrodynamic flow.

way, subject to the shape or form of the hull. This situation is most noticeable when it is observed with R_n increasing from a laminar flow regime; the transition to turbulence moves quickly from the stern to the point of maximum beam near amidships. Further increase in R_n brings the transition point more slowly forward.

The flow lines from the bow, back to the maximum width where inward curvature sets in are crowded. From this region aft, they open out into a pattern of more expanded and slower flow, and, at some point in the after region of the conventional ship form, may actually tend to separate from the hull. Beyond this point of separation, the water becomes extremely confused, and swirls and eddies are very much apparent. The drag that results from this separated flow becomes a significant portion of what is called *eddy resistance*.

Historically, eddy resistance has been lumped together with wave-making resistance simply because it is not a type of frictional resistance whose behavior and effect can be dealt with in a similar way. It is a comparatively small part of total resistance. Since wave-making resistance is a function of form, as eddy resistance obviously is, they are naturally associated and related. However in the design process, they should be of separate concern. Eddy resistance is most certainly, on the other hand, associated with the formation of a stern wave where they both originate in the low-pressure regions of the stern.

MEANS OF REDUCING FRICTION

The true nature of turbulent flow formation in the boundary layer is not perfectly understood. The mechanism of turbulence however is being exhaustively studied by many hydrodynamicists and research students. Some of this study, with associated experimentation, is of great interest, and some promises encouraging possibilities.

Basically, the mechanism of turbulence in the boundary layer is one of small pressure fluctuations stimulated by a wave phenomenon whose frequency is approximately 100 cycles per second. The intensity of these pressure fluctuations is indicative of the turbulent-wave amplitude, and the energy involved in its generation. An investigator named Max Kramer reasoned that the rigid surface of the hull tended to augment and promote these oscillations in the boundary layer and thus accelerate the transition from laminar to turbulent flow. He also concluded that a more pliant surface, such as that existing in the skin of a porpoise, would suppress or inhibit this dynamic instability in the boundary layer.

Kramer consequently developed a rubberized, pliant material called *Lamiflow* whose flexible surface was a good imitation of porpoise skin. Composed of an inner and outer layer and separated by small rubber pillars and a liquid of carefully controlled density, this material was stretched over torpedo-like forms and towed in resistance measuring tests. The results quite remarkably indicated reductions in frictional resistance measuring tests. The results claimed by the inventor indicated reductions in frictional ships' bottoms has understandably slowed its use and popular acceptance. Further development or promotion of Lamiflow is not known to the author.

A much more active program of study presently exists to discover the means to change the physical character of the fluid in the boundary layer. Solutions of certain substances (of which there are a number available), described by chemists as *non-Newtonians* or *long chain polymers,* when injected into the boundary layer, have a strong inhibitive effect on the pressure fluctuations in the boundary layer. Frictional resistance reductions up to 30 percent have been frequently measured with much greater reductions promised with the development of improved techniques of injection. One of the most encouraging factors in the use of these injected polymers is that the concentrations involved are so very small—generally only a few parts per million.

From the standpoint of any possible application to ships, however, the question must be asked, cannot this be likened to the need for transporting an additional "fuel," and if so, is the resulting augmentation of speed more economical?

Returning to the boundary layer surrounding a moving ship, we are necessarily confronted with uncompromising natural phenomena, some of which offer (as above) encouragement for exploitation but most of which primarily require understanding and recognition in design. A most interesting detail of the boundary layer is the nature of a nearly stagnant layer of water immediately next to the skin of the ship. The existence of this sublayer or laminar film is of more importance in small vessels and in sailing yachts; nevertheless, its presence deserves attention.

The laminar film covers slight roughness and encases small protuberances on essentially smooth bottoms making a hydrodynamically efficient wetted area. The thickness of this sublayer decreases as the Reynolds Number increases, and

speeds are soon reached that cause the roughness and grain of the surface to penetrate the film. The surface, consequently, takes on a changing roughness character with an increasing friction coefficient.

From the practical point of view, the effect of surface roughness on frictional resistance must be stressed. The smoothness of a vessel's bottom, including the absence of rivet heads, fastening heads, welding beads, roughly applied bottom paint, etc., is the most important current factor in the reduction of frictional resistance. It is also important to remember that the resistance caused by these factors increases rapidly with speed.

OTHER RESISTANCE FACTORS

We have seen in the foregoing that the total resistance opposed to the propulsive force of the ship is mainly composed of the energy in the self-generated waves and in the fluid friction surrounding the ship's immersed and moving hull. There are other factors and components of the total resistance that, under some conditions, present formidable opposition to forward motion.

Eddy resistance has already been mentioned, and it will be sufficient only to add that eddies are produced as a phenomenon of separation in the regular flow pattern around the hull. This separation exists primarily and in normal speed regimes where appendages or sudden changes in contour or shapes in the hull are present. Particularly in the after portions of the underbody, which is sometimes referred to as the *run,* the existence of excessive curvature located in an expanding flow pattern inevitably produces a breakaway of the flow. The eddy resistance, here produced, exists together with the wave-making resistance of the stern wave which forms in the same region of lowered pressure. These are two different components to be dealt with separately but whose magnitudes originate from the same or similar causes.

Air resistance becomes a factor of increasing importance in higher speed ships of proportionately large superstructures. Attention is being paid more consistently in modern ships of all sizes to the shape and fairing of superstructure, stacks, masts, etc. Wind tunnel tests of waterline models are most helpful in evaluating this reduced wind resistance. Where speeds in excess of 20 knots exist, it becomes economical to fair the super-structure and optimize, within functional limitations, its *air drag* character.

Shallow water produces resistance problems not existing in deep water and such problems become theoretically effective at depths equal to $10T (V/\sqrt{L})$, where T is the vessel's mean draft. The shallow water problem becomes far more noticeable in cases where the water is of the depths that exist in many harbors and particularly canals. Between the bottom of a canal and the bottom of a ship, the channeling effect of the water must increase its velocity, at the same time decreasing its pressure. This produces increased friction due to both higher flow rate and sinkage, and thus increases the wetted surface. Such restrictions produce a blockage effect that in turn changes the character of the self-generated wave. This situation is difficult to define or evaluate because of the infinite combinations of water depth, vessel size, etc. However, there is a limiting relation of speed to water depth alone where the shallow water effect increases resistance due to the changing wave-making phenomena. This is $\dfrac{V}{\sqrt{gh}} = 1.0$; ($h$ = water depth). Where the increased drag is due to the shallow water effect alone, it will finally begin to decrease if the ship has sufficient power and is of the appropriate shape to overcome it.

Rough water, most positive and erratic of all the considerations that oppose the propulsive force, is the most difficult to analyze. Obviously because of its infinite and random nature as well as its natural origins, rough water cannot be predicted in a deterministic way. Not surprisingly, however, it can be dealt with in analysis by computers.

The nature of sea waves and sea conditions will be discussed in chapter 12. It will be sufficient to note here the manner in which the ship's resistance is increased because of motion in rough water and, for the moment, avoid the complexities of controlling or inhibiting the motion. Actually, the natural sea waves that are encountered

Figure 5–14. Energy Dissipation by a High-Speed Hydrofoil Model in the U.S. Naval Academy Towing Tank

have two effects in increasing resistance. The first is a function simply of their size and the force of moving water in parts of them that act against the ship's forward motion. The second effect is the motion they induce in the ship, either pitching, rolling, or heaving that adds to the wetted area as well as the localized increased water volume to be displaced. In the design process, both of these effects are considered with consequent functional limitations to the extent that the designer feels is necessary and possible. Obviously, little attention is given to the matter in the design of, say, a harbor ferry or river barge. Small protected-water vessels are known to have their

limitation. However, in the design of seagoing craft, the means to provide for the action and motion of the sea are not unlimited. As a matter of fact, assuming the strength factors are attended to, the necessary forms, which include a fine and easy entrance, with adequate sheer are difficult to describe geometrically in terms of seaworthiness. However, such sea-kindly forms as fishing trawlers are universally recognized for their advantages in heavy seas. Unfortunately, when compared in calm or moderate seas with certain conventional ship forms of a greater length/beam ratio and generally less curvature, they do not perform as well.

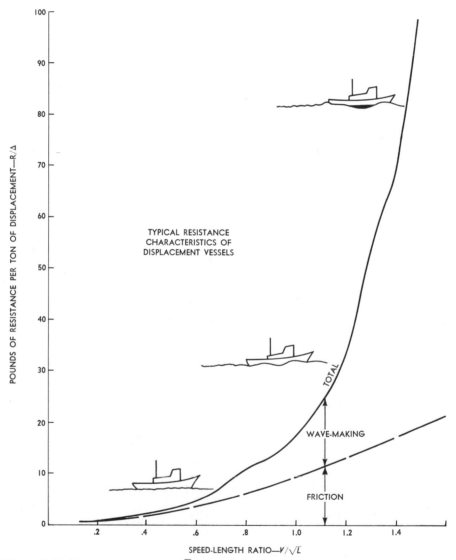

Figure 5–15. Resistance Versus $V/\sqrt{L}$ in a Characteristic Speed-Power Curve for a Displacement Ship (Note the Ship-Wave Profiles)

Such considerations simply point up the most fundamental of design principles; that any single ship concept must always be a compromise. No single ship can be designed for all things; it must emphasize the features involved in those functions it performs and the probable environment that will be encountered.

Resistance Characteristics in Submersibles

As pointed out previously in the discussion of hydrostatics, a submarine operating on the surface behaves as does any surface craft. It is subjected to the same force phenomena when moving through the water. However, in considering the modern submarine, the operational requirements are such that the time spent on the surface is limited almost entirely to the time in port. These same operational requirements, as will be seen below, produce submarines whose total design of systems and configuration are wholly oriented to the three-dimensional, highly pressurized environment deep beneath the sea's surface.

Prior to World War II, the configuration of submarines was the result of a compromise between surface and subsurface operation. Because of their dependence on surface oxygen for cruising operation and their limited battery power for extensive submerged operation, their hull form was a concession to the existence of wave-making resistance. They were long and narrow, having an L/B ratio of about 11.5, with a center of volume approximately amidships. The bow configuration was a modified surface ship's bow, and there was considerable flat-deck sur-

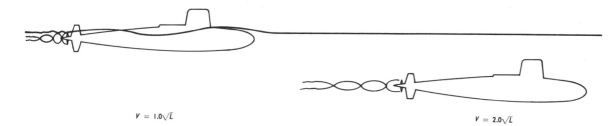

$V = 1.0\sqrt{L}$

$V = 2.0\sqrt{L}$

Figure 5–16. Submarine Wave-making Characteristics

Figure 5–17. A Navy Attack Submarine Cruising on the Surface Creates a Deep Bow Wave, engulfing its forward quarters. This is a large expenditure of propulsion energy.

face with many unstreamlined appendages. The eddy-making resistance submerged was considerable because the craft was essentially a modified surface ship capable of submerging for short periods.

The use of nuclear power has permitted the modern submarine to become a true subsurface ship. It is no longer dependent on the surface for oxygen to supply the engines. The crew breathes revitalized air, and the subsurface operation is limited more by personnel endurance. The present hull shapes are completely clear of appendages except for the necessary control surfaces at the stern, the propeller, and the streamlined sail enclosure. The basic configuration is that of a surface of revolution whose center of volume is forward of amidship, and it has an

L/B ratio of approximately seven (slightly greater for Polaris submarines).

Thus the modern submarine's surface resistance characteristics are completely subordinate to the speed and maneuverability requirements of submerged operations. The eddy resistance is reduced to a minimum and the total resistance submerged is almost completely frictional except for eddy or form resistance, similar to that of aircraft.

The modern submarine experiences no wave-making resistance whatsoever when submerged more than three diameters from the free surface. This means that the total submerged resistance, including all of the frictional resistance of deck and sail as well as form and eddy drag, is only a comparatively small fraction of its total resistance at the same speed on the surface.

Figure 5–18. A Tank Test Model of the Submarine Hull shown in Figure 5–17 at the equivalent model speed, showing the same bow wave, which is here evaluated. (U. S. Naval Academy Ship Model Towing Tank.)

CHAPTER 6

Propulsive Forces and Propulsion Systems

The first efforts to use mechanical forces to propel ships were applied in a tentative way, with indifferent success, probably more often and earlier than is generally realized. The continual frustrations with the unreliable and inadequate force of the wind on sails forced men to search for other means to move ships in the water from the earliest days of history. Aside from the simple paddle or manned oars, there is evidence that pre-Christian Romans used paddle wheel propelled boats (whose source of power was oxen) to transport soldiers to Sicily. Paddle wheels were used apparently by the Orientals as early as the seventh century, and, of course, Leonardo da Vinci designed many mechanical devices for propelling ships.

True mechanical propulsion, however, deriving its power from the energy conversion in a steam engine, came gradually very much later through many frustrating failures. It is very difficult to say where and when such propulsion was first successful, but it is earliest recorded that in 1783, at Lyons, France, a barge-like boat 148 feet in length, equipped with a horizontal double-acting steam cylinder that drove side paddle wheels was able to move against the current of the Rhone River. This vessel was aptly named the *Pyroscaphe,* and the inventor-designer, Claude de Jouffroy d'Abbans, is generally accepted as the successful pioneer in the application of steam-powered propulsion to ships. In America, John Fitch of Philadelphia built and experimented successfully with steam-powered vessels as early as 1785 and can be credited with the building of the first commercial steamboat. In 1790, his steamboat, the *Experiment*, began carrying passengers between Philadelphia and Trenton on a regular schedule. His vessel was not propelled by paddle wheels, however. Her 18-inch single cylinder engine and fire tube boiler powered three "duck leg" paddles at the stern which moved the 60-foot boat at the respectable speed of eight knots. James Rumsey, of Berkley Springs, Virginia, had produced a steam-powered boat in 1787 which was propelled by a water jet. While this boat was intended for ferry service on the Potomac, she was laid up after a successful public demonstration where she attained a speed of approximately 4½ knots.

It is interesting to note that in these early historic efforts, the propelling devices were all dissimilar. The paddle wheel, the mechanical oar and the water jet all achieved some degree of success a full half century before Archimedes' screw propeller was successfully adapted by John Ericsson and the U.S. Navy.

There are by this time a great proliferation of types and styles of ship propulsion devices. Many other unusual, impractical, and inefficient devices have been invented, tried, and discarded. Of the first devices used successfully, the paddle wheel has subsided very slowly into near obscurity after its early successful use and universality. While it still may exist in some remotely located riverboats and special purpose craft, it has certainly passed its days of significance. Fitch's walking oars were never used again. The water jet has enjoyed a recent successful rebirth and is used with increasing promise (it will be discussed subsequently in this chapter). The marine propeller with its many variations is the prime propulsive device of modern ships. Before a more detailed and technical discussion of these and other devices that provide the thrust that counters the resistance forces, it is necessary to understand the components of transmission and associated losses in a definitive way.

Propulsive Forces

The resistance to motion, discussed in the preceding chapter, must be overcome by a propelling force. This propelling force is derived from a system within the ship for the conversion or liberation of energy. For the purposes of naval architecture, we need only note this machinery primarily as a power source. (See chapter 7 also.)

The types of propelling machinery normally used by ships are the diesel engine, the gas turbine, and the steam turbine. The diesel engine and gas turbine are increasingly used in combination. (They are discussed subsequently in chapter 7 in this connection.) The steam turbine is well suited to the largest power plants, produces a uniform turning effort, and is capable of relatively high efficiencies, long endurance, and reasonable maintenance. It has the inherent disadvantages of large space requirements, intermediate energy conversion with its secondary working substance, mechanical nonreversibility, and high turbine speed. These latter two disadvantages necessitate a separate, low-efficiency astern turbine of reduced power and large, heavy reduction gearing to the propeller shafts. The speed reduction is of prime necessity to allow both the turbine and the propeller to operate in their most efficient speed range.

To discuss further the power transmission from the ship's power plant to its terminus, it is useful to include certain traditional expressions and relationships in order to assign the propulsive losses or efficiencies or both. The following definitions must therefore be used (see figure 6–1):

- *Brake horsepower, BHP,* is the power at the engine.
- *Propeller horsepower, PHP,* is the power delivered to the propeller. It is equal to the effective horsepower, plus the power losses in the propeller and the losses in the interaction between the propeller and the ship.
- *Shaft horsepower, SHP,* is the power measured in the shafting within the ship by a torsionmeter as close to the propeller or stern tube as possible. It is equal to the *PHP* plus the bearing losses between the propeller and the torsionmeter.

- *Propulsive coefficient* is

$$\eta_d = EHP/SHP.$$

- *Propulsive efficiency* is

$$\eta_b = EHP/PHP.$$

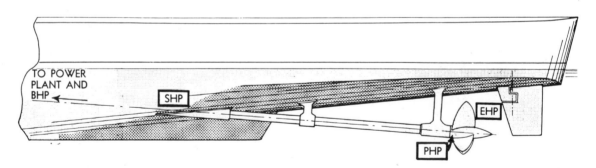

Figure 6–1. Power Relationship Along the Propeller Shaft

• *Transmission efficiency* is

$$\eta_s = PHP/SHP.$$

• $\dfrac{EHP}{SHP} = \dfrac{EHP}{PHP} \times \dfrac{PHP}{SHP}.$

Propelling Devices

Of the successful types of propulsive devices presently in use to a greater or lesser degree, the following may be grouped in four distinct categories:

• Screw propellers
  a. Fixed-pitch screws working in open water.
  b. Controllable-pitch propellers.
  c. Shrouded screws working in tunnels or sleeves.
  d. Contra-rotating propellers.
• Paddle wheels—either side or stern mounted with fixed or feathering blades.
• Jet propellers
  a. Water jet through submerged nozzle.
  b. Water jet through surface nozzle.
• Vertical axis propellers
  a. Kirsten-Boeing propeller.
  b. Voith-Schneider propeller.

These above types will be individually discussed in the immediately subsequent sections.

SCREW PROPELLERS

Because the most universally used propeller is the screw propeller (referred to henceforth, in keeping with common practice, as a *propeller*), it will be discussed in greater detail along with some general propulsive theory that is applicable to other types of propellers as well.

It will be useful to consider first the propeller itself in general terms and some associated terms and definitions.

A propeller has two to six blades projecting from a hub which is keyed to and driven by the propeller shaft. There are two general types of marine propellers in use today. Fixed-pitch propellers have blades which are either an integral part of the hub or are bolted to the hub. In this type of propeller, the position of the blades relative to the hub cannot be altered—with the exception of minor adjustments which may be made during the assembly of some of the bolted-blade types. Controllable-pitch propellers are provided with a mechanism for altering the position of the blades relative to the hub at any

time. In the following discussion, refer to figure 6–2 which shows a three-blade propeller of constant pitch.

• A *right-handed propeller* is one which rotates clockwise when viewed from astern (counterclockwise when viewed looking aft as in figure 6–2) when driving the ship ahead. A left-handed propeller rotates counterclockwise when viewed from astern while driving the ship ahead.
• The *pressure face* of a blade is the after side when going ahead.
• The *suction back* of a blade is the surface opposite the face.
• The *tip* of a blade is the point farthest from the axis.
• The *leading edge* of a blade is the edge which cuts the water first when going ahead. The *following* or *trailing edge* is opposite the leading edge.
• The *diameter* is twice the perpendicular distance from the axis to the blade tip or is the diameter described by the blade tips.
• A *helicoidal surface* is a surface generated by a line (the generatrix) at an angle with an axis through one of its extremities that revolves about this axis at a constant angular rate and advances along the axis at a constant linear speed. In its most simple form, the pressure face is a portion of a helicoidal surface with the axis along the propeller shaft. Any surface of the thread of a machine screw is a helicoid.
• The *pitch* of any point on a blade is the distance moved parallel to the shaft axis by the generatrix of the helicoidal surface through the point in 360 degrees of rotation. The pitch of point C in figure 6–2 is the distance, FE, for one revolution. When the pressure face is a helicoidal surface, each point on the pressure face has the same pitch, and the propeller is said to be constant or of uniform pitch. It may be seen in figure 6–2 that each point on the developed blade section has the same pitch as point C. Because it is a constant pitch propeller, every point on other blade sections will have the same pitch as point C. If the pitch increases from the leading to the following edge, the pitch is axially increasing. If the pitch increases from hub to tip, the pitch is

termed radially increasing. When the pitch of the blade varies from point to point, the pressure face is not a helicoidal surface.

The theory of propeller design with variable pitch over the blade is a particular and specialized adaptation. To summarize the purpose of such design it is sufficient here to say that: (1) when the pitch varies between leading and following edges, the propeller will be adaptable to a greater range of ship's speeds, and (2) when the pitch varies between root and tip, the propeller will take advantage of the variation in velocities of the wake current around the propeller. The former modification extends the range of efficiency and the latter increases the peak efficiency.

SLIP AND THRUST

There are many mechanical devices that employ the principle of advancing an object by means of a rotating helical screw; some common examples are wood screws, worm gears, and many types of positive displacement pumps and compressors. In almost all of the above examples, the primary energy losses are frictional, and the velocity of the object or fluid which is moved is equal to the axial velocity of advance of the helix as determined by its pitch. However, in the case of a ship and its propeller operating in open unobstructed water, the axial *advance per unit time of the propeller's helix is not in any case equal to the velocity of the ship.* This difference in velocities, which is called slip, is the result of the fluid shear caused by the acceleration sternward of the mass of water ahead of the propeller. Actually, the slip referred to above is *apparent slip* and is more precisely defined as a ratio, thus

$$S_a = \frac{(pn) - v}{pn}$$

where

S_a = apparent slip ratio
p = pitch in feet
n = rpm
v = ship's absolute speed.

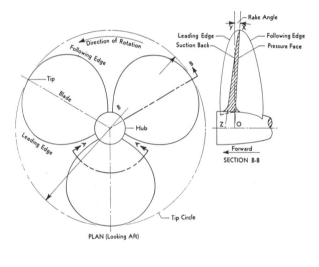

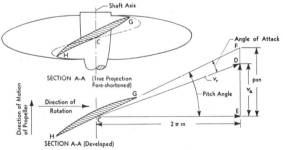

Figure 6–2. Propeller Definition Diagram (Three-Bladed, Right-Hand, Constant Pitch Propeller)

The above expression is not altogether representative of the actual amount of slip, because the water surrounding the ship, particularly in the vicinity of the propellers and wake, is disturbed and has its own absolute velocity. It is with relation to this water in which the propeller is working that the true slip must be expressed. This is also expressed as a ratio as follows:

$$S_r = \frac{(pn) - v_a}{pn}$$

where S_r = true slip ratio
v_a = speed of the propeller relative to the disturbed, surrounding water.

From the above expressions it may be seen that with the water in the wake traveling in the same direction as the propeller, v_a will be less than v and the true slip ratio will be greater than the apparent slip ratio.

The relationships between true slip, apparent slip, wake, and the propeller and ship velocities may be seen in figure 6–4.

The force produced by the ship's propeller that overcomes the resistance of the ship is referred to as the propeller's *thrust*. Without the slip described above, there would be no thrust. The concept of thrust recognizes it as the result of change in momentum of the fluid from a point ahead of the propeller to a point astern of the propeller. Because the propeller operates in an unbounded volume of working fluid, it is difficult to resolve the thrust equation to terms of specified

Official U.S. Navy Photograph

Figure 6–3. Three-Bladed, Left-Handed Propeller Installation, Port Shaft—DD-710 Class

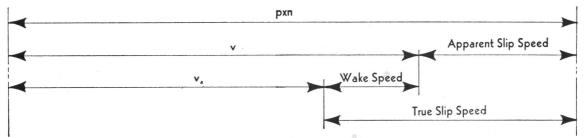

Figure 6–4. Relation of Speeds in Way of Propeller

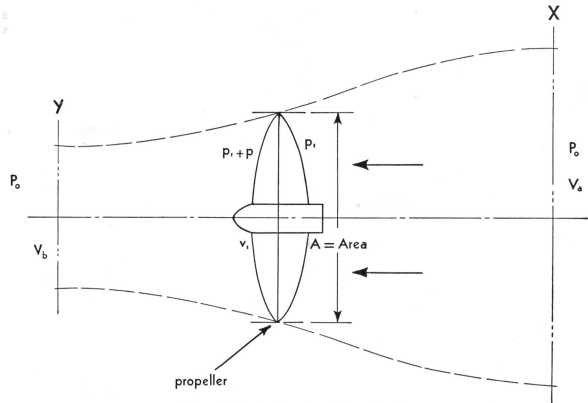

Figure 6–5. Active Boundary of Propeller Jet

dimensions as is done in pumps, turbojet engines, etc. However, we may consider the boundaries of the water set in motion by the propeller as being limited, as in figure 6–5 by the dotted line. We must assume here that the water ahead of section X is at pressure p_o and at section Y is also returned to p_o. Assuming that there is no interchange of water between the inside and outside of this imaginary tube, the thrust may be expressed as

$$T = \rho \, AV_1(V_b - V_a)$$

where

     ρ = water density (mass)
     A = area of the projected propeller disc
     V_1 = velocity through the propeller
     V_a = velocity ahead of the propeller at X
     V_b = velocity behind the propeller.

The expression, as given above, is oversimplified because of the nature of actual propeller installations, and certain assumptions become necessary. However, it does emphasize the basic concept of the axial momentum theory, where the reactive thrust of a fluid is equal to the mass multiplied by its change in velocity. It may be seen, then, that if the velocity v_a were the same as the maximum velocity possible at the propeller (pitch times rpm) resulting in a zero slip, there could be no change in velocity across the propeller; thus the thrust would be zero.

In terms of power we may arrive at an expression for thrust power by multiplying the thrust by the velocity V_a, thus

$$P_t = Tv_a/550 \; HP$$

In order to arrive at an expression for propeller efficiency, it will be necessary to define power delivered to the propeller as:

$$P_d = 2\pi Qn/550 \; HP$$

where

     Q = propeller shaft torque at the propeller
     n = rps

The propeller efficiency, then, is the ratio of output power to input power:

$$\eta_o = \frac{Tv_a}{2\pi Qn}.$$

Before leaving the general discussion of propeller theory, it will be advantageous to point out by means of figure 6–6 the relation of the propeller blade section to the acceleration of the water around it. It is obvious that the rear surface or pressure face of the blade increases the pressure of the water on and near that surface in imparting a positive thrust. The opposite surface of the blade or suction back creates a negative pressure distribution, as indicated in the figure, that may amount to a greater pressure differential than on the pressure face. Together, the total pressure differential on both sides of the blade account for the increase in velocity of the water and for the lift or forward thrust on each blade from which the overall thrust is derived.

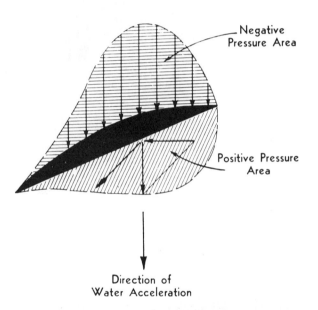

Figure 6–6. Pressure Distribution About Propeller Blade Section

Propeller Action

Various theories have been advanced to explain actual conditions encountered in propeller operation. The circulation theory gives the best explanation of the phenomenon. This is discussed very briefly in its relation to the forces on a blade section such as in figure 6–2. The section is advancing along the line, CD, with a velocity, v_r, which is the resultant of the speed of rotation, $2\pi rn$, and its axial advance, v_a. Similar to an airfoil, the blade section is advancing with an angle of attack, $\angle FCD$. An unsymmetrical body, such as an air foil section of a propeller blade, when placed in a parallel fluid flow, will disrupt the symmetry of this flow. Upon measuring the velocities of the fluid adjacent to different parts of the blade, it has been found that there is a higher velocity on the back than on the face. The circulation theory indicates that the new unsymmetrical flow can be represented by a counter-clockwise circulatory flow superimposed on the parallel water flow past the blade section. The vector sum of the circulatory flow and a parallel flow will produce the high velocity region on the suction back and the low velocity region on the pressure face of the blade. The velocity variation will be proportional to the strength of the circulation flow.

By Bernoulli's law, a high velocity region means low pressure and vice versa. Therefore, we have high pressure on the pressure face of the blade and low pressure on the suction back. The resultant force due to this pressure difference resolved along the shaft axis is the lift or *thrust* of the propeller. The component at right angles to the shaft is the required force which produces the torque.

The pressure distribution from the leading to the following edge of both the pressure face and the suction back is irregular. The pressure reduction on the suction back is greater than the pressure increase on the face indicating that the greater portion of the propeller thrust is contributed by the suction back of the blades.

CAVITATION

When the minimum value of the absolute pressure on the back is reduced below the vapor pressure of the water, which will occur at relatively high propeller speeds, vapor pockets or cavities are formed which disrupt the flow and reduce the propeller efficiency. This phenomenon is known as *cavitation*. When the vapor pockets collapse on the blade surface, erosion of these surfaces results and noise is emitted. Advanced cavitation produces a very slow increase in thrust for increasing shaft horsepower while speed of rotation increases more rapidly than usual. Fully developed cavitation noise is violent and can be heard easily in the vicinity of the stern.

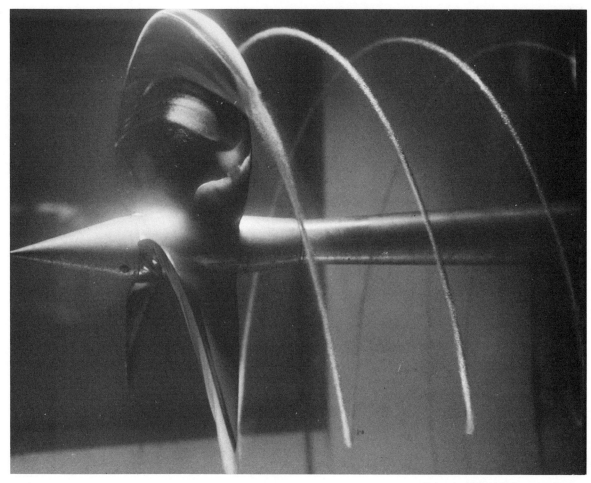

Figure 6–7. Tip Cavitation on a Common Three-Bladed Propeller in a Testing Tunnel at the Admiralty Experimental Works, Haslar, England

PROPELLER DESIGN

It is possible to design a propeller by means of the circulation theory. At the present writing, this method requires the application of certain corrections to give agreement between calculated and test values. The failure of the theory to substantiate experiments without some corrections indicates that the theory is at present incomplete and that its further development is necessary. The method of propeller design by chart is the most common and produces very satisfactory results. Tests of the model propeller are performed in open undisturbed water by varying either the propeller rpm or the speed of advance and measuring, in addition to rpm and speed of advance, thrust and torque. These data are converted to a set of nondimensional coefficients (constant irrespective of propeller size) and plotted.

Common parameters that are used in propeller design and are a means of comparing various propellers' performance must be familiar to all designers. Some of the most frequently used are:

• Thrust coefficient

$$K_T = \frac{T}{\rho\, n^2 D^4} \quad \text{or} \quad \frac{T}{V_a{}^2},$$

where T = thrust in pounds

ρ = mass density of water

v = velocity of water in feet per second

D = propeller diameter in feet

V_a = speed of advance in knots.

n = revolutions (rps).

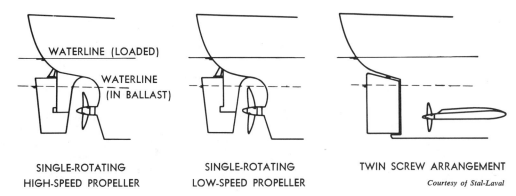

SINGLE-ROTATING
HIGH-SPEED PROPELLER

SINGLE-ROTATING
LOW-SPEED PROPELLER

TWIN SCREW ARRANGEMENT

Courtesy of Stal-Laval

Figure 6–8. Modern Propeller Arrangements and Propeller Sizes for Ships of Similar Size and Power

- Torque coefficient

$$K_q = \frac{Q}{\rho\, n^2 D^5}$$

where n = revolutions (rps).

- Advance coefficient

$$J = \frac{V_a}{nD}$$

- Propeller loading

$$\sqrt[4]{\frac{K_T}{J^4}}$$

- Pitch ratio

$$\frac{P}{D}$$

- Basic variable

$$\delta \quad \text{or} \quad B_p = \frac{nD}{V_a}$$

These coefficients are used chiefly in plotting the design criteria for series propeller tests and in the construction of the design charts.

A series of design charts have been developed by model tests for groups of propellers with varying pitch ratio. Within each group, other characteristics, such as number of blades, mean width ratio, blade thickness fraction, and shape, are varied. The usual design problem is to determine from these charts the propeller which will give the best efficiency by entering with the known information and any restrictions on the design, such as maximum diameter. This design method restricts the propeller to similarity with a prototype and will result in the design of the most efficient of the group, but not necessarily the best propeller for the specific requirements.

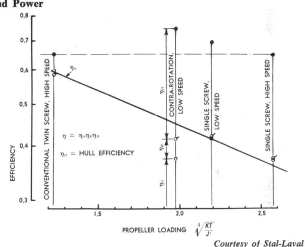

Courtesy of Stal-Laval

Figure 6–9. Comparative Efficiencies for Contemporary Design Propeller Combinations and Arrangements

FULLY CAVITATING PROPELLERS

Although cavitation produces serious blade erosion as well as a breakdown in developed thrust with advancing power, it has been shown in laboratory tests that a blade with complete cavitation over its back is superior at higher speeds. This phenomenon is based on the fact that with complete separation over the back of the blade and no water contact, there can be no further pressure reduction or increasing cavitation effect. On the face of the blade, however, pressure continues to increase with increasing rpm as does the total thrust. In such applications at high speeds, there are no unsteady and vibratory forces caused by intermittent cavitation, and there is no erosion of the blades because the bubbles collapse in the wake. Such propellers are designed with a sharp wedge-shaped blade section to produce clean, complete cavitation. They are less efficient than the conventional subcavitating propellers, but in the high-speed regimes for driving craft in the range of 40 to 80 knots, they are a practical alternative.

Courtesy of Swedish State Ship Testing Laboratories

Figure 6–10. Supercavitating Propeller Model in Homogeneous Flow

INTERACTION BETWEEN HULL AND PROPELLER

Up to this point, the resistance of the ship and the action of the propeller have been considered apart. It is now necessary to consider the interaction between the hull and propeller when the ship is self-propelled. In the discussion of resistance, a *wake* or *wake current,* was mentioned. This wake, which is the motion of the water immediately surrounding the ship relative to undisturbed water, is considered positive when moving in the same direction as the ship. It is the algebraic sum of three components: the frictional wake, the streamline wake, and the wave wake. It is equal to $v - v_a$. The wake speed is customarily defined as a fraction of the ship's speed, v. Thus,

$$v - v_a = wv, \qquad v_a = (1 - w)v$$

where w = wake fraction.

The propeller of an actual ship does not work in undisturbed water as in an open water propeller model test, but in water disturbed by the wake current it experiences a change in the relation between thrust and torque from the open water condition. The ratio between thrust and torque, as measured in self-propelled and open water tests, is called the relative rotative efficiency, η_r. Values of η_r range from 95 to slightly over 100 percent.

The propeller acts on the ship by increasing the water velocity near the stern and creates an augmentation of resistance. For a given speed, the propeller thrust, T, is greater than the ship's total resistance, R_t. The quantity, $T - R$, is called the thrust deduction and is normally expressed as a fraction of the thrust.

$$T - R_t = t\,T, \qquad \text{or} \qquad R_t = (1 - t)T$$

where t = thrust deduction coefficient

     $1 - t$ = thrust deduction factor.

The net effect of the wake and thrust deduction on the hull is called the hull efficiency, η_h.

$$\eta_h = \frac{1 - t}{1 - w}$$

In general, values of t and w are of the same magnitude. Hence, the hull efficiency is usually in the vicinity of 100 percent. Collecting these thoughts, we may express the ratio, $\dfrac{EHP}{PHP}$ (propulsive efficiency), as the product of the propeller, hull, and relative rotative efficiencies.

$$\frac{EHP}{PHP} = \eta_o\,\eta_h\,\eta_r$$

where η_o = propeller efficiency as determined from the design charts mentioned before.

In propeller design, the wake fraction, thrust deduction coefficient, and the relative rotative efficiency must be determined by special tests or estimated from past performance. It is desirable to locate the propellers near the hull in the region of greatest wake intensity. Thrust deduction decreases with an increase in distance between the hull and propeller and is probably reduced to a very small value when this distance is one propeller diameter. However, in actual design, very little consideration can be given to the location of the propeller to reduce thrust deduction. The propeller is normally located with a maximum diameter and the minimum acceptable tip clearance from the hull and a suitable submergence to prevent surface losses. Many other considerations enter into the location of the propeller, including elements of the machinery design and internal hull arrangements.

A single propeller located on the centerline is the most efficient for normal ship forms. The number of propellers is usually determined by limitations on propeller diameter, size of individual propelling plants, the greater immunity to complete breakdown, and ability to maneuver with twin or quadruple screws. The choice of the number of blades is usually between three, four, or five blades. Three-bladed propellers are usually more efficient, but four- or five-bladed propellers allow a smaller diameter. The selection of the number of blades may be dictated by hull vibration considerations.

CONTROLLABLE-PITCH PROPELLERS

In some types of propulsive power plants, such as large marine diesels and gas turbine plants, it is difficult to reverse the direction of the shaft. To reverse the direction of the shafts often requires large and expensive reversing mechanisms and generally involves an appreciable interval of time in any type of plant. In addition, the efficiency characteristics of the power plants are such that a peak is reached at a given rpm. To assist in overcoming these difficult features, there are in use, in many large ships, propellers that are equipped with blades which rotate from full ahead pitch to full astern pitch. The mechanism that accomplishes this consists of a servo mechanism from the bridge controlling hydraulic pistons which in turn transmit motion through linkages

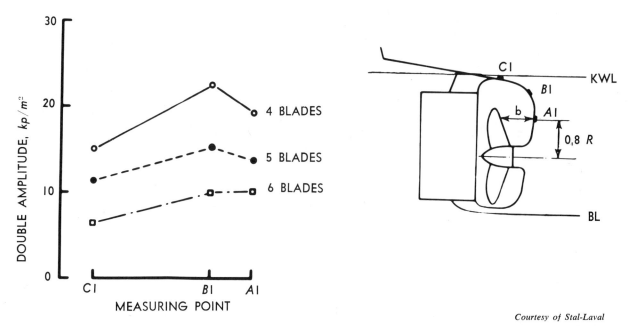

Courtesy of Stal-Laval

Figure 6–11. Effect of the Number of Blades on the Pressure Impulse Amplitude (Vibration)

Variations from designed dimensions are usually evidenced by abnormal vibration. Imbalance, pitch variations between blades, failure of blades to track (corresponding points on all blades lying in a circle whose plane is normal to the propeller axis), and radical variation in blade thickness result in increased vibration. Such variations usually decrease propeller efficiency and frequently cause cavitation. If surface erosion is noted when in drydock indicating cavitation, the propeller dimensions should be checked.

or hydraulic lines in a hollow propeller shaft to a geared drive or piston in the hub of the propeller. This mechanism in turn transmits the motion to each blade equally to change its pitch. (See figure 6–12.)

The controllable-pitch propeller, in addition to full reversing without changing the direction of the shaft rotation, extends the range of propeller efficiency, which in a fixed-pitch propeller has a characteristic peak at a given rpm. The proper pitch may be adjusted for every engine speed. Such a feature is particularly advantageous for tugboats, landing craft, and mine sweepers where high torque absorption is important for various ranges of ship speed and engine revolutions.

PROPELLER SHROUDING AND CONTRA GUIDES

Because of the interaction between the water in the "jet stream tube" (see figure 6–13) and the surrounding undisturbed water, it is possible to recover some of this energy along with the tip losses of the propeller by surrounding it with a short cylindrical tunnel or nozzle. This shrouding, as it may be generally termed, directs the stream of incoming water directly into the propeller disc area effecting generally a greater change in velocity of the water and increasing the propeller efficiency. This shrouding should be provided with the necessary structural dimensions and material to make it a true, streamlined tunnel in the form of a nozzle. (A very well-known device of this sort is the patented Kort Nozzle.)

direction, since they are effective on only half of the propeller stream. Such devices are called contra guides.

It should be noted that contra guides increase the efficiency when the ship is going ahead, but they give a corresponding decrease in thrust when going astern and are therefore seldom used in ships where maneuverability is very important.

COUNTER ROTATION

In the further pursuit of a means to recover the rotational losses imparted to the stream of water through the propeller, coaxial propellers (two or more propellers on one axis) have been used in a limited way in the past. They are more recently enjoying a new significance for large ships where increased rpm is impractical but increased blade loading is unavoidable.

It is not possible, of course, to recover all of the rotational energy lost by the first propeller on the shaft. Because of the interference between

Courtesy of Morgan Smith Co.

Figure 6–12. Controllable Pitch Propeller—Full Ahead Position (left), No Thrust Position (middle), and Full Reverse Position (right)

Because of the rotary motion imparted to the water as it passes through the propeller from slightly ahead of it, some of the effective velocity component is lost by virtue of the water's rotational motion. To assist in straightening out this helical motion, some propeller shaft struts and some types of rudders are shaped to direct this stream out of a rotational path. In the case of some rudders directly in the propeller stream, the upper half is angled several degrees in one direction and the lower half angled the same amount in the opposite direction. Shaft struts nearest the propeller are similarly angled but only in one

propellers caused by the aft propeller working in the disturbed wake stream, the propeller efficiency is lower than for a single propeller of the same loading. The propeller circle is reduced in diameter, however, and the overall propulsive efficiency is higher because of the increased hull efficiency and relative rotative efficiency. (See figure 6–14.) These generalizations are valid primarily for comparatively low rpm. Counter rotating propellers are inadvisable for higher speed rotations because of the effects of cavitation of the forward propeller on the after one. In addition, the required gearing and concentric

Courtesy of Dravo Corp.

Figure 6–13. Kort Nozzle on Twin Screw Towing Vessel

Courtesy of Swedish State Ship Testing Laboratories

Figure 6–14. Conventional (left) and Contra-rotating (right) Propeller Models in Test Tunnel
(Note Incipient Cavitation)

drive shafts make an expensive and complex installation that may be an important consideration in the life cycle costs.

In designing counter rotating propellers, the pitch of the after propeller must be greater than that of the forward to be compatible with the increased water velocity entering it. Also, to avoid

vibration problems, the number of blades should be different on each of the two propellers so that no more than two blades are passing each other at any time.

An additional analysis indicating recent significant research in the application of counter rotating propellers is contained in chapter 9.

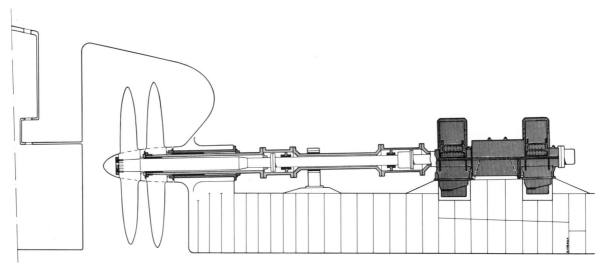

Figure 6–15. Installation of Contra-rotating Propellers

Other Propulsive Means

WATER JET PROPULSION

Water jet propulsion in its modern sense can be defined (or better described) as the propulsive force provided by the jet-reactive thrust of high velocity water expelled through a nozzle. The theory is similar to the basic momentum theory reviewed in connection with the marine propeller and is an extension of it. The application is most common to the propulsive drive of jet aircraft. Rather than using air as the working substance, however, water is fed into an internal high-powered pump or impeller which adds energy in the form of high velocity and expels it aft through the nozzle. It might also be thought of as an internal, ducted propeller.

As an alternative to propeller cavitating problems for high-speed craft and some special purpose craft, the water jet, driven by gas turbines, has shown considerable promise. It is presently being used in the most recent naval hydrofoil craft, and in this application, it largely eliminates the shafting and gear losses as well as cavitation losses of propeller installations.

In the lower speed ranges, water jet propulsion is inefficient. Because thrust depends upon a change of momentum, the jet develops less thrust at low and intermediate speeds than do conventional propellers because of its inherent difficulty of handling large enough volumes of water. How-

ever, as speed increases, the characteristics of jet propulsion show an increase in propulsive efficiency, whereby the opposite is true for conventional propellers. (Chapter 7 reflects this comparison in the options of power choices.) Consequently, water jet propulsion is of advantage in these higher speed regimes not only for hydrofoil craft but also possibly for larger ships where it might be combined with a practical means of boundary layer ingestion.

Fig. 6–16. Gunboat Tucumcari (PGH-2) at 40 Knots. This propellerless hydrofoil is the largest water-jet propelled craft operating in the world.

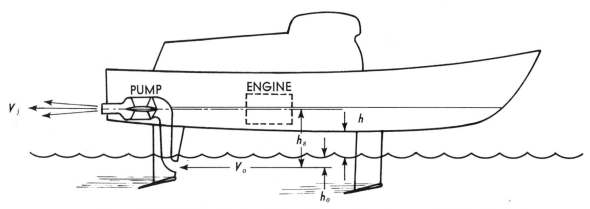

Figure 6–17. Definition Sketch of Water Jet Propulsion System with Hydrofoil Craft

A schematic diagram showing a typical water jet installation is given in figure 6–18.

While the water jet in the past was confined to lower speeds and powers and hence deemed a poor means of propulsion, its future is now much brighter where it can be combined with higher powered, lightweight gas turbines.

A further attraction to water jet propulsion is the nearly total lack of any projecting appendage below the hull. This advantage has been profitably used in many small craft that must operate in shallow, restricted waters.

VERTICAL AXIS PROPELLERS

A later development in the field of marine propellers is a device which is generally referred to as a *vertical axis propeller.* There are two types of vertical axis propellers, which differ only in details of operation but are based on the same basic theory. These are known by the names of their inventors: the Kirsten-Boeing propeller and

the Voith-Schneider propeller. Both of these propellers consist of four or more blades projecting from a circular disc whose axis is vertical and is generally flush with the bottom of the hull. This disc is geared to the propeller drive shaft, and as it rotates, the blades are capable, by means of cam action, of maintaining a positive angle of attack when they are in a fore and aft line with the axis and a zero angle or flat surface to the stream when in the athwartships position. The position of the cam with respect to the disc may also be varied so that reverse or side thrust may be produced. This type of device provides generally a very versatile propeller with both turning and reverse action that eliminates the need for both a rudder and reversing mechanisms at the engine. Here again, the efficiency of this device is not as high as the screw propeller, but it has maneuverability characteristics that are superior to any other type of propeller. It has been used with considerable success in small harbor craft,

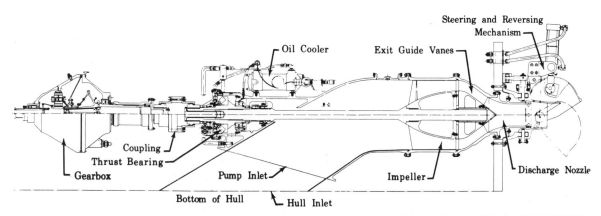

Courtesy of Pratt & Whitney, AIAA/SNAME

Figure 6–18. Seajet 12-1

patrol boats, and towboats where the maneuverability feature is highly desirable. Figure 6–19 shows a typical installation of a vertical axis propeller used in an Army towboat where maneuverability in both pushing and towing is of maximum importance.

ELECTROMAGNETIC PROPULSION— (MAGNETOHYDRODYNAMIC SYSTEMS)

There are some propulsion systems seemingly in the realm of the esoteric and improbable that should not be disregarded because of this. It was not too long ago that water jets fell in such a category. For a number of years, it has been proposed that certain types of craft, particularly submersibles, could be advantageously propelled by the direct application of an electromagnetic current.

Any propulsion system for watercraft (except sails) is ultimately a pump that imparts momentum to the water in the direction opposite to the vessel's direction of motion. The thrust on the ship is the reaction that is equal and opposite from the action force on the water. The same principles are equally true in the electromagnetic or magnetohydrodynamic systems.

The simplest form of propulsive duct for these electromagnetic systems is the impression of a direct current voltage across electrodes that span or surround the duct of water. In such a case, the electric and magnetic fields are at right angles to each other and the force field imparted to the water is then through the magnetic field. This is the force that would normally be imparted to the rotor in a direct current electric motor. The duct serves as a pump without blades or vanes, the force on the water being a direct one acting throughout the flow where the electric current flows in the presence of the magnetic field.

There are variations of this simple analysis which, in general, can be resolved into four basic choices. The system as described above can be simply identified as the crossed-field internal duct. Instead of the cross-field system, the induction method can be used where the magnetic field is produced by energizing a number of induction

Courtesy of Dravo Corp.

Figure 6–19. Vertical Axis (Voith-Schneider) Propeller Installation on a U.S. Army Towing Vessel

coils successively by alternating current. Circulating currents are thus induced in the sea water in contact with the magnetic field, thus producing the reactive thrust.

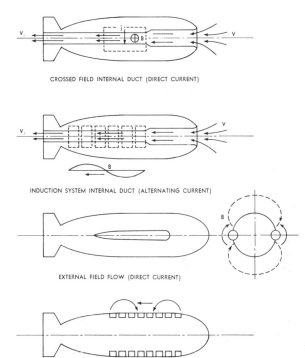

CROSSED FIELD INTERNAL DUCT (DIRECT CURRENT)

INDUCTION SYSTEM INTERNAL DUCT (ALTERNATING CURRENT)

EXTERNAL FIELD FLOW (DIRECT CURRENT)

EXTERNAL FIELD FLOW (ALTERNATING CURRENT)

Figure 6–20. Methods for Electromagnetic Propulsion

Either the induction system or the crossed-field system can be designed to produce an internal flow through a duct-like jet or an external field flow system applying comparatively smaller forces to the larger surrounding body of water.

There are and have been some inherent disadvantages to electromagnetic propulsion, one of which is the poor efficiency of energy conversion of permanent magnets. Super conducting magnets of more contemporary design have solved this difficulty in more recent designs. There still remains the large size of the required propulsors needed for surface ships with their accompanying drag, the great weight of the coils necessitated in the induction system, the stresses on the structure resulting from the forces produced, the heat transfer problems, and a formidable list of associated mechanical and design problems. However, there are no simple nor perfect propulsive devices for ships to say nothing of other mechanical systems. No one knows better than the engineer or designer that we live in an imperfect world.

The universally used marine propeller, originally fashioned after the old pump of Archimedes, has been evolved, developed, and subjected to the most sophisticated analysis, testing, and design, and in its contemporary state, still does not perform well at speeds beyond 40 knots. There are no other propulsive devices without severe limitations, and there is no reason to assume that the electromagnetic means will be any better or as good.

It does, however, offer an interesting alternative that, with further development, may prove to be very applicable to submersible craft where there is an attraction for silent, appendage-free low-drag hull forms.

Model Testing an Escort Type Ship with a Gravity Dynomometer

CHAPTER 7

Propulsive Requirements and Power Selections in Ship Design

The Importance of the Ship's Power Choice

At some point very early in the ship design process, a specific decision must be made on the choice of the power plant. (See the design spiral in figure 13–7.) It is difficult, of course, at such an early stage to be completely specific on a particular type of power unit or plant. So much depends upon the size and exact configuration of the hull. And, in turn, a considerable portion of the size and configuration of the hull is determined by the power plant choice. This, of course, is the justification for the circuitous planning that generates the design spiral.

It is traditional that the naval architect does not involve himself in the details of machinery design or the intricacies of the power plant. These are the specialties of the marine engineer. On the other hand, the naval architect is not absolved of the responsibility for an engineering knowledge of the processes, components, and performance ranges of the varieties and combinations of both internal and external marine propulsion machinery. It cannot be emphasized too strongly that the selection and placement of the proper propulsion machinery is in the province of the naval architect. The equipment that powers and propels the ship is a very basic part of the *whole ship,* whether that equipment is masts and sails, steam

turbines with nuclear reactors, diesel engines, gas turbines, or any of the other prime movers in their nearly infinite combination of sizes and arrangements. The main propulsion machinery with its fuel supply is always a critical weight and volume consideration, a factor that is basic to the design. This weight and volume affects immediately the necessary performance characteristics such as cruising range, maximum speed, "go or no-go" capability, as well as the buoyancy and stability adequacy. This chapter will attempt to outline the choices and directions and a few of the guidelines available to the ship designer in these fairly critical determinations.

Sooner or later in the process of new ship design, the necessary speed-power spectrum must be determined in a very quantitative form. This determination is originated through a customary model basin test. Such a test, of course, requires a specific hull configuration, which in itself is an indication that the design process has progressed to a stage of rather exact dimensional criteria. In new design, as it has been pointed out in preceding chapters discussing preliminary design and planning, model testing is essential, and frequently various configurations are used to determine the best hydrodynamic characteristics. The nature of these powering tests as well as the detailed theory is fully described in chapter 5. While the *model tests* are not the first or most preliminary efforts for power determination in the whole process nor yet the ultimate and final efforts, they are, nevertheless, the most basic and definitive sources of information.

The value of model testing lies ultimately in its true correlation with the corresponding speed-power characteristics of the parent ship and the verification of the actual ship performance.

The discussion will return to the necessary early power estimates prior to the model test and the various approaches to power plant selections. At this point it will be more helpful to examine further the disposal of model test results and the full scale correlation in the ultimate ship operation.

Model Testing

In light of improved model testing techniques together with the facilities available for rapid and accurate data acquisition and data processing, it is presently a reasonable assumption that the power required, expressed in the form of effective horsepower (EHP), is essentially valid.

The actual model test procedure is customarily based upon the theories of William Froude (chapter 5) and, aside from minor techniques, is essentially the same in all countries. The international Towing Tank Conference (ITTC), which meets approximately every five years, has established standards and uniform procedures that promote correlated exchanges and comparisons of model test results on an international basis.

Beginning with Froude's Law of Comparison between ship and model in terms of total resistance (R_t), residual resistance (R_r), and frictional resistance (R_f),* recall that at corresponding speeds

$$\left(\frac{V_s}{\sqrt{L_s}} = \frac{V_m}{\sqrt{L_m}}\right)$$

$$R_{r_s} = R_{r_m} \frac{\Delta_s}{\Delta_m}.$$

To continue toward the solution of the ship's total resistance, the frictional resistance is dealt with by direct computation for both model and ship individually. Various investigators have established empirical formulae for frictional resistance or the coefficient of frictional resistance. Formulae are practicable in this case because frictional resistance is very largely independent of the shape. A modern frictional resistance formula recommended as a standard by the American Towing Tank Conference in 1947 and 1950 is the Schoenherr Formula:

$$\frac{.242}{C_f} = \log_{10}(R_n C_f)$$

to obtain R_f from

$$R_f = \frac{\rho}{2} S v^2 C_f.$$

The ITTC in its 1957 conference approved a more recent formula based on a *correlation line*. This most recent modification is expressed as

$$C_f = \frac{.075}{(\log_{10} R_n - 2)^2}.$$

We are now in a position to summarize and arrange an orderly step-by-step procedure for determining total effective horsepower of a ship from its model test as follows:

MODEL RANGE

- Measure by actual towing test the total resistance of the model (R_{t_m}) at a series of speeds for which $V_s/V_m = \sqrt{\lambda}$. ($\lambda = L_s/L_m$)
- Determine R_{f_m} by empirical computation such as above.
- Obtain R_{r_m} by subtracting R_{f_m} from R_{t_m}.

SHIP RANGE

- $R_{r_s} = R_{r_m} \dfrac{\Delta_s}{\Delta_m}$, at $V_s = V_m\sqrt{\lambda}$ (Froude's Law).
- Determine R_{f_s} similar to R_{f_m} above.
- $R_{t_s} = R_{r_s} + R_{f_s} + R_a$ (A correlation allowance, R_a, must be added here for the ship.)

---

*It should be noted that in some towing tanks, particularly those used in research rather than testing work, the adoption of terms *viscous* resistance and *wavemaking* resistance in place of the more categorized *frictional* and *residual* notations for resistance appears to be useful terminology. Thinking in these terms may be more helpful in sorting out some of the more troublesome but small components of resistance that will be noted in the following discussions.

Note that R_{f_s} is the frictional resistance of a smooth ship. The correlation allowance, R_a, is obtained by testing actual ships. We will adopt a value, for our purposes, as:

$$R_a = .0004 \left(\frac{\rho_s}{2} S_s v^2 \right).$$

- R_{t_s} is now directly converted to *EHP* by

$$EHP = \frac{R_{t_s} v}{550}$$

While the above is a step-by-step indication of the model-ship power determination, it is common practice to use resistance coefficients as an expression of resistance values, such as

$$C_t = \frac{R_t}{(\rho/2) S v^2}$$

where $C_t = \phi_1 (R_n, F_n, r_1, r_2, \ldots)$.

The coefficients are further used to express residual and frictional resistance as follows:

$$C_f = \phi_2(R_n) = \frac{R_f}{\frac{\rho}{2} S v^2}$$

$$C_r = \phi_3(F_n) = \frac{R_r}{\frac{\rho}{2} S v^2},$$

and therefore

$$C_t = C_f + C_r = \frac{R_f}{\frac{\rho}{2} S v^2} + \frac{R_r}{\frac{\rho}{2} S v^2}.$$

These coefficients are nondimensional, and it is the practice to use them in the computations instead of the actual resistance values.

The procedure using these coefficients is as follows:

1. From the test value of the model's total resistance, compute C_{t_m} from the relation shown above.
2. Determine C_{f_m} from the ITTC formula or tables.
3. $C_{r_m} = C_{t_m} - C_{f_m}$.
4. For the same value of speed-length ratio, $(V/\sqrt{L})$, $C_{r_m} = C_{r_s}$. The values of C_{r_m} are generally plotted versus $V/\sqrt{L}$, and then any values may be selected after determining the ship's desired speed. See figure 7–1.

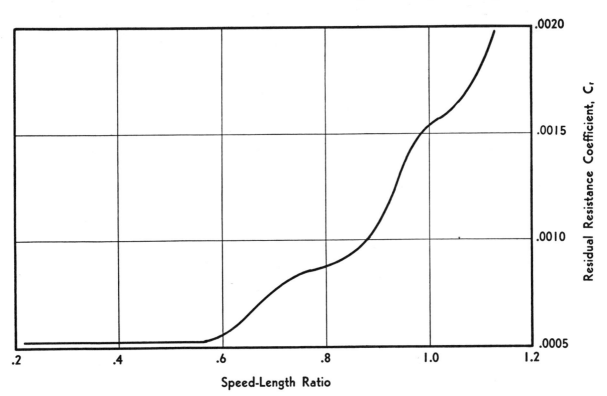

Figure 7–1. Curve of Residual Resistance Coefficient Versus Speed-Length Ratio

5. Determine C_{f_s} similar to C_{f_m} above. (Assuming 59°F seawater temperature.)

6. Then, $C_{t_s} = C_{f_s} + C_{r_s} + C_a$

C_a is a correlation allowance coefficient determined by actual trials of similar ships. (See below.)

7. Compute $EHP_t = \dfrac{\dfrac{C_{t_s}\, \rho v^3\, S}{2}}{550}$

Figure 7–2 is a final plot of EHP_t and EHP_f which is made when the above procedure is completed for the entire range of speeds.

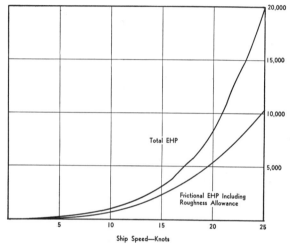

Figure 7–2. Typical Curves of Frictional and Total Effective Horsepower Versus Speed for a Large Displacement Ship

Figure 7–3 illustrates graphically the relationship of the resistance coefficients throughout the model and ship range. The resistance coefficient curves plotted on coordinates of the coefficient versus Reynolds' Number show the resistance characteristics of the ship and its model operated at the same speed-length ratio. It will be noted that both curves for C_r (for ship and model) are identical when referred to the curve of C_f. For the ship range, the C_r curve is displaced upward by the constant value of C_f plus the correlation allowance.

ROUGHNESS AND CORRELATION ALLOWANCE (C_a)

Surface roughness varies from ship to ship, depending on irregularities in plating, butts, butt straps, rivet heads, type of paint, etc. The most satisfactory method of determining correlation allowances, C_a, is through an analysis of data from carefully conducted full-scale trials. Pending such an analysis, a nominal correlation allowance of .0004 has been adopted for all ships at all speeds. The significance of roughness is indicated by the fact that for an aircraft carrier, the C_t will be .0035; C_r, .0016; and C_f, .0013. The roughness allowance currently established at .0004 may vary from .00001 to as much as .0010. (With very large ships, this allowance may even be negative.)

The curve referred to in figure 7–3 as the C_f curve is actually called the *frictional resistance correlation line,* and its configuration depends upon the frictional resistance formula selected. Correlation lines used in the expansion of model data to full-scale are very similar in most model testing establishments, but their standardization is subject to much discussion and constant scrutiny. There is considerable variation in this "scale effect"; for example, variation exists in unusual hull forms such as full, round hulls or sailing hulls. The lack of a fully developed turbulent boundary layer is troublesome in good correlation analyses, as is interaction between model and tank walls.

This lack of consistency in C_a can be also attributed to the erratic behavior of, or lack of suitable theory for determination of the phenomena existing in and around the boundary layer in the actual ship. Some of these factors that do not reproduce well in the model might well be found in the eddy resistance, separation resistance, or viscous pressure drag. The whole problem, while it does not affect the validity of model testing or the reliability of the powering results within reasonable tolerance, is a most challenging one for the serious research student.

APPENDAGE RESISTANCE

Most preliminary model testing and often entire model tests are carried out on *bare hull* models. This means models are used that do not include such real ship appendages as bilge keels, propellers, struts, shafts, or bossings and that are often without rudders. Obviously, such appendages contribute to the total resistance and required power, and complete model tests will determine both the total resistance values with and without appendages. Many model tanks handle the appendage resistance simply as a percentage increase based on the ratio of the bare hull resistance to the hull resistance with

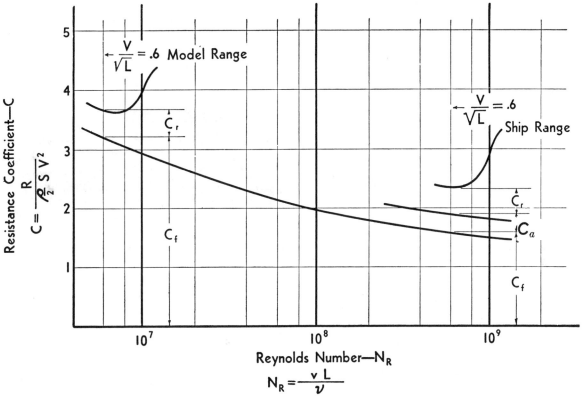

Figure 7–3. **Coefficients of Resistance Versus Reynolds' Number**

appendages. The percentage on the basis of model tests, because of the variation of scaling effects in eddy and viscous pressure drags, is sometimes arbitrarily reduced by a factor of two when applied to the ship's resistance. There are few rational methods to accurately determine appendage resistance other than full-scale testing which is most often impractical. In any case, it must be considered and included for the final determination of *EHP*.

Estimate of EHP from Standard Series

In the earlier stages of the design process when it is not feasible to define the hull form or when designers do not have model testing facilities readily available, it is possible to make reasonably accurate power calculations by using preplotted model series data. The oldest and most traditional of such sources is *Taylor's Standard Series*. This data was originally compiled and arranged by Admiral David W. Taylor in the early part of this century and was based on model tests of a series of uniformly varied models of similar geometry. It has since become a classic reference

tool and has set a pattern for other similar series data. The original Taylor's Series was revised in form in 1954 to bring the data into closer accord with more current methods of computation and is presently available under the title *A Reanalysis of the Original Test Data for the Taylor Standard Series,* Taylor Model Basin, Report No. 806. It should be understood that the parent model on which this data is based was a hull form with the old-style cruiser stern, which is a sharp stern form. This form undoubtedly produces a variation in residual resistances in the upper speed ranges from the more contemporary naval hull forms with transom-type sterns. There are, however, series test data available on hulls with transom sterns as well as trawler hull forms and other more modern hull forms. The Taylor's Series data still serve very well, however, for a great many types of cargo ship forms and conventional moderate speed ships. From these series data, the designer can obtain for desired speeds the residual resistance coefficient, C_r, when entering with beam-draft ratio, prismatic coefficient, and volumetric coefficient. His computations, then, for *EHP* follow the procedure presented in the preceding section and are dependent for their validity on the *series value* of C_r.

These preliminary power determinations from series data are normally made during the feasibility study phase of the design and are particularly helpful in determining power requirements in connection with cruising range, cost analysis, and performance requirements.

Operational Factors Relating to Power

There are a number of other factors that must be considered and allowed for in power determination and selection that are encountered in operation. Customarily, speed-power tests in model basins are made in flat, calm, fresh water. The allowance for seawater is made in the calculations to full scale as noted. The effects of shallow water, rough water, and wind resistance were briefly noted in chapter 8; however, in order to emphasize the order of magnitude to be expected and possible allowances, they will be mentioned in the context of quantitative allowances here. Other factors, such as displacement changes and trim changes, must be considered in the design process where the mission and employment of the vessel indicate the importance of these variables.

DISPLACEMENT

Changes in displacement will alter the form and amount of the wetted surface from the still-water condition. Reduction in displacement almost certainly will decrease resistance. Very light displacements may require an accompanying trim by the stern to avoid a serious decrease in propulsive efficiency resulting from the propeller tip circle being so close to the surface that the blades draw air in smooth water and from the propeller breaking the surface and racing in a rough sea.

TRIM

A change in the still-water trim will alter the underwater form at the extremities of the ship. The effect on resistance depends on the hull form and on the speed. Trim by the stern may cause additional eddy resistance at low speeds where wave-making resistance is a minor item. At higher speeds, where wave-making resistance

is predominant, trim by the stern may result in less resistance. Trim by the stern has some advantages in that it generally improves directional stability, and in rough weather, it is desirable to secure greater immersion for propellers and greater freeboard forward.

CHANGE OF TRIM AND SINKAGE

When a ship is underway in calm water, there is a change of level of the bow and stern from the condition in response to the elevation and depression of the water level about the hull resulting from the bow and stern wave systems. Up to moderate speeds, the ship usually experiences a body sinkage or squat without any appreciable change in trim. At higher speed, the sinkage at the bow ceases, and the bow begins to rise, while the stern continues to settle. Squatting and changes in trim do not increase resistance but are symptoms of increased wave-making resistance.

FOULING

In design work, the wetted surface of the ship is considered to be perfectly clean. The effect of fouling is to increase the roughness of the wetted surface and, consequently, the frictional resistance. The extent of fouling may be such that it could increase the clean-bottom resistance by 50 percent. The rate of fouling by sea growth on a ship's bottom is a variable function depending upon local conditions, water temperatures, salinity, and the amount of time the ship remains in port. It is difficult to predict or allow for. However, with the types of anti-fouling paint currently in use on steel-hull U.S. Navy vessels, fouling has been reduced so greatly that ships are normally docked for cleaning and painting only during routine overhaul (normally every eighteen months) rather than being docked each nine months.

WIND RESISTANCE

The air resistance, mentioned previously in chapter 5, considered only the relative wind due to the ship's motion. High head winds will cause appreciable increases over the still air resistance, mainly because of the eddy-forming features of superstructures of conventional design. A head wind having a velocity in the range of one to two times the ship's speed will result in a wind resistance of about 10 to 20 percent of the ship's water resistance. Streamlining the superstructure can undoubtedly reduce the wind resistance caused by winds from dead ahead. However, unlike an airplane which advances directly into the air stream, the wind more often strikes the superstructure from an angle than from dead ahead. It is extremely difficult to provide effective superstructure shapes for these variable conditions. The wind resistance may reach a maximum value of about 130 percent of the dead ahead wind resistance when the relative wind is about 30 degrees on the bow. In addition to wind resistance, wind may cause a further increase in resistance if it strikes at an angle requiring a permanent rudder angle to maintain the ship on the desired course.

ROUGH WEATHER

In rough weather the ship's resistance will be increased. The amount of increased resistance is extremely difficult to evaluate because it will vary with the relative size, speed, and course of the ship and the waves. Model tests are frequently made in towing tanks equipped with wave-making devices, and such tests for powering are becoming increasingly common, to the point that they are considered a part of the total spectrum of the speed-power characteristics together with the tests for various displacements and trim conditions. In head sea conditions, there will be some critical speed or rate of encounter of a wave system of a particular wave length, L_w, usually where $\lambda \approx 1.0$ to 1.25, that will produce a maximum pitching motion. It is under this circumstance that powering conditions are most disadvantageous, not only because of increased resistance but also because of the reduced propulsive efficiency.

SHALLOW WATER

In shallow water, the restricted passage for water flow around the hull brings about greater water velocities, greater pressure differences, and hence waves of greater height. This normally produces an increase in wave-making resistance. However, as the speed of high-powered ships in shallow water is increased, a critical speed is reached, depending on the ship's length and speed and the depth of the water, where the difference between shallow-water and deep-water resistance

becomes a maximum. At speeds higher than the critical speed, the increase in shallow-water resistance diminishes rapidly to zero, and the ship may, at extreme speeds, actually encounter less resistance in shallow water than in deep water.

It is difficult to say at just what depth the effect of increased resistance due to shallow water begins to become effective. Because of the variables, such as speed and draft, which are both functions of this increased resistance, it must necessarily be a dependent relationship. However, if the speeds are moderate (below the critical range mentioned above), it is possible to state an effective depth-speed relationship as

$$V = 0.4 \sqrt{gh}$$

where V = speed in knots
h = depth of the water in feet.

The above equation indicates depths of water that are not ordinarily thought of as shallow water. However, based on model tests, the effect of increased resistance can be detected as beginning at these drafts. For power and standardization trials, a location is usually selected where the depth of water is greater than that given by the equation above.

Sinkage and changes in trim are greater for any given speed in shallow water than in deep water. To avoid touching bottom in channels where the depth of water affords only a minimum clearance, ships should proceed at very low speeds.

POWER LOSS

As must be evident from the foregoing discussion, the means for determining the power requirements during the design process are imperfect. The difference between the actual power that the ship expends and that which was predicted in the design lies somewhere in the so-called correlation allowance or roughness coefficient, C_a. In terms of percentage error this difference may vary from a very negligible fraction up to four or five percent. Normally where the hull form is not unusual and where the model testing procedures are thorough, an error of no more than one percent can be expected.

From the foregoing discussion in this chapter and the preceding chapter on propulsion, the difficulty of proceeding from the *effective horsepower,* determined by model test, to the *brake horsepower* at the engine is an arduous road. There are many losses through this long energy transmission including mechanical, thermal and fluid losses, many of which evade precise analysis.

The most troublesome power losses to account for are those fluid losses through the propeller. The performance characteristics of a propeller in a hydraulic test tunnel, where it can be tested and analyzed, cannot very closely duplicate conditions when installed in its operating position on the ship. The thrust deduction and the wake phenomenon often are of the opposite effect and tend to cancel. They are also erratic at varying speeds, however. There is no completely satisfactory method of analysis for a quantitative measure for these factors. The best approach available to the designer is to use the best figures available from full-scale power trials of similar ships, using allowances from experience where there are design dissimilarities. Self-propulsion tests, where the facilities are available, are often relied upon.

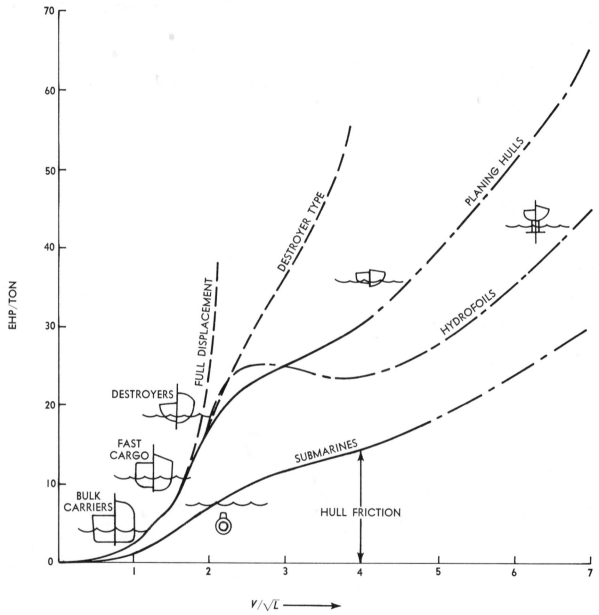

Figure 7–4. Speed-Power Trends for Ship Type Ranges

Another difficult determination is the power delivered at the propeller. Because at this point the propeller shaft is outside of the ship, it is not practical to make torsion measurements under operating conditions. However, by adding the best estimates of the fluid losses through the propeller to the effective horsepower, calculating the strut bearing or stern tube bearing losses, and proceeding through the internal shaft bearings and gear losses, the designer can arrive at the engine requirements with only a slight depression in his confidence. But in this present day of computer memory banks and rapid data processing, there is substantially less opportunity for error. The great mass of accumulated data on performance characteristics that contain accurate trends for the power losses for a multiplicity of designs are now providing opportunities for far more thorough analyses than ever before could have been contemplated.

Power Sources—The Designer's Choice

To quantitatively determine the amount of necessary power for the required spectrum of speeds and operational missions is by no means the end of the power selection problem. It has been described how the designer refines this determination through a thorough model test schedule. He must have before this time in the process of the design decided what type of prime mover or engine combination would deliver this energy. When ships were first mechanically propelled, and perhaps for a century thereafter, there was little choice other than a reciprocating steam engine with a boiler. Near the turn of the century came the steam turbine and the diesel internal combustion engine, followed closely by combined electric drive, both turbo-electric and diesel-electric. Later in this century the gas turbine has been advanced to a practical power source and is increasingly in use with an ever-brightening future.

The most sophisticated of marine power plants perhaps is the combination of a proper choice of two basic engines, such as gas turbine and diesel, either through two different propulsors or a single propulsion system.

All of the power systems noted above have their individual characters, their best operating efficiency characteristics, their specific weights (pounds per horsepower), their characteristic fuel consumption rates and their power limitations. These factors are obviously most important to the designer who must be intimately concerned with weight, volume, cruising range, and speed.

TYPES AND CHARACTERISTICS OF POWER SOURCES

All of the marine power plants currently in use and to be contemplated for use fall under the classifications of the following basic thermodynamic cycles:

Brayton cycle—gas turbines
Otto cycle　—internal combustion, reciprocating gasoline engines
Diesel cycle　—high-speed diesel engine, rpm > 1000; low-speed diesel engine, rpm < 1000
Rankine cycle—steam turbine

For comparative purposes here, it is unnecessary to describe the above cycles further or to subdivide them into their various arrangements—closed, open, regenerative, etc. The inherent operating characteristics are common to all, and these characteristics contain the key to the choices available to the ship designer.

The performance parameters which interest the ship designer most in the early stages of design when he is on the outer edges of his design spiral and where power-type selections are made are principally

- Horsepower ranges
- Specific fuel consumption, (*SFC*) lb/hp hour
- Specific weight, (Sp.wt.), lb/hp.

There are other performance parameters of nearly equal, but actually secondary, interest that must be investigated simultaneously with the above characteristics. Among these are the

- Initial and life-cycle costs
- Maximum-to-continuous power ratio
- Maintenance and repair requirements
- Lubricating oil consumption rates

It is apparent that when weighing the total effectiveness of these powering systems for a specific ship design, that problem immediately becomes one of optimization with all of the other ship design factors. Such optimization in modern design technique becomes a problem for computerized solution. As such, it is discussed in chapters 1 and 14. This discussion must be more simply confined to the built-in performance ranges to be found and to be expected in the available marine power plant types.

In terms of total horsepower requirements, the selection is most straightforward, and for very large displacement type ships requiring maximum horsepower, there is very little choice. However, as ship size may be limited and speed and cruising range become more critical with mission, the selection becomes more acute. The following arrangement according to power ranges indicates the order generally accepted for the basic system types:

	Horsepower		
Steam turbine	35,000	—	100,000+
Gas turbine	500	—	40,000
Diesel	25	—	25,000
Otto (gasoline)	10	—	500
Turbojet (aircraft type)			3,500 (max.)

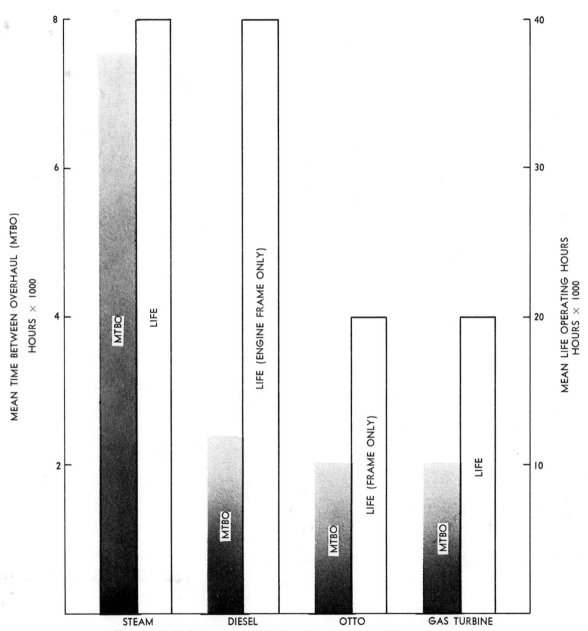

Figure 7–5. Maintenance and Lifetime Characteristics of Various Engines

The above types and ranges are considered in the context of surface craft. For submarines using nuclear fuel, the cycle is the steam (Rankine) cycle, generally of low to moderate pressure using little or no superheat, and the engine powers are lower than those indicated. Because of the necessity for atmospheric air in all other cycles, the nuclear fueled submarine is presently limited to the steam cycle, and its power must be designed to fit the submarine's requirements.

Figures 7–6 and 7–7 indicate the characteristic ranges of specific weights for the gas turbine, diesel, and Otto cycles compared with their maximum power ranges. It will be noticed at once that total power requirements do not affect the specific weight of the gas turbine type except at very low power. Otherwise, it is essentially constant and is the most attractive, in these terms, by far. Because of the many auxiliary and independent power plant components of the steam cycle, it is difficult to compare the steam engine on the same basis as the other type engines. Needless to say, its weight characteristics are the highest.

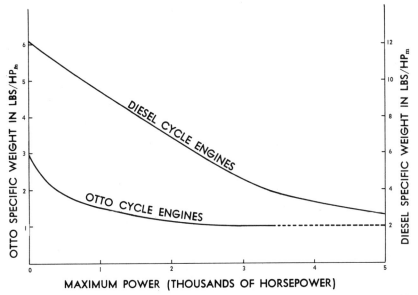

Figure 7–6. Recommended Characteristics of Lightweight Otto and Diesel Cycle Engines

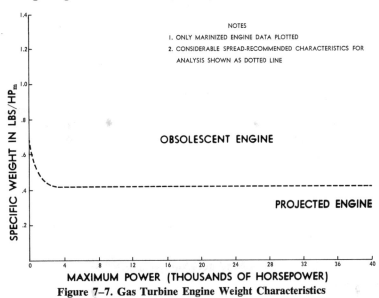

Figure 7–7. Gas Turbine Engine Weight Characteristics

Figures 7–8 and 7–9 show the relative fuel consumption characteristics of various types of cycles and indicates the increasing attractiveness of the two turbine types in the high power ranges.

The above characteristics reflect the best operating speeds and loads of each type. It is an important consideration in many ship designs to determine the variations of fuel consumption at partial rated power. These characteristics are shown in figure 7–8.

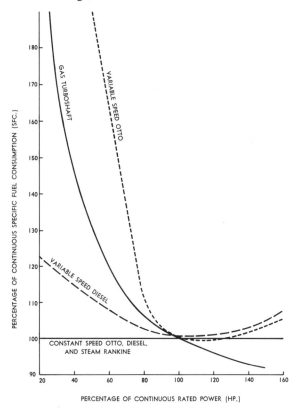

Figure 7–8. Fuel Consumption Characteristics

Gas turbines are perhaps most sensitive to environment in terms of atmospheric air temperature. Their power output will drop as inlet air temperature climbs. This feature is indicated in figure 7–10. At the same time, it must be pointed out that the steam cycle's efficiency drops when the cooling water temperature in the condenser rises, which is also a function of its operating environment. It should also be pointed out that gas turbine fuel costs may be as much as 30 percent greater than those for steam power plants.

In terms of maintenance and repair, there is no question of the steam system's great superiority. Both life cycle and time between overhaul are more than double any of the other engine types, except perhaps the life duration of the diesel cycle engine frame. It is worth some additional explanation in reference to this notation of frame life. Both the diesel and gasoline (Otto cycle) engines are self-contained reciprocating engines with a multiplicity of moving parts as well as stationary parts. The engine frame referred to is the familiar engine block in the smaller engines and its equivalent in the large horsepower diesels which are universally built in cylinder modules.

The frame life is extremely long because of its necessary rugged strength. It is most difficult to measure the frame's rate of deterioration because the only progressive deterioration normally evident is the rate of corrosion caused by seawater cooling, or, where applicable, freshwater cooling. However, in the lifetimes of most marine diesels or gasoline engines, the replacement of worn parts and expired subsystems goes on at a steady monthly and annual rate that even applies to the replacement of such major parts as cylinder liners, main bearings, valves, crankshafts, etc.

Figure 7–5 indicates a comparison of each major marine powering system's life expectancy and maintenance.

It is most evident at this point that some power plants have advantages not possessed by others, and, in turn, there are virtues in the others lacking in the first. No system can meet every requirement. Consequently combined systems are necessary for the special craft required to keep at sea for long periods of cruising at comparatively low speed and low power and yet have the reserve muscle for high speeds of short duration.

CODAG

In recent years, the *CODAG* (combination diesel and gas turbine) system has been increasingly used in the most modern ships from comparatively small patrol craft to larger destroyer-type escort craft, Coast Guard cutters, rescue craft, etc. The control of the two modes of operation in CODAG systems is described in chapter 8 in connection with the highly maneuverable USS *Asheville* class.

Choosing Power in Naval Ships

In the evolution of design and construction of new ships, naval engineers in the technical branches of the Navy Department have adopted

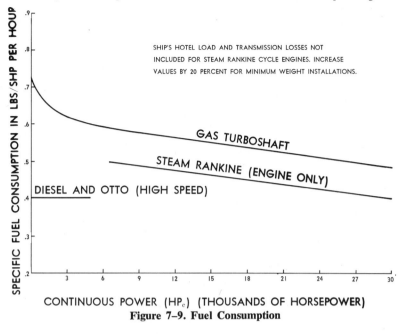

Figure 7–9. Fuel Consumption

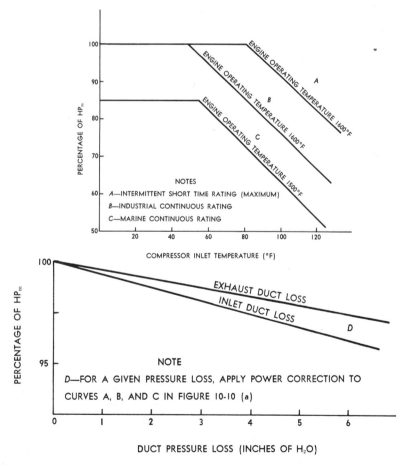

Figure 7–10. Gas Turbine Engine Performance—Effect of Operating Temperature (top) and Effect of Duct Pressure Losses (bottom)

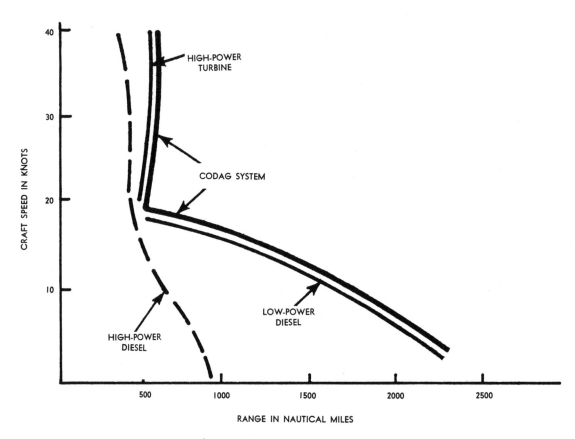

Figure 7–11. Engine Comparison—Range Versus Speed

a pattern or sequence of processes to determine the power requirements as accurately as possible. It is believed that these processes, which involve both valid theoretical approaches and empirical values based on comparative data and experience factors, are as complete and as reliable as those used by any designers or shipbuilders. There are, of course, as has been pointed out earlier in this chapter, a number of areas where basic knowledge is very thin or not available in current technology. It is these areas that remain to the researchers and will ultimately be narrowed to the benefit of future naval architects.

The sequential phases of power selection used in the Navy are briefly outlined below. They begin in the earliest planning stage.

INITIAL REQUIREMENTS FOR SPEED AND ENDURANCE

The initial speed and endurance requirements are determined as outlined in chapter 1 and are

the mission-related factors evolved through *operations analysis* and *cost effectiveness* study rather than from precedent or arbitrary decision, as was often the method in earlier approaches.

Some of the considerations during this phase are: full power speed (trial conditions), sustained speed capability, and speed profile (estimated ratio of operating times to speeds).

ESTIMATE OF EHP AND SHP IN THE PRELIMINARY DESIGN PHASE

Early estimates for *EHP* are largely based on the hull form coefficients derived from the preliminary design dimensions and the use of the updated Taylor's Standard Series procedures as outlined earlier. *SHP* values are projected then from *EHP* values by using predicted propeller efficiencies and best estimates of propeller-hull interactions. Many standardized Navy Calculation Sheets are used in this phase.

MODEL TESTS FOR EHP

Model tests for *EHP* may proceed and overlap the processes above and those following. They generally begin during the preliminary design phase and continue in a refining process through the contract definitions.

FULL POWER AND FUEL RATE REQUIREMENTS

This very necessary information is determined from several basic source data including data from previous ship trials and their fuel consumption reports showing fuel consumption versus rpm and fuel consumption and cruising radius versus *SHP*. Also important in this data consideration are the typical curves of speed, *SHP,* and rpm and finally the comparison with the predicted performance from model tests. The *standardization trial curves* are prepared in this phase of power determination.

MODEL-SHIP CORRELATION

The model-ship correlation phase is perhaps the most controversial of all and contains the various indeterminate factors caused by lack of valid hydrodynamic information. Previously in this chapter, there was some discussion of the roughness allowance, now called the *correlation allowance*. For most ship design purposes, this factor can be set at a more or less arbitrary factor as explained. However, the bottom roughness does affect this value, and with the various types of bottom coatings used by the Navy, it is considered important enough to consider the exact coating to be used. The table below, determined by test, indicates the variation of C_a with several bottom paints.

Type Paint	C_a
Hot Plastic	0.00085
Cold Plastic	0.0005
Vinyl Resin	0.0004
Zinc Chromate*	0.0005

At this stage, the model basin has made a series of more refined model tests including a regime of bare hull resistance tests, appendage tests and at least two sets of self-propulsion tests. For the self-propulsion tests, the method used

*Zinc chromate is not a practical operational bottom paint.

requires the model to be towed by the carriage using a force equal to the difference between the model frictional resistance and the ship frictional resistance scaled to the model. This carriage towing force, known as *the overload ITTC loading* or D_f, is determined by the equation

$$D_f = \frac{\rho}{2} Sv^2 \left[C_{fm} - (C_{fs} + C_a) \right].$$

It should be noted here that the self-propulsion tests are used basically to determine the predicted *SHP* for the ship throughout its speed-power spectrum.

FACTORS AFFECTING ABILITY TO SATISFY FULL POWER REQUIREMENTS

There are a number of external factors that inhibit or reduce the capacity of the ship's propulsive system to satisfy the full power requirements. Among these, the most significant are

- Shallow water effects
- Rough water effects
- Hull fouling
- Injection temperature

Both shallow water and rough water effects on resistance have been previously discussed, and their contribution to power prediction is accordingly applied at this stage.

Hull fouling by sea growth is dependent upon the type of bottom paint and the operational environment. These factors can be applied from available source data in terms of prepared tables and curves based on actual tests.

The effect of cooling water injection temperature is simply a correction to *SHP* for variation to the steam plant's power cycle from that temperature used to compute the predicted plant power. As such, it must be taken into consideration together with the above three factors as considered variables to the ideal predicted conditions.

FINAL CONSIDERATIONS

The ultimate choice of the power system, as can be seen in the foregoing, depends upon a multiplicity of factors and for the larger vessels, in the absence of predetermined design direction of sister craft, will increasingly depend upon the optimization procedures conducted through computer-aided analysis.

Courtesy of David Taylor Model Basin

Figure 7–12. Self Propulsion Test Model. This model is being ballasted to its proper water-line in the trimming canal. The model is also weighed on platform scales to ensure that the displacement is correct.

The designer's experience and knowledge, in working with the external fluid losses of the propeller and the energy losses in the engine through the mechanical losses of gears and bearings, will largely direct his planning. He is continually aware of the very small proportion of the total energy supplied that is available in the reactive thrust of the propeller's water column astern to overcome the ship's total resistance. He is aware, too, of the relative weights and sizes of the great reduction gears necessary to bring the speeds of turbines to the required revolutions of the propeller shafts. (See figure 7–13). He knows in this connection also that in large vessels this required space is not a difficult problem, and that the gear losses are often compensated for to a large extent where the reduction of speed is designed to the best propeller size and, consequently, improved propeller efficiency. This is too

HIGH PRESSURE
TURBINE

Courtesy of Stal Laval

Figure 7–13. Reduction Gear Needed for Contra-rotating Propellers in a Steam Turbine-Powered Ship

frequently not the case in large diesel-powered ships where direct drive engines turn too fast to achieve their rated power and thus require smaller, less efficient propellers.

Cruising range will always be coupled to fuel consumption and fuel capacity. These two factors taken alone reduce the choice in larger plants over 25,000 horsepower to a nearly arbitrary decision between diesel and steam systems.

Nuclear fueled plants, of course, provide an unparalleled cruising range. This advantage, as attractive as it is, is not entirely free and clear. (See figures 7–15 and 7–16.) Other than the extremely high initial cost, which is prohibitive for all but government and subsidized vessels, the weight of the reactor and its heavy shielding is approximately the equivalent of the liquid fuel weights of the more conventional plants.

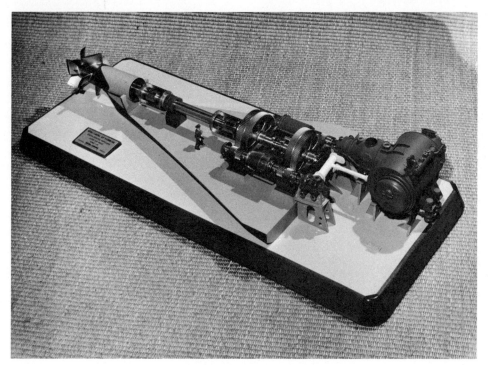

Courtesy of Stal Laval

Figure 7–14. Relative Sizes of Reduction Gear, HP Turbine, LP Turbine, and Condenser in a Turbine-Powered Merchant Ship

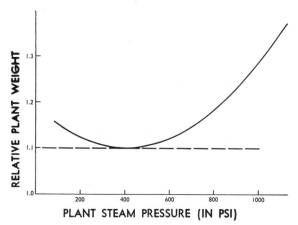

Figure 7–15. Effect of Selecting Steam Pressure on Nuclear Plant Weight

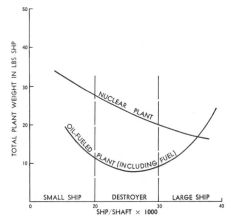

Figure 7–16. Variation of Plant Weights (Nuclear versus Oil)

Official U.S. Navy Photograph

USS Long Beach Testing High-Speed Turns During Trials

CHAPTER 8

Maneuverability and Ship Control

The Ship's Rudder

The rudder is the most important ship control surface and certainly it is the oldest. This vital device, or its equivalent at the ship's stern, has been in use since pre-history. In the earliest archeological pictorial evidence of man's watercraft, there are very prominent steering oars with wide, rudder-like blades held to the stern. There is no doubt about the antiquity of this appendage; there should be, also, with all of this obvious experience, some evidence of its improvement.

Actually, in a technical sense, there has been a great deal of improvement in the rudder as an effective control surface; in a basic sense, there has been very little change in its nature and usage.

Historically, there have been only about three fundamental design changes in this steering appendage. The first change took place sometime during the thirteenth century when the long, heavy steering oar, swiveled on the side near the stern (and which had been so effective, apparently, as to dissuade mariners from making any real change for nearly 5,000 years), was replaced by a hinged, centerline blade hung on the stern post. Not until the era of iron ships in the latter part of the nineteenth century did the

rudder ever penetrate the hull below the waterline, and only in very recent decades has the rudder begun to be disassociated completely from the last vestiges of a stern post and become a truly separate control surface. There have been perhaps a few isolated and singular exceptions to the above historical trend, but they have been only exceptions to the overall acceptance and general adaptations of the device.

In its presently most adaptable form on large and even small ships, the rudder is a fin or spade-like projection under the counter and below the waterline, generally placed as far aft as practicable. It is hung on a circular, solid shaft called a *stock* that penetrates the hull through a stuffing box and bearings. It often has a fixed, faired, foil-like section ahead of it which is firmly attached to and part of the ship's structure. This is called the *rudder horn* or *rudder skeg;* it may extend the full or partial depth of the rudder. In any case, it serves a double purpose: to help support the weight and thrust of the rudder and to improve materially the hydrodynamic effectiveness of the rudder. The basic rudder dimensions and nomenclature are shown in figure 8–1.

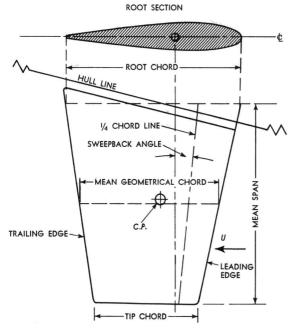

Figure 8–1. Basic Rudder Definitions

FORCES ON THE RUDDER

For purposes of definition and subsequent discussion, it is relevant at this point to discuss very briefly the forces that are generated at the rudder when it is turned at an angle to the direction of the stream of water in its vicinity. Figure 8–2 indicates a normal rudder section in such a situation at angle α.

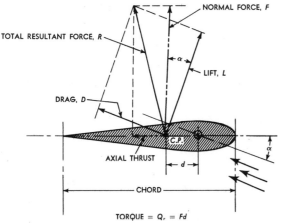

TORQUE $= Q_r = Fd$

Figure 8–2. Rudder Force Nomenclature

The total resultant force, as shown in the diagram, is the result of the combined action of the fluid flow over and around the rudder surface. Its magnitude and direction combine the differential pressures created by the variation in velocities of the water on both upstream and downstream surfaces of the rudder, as well as the impact force of the water, the viscous drag, the induced drag, and the eddy drag. These factors are all either the result of transient flow phenomena basic to all foils in a fluid or those introduced into the design. This total resultant force can be resolved into a lift component, *L,* and a drag component, *D,* perpendicular and parallel to the direction of motion. For purposes of rudder design and analysis, the component of the total resultant force which is normal to the centerplane of the rudder is called the *normal force, F,* and when multiplied by the distance, *d* (between the rudder axis and the locus of action of forces or center of pressure), produces the *rudder torque, Q_r.* These forces will be considered in the subsequent discussions of turning and rudder analysis.

AREA AND SHAPE OF RUDDERS

There is no fixed rule for the determination of the size of rudders due to the difference in maneuverability required for different ships. In practice, rudder area, expressed as a fraction of the product of the length and draft or centerline plane area, is often selected by comparison with another similar ship which has the required maneuverability. The ratio of rudder area to the product of length and draft for destroyers is usually about .025, while for a cargo ship, the ratio is usually about .017.

Apart from the aspect ratio, the outline of the rudder has little effect on the rudder force. The *aspect ratio* is the ratio of the rudder height to rudder length. Short, high rudders (i.e., rudders of high aspect ratio) produce larger rudder forces than long, low rudders of the same area at the same small rudder angle. However, high aspect ratio rudders will stall or "burble" at moderate rudder angles, with an accompanying decrease in the rate of rudder force increase for increasing rudder angles beyond the stalling point. *Stall* is the name generally given to the change from the initially smooth streamline flow on the downstream side of the rudder to an irregular eddying flow caused by separation. This phenomenon limits the usefulness of rudders with high aspect ratios. On the other hand, rudders having low aspect ratios will not stall until greater rudder angles are reached and will usually attain a greater rudder force than rudders of high aspect

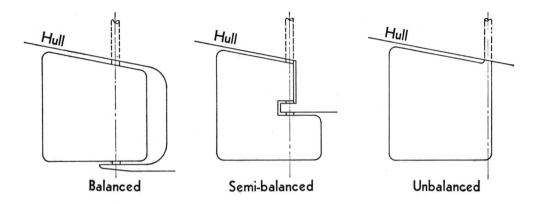

Figure 8–3. Rudder Types

ratio before stall occurs. Rudders are normally designed with an aspect ratio approximately equal to or slightly greater than 1:1, where the rudder angle for maximum rudder force is about 30 to 35 degrees.

The rudder consists of two parts: the flat part or blade, against which the water pressure acts, and the shaft or stock, which transmits the motion of the steering gear to the blade. In the case of warships, a principal concern is to get sufficient blade area totally below the waterline, with the bottom and trailing edge above the base line and forward of the tangent to the after contour of the ship.

The general types of rudders are unbalanced, semibalanced, or balanced as shown in figure 8–3. The blade of an *unbalanced rudder* is entirely aft of the stock. In a *balanced rudder,* a portion of the rudder area, disposed symmetrically throughout the rudder height, is forward of the stock. In a *semibalanced* rudder, the area forward of the stock does not extend to the full height of the blade aft of the stock. Hence, the upper portion of a semibalanced rudder may be considered an unbalanced or hinged rudder, and the lower portion a balanced rudder.

Disposing a portion of the blade area forward of the stock reduces the torque. Since the center of pressure moves toward the trailing edge as the rudder angle is increased, it is not possible for the stock and center of pressure to coincide at all rudder angles. Balanced rudders are normally designed to be balanced (i.e., have the center of pressure coincide with the rudder stock) at about 15 degrees of rudder angle.

Figure 8–4 illustrates the relationship of force, location of center of pressure, and torque on a balanced rudder. It will be noticed that the location of the center of pressure is a function of the rudder angle and moves aft as the rudder angle is increased, being on the axis of the rudder at about 15 degrees. The product of the force on the rudder and the distance to the center of pressure from the axis produces the torque variation shown in curve 3 of figure 8–4. This curve actually represents the mean torque on the rudder and not the actual torque required by the steering engines. Because of friction, the actual amount of torque required by the steering engine varies not

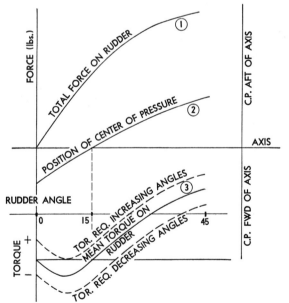

Figure 8–4. Rudder Angle Versus Force, Center of Pressure, and Torque

Courtesy of Newport News Shipbuilding Co.

**Figure 8–5. Typical and Efficient Modern, Double-Plate, Semi-balanced Rudder (on horn)
in a Single Screw Ship**

only with the angle but with the increasing and decreasing angle. The actual torque supplied is indicated by the dotted curves above and below curve 3.

A streamlined double-plate rudder develops more rudder force and has less resistance than a single-plate rudder. Considerable attention to the design of the rudder post and rudder will materially reduce resistance (see figure 8–5). Modern destroyers are fitted with twin semi-balanced rudders to avoid the space limitations of a single rudder and to enjoy the greater effectiveness when each one is located in the race of each of the twin screws.

Factors Affecting Steering

The portion of a ship's hull aft in the vicinity of the keel and just forward of the propeller is in

the form of a vertical fin-like surface apparent in the sharp V-shaped sections. This fin-like surface is called the *deadwood* and, of course, is not the same either in extent or shape from ship to ship. It may be extensive and predominant in some types of ships, particularly single screw, ocean-going vessels, or it may be extremely limited in other types. Its purpose, in any event, is to provide the desired degree of directional stability. The turning resistance is greatly increased by a large amount of deadwood or skeg area, and the ships with a small amount of deadwood tend to yaw in a heavy sea. In large ships where directional stability is a critical factor, as for example, aircraft carriers, it is often found necessary to provide twin skegs, spaced side by side on each side of the centerline. (See figure 8–6.) In ships such as destroyers where high-speed maneuverability is desirable, a proportionately smaller amount of deadwood is used.

Ships with large moments of inertia about their pitch and yaw axes are less sensitive to small sea disturbances and will steer better in moderate seas.

The effectiveness of the rudder and the time required to apply the rudder affect the steering characteristics. To avoid the building up of a large angular momentum due to a disturbing force, the helmsman must detect and oppose the initial tendency to yaw.

Most ships steer erratically in a following sea because the decreased relative speed between waves and ship allow any athwartship component of the wave force a greater time interval to act on the stern. Also, because of the orbital motion of the water particles in a sea wave (see chapter 12), the rudder force will fluctuate between high and low values and actually in one wave cycle may go from positive to negative values. This phenomenon is most apparent when the ship is moving in the same or nearly the same direction as the predominant wave system where the speed of the wave system is only slightly greater.

Wind striking the ship from an angle will tend to blow the ship off course. Ships with high forecastles are very difficult to turn into the wind.

Steering is also influenced by the depth of water, narrow channels, the number of propellers, and the relative position of rudders astern of the propellers. Propellers extending below the keel line greatly increase the resistance to turning.

FLOW AROUND RUDDERS

The flow phenomena and resultant forces on the rudder are generally treated through the same theories as those used in basic aerodynamics. There are, however, some marked differences and special considerations that combine to evolve a more complex and variable situation for a rudder performing its function for a ship. Because of the natural location of the rudder on the ship in the vicinity of the stern, aft of the propellers and generally either wholly or partly in their race, often in the zone of separation where strong eddy currents exist, and where ship motion and sea state produce oscillating forces and velocities, it can be truly said that a rudder operates in a most complicated environment. Basically, there are three hydrodynamic flow phenomena to which a rudder is subject even when operating in a free

Official U.S. Navy Photograph

Figure 8–6. Twin Skegs and Rudders on Large Carrier

stream from the interaction with the ship. These are *hydrodynamic stall, cavitation,* and *aeration.* These phenomena may exist separately or, in the case of aeration and cavitation, together. They all inhibit or, occasionally, destroy the effectiveness of rudder action.

Stall is the same phenomenon encountered on an aerodynamic surface. It is the sudden discontinuity of lift on the downstream surface of the rudder caused by an increasing angle of attack to the critical angle where separation occurs and when the normal flow pressures can no longer exist.

Cavitation and *aeration* are functions of the magnitude of pressure reduction on the downstream side of the rudder. Aeration is often caused on the rudder when it becomes, either by design or motion in the sea, too close to the surface and air is pulled down from the atmosphere to the low-pressure region of the rudder. Cavitation is the same phenomenon as that produced under certain conditions on propeller blades and hydrofoil surfaces due to increasing

reductions in pressure leading to the vaporization point. (It is discussed in chapter 6 in more detail.) It not only inhibits lift or rudder force but produces erosion on the metal surfaces in its vicinity.

These hydrodynamic flow phenomena, where the rudder is actually operating in its real environment on the ship, are most difficult to predict. Scaling factors in model tests become most difficult because all of the above phenomena are governed by different laws of similitude as well as influenced by flow velocities induced by the turning ship. Model tests are helpful in qualitatively determining rudder effectiveness, and freestream rudder experiments in flow channels at high Reynolds Numbers and in turbulent flow are often reliable, particularly where the parent hull flow conditions have also been investigated.

Figure 8–8 shows photographs of rudder models in the Naval Academy flow channel where aeration is plainly evident. There is evidence also in these photographs of incipient cavitation.

TURNING

When a ship is underway on a straight course in still water, the streamline flow about the rudder is generally symmetrical with respect to the centerline plane with no athwartship component of the water force. When the rudder is moved from its midposition, the symmetry is disturbed and a force acting at the center of pressure of the rudder is introduced. This results in a path of motion of the ship's center of gravity such as indicated by figure 8–9 and also results in a heeling of the ship. The initial motion of translation is a spiral curve which steadies to a circular path when the ship has turned approximately 90 degrees.

The distance moved by the center of gravity in the direction of the original course and at right angles to the original course from the point where the rudder is started over until the heading has changed 90 degrees, is named *advance* and *transfer,* respectively. The distance at right angles to the original course gained by the center of gravity in turning 180 degrees is the *tactical diameter*.

In turning, the ship moves with the bow inside and the stern outside the tangent to the path of the center of gravity. The angle between the tangent to the turning circle and the centerline of the ship is called the *drift angle*.

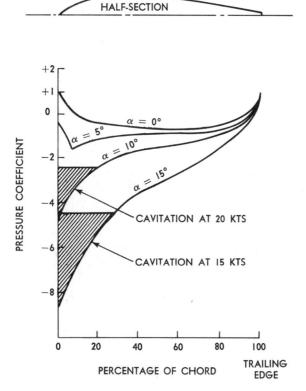

Figure 8–7. Pressure Distribution on a Typical Rudder

Figure 8–8. Rudder Profile Test in Naval Academy Channel. All rudders have same area.

(Top Left) Rectangular shape; aspect ratio = 1.0; α = 25°. Note aeration pocket forming.
(Top Right) Rectangular shape; aspect ratio = 2.0; α = 35°. Full stall is nearly reached.
(Bottom Left) Semicircular shape; aspect ratio = 2.0; α = 35°.
(Bottom Right) Semicircular shape; aspect ratio = 2.0; α = 40°. Note aeration and vortices of stall.

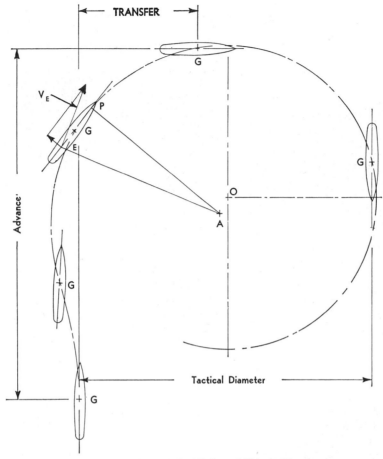

Figure 8–9. Motion of Ship in Turning

When the ship assumes its drift angle, there is a point on the centerline between the bow and the center of gravity at which the resultant velocity (rotation plus translation) is directed along the centerline (i.e., no component is at right angles to the centerline). To the observer aboard, the ship appears to rotate about this point, which is called the *pivot point*. The pivot point is normally located about one-third to one-sixth of the distance from the bow to the center of gravity. The *rudder angle* is the angle between the centerline of the ship and the rudder.

In figure 8–9, point A is the instantaneous center of the turning path when the ship is in the position indicated. The instantaneous velocity, V_E, of point E is normal to the radius, AE. It should be evident that the instantaneous velocity of point G, being normal to the radius AG (not drawn), will be tangent to the turning path. Further, it should be evident that the instantane-

ous velocity of point P will lie on the centerline of the ship, inasmuch as the radius, AP, is normal to the centerline. The point, P, is the pivot point. When the ship has steadied to a circular path, the instantaneous center becomes fixed at point O.

Forces on the Ship

When the rudder is put over to an angle, θ, a rudder force acting at the center of pressure of the rudder is generated. This force may be resolved into components normal to and along the rudder surface. The force parallel to the rudder surface has little effect on the turning action and may be disregarded. Considering figure 8–11, the rudder force, P, is shown acting normal to the rudder. This force may be resolved into an equal and parallel force, P_2, and a couple, $P\,D$, acting at a point, C. Point C is in the horizontal

Official U.S. Navy Photograph

Figure 8–10. USS Halsey (DLG-23) Making a Normal Maneuvering Turn in the Golden Gate Channel. A ship must be well designed and model tested to attain control such as this. Note the wave pattern in the ship's wake.

plane containing the rudder's center of pressure and is directly below the ship's center of gravity. The force, P_2, may be further resolved into P_2 cos θ and P_2 sin θ, which are perpendicular and parallel to the centerline respectively.

1. *Initial Phase.* The initial phase of the turn begins when the rudder is put over. Under the influence of force P_2 cos θ, the ship

accelerates in an outward drift away from the center of turning (to port in figures 8–9 and 8–11). The force, P_2 sin θ, opposes the motion, and a reduction of speed results. At the same time under the influence of the couple, $P\,D$, the ship begins to rotate about a vertical axis through C. This rotation is in the direction of the desired turn

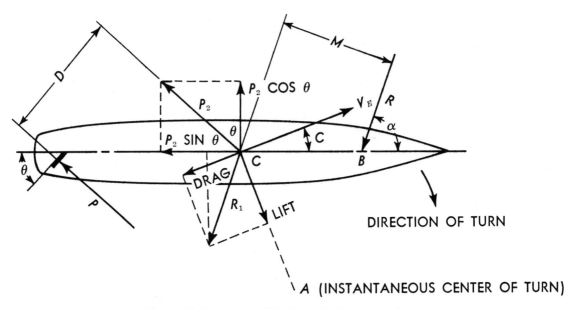

Figure 8–11. Forces on a Ship Caused by Rudder Action

as indicated in the figure 8–11. The initial phase is over as soon as the rudder has overcome the ship's rotational inertia, and the ship has rotated through an angle that allows hydrodynamic forces to develop.

2. *Second phase.* As the ship rotates, the direction of the instantaneous velocity, V_E, rotates through an angle of attack, β, from the ship's centerline. The force, P_2, and the couple, $P\ D$, continue to act, but the pressure distribution about the hull changes. The translation of the ship with the angle of attack, β, produces a pressure increase all along the outward (away from turning center O) side of the ship, thus creating a force, R, acting at some point, B, and inclined at an angle, α, to the ship's centerline. This force may be resolved into an equal and parallel force, R_1, and a couple, $R\ m$, acting at point C. The force, R_1, may be further resolved into *lift* and *drag,* which is perpendicular and parallel to the direction of the instantaneous velocity. Note that lift and drag are defined in exactly the same way as they are on propeller blades and rudders because of the essential foil shape of the ship moving through a fluid medium at a specific angle of attack.

During the second phase, the couple $R\ m$ aids the couple, $P\ D,$ and the turning motion is accelerated (if B is forward of C, which

is the usual case). As this occurs, the ships angle of attack increases, point B moves aft, and the turning tendancy of the couple $R\ m$ is reduced. This accounts for the S-shaped path during the first 90 degrees of the turn. During this phase, the ship is also being influenced by the lift and drag components of R_1. The ship is being further slowed by the drag and is being accelerated toward the instantaneous center of the turn. Thus the ship, which accelerated outwardly in the initial phase due to $P_2 \cos 0$, begins to accelerate inwardly as the lift becomes greater than $P_2 \cos \theta$. It can be seen that the second phase is a transition between the initial phase and steady turning.

3. *Steady Turning Phase.* Eventually B moves abaft the center of gravity, and equilibrium is established between the rudder couple, $P\ D,$ and the lift couple, $R\ M.$ The ship settles, then, on the circular portion of the turning path. The forces, P_2 and R_1, continue to act at constant values. The ship continues to be slowed and accelerated toward the center of the turning circle. In the steady turning condition, this inward acceleration becomes constant, and the ship maintains a turning path of constant radius.

In discussing the heeling forces on a ship in a turn, it is necessary to consider a component of R_1 other than lift and drag. This is $R_1 \sin \alpha$, the

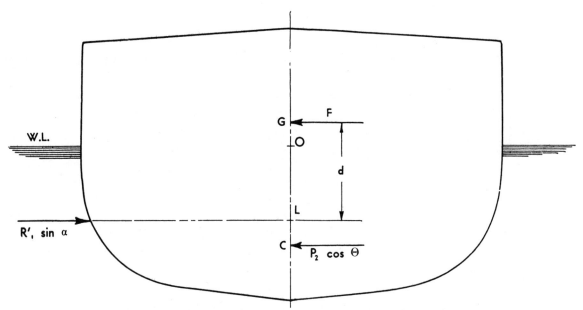

Figure 8–12. Heeling Caused by Rudder Action (Viewed from Aft)

component perpendicular to the ship's centerline. In figure 8–12, $R_1 \sin \alpha$ is assumed to act at L, the geometric center of the immersed centerplane, and produces an inward force which opposes the outward drift due to $P_2 \cos \theta$. These forces, because of their lack of vertical agreement, result in a heeling action. The discussion of heeling action will follow the same three phases discussed above.

1. *Initial Phase.* During the short time interval immediately after the rudder has been put over, the transverse component of rudder force, $P_2 \cos \theta$, acting at the center of pressure of the rudder, produces an inward heeling moment whose arm may be assumed to be $\overline{OC}$. (This is a fair assumtion for most ships, because at small angles of heel, the heeling axis is very close to the waterplane and near the center of gravity.) The moment of rudder force at this phase, acting as a heeling moment, is $\overline{OC}\, P_2 \cos \theta$.

2. *Second Phase.* The component of the force on the hull, $R_1 \sin \alpha$, gradually builds until it becomes greater than $P_2 \cos \theta$. As it builds, a heeling moment counter to $\overline{OC}\, P_2 \cos \theta$ is developed, and the net heeling moment in the second phase of the turn is

$$M_1 = P_2 \cos \theta\, \overline{OC} - R_1 \sin \alpha\, \overline{OL}.$$

This net moment results in an inward heel,

because at the beginning of turn, $R_1 \sin \alpha$ is zero. As $R_1 \sin \alpha$ begins to grow in magnitude, the inward heel diminishes and an outward heel may begin (most usually in warships and higher powered ships of ample freeboard).

3. *Steady Turning Phase.* The steady turning phase can best be analyzed by considering the centrifugal force resulting from the ship's inward acceleration toward the center of the turn. When the ship has settled into a steady (circular) turning path, the centrifugal force of the mass of the ship is acting at the ship's center of gravity, G. This is the amount,

$$\frac{\Delta v^2}{gr}. \quad \text{(in tons)}$$

The ship, being in a steady path, indicates that a state of equilibrium has been established between the outboard forces at G and C and the inward resisting force at L. According to figure 8–12, the centrifugal force would be acting counterclockwise about point L, while the transverse component, $P_2 \cos \theta$, is still acting in a clockwise direction. Thus, taking our moments about L, we have the net heeling moment

$$M = \frac{\Delta v^2}{gr}\, \overline{GL} - P_2 \cos \theta_r\, \overline{CL}.$$

Official U.S. Navy Photograph by O. V. William

Figure 8–13. USS Enterprise (CVAN-65) Making a High-Speed Turn. Note the heeling angle, which can become operationally dangerous when the forces involved are not understood.

The greatest angle of heel is reached immediately after the change from inward to outward heel because, due to its mass inertia, the ship rolls past the position of equilibrium. If, in a high-speed turn, the rudder is returned amidship at this instant, the inward heeling moment disappears and a dangerously large outward heel may result. This fact deserves some attention because the helmsman, fearing too large a heel, might be inclined to remove the rudder angle, whereas the only safe action would be to reduce speed.

At the equilibrium angle of heel, the algebraic sum of the three heeling moments is equal to the ship's righting moment. The angle of heel is dependent on the relative location of points $C, L,$ and G of figure 8-12 and rudder angle, speed, and metacentric height.

Other Control Surfaces

Stabilizing fins that could be controlled were patented in 1889 by John Thornycroft in England but were not actually applied until about twenty-five years later. Since World War II, there has been an ever-growing application of controllable fins, and an impressive list of large ships have been built with or have had the devices installed in them. Credit for the successful current development of this type of device must be shared, most probably, by the Denny-Brown Co. of the United Kingdom and the Sperry Gyroscope Co. of this country.

Briefly, the device consists essentially of a projecting fin (actually one on each side of the ship) at the bilge line and somewhat forward of amidships. (See figure 8–14.) This fin is retractable either axially or radially and, when fully extended, can rotate within a limited arc in a similar manner to a stabilizing fin on an aircraft or the diving planes on a submarine. In the more recently

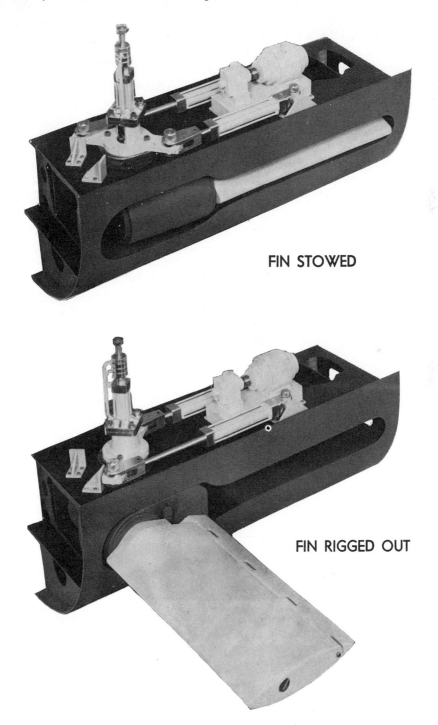

FIN STOWED

FIN RIGGED OUT

Courtesy of Sperry Gyroscope Co.

Figure 8–14. Active Fin Stabilizer—"Gyrofin"

developed fin, tail flaps are fitted to the fin's after edge to produce a shaped hydrofoil section that will produce the most effective vertical force (either upward or downward) when the angle of attack is reversed. The angle of attack of these fins is controlled through a shaft connected to motors inside the ship. A gyroscopic sensing device actuates the motors, creating a response to and, in fact, anticipating the wave's roll force. The transmission of motion to the fins produces at the proper time the desired angle and results in a force at the fins opposing the heeling or rolling force of the waves. The port and starboard fins operate simultaneously with a 180 degree phase relationship, thus producing a total correcting moment opposite in direction to the rolling moment. Figure 8–15 shows a typical comparison under given sea conditions of unresisted rolling and rolling under control of a fin stabilizer of the type described above.

With the rather impressive results and public popularity of anti-roll fins, it quickly became apparent that the motion of pitch should also be dealt with, and, accordingly, anti-pitch fins have been developed and tried. Unhappily, these fins installed at the bow have not been, to any extent, practical or successful. Because of the nature of the lower stem of a ship and the tendency in a seaway for unsymmetrical flow conditions to exist on either side, vibrative forces result from the extreme pressure differentials. In most cases, these anti-pitch fins were, when used on large vessels, fixed and unmovable (unlike the bow planes on a submarine). They were most vulnerable to damage and frequently were torn off in

heavy sea conditions. For these reasons, their use has not continued, and some other more effective solution to dampen pitch motion will have to be sought. To an extent, the large bulbous bow now being designed into most large and some smaller vessels is a fairly effective pitch reducer.

Vertical Control

Submersible vessels must be controlled when submerged in a vertical plane as well as a horizontal plane or, as in actual operation, a three-dimensional mode which is the resultant of combined horizontal and vertical control. To accomplish this, the modern submarine has at the stern both vertical and horizontal control surfaces. Frequently, these are arranged in a symmetrical design and oriented equally in shape and area above, below, to port, and to starboard of the centerline axis. The vertical surfaces, which are the traditional rudder surfaces, are both active when submerged, but only the lower one is immersed when the submarine is on the surface. The horizontal surfaces, known by their traditional name as the *stern planes* or, in more modern terminology, sometimes as *stabilizers,* may be controlled separately or together. In the older types of submarines, bow planes are used together with stern planes in controlling the vertical attitude and pitch angle. The shape, area, and location of these control surfaces depend upon the size, speed, and other operational requirements of the submarine, and a detailed discussion of them must be left to a more specialized treatment of submarine design. However, the

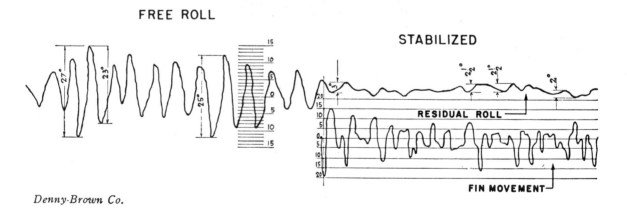

Denny-Brown Co.

Figure 8–15. Actual Rolling Record With and Without Fins Operating

nature of the basic problems of vertical control may be cited briefly by examining figure 8–16, which shows the sequence and time history of a submarine in a simple change of depth maneuver.

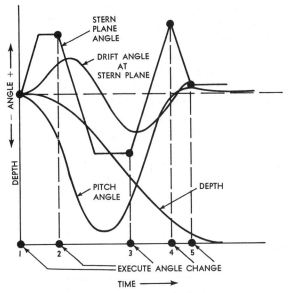

Figure 8–16. Submarine Time-Depth Change History

It can be seen in particular that the pitch angle, which is the submarine's attitude relative to the horizontal, progresses through a cyclic change from negative to positive angle throughout the process of changing depth. Thus it changes from down angle to up angle at about half of the depth change, so that while the submarine is still increasing depth during the last half of a dive, it is at an up angle. The pitch angle and depth finally level off together with the stern plane angle, which maintains, together with pitch angle, a slightly positive value at the increased depth to counter the tendency of the boat to sink further due to compressive buoyancy change.

Directional Control Systems at Low Speeds

All control surfaces, such as rudders and stabilizing fins, are by design, forms of hydrodynamic foils. As such, they depend for their effective control force upon the relative motion of the water over their surface. When a ship is maneuvering in close quarters in a harbor at low speed or underway with no way on, the necessity for directional control still exists. As ships have grown larger and more unwieldy due to their greatly increased inertia mass, the task of maneuvering them in restricted water at low speeds has

required the services of small, relatively high-powered tugboats acting at various locations along the ship's length. This process, as effective as it may be, is not as efficient nor as dependable as the ship's own self-contained systems, if she is able to supply these localized and directional thrusts. Consequently, there was introduced some years ago (for large passenger vessels originally) directional control systems called *bow thrusters*. The original bow thrusters consisted basically of ducted or tunneled propellers where the duct or tunnel was literally a transverse tunnel through the ship near the bow in a deep **V**, narrow, forward section. Within this bow tunnel was installed a reversible propeller or propellers that, operating as propeller pumps, threw a relatively large mass flow of water to either side. This is essentially the nature of currently used bow thrusters which are becoming increasingly popular and are designed into many ships, both large and small (see figure 8–17).

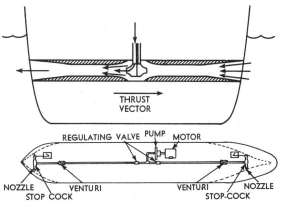

**Figure 8–17. Directional Control Thrusters—
Arrangement of Ejector Bow Thruster (top)
and Bow and Stern Thrusters (bottom)**

With the great increase of very large tankers and bulk cargo ships, the problem of directional control at low speed has become an increasing concern. New designs for better control in low-speed modes have been developed using not only bow thrusters but also similar stern thrusters as well together with better propulsion devices. These devices, consisting mainly of a single, shrouded propeller where the shroud is movable and acts as a rudder, not only have improved the maneuvering characteristics but also have been able, in a well-designed after body for low-speed operation, to reduce the *SHP* by as much as 15 percent.

Both bow and stern thrusters have been varied and improved by replacing the tunneled propellers by single- or two-stage ejectors or by high-velocity nozzles. The latter design, using nozzles, permits the elimination of the cross-hull tunnel and provides a system that is perhaps less efficient but much more economical and trouble free.

Control by Automation—Its Impact on Design

It become apparent to ship operators in the early part of this century that manual steering and course keeping was both costly and less effective than desired. Such steering required two helmsmen, at least, per watch. The human response mechanism is unable to cope with the motion of a ship in a seaway to produce other than an erratic track through the water. Because of these straightforward motivations, there came into being the first of all ship automated systems, the *auto pilot* or, as the seaman of the day referred to it, the "iron mike."

This compartively simple steering control system consists, in its simplest form, of a course indicator together with a course-set device which signals any discrepancy in either direction to a relay. This starts the steering mechanism which responds with an appropriate rudder angle until the discrepancy is eliminated and the signal ceases. In the intervening years since the auto pilot's first introduction, many sophistications have been added, such as feed-backs indicating the rate of the change of the heading. This allows the steering mechanism to anticipate the magnitude of the correction and to correct for overswing with the easing and, if necessary, reversing of the rudder angle.

This comparatively simple error-response system for automatic steering, however, is by no means the system (or systems) that is referred to presently as *automatic ship control*. Ship control, in the current systems of automation, is a far broader concept which is intended to, and does materially, reduce the number of personnel required for manual operation. It not only performs the routine and prosaic tasks of course-keeping, but also provides a system for remote control of propulsion and auxiliary machinery from the bridge or the control center. This includes automated control of most traditionally manned stations for main engine operation, with control for boilers, feed water, fuel oil, and auxiliaries which are pertinent to speed and maneuvering changes through all ranges of ahead, stop, and backing procedures. It further includes monitoring of the systems and, on some vessels, the central controlling of docking and line-handling winches.

What such control involves can be better un-

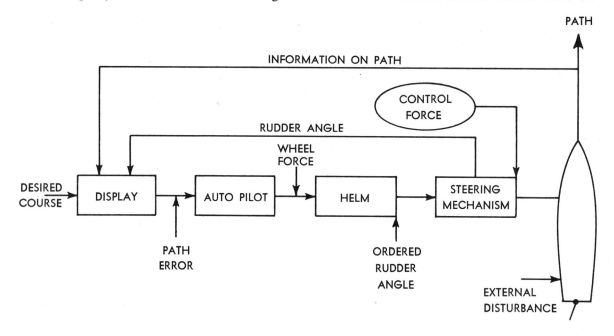

Figure 8–18. Simple Ship Control System (Typical Flow Pattern)

derstood by the systems diagram and analysis shown in figure 8–19. This illustration is essentially a basic and simple study for elemental automatic control. The customary scope of naval architecture does not normally include the design of machinery or such internal systems, and these details and functions will, accordingly, not be treated here. However, the impact of automatic ship control on the design of ships must not be lightly passed over.

The primary motivating factor of ship automation is, of course, centered in the economics of operation and maintenance. The reduction of crew, both for naval vessels and commercial vessels, is of vital concern in the successful continuance of ship operation. Automation is the only rational solution to the labor problem for ships of conventional missions and configurations. As an example, for cargo vessels of the *Mariner* class, the conventional steam-powered unautomated ship requires a crew of approximately 55 men. Fully automated, such a ship can operate with a crew of 14 men or, with gas turbines instead of steam turbines, perhaps only 10 men. From the point of view of economy, such a ship without automation at best makes a cash return to the owners of only 0.5 percent per annum and, on the projected wage scale of a few years hence, will be operating at a deficit. With automation, this ship can assure the owners of a cash return of 1.4 percent—perhaps, this is not spectacular, but it is an assurance of continued economic vitality, and this factor alone must be a primary consideration for the continuance of a merchant fleet and reflect the increase of overbearing operating costs of a naval fleet.

The designers of ships are, of course, acutely aware of the enormously increased costs of ships with complex automated systems. They must also be aware of the requirements imposed on them both by the new requirements in the command control of such ships and by the competitive rationalization of such costs. Such ships must be given every advantage in design for improved

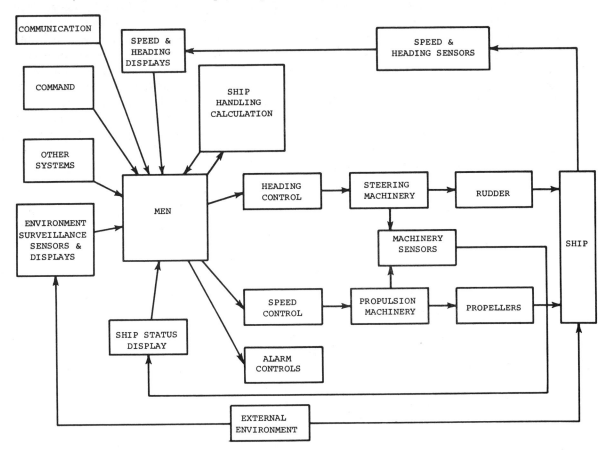

Figure 8–19. Typical Destroyer-Type Ship Control System

hydrodynamic character and responsive maneuverability by the *effective* design and application of the elements cited earlier in this chapter for directional control. They must have improved control stations derived from the increased utility of space aboard the ships. (This can, to a large extent, be done through the economy of the reduction in living space required by previously large crews.) Thorough and complete designs prior to construction must include the most efficient accommodation of these control systems, particularly by taking advantage of the new shipbuilding "block" methods, where all of the interior systems are complete and included in the subassembly process.

Finally, the designer must increase the tempo of his traditional search for more economical construction within the requirements of the vessel's design, whether it be in new, more economical materials, construction methods and techniques, structural simplifications, or improved configurations.

There is an inherent complexity in steam turbine propulsion machinery involving the various major components, such as the fuel oil system, the boiler with its feed system and steam cycle, high- and low-pressure turbines with astern elements, etc., that obviously requires a most sophisticated and complex system for automatic control. Primarily because of these basic reasons together with required warm-up times and lead times for increased boiler output, the steam plant is not as well adapted to automation

as the diesel or gas turbine plant, where the energy transfer from fuel to engine is direct, and power changes can be absorbed almost at once. It therefore follows that automation is far more economical and effective when applied to diesel and gas turbine driven ships.

In this connection, it is worthwhile to briefly cite an example of a well-automated, small naval vessel which combines diesel and gas turbine power. Such power plants are often called CODAG (*co*mbined *di*esel *a*nd *g*as) and make use of the diesels for continuous lower power cruising requirements and the gas turbine for the high-power, more intermittent full-speed requirements.

In such a design, the machinery space is greatly reduced compared to an equivalent steam plant or total diesel installation. The PGM-84 class encompasses the fastest and most maneuverable ships in the world and achieves this in an integrated, total design by using an aluminum hull structure, fiberglass superstructure, CODAG power, and automated engine and ship controls. This ship is only one of many of a similar type operating now in the Navy and the Coast Guard. (These CODAG-type ships are also used in the navies of several northern European countries.)

The power plant of the PGM-84 consists of two 750 horsepower diesels with 12-cylinder engines and a single 14,000 horsepower gas turbine, which drives, through a gearing arrangement, twin controllable pitch propellers. This arrangement is shown in figure 8–20, indicating both diesel drive and gas turbine drive. The pneumatic

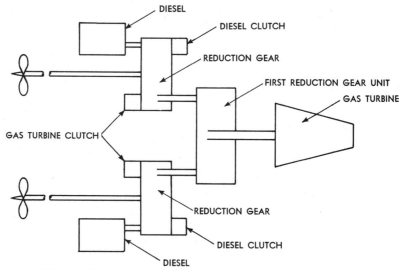

Figure 8–20. Diesel versus Gas Turbine Mode in PGM Propulsion

control system on this ship permits engine control from either the pilot house or the machinery space. There are three propulsion control levers and three control modes:

- *Diesel mode*—two levers control the diesel speed simultaneously with the propeller pitch.
- *Gas turbine mode*—one lever controls the turbine speed and the pitch of both propellers.
- *Gas turbine maneuvering mode*—the turbine lever controls the turbine speed while each diesel lever controls the pitch of one propeller.

Two additional control outlets select the desired propulsion mode. The turbine may be started from either the operating station, which automatically engages the turbine clutches, brings the diesels to idle, and transfers control from the diesel mode operation to the turbine mode with appropriate control levers. Such systems as this are extremely flexible and responsive; however, because of the large amount of power available at the operator's rapid change of order, there must be numerous safety features to block overloading and misoperation.

The displacement of the PGM–84, whose block dimensions are 165 ft. x 24 ft. x 9.5 ft., is only 240 tons. Her specific power for full speed is thus nearly 60 h.p./ton, nearly three times that of a destroyer. Needless to say, her hull is designed as a planing hull but with a rather high length to beam ratio and with fairly deep **V** sections which results in essentially good rough water characteristics.

Such a ship is a most modern and successful concept when adapted to a mission requiring speed, maneuverability, seakeeping, and minimum manning.

Official U.S. Navy Photograph by PHC R. C. Veeder, USN

Figure 8–21. Automatic Central Control Panel of the USS Gallup (PGM-85). This system shifts from diesel to gas turbine drive in a few seconds providing acceleration to a maximum speed of 40 knots.

The Camera Records a Sphere Dropping into the Transparent Wall Tank at David Taylor Model Basin

CHAPTER 9

Ship Research and Design in a Modern World

Until the middle of the past century, successful development and implementation of ship design has come about through the obscure adaptations of the builders, sailors, and owners of the ships. No one can say exactly which ship was first built with a keel to give the hull its original and needed longitudinal strength. It is not known what ship first used a centerline rudder instead of the universally used steering oar. The development of sailing rigs from single sails on single masts to the multiplicity of masts and sails on nineteenth-century ships was not the result of scientific research.

Ship research in a serious sense did not really make a discernible impact on ship design until William Froude presented his first findings in 1872 concerning the water resistance and powering of vessels and the relationship of the resistance of towed models to their parent ships. Since that time, the greatest and most significant contributions of research to ship design have been concerned with hydrodynamics and have had as the primary investigative instrument the ship model towing tank. It is difficult to say exactly how many towing tanks there are in the world today. Each year a few more are added, and the older ones are continually being improved and are

growing more sophisticated. It is not the purpose here to describe the many towing tank establishments, their similarities, or their variations in size or capacities. The author has visited a great many ship hydrodynamic research facilities with towing basins in this country and abroad, and the most impressive thing of all is that they are all so unlike in design, aside from some common and irrelevant mechanical details.

Towing Tanks

The primary function of towing tanks was noted in chapters 5 and 7. In most state-owned or government-operated tanks, the work being done falls more frequently into the categories of routine tests and specific determinations. The hydrodynamic facilities with towing tanks in educational institutions, on the other hand, are concerned with the basic problems of ship hydrodynamics and can be more readily identified with true research functions.

In this latter connection, it might be useful to describe a recent and modern design of a hydrodynamic laboratory with emphasis on its towing tank facilities. This towing tank is both a teaching and a research facility and represents the highest order of mechanical and electronic

Figure 9–1. Powering Test on a Destroyer-type Model Hull Fitted with a Bulbous Bow in the U.S. Naval Academy Towing Tank. This is a conventional test to determine speed-power characteristics for specific hull forms. This towing tank test and research facility is 85′ x 6′ x 4′ and is equipped with very complete electronic controls and data acquisition systems.

Official Photograph, Naval Ship Research and Development Center

Figure 9–2. The Navy's Seakeeping Basin at the Naval Ship Research and Development Center where ship's motion characteristics and seakeeping ability are model tested. This 16-foot long model is of a high-speed replenishment ship. The model and carriage can be oriented in any direction to the regular or irregular seas by the movable bridge-like structure above.

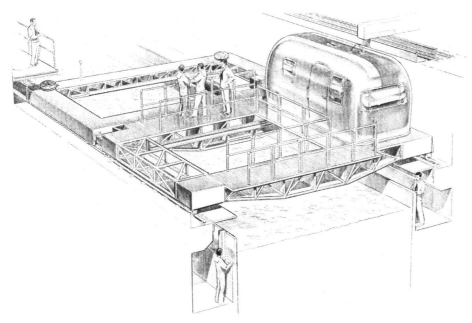

Figure 9–3. Standard carriage used in new high performance towing tank at the U.S. Naval Academy.

sensitivity. It is the result of several years of design planning for incorporation into the new engineering building's laboratories at the United States Naval Academy.

Naval architecture and marine engineering have long been taught at the U.S. Naval Academy. Since 1956, an 85-foot towing tank has been in operation, both as a teaching laboratory and, increasingly, as a research tool for midshipmen and faculty. Included in the Engineering Studies complex is a modern hydromechanics laboratory centered about a 380-foot towing tank with hydroacoustic capabilities. The laboratory includes a circulating water channel, a 120-foot towing tank, a ship stability and model ballasting tank, a wind-wave tank, and a 380-foot high performance towing tank. (See figures 9–3, 9–4, and 9–5.)

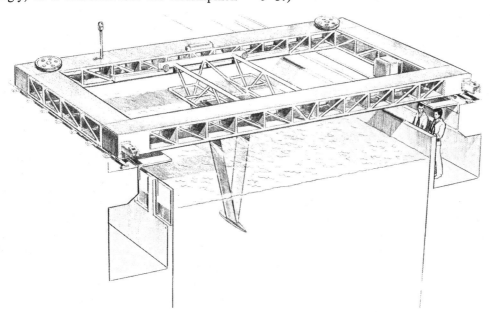

Figure 9–4. High-speed carriage used in the high performance towing tank at the U.S. Naval Academy. (Dimensions, 380 feet by 26 feet by 16 feet.)

This new tank embodies a high-speed carriage and is designed for a maximum steady-state speed of 30 knots, with a steady-state run of five seconds duration. This speed is required to achieve Reynolds Numbers of interest in the study of near field-flow noise, while the length of run is required for the gathering of sufficient statistical data to allow reasonable confidence levels. In order to achieve this high speed in a relatively limited length of run, the carriage is propelled by off-board electric motors attached to the carriage by pretensioned steel cables. Speed control is exercised from a central control room on shore.

The tank width is 26 feet and the water depth is 16 feet in order to minimize blockage and shallow water effects. The facilities include water treatment, water temperature control, air conditioning, underwater observation and photography provisions, and a drydock and carriage rigging area.

The tank includes the conventional equipment found in most towing tanks. A large (16 x 20 feet) 15-knot carriage incorporating an 11-foot square central well provides ample observation room for groups of midshipmen. This large carriage has no direct attachment to the towing cable system already mentioned, but is rigidly linked to the high-speed carriage and is towed at speeds up to 15 knots. Carriage control can be on board or from an on-shore control. Since this carriage is intended for teaching, as well as research concerning resistance and seakeeping, it is of heavy box girder construction with an unobstructed view and rides on vibration-damped steel wheels. A precise digital speed control powering four electric motors is used. (See figure 9–5.)

The wave maker is capable of random sea generation and of operation with varying water depths. The wave maker is an articulated flap-type generator which is electro-hydraulically actuated and can be controlled manually or by a local dedicated digital computer system. The rigid beach is segmented to permit unobstructed runs and to offer a variable slope for optimum damping and for the study of near-shore wave phenomena.

Since a primary purpose of the tank is the study of flow noise, acoustics play a large role in its design. Noise due to the carriage, models, and towing struts is isolated from the model being studied. Acoustic material lining the tank walls reduces external and reflected internal noise.

The rails are cantilevered from the building's structure and are independent of the tank, thus isolating the wheel noise and reducing the required span. The tank structure is isolated in a similar manner from all contact with the building.

The high-speed carriage is specially designed for acoustics tests. Design parameters include velocity, acceleration, time rate of change of acceleration, and vibrational levels. The carriage is a lightweight damped structure riding on teflon slippers. The carriages have been designed to allow interchange of all major dynamometry and instrumentation modules so that most tests can be run on either carriage.

Data transmission from the carriages to a central control room on shore is either by trailing cable or by a noise-free wave guide system. Data storage devices include on-board and shoreside magnetic tape systems as well as core and disc computer memory. The data reduction function considers real-time statistical analysis, data storage for a digital computer, and the interfacing with a time sharing computer system.

Figures 9–3, 9–4, and 9–5 indicate the structure, dimensions, and configurations of the towing tank and its components. This entire hydromechanics laboratory is one of the finest and most capable installations for pedagogic research study. While there are many towing basins that are larger, they are also more unwieldy and require far more operating personnel, complicated schedules, and expensive maintenance. There are similar facilities that have greater emphasis in one or another phase of hydromechanic study, such as special seakeeping basins with complex wavemakers and large, very powerful propeller tunnels and water channels. Such laboratories are generally weak or lacking altogether in other equipment and reflect the special interests of one or two outstanding researchers. For general student involvement and use in connection with ship design study, however, the hydrodynamic laboratory should be well-balanced to serve the interests of all. The Naval Academy's hydrodynamic laboratory is such a facility with a strong leaning toward hydroacoustic study. This feature must be considered as an investigative technique in boundary layer and flow phenomena study and as a means toward the goals of improved speed-power characteristics of ships, a fundamental part of ship design.

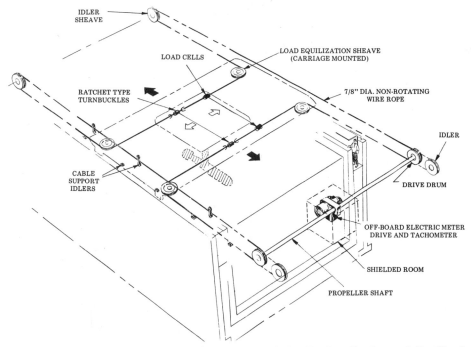

Figure 9–5. The Schematic Powering Arrangement of the Towing Carriages of the Naval Academy Towing Tank

Organizational Ship Research

While it is axiomatic that research does not thrive when too closely supervised or directed, it does require some sort of organizational sponsorship in order to avoid serious duplication, pursue the most significant problems, and receive the necessary grants and funds. There are, of course, a great many organizations, including educational institutions, private foundations, and government offices, that provide this organizational attention for researchers. Of these various interests, those perhaps most intimately associated with ship research in the United States are the Office of Naval Research (Navy Department), Stevens Institute of Technology (Davidson Laboratory), Massachusetts Institute of Technology (Department of Naval Architecture and Marine Engineering), University of Michigan (Department of Ocean Engineering), and the Society of Naval Architects and Marine Engineers. There are other institutions, of course, but the above are the most important because of the contributive research work they have accomplished. All of the above-named organizations function in different ways; for example, the Office of Naval Research is primarily supervisory and administrative, by maintaining programs through the Naval Research Laboratory, Naval Ship Research and Development Center, and other naval laboratories and facilities, as well as by funding individuals and other institutions having appropriate facilities. Its operational influence, needless to say, is enormous.

It is not practical to attempt to cite the current research programs in progress that pertain to ships; however, it might be useful to describe the functioning of the ship research program being carried on by and through the Society of Naval Architects and Marine Engineers. Within this professional society there exists a committee that directs a detailed and explicit program whose structure is indicated in figure 9–6. Note that there are six main branches or categories under which the specific studies are grouped; viz, *Hull Structure, Hydrodynamics, Ship's Machinery, Ship Technical Operation, Marine Systems,* and *Ship Production.*

The financial support for the research endeavors carried out under this organization is obtained from annual voluntary contributions from every segment of the marine industry, mainly from shipbuilding companies, shipping firms, ship suppliers, and ship designers.

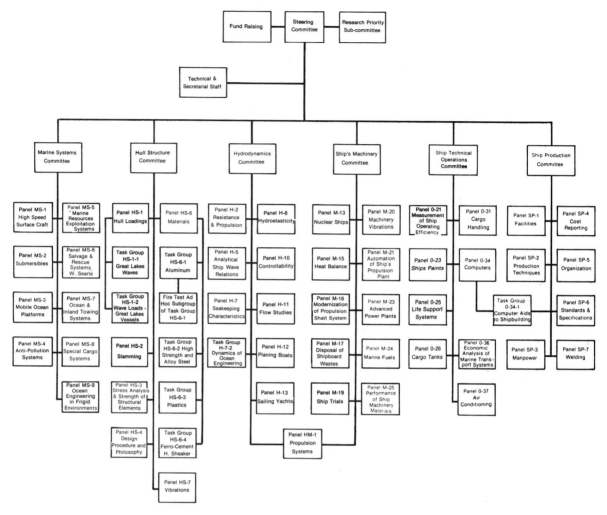

Figure 9–6. Organization Chart of the Research Program Sponsored by the Society of Naval Architects and Marine Engineers

The results of the various research projects are reported and made available through the Society's publications, *Marine Technology, Journal of Ship Research,* and their annual *Transactions.* The information is available to all members of the Society and to the marine industry. It is not necessary to be a member of the Society to either participate in the research program or to receive the information.

Research Emphasis

While it has been stated above that ship research has and does to a large extent involve hydrodynamic study that centers about towing tank facilities, there has been in recent years a rapid expansion of investigation in all facets of ship construction and operation. Such investigation is immediately apparent in the brief description of organizational research described above. Research in hull structure, machinery and ship control, and operation are equally considered, not only by the Society of Naval Architects but also by other organizations. In addition to all of the research directly associated with ship design, there is a multitude of peripheral and indirectly associated investigations proceeding, such as computer applications to increase design facilities and improve construction techniques, to mention only two of the most important areas.

For purposes of categorizing and indicating the directions, the emphasis, and the significance of ship research, the total effort should first, perhaps, be subdivided into three primary concerns; viz.,

1. Current operational problems
2. Future ship capabilities development
3. Abstract investigation

Unquestionably there is some amount of overlap; however, the division is a valid one. Under the first category can be found the greatest number of active programs and, some would insist, the most significant. This is probably true because funds are more quickly and abundantly available from the shipbuilding industry and ship owners for solutions to their current problems and the improvement of operational economy. In this area, there exists, for example, the extensive investigations for the improvement of hull forms for displacement-type hulls with the view toward the reduction of wave-making resistance, the development of computer programs aiding ship design and building, the investigation of sea-keeping characteristics, and the study of propellers and propulsive arrangements. These are but a very few of the broader fields, and it would be of doubtful value to cite more examples because the list is very long and is ever lengthening.

In the category of developing future ship capabilities exists the tenuous, imaginative and often more theoretical efforts. Such research as this is seldom funded or supported as in-house projects by shipbuilders and frequently takes a low priority in organizational research. Such studies might be involved in current basic ship problems, but the procedures would deal in terms of future concepts. Or, on the other hand, such research might deal in open-ended types of projects which are directed toward no specific single determination, either positive or negative. Banking a large amount of hydrodynamic data on series hulls for standards in future references and applications is an example of the more prosaic type of study in this category. Taylor's Standard Series is the result of such research begun early in this century and is being supplemented by data acquisition on Series "60" hulls, trawler-type series, planing hulls, submerged bodies of revolution, and others whose typical basic forms tend to classify them as being adaptable to such codifi-

cation. At this point, it should be emphasized that the process of data acquisition in itself cannot be recognized as research. However, data acquisition is certainly a part of most research projects, and in the case of series hulls, it becomes ultimately a useful rationalization and contributes to the knowledge of the behavior of the previously unknown parameters and coefficients. Projects in this category are most frequently guided by government agencies or educational institutions and, as in the case of series hull studies, by organizations such as the Society of Naval Architects and Marine Engineers.

In the third category—abstract and contributive investigations—there are generally no immediate problems that actually activate the research. Theoreticians often work individually on concepts and proposals. The product of their work is most frequently expressed via mathematical models of physical phenomena. Such work can become the tools for researchers in the first two categories. This research generally requires little or no laboratory support, is most frequently carried out in educational institutions by faculty or under faculty direction, and is often conducted by specialists who are only indirectly involved in ship design or the shipbuilding industry. It must be recognized, however, as a most important source of knowledge.

Containerization in Ship Design

There is much research continuing in ship design that falls in the first category of research (current operational problems) that has little to do with laboratories and is not scientifically centered in hydromechanic problems. Such research and development involves the pure economics of the operation of seagoing carriers. Recently, most forward-looking shipbuilding companies have concerned themselves with the development of ship types that are designed to solve some of the most troublesome operating problems of the shipowner. Many of these problems involve port losses, such as slow turnaround because of limited port facilities, high cargo handling costs, etc.

These universal problems have caused the development of the concept of the *transport unit* ship from the older idea of the *storage unit, cargo hold* ship, and this concept has resulted in the various and popular ships known generally as *container ships*. A more rapid but less efficient (volume-wise) variation, the roll-on/roll-off ship, used in connection with efficient land transport, speeds up the turnaround, but still depends upon port accessibility and berth availability. This port congestion problem is becoming increasingly serious and is being met with the concept of a *barge container ship* (see figure 9–8). These floating containers or barges are simply large containers built on the same module as the standard truck-

Courtesy of Swedish State Ship Research Station

Figure 9–7. Shrouded Propeller Test (top) and Coaxial Propeller Test (bottom). Note the cavitation helix in bottom illustration.

size containers and fitted in pre-built slides and racks in the barge carrier ships. They are discharged from the ship directly overboard, either from a moving deck gantry over the stern or from a stern ramp. The ship is thus independent of piers, dock labor, or congested ports and needs only a relatively protected anchorage. Such ships can be designed to accommodate both standard containers or barge containers separately or together in various combinations.

Barge container ships are not an isolated technical product, rather they are part of a complete transport system. Because of this, their designs are researched and analyzed by special computer programs to meet the demands of prospective owners. Some of the factors considered by the computer are cargo intensity over a year, whether the barges will carry from port to port or customer to customer, and the probability that the

barges will be forwarded over different distances, be detained for different reasons, and be returned at different times. The data is supplied by the customer, and the plotted results of all calculations show the most economic barge transport system—not only for the number and size of the carriers but also for their speed and schedules.

When the entire transport chain is considered, from the origin of the goods to their destination, the higher investment for a barge container system can be adequately justified by faster, safer cargo transport and by a higher earning capacity because of the increased number of round trips made possible. A major problem awaiting solution is the logistics of empty containers and barges, both aboard ship and at the delivery terminals.

This type of research reflects the most modern concepts and contemporary methods of work study with its economic and manning implica-

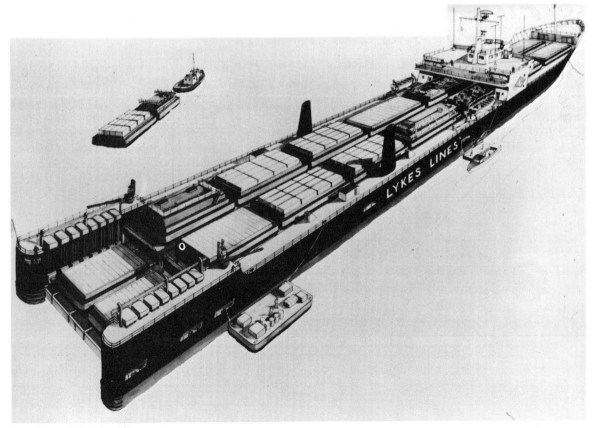

Courtesy of Lykes Brothers Steamship Co.

**Figure 9–8. New Type of Ship Developed for Large Container-Barge Transportation System.
This ship concept, called a LASH (Lighter Aboard SHip), is largely the result of the analysis
and research of economical sea transportation.**

tions that are directly applied to ship design. It is a direct result of changing operational and economic requirements.

The Impact of Research Upon Design

It is incumbent on every modern ship designer to keep current with the professional literature and remain alert to the many useful contributions from such outlets as hydrodynamic symposiums, professional society technical sessions, and other technical media of both marine and non-marine sources.

While most designers have little opportunity to engage directly in research themselves, they cannot afford to ignore its movement and impact on their professional product. It is no longer possible to practice naval architecture in isolation as it was practiced earlier in this century. An education in the hydromechanic principles of ship design, a sound basis of engineering fundamentals, and a reliance on experience and knowledge of past design criteria are by no means enough in this sprawling technology.

In past decades up to the perhaps mid-twentieth century, there was very little evidence in the existing ship designs of the contributions of research. There were, however, some that must be pointed out merely to indicate that even the comparatively little ship research then conducted was used. It is needless to repeat the overwhelming contributions of William Froude in the mid-nineteenth century. This was research of the most fundamental sort and surely convinced designers and shipowners alike of its great value.

Admiral David Taylor, in the first decade of this century, accomplished his famous investigations of systematically varied hull forms, and the results have been used and extended by the world's ship designers since. It was also during these investigations that he discovered the advantages of the bulbous protrusion at the lower forefoot of the ship. This bulb-type bow was immediately adopted, proven and consistently used since then on our larger, higher speed ships.

Research in the ship's structural material, progressing from iron to steel, has made possible the greatly increased size of ships. Research and study in propulsive devices, namely, the screw propeller, has contributed greatly to improved propulsive efficiencies. However, there was a comparatively slow and reluctant change in design before World War II, mainly because of the conservatism of shipbuilders and owners evidenced by their resistance to invest capital on the basis of untried ideas developing from research alone. This reluctance is difficult for progressive and impatient designers to understand. When viewed in the context of the experience existing then, it may be more understandable. The greatest disasters had occurred to ships that were the product of imaginative designers attempting to improve the product—the experiences of the *Great Eastern* and the *Titanic* were very vivid in the minds of the shipowners of that era.

In the ship design and shipbuilding world today, it is difficult to cite a single example of a modern vessel that is not substantially the result of, or does not include some major feature resulting from, research effort. To name only a few of the most obvious examples, we must note, first, nearly every modern warship. Since the Navy maintains the largest and most active ship research organization, it naturally follows that the vessels it builds are the embodiments of the fruits of its research efforts. This research is evident in their exterior configurations and in the complexities of all their subsystems. Without technological research and designers who share the resulting knowledge, the Navy would be merely duplicating the ships of World War II. The outstanding examples are the nuclear submarines, the supercarriers, the surface effects ships, and dynamically supported craft.

The modern supertankers, whose structures and configurations are less noticeably the result of research, universally employ the Inui bulbous bow or a similar variation. They are produced in shipyards utilizing the most revolutionary methods, which are largely the result of research. Their designers have, in most cases, oriented their designs toward the production requirements which frequently affect their hull form. In this connection, the Japanese have currently developed a new "flat flow" after body (see figure 9–10) for supertankers that appears to have totally acceptable hydrodynamic characteristics and has no complex curvature in the conventionally complex stern configuration. These supertankers are very economical to build.

It would be possible to continue for page after page listing examples of ship design resulting directly from research, but it need not be done for the sake of substantiating such an obvious and commonly accepted fact. However, it would be perhaps neglectful not to mention one triumph of research that has advanced and maintained this nation's prestige in a special world of marine design.

The Davidson Laboratory at the Stevens Institute in Hoboken has been involved, among many other things, in research in sailing yachts since the early 1930s. Their spectacular success in developing, through model testing research, successful defenders for the *America's* Cup races is quite well known. Not as well known, perhaps, is the impact that some of these 12-meter racing boats have had on the subsequent designs of nearly all ocean racing sailboats.

Unfortunately, some boat designers and builders lack somewhat the full appreciation of hydrodynamic design, and some of the features that became evident on several of these 70 foot, slim, racing 12-meter boats have shown up on a number of 25-foot day-cruising boats. It is of considerable interest to observe that the popularity of the separated rudder and keel fin on modern sailing boats, together with their proven efficiency, is an outgrowth of the research study carried on first at Stevens for *America's* Cup boats. Research continually goes forward in this special and fascinating part of naval architecture in the towing tanks at Stevens, M.I.T., and even in a limited way at the Naval Ship Research and Development Center. The hydrodynamic and aerodynamic forces involved in the varied conditions of sailing

Bell Aerospace Co., Division of Textron

Figure 9–9. A Designer-Artist Concept of an Intensive Research effort to develop a large, 2,000-ton surface-effect ship

pose some very interesting and also some in-soluble problems. The results of this research, as they slowly filter down to the designer, will ulti-mately become evident in new rigs, new materials, and improved underwater form in many types of vessels.

Research Trends

Probably the greatest amount of ship-oriented research is concerned with some aspect of hydro-dynamics. While hydrodynamics investigations have been conducted consistently since the work of Froude and have resulted in many interesting developments, researchers are most heavily influ-enced now by the changing operational require-ments of ships. It should be immediately added, of course, that these changing requirements influ-ence all areas of research as well.

One of the significant areas is in the study of propulsive devices. Of all the past and present devices that have been used and are being used, the marine screw propeller is the most versatile and is the most widely used. Yet with all of its successful applications, it still presents many troublesome characteristics. Its most serious prob-lem is that of cavitation, which is closely coupled

with high rotative speeds. This phenomenon has been discussed in other chapters in this book, particularly in chapter 6 and in connection with high-speed craft in chapter 15. However, there is a pressing demand currently for more efficient propellers in the low-speed range which has come about with the development of the large single screw supertankers.

To cite this problem briefly is to note first that the growing size of tankers has been accom-panied by a radical deterioration of propeller efficiency. The open water propeller efficiency for an 18,000 ton tanker is about 60 percent at 110 rpm; the corresponding efficiency at the same rpm for a 150,000 ton tanker is about 40 per-cent. This difference results from the fact that the larger vessel's propeller speed is relatively higher than the smaller vessel's, and according to Froude's law of comparison, the larger vessel should have a propeller speed of closer to 60 rpm to be comparable in efficiency. This lower speed means further reduction gear losses, or, with higher propeller loading because of increased power, a cavitation risk. This higher loading is also prevalent in the new, fast, single screw, dry cargo vessels. Obviously, a newer and better

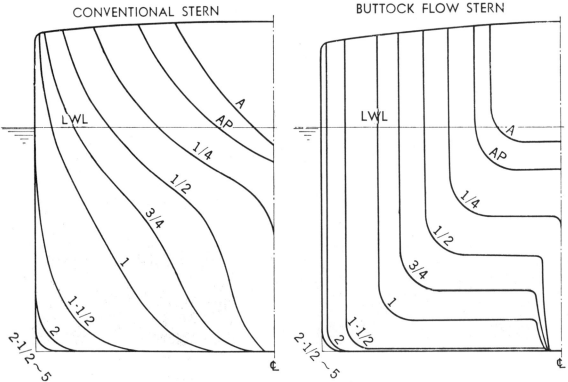

Figure 9–10. Conventional Stern (left) and Flat-Flow After Body (right).

marine propulsion system must be devised that still retains the practicability, ruggedness, and protectiveness of the single shaft propeller system with its greater hull efficiency. These basic but developing requirements have caused researchers to consider and to study the contra-rotating propeller system. The ducted propeller also (see chapter 6) has shown some promise for this application. However, the ideal solution has not yet been devised. There will be undoubtedly more single-shaft ships with low-speed contra-rotating propellers, even with their complex gearing. We may also expect to see more low-speed ducted propellers. See figure 9–7 (a).

The stimulation of deep-sea research has brought with it many hydrodynamic problems other than propulsive and speed problems. These will be covered in chapter 15. The sporadic funding for this type of research and associated submersible craft have created a confusing array of designs. Perhaps the most impressive example is the trend in ship research to adapt design to changing operational requirements.

The most persistent operational requirement, both now and in the past, and probably as far into the future as can be seen, is the demand for *better sustained speed in all weather conditions.*

This demand requires not only higher speed through the water, but also implies successful negotiation of bad weather conditions. This means essentially larger sea capable ships or a proliferation of smaller, specially designed ships (e.g., hydrofoil craft, SWATH's, etc.) which are able to move more efficiently at higher speeds. More and more, larger bulk cargo ships can satisfy some of the demand for volume transport. But other commerce on the sea and naval ship development will continue to call for faster ships. Through no fault of his own, the ship designer must sit in the shade of the statistics that show that commercial aircraft speeds have multiplied six-fold in this century while average ship speeds have hardly increased at all.

The ship designer has struggled against the formidable barrier of the wave-making phenomena of displacement ships for many decades with comparatively little success. It would now seem that the most promising and active fields of ship research are those that steer away from this impossible dream. To either submerge below or surmount the surface is the apparent direction for a more positive increase in seagoing speed, and in this direction, research is most promising.

The increased study of ship motions and sea state that complies with the requirements for increased all-weather operational ability is in progress.

Research will continue in systems analysis and control, subjects which are perhaps less glamorous than others but no less required as ships grow in automation, size, speed, and complexity. And, most significantly, it must not be overlooked that the ever-increasing use of computers will rejuvenate research progress that has stagnated because of the lack of previous data processing capabilities. For example, it is even now possible to numerically and graphically duplicate complex fluid-flow systems by computerized processes. This facility alone suggests a great number of possible applications to uncompleted investigations as well as new studies of boundary layer and turbulence problems.

With all of the technological possibilities existing and multiplying in modern usage, which includes rapid data processing and electronic instrumentation for data acquisition, the primary problem for the ship designer becomes one of knowledge assimilation. The role of the designer in this expanding and bulging science is rapidly crystallizing into that of restricted specialization. While he must know the processes and nature of overall design, his practice and his professional knowledge are forced, through the paper explosion of technical reports, toward limitations of individual competence. It may be sooner than we expect when only a handful of naval architects still exist who are capable and competent to design a whole, seagoing vessel.

**PHM-3, One of the U.S. Navy's new Pegasus Class Patrol Combatant Missile Ships (Hydrofoil)
in the Hangar while under Construction.**

CHAPTER 10

Shipbuilding Methods

Except for the brief period of mass-produced cargo ships and smaller craft during World War II in the United States, the process of shipbuilding has been traditional, methodical, and conservative. In most cases it was and still is a slow, laborious, and very expensive process. For custom-built or one-of-a-kind ships with complex systems, such as naval vessels, the construction process requires upwards of two or three years.

In today's technology, this consumption of time, use of skilled labor, and employment of expensive facilities is nearly prohibitive. In order to properly describe and appreciate modern, evolving shipbuilding methods, it is of some value to briefly describe the classical and traditional approach, used in the past and even, in some places, still in use here and abroad.

The Older Method

During the latter stages of the design process and after the building contracts have been signed, the shipyard begins the building process with the most fundamental elements of the design—the lines drawing and the table of offsets. This beginning proceeds, of course, simultaneously with many contributing activities, such as the structural plan study, equipment lists, etc., together with the ordering of steel and other required materials.

The lines of the ship are lofted full size in the mold loft (see figure 14–2); intermediate stations, bulkheads, and frames are located on the lofting and patterns are made; a shell expansion plan is made (often with help of a large half-model of the hull called a plating model); and the building and launching ways are prepared. It is literally some months before the keel is actually laid, and the ship's structure begins to be evident. Together with the slow growth of this structure is the necessary construction and growth of the surrounding cradle and scaffolding which nearly hides the ship itself.

During the early part of this century, when steel welding techniques were being expanded, welded ships soon proved stronger and more economical. However, because of the necessity of welding downward, that is, on top of the material being joined, it was necessary to prefabricate large sections of the ship's bottom before placing them in position. This practice led soon, and was stimulated by the mass production requirements during World War II, to large subassemblies. The modern practice of building ships sectionally in large subassemblies was here begun. Its application was largely restricted to ships of a single design in series. The extensions and variations of this system, together with automated and computer-directed tools, are the basic ingredients of the most advanced methods of shipbuilding today.

Economic Impact on Building Methods

Before describing in more detail the contemporary shipbuilding techniques, it is better at this point to explain briefly some causes for wide variation in shipbuilding methods today and to note that while some shipyards are highly automated and streamlined, others employ interesting composites between automated methods and the traditional employment of skilled labor. Still others appear to have made very few concessions to modern technology.

The explanation for this lack of conformity lies almost wholly in the realm of economics and basic shipyard capacities. Briefly and simply, the most elemental economic factor is the desire and ability to offer a continuing supply of ships at the most competitive price. It is no obscure economic law that recognizes the advantages of production in multiple-identical units, and this law applies very nicely to ships. However, with ships being as they are of diverse types and applications as well as of extremely high unit cost, there is introduced a restriction to mass production techniques, and shipyards must choose between the advantages of diversification on one hand an specialization on the other.

Graphically, a very simple chart may explain this situation, which exists not only in the shipbuilding industry but also in most industrial enterprises. Note in figure 10–1 that the cost-production curve is very nearly hyperbolic but that the tendency is clear at some production quantity for the cost to level off and become more or less fixed. If this simple comparative analysis were applied to ships of various sizes and types, the result would be more accurate if it reflected

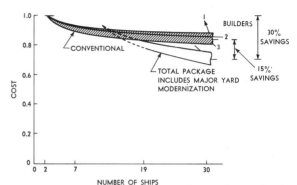

Figure 10–2. Typical Acquisition Costs—Conventional Versus Total Package Procurement

an envelope or range of variables as in figure 10–1. Near the upper edge of the envelope would, of course, be the more complex types of ships, such as warships, passenger vessels, and special purpose craft. The lower limits would characterize the costs of the simpler bulk cargo carriers and traditional, simply finished working craft.

A shipbuilder must decide, based on this type of analysis, at what point his operation can survive financially. In the labyrinths of cost analysis, he will undoubtedly find frustration when he must compare the amortization costs of automatic computer-tape operated plate-cutting machines with labor costs of cutting torch operators, or, on the other hand, the expansion costs of numerous subassembly shops compared to the occupation time of a dock by a ship and the cost of a large building dock or expensive building ways. Solutions of such problems are mostly transitory and depend upon estimates of future units to be built. These decisions do require the involvement of the ship designers and naval architects, even down to the hydrodynamic analysis of ship forms. It is not intended here to delve further into economic factors, nor has the time yet arrived when the designer is required, in addition to his other talents, to be a professional economist as well. However, it may be of interest to cite several examples of modern shipyards, compare their methods, and examine briefly their technical means of dealing with common economic problems.

Developing Newer Methods

Probably the most interesting of the world's shipyards as well as the first to develop advanced techniques of automation and subassemblies is the Arendal (Sweden) yard of the Götaverken

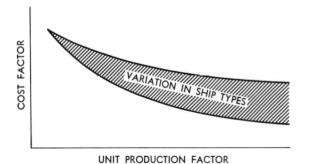

Figure 10–1. Cost Versus Quantity

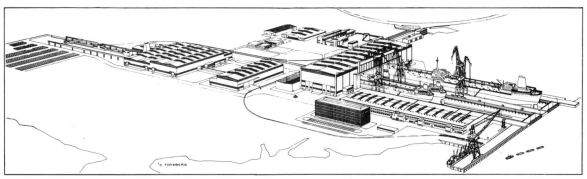

Figure 10–3. Götaverken's Arendal Yard. This uniquely planned shipyard has had a considerable impact on shipbuilding methods throughout the world.

Industries. The industrial group owning and operating the shipyards of Götaverken is a heavy industry complex whose industrial activities include diversifications from paint manufacture to bridge building. Such involvement is not a distractive handicap where shipbuilding is involved, for it means control over the great variety of services and equipment required in most ships. Also, Götaverken Industries has always been basically and historically involved in the operation of traditional shipbuilding and repair yards.

It was therefore of considerable interest when, in 1962, Götaverken Industries embarked on a most revolutionary system for the construction of the largest of ships. This new shipyard was not the reconstitution of an old and established site but was literally carved out of the solid rock and ground in a new and undeveloped area remote from the shipbuilding centers of Gothenburg, Sweden. The construction system which formed the basis of this new yard's revolutionary approach is the "straight through" assembly line coupled with optimum automation.

By referring to figure 10–3, showing a perspective view of the yard, it can be seen that the launching docks where the new and finished ships emerge are at the end of a long line of shops and an assembly hall which is at the inboard end of the docks. The plates and structural bars begin their journey from the storage yard at the opposite end of the shipyard, where they are picked up by very large straddle-lifts with magnetic pickups. The material moves first into the shot-blasting plant where it is cleaned, and continues on to the painting and marking shops while always being handled, sorted, and processed automatically. The direction of the plates and

structural shapes from these shops is controlled further by the plate shop boss who is isolated in a strategic control room with a number of closed circuit television viewing screens and a multiplicity of selector controls with which he can observe as well as direct the progress of the material. In the plate shop, the plate material is automatically

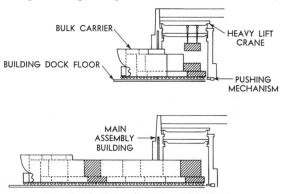

Figure 10–4. Application of the Block System in Shipbuilding

cut to shape, and where bending or pressing is required to produce the three-dimensional shape necessary in the ships hull, the plates are formed in gigantic presses with capacities of 2000 tons. From the plate shop, the material is moved on conveyors to the welding shop where the subassemblies take shape.

The routine and straight welding is done by machine and, uniquely in Sweden, a "one side" through-weld has been developed which reduces the welding time to nearly half of that of previous methods. The small assemblies are joined to larger assemblies, creating large and recognizable portions of the ship. These large subassemblies are completed internally with all compartmentation, piping systems, and furnishings (except for the main propulsion engines) at this stage which accounts for the minimal fitting-out time after launching (only eight days to two weeks). Beginning with the stern section first, these large subassemblies are lowered into place at the end of the building dock, which extends into the assembly hall and is completely sealed off from the weather. As further assemblies are completed and attached, the ship is allowed to "grow" by moving the completed portion out of the assembly hall along ways in the bottom of the dock. This process is accomplished by large hydraulic rams which push the ship along the building dock in increments, moving it periodically about 60 to 80 feet every two or three days.

The end sections of the ship, being more complex because of the ship's form, steering and rudder gear, and equipment and furnishings, consequently require more working time. These sections are therefore in the assembly hall for longer periods than the sections of the long, parallel middle body. The entire process, however, from the beginning of a large tanker until its final completion and sea trials, takes some 19 to 20 weeks. This is about half of the time required by conventional shipbuilding methods using twice the amount of labor.

Arendal Shipyard's approach to the problem of economic shipbuilding and survival in the very competitive world shipbuilding market is unique.

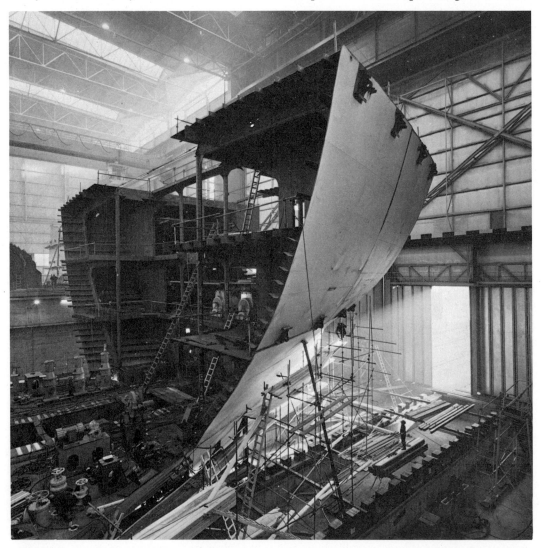

Courtesy of Götaverken Shipyard

Figure 10–5. Götaverken (Arendal Yard) Assembly Hall

They have planned and created a shipyard and building process where all other considerations are subordinated to the overriding purpose of establishing a straight-flow production line with a high degree of automation and with all phases of construction carried out indoors. This was achieved in Sweden with an investment of about $37 million from 1959 to 1961.

It is interesting to note that the Swedish shipbuilders of Arendal have made no compromise with the shape and form of the ships they build. While it is true that the efficient function of the yard depends on specialization in large tankers and bulk carriers built in series, it is also possible to apply the same principles to other types where a series of identical hulls is ordered. The system has been explored and considered by the Naval Ship Systems Command of the Navy Department, particularly in connection with the building program for the contemplated FDLs (Fast Deployment Logistics Ships).

It is interesting in a contrasting light to note how other leading shipbuilding nations in Europe have coped with the same problem of mounting labor costs to provide large ships more efficiently built. In every other case where there is a serious attempt to reduce costs or maintain them at competitive levels, the attempted solution lies in the design of the ship's hull itself.

For example, first of interest might be the product of the large industrial and shipbuilding complex of Burmeister and Wain of Denmark. This shipyard, which is operated by one of the largest and most progressive industries in Scandinavia, has developed a hull configuration that is adaptable to computerization as well as less complex fabricating techniques. This hull configuration for large tankers contains a minimum of curvature and eliminates altogether complex curvature. The curved surfaces that do exist in the bow and stern sections and along the turn of the bilge are all developable surfaces (capable of being rolled out flat), being portions of cylindrical or conic surfaces. Such a surface is clearly evident in figure 10–6, which shows the upper flaring bow of a 80,000-ton tanker.

Figure 10–6. Bow of Burmeister and Wain Tanker in Building Dock. The elements of the forward portion of this ship show, through the use of conic and cylindrical surfaces for ease in bending, the effect of computerized design for simplification in construction.

The plating of the subassemblies of these curved sections does not require any heating or difficult pressing to be shaped. For many of the sections, the plating is simply placed on a grid of pedestal-like spindles whose contact points have been pre-positioned by computer to conform to the hull lines, and the plates assume their curvature then under the forces of gravity and are welded together and joined to the structural frame in this position. (Japanese shipyards employ a very similar technique in this type of assembly.)

Using such basic geometric surfaces of curvature as the cone and cylinder together with the computerized position allows automatic welding, something that was once considered impossible.

The Burmeister and Wain shipyard is a versatile shipyard and does not, of course, confine its building to this one type of ship. However, the current design solutions are quite naturally developing building techniques that are adaptable and effective only where a series of similar or identical ships are built and where assembly line and multiple unit fabrication can force costs down along the decline of the curve introduced in figure 10–1. The Burmeister and Wain yard has accordingly developed another special ship-type which enjoys considerable popularity, particularly in the Soviet Union. The fish-factory ship, designed by Burmeister and Wain together with the ship's Russian owners, is a most effective and complex ship system. This particular ship is nearly 6,000 tons in displacement, about 340 feet in length, and 52 feet in beam. She is propelled by diesel engines of 3500 horsepower with a speed of about 14 knots. The ship is able, by modern stern-trawling methods, to catch and process completely some 2500 tons of fish. Such ships not only clean and process the edible portion of fish, but also convert scraps to fish meal and fish livers to valuable oil. In addition, the complex communication gear, together with capabilities for 60-day cruises, make these ships most useful instruments for the Soviet intelligence network as well as for oceanographic research. Burmeister and Wain have delivered over 25 of these ships at this writing, and under series assembly-production

Figure 10–7. Soviet Stern Trawler Factory Ship Under Construction. This ship, for the most part, was built in block sections or large subassemblies indoors in a gigantic assembly hall. It was then assembled and occupied the building dock shown here for only two weeks before launching.

methods, the assembly process in the building dock requires only two weeks. (See figure 10–7.)

The final assembly process of ships in the Burmeister and Wain building dock is similar to that of most modern shipyards and differs from the *extrusion* method developed by Götaverken Arendal yard mainly by in-place block assembly through the use of a great rolling gantry crane capable of handling subassembly sections of blocks up to 600 tons. Two large assembly shops are located at the head of an 800 foot long building dock, similar to that of Arendal, where the block subassembly sections are completed indoors, but instead of joining them together within this enclosure, they are picked up by the huge gantry and rolled out over the dock and lowered into position for in-place joining. This method is also used in many Swedish, German, and Japanese yards and is the keynote to the comparatively brief occupancy of the building dock and the resultant efficient use of space and time.

The ultimate in the subordination of hull configuration to construction simplicity is the *Pioneer multi-carrier system* developed by the Blohm and Voss Shipbuilding Yard in Hamburg. This old and versatile yard, which has built such famous ships as the great battleship *Bismarck* of World War II, has developed a cargo ship of multiple, flat surfaces. The hull shape consists exclusively of flat, polygonal and partly congruent plates set together at diverse angles, resulting in a polyhedron whole. (See figure 10–8.) While this ship as a system is described more fully elsewhere the brief discussion here deals only with the justification of its form for construction.

It is not entirely fair to describe the Blohm and Voss *Pioneer* ship's unique shape and other unorthodox features as being solely adapted for ease of construction. Actually, that is undoubtedly of primary consideration, but the entire ship system is of far broader interest and application. The ship is a variable assembly of optional modular units, with the bow and stern sections being more or less standardized. The sections of the parallel middle body are basically rectangular in all directions except for the inclined (45 degrees) surface at the bilge. These modular sections are prefitted for either general cargo, bulk cargo, container pallets, or convertible general/bulk cargo. The size of the ship can be varied by using different numbers of parallel middle body units. By using four units, the deadweight tonnage can be increased to 24,750 tons. The primary saving in a ship of this distinctive type is in the elimination of both complex and simple curvature of frames and plates, elements that require special machinery, highly skilled labor, and much additional time. Blohm and Voss argue that the minor differences in hydrodynamic efficiency and powering are far less significant than the saving in construction and the operational savings in the ship's adaptability. Also, they point out that one of the smaller variants can be increased in size to a larger variant in minimum time at minimum expense. The change takes about five days.

In these three different methods described, i.e., the Arendal system, the Burmeister and Wain system, and the Blohm and Voss multi-unit polyhedron, there is a common factor of approach, one that is so basic to industrial production that it is surprising that it was not used in steel shipbuilding from the beginning. This factor stems from the incontestable fact that the labor required to build a ship is of a great multiplicity and diversity of skills. To build most efficiently, then, these skills must be employed on a continuous time schedule with all skills employed simultaneously. The integration of production also requires a straight-line work flow, and this is being slowly achieved or planned in the most modern shipyards. It is of lesser consequence whether the ship erection is accomplished by the Arendal extrusion method or the more common in-place method.

There is another noteworthy shipbuilding operation in Sweden which has perhaps been overshadowed by the unique Arendal system, and that is the Kockums Shipyard at Malmö. The Kockums yard is capable of building ships over 200,000 tons (dwt). The efficiency of this yard derives from its automated plate and shape processing as well as its straight-line production system. This yard also employs mechanical rollers for the movement of material as well as automatic cutting and welding in small subassemblies and large structural beams. The building and erection dock is served by a very large gantry capable of handling assembly sections up to 800 tons.

Much of the flexibility inherent in these Swedish shipyards has proven attractive to other shipyards particularly in Germany, Denmark, France, and Japan.

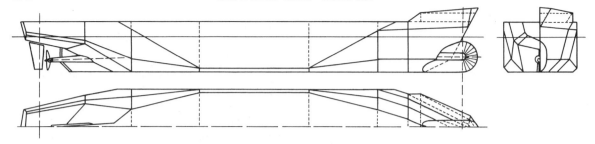

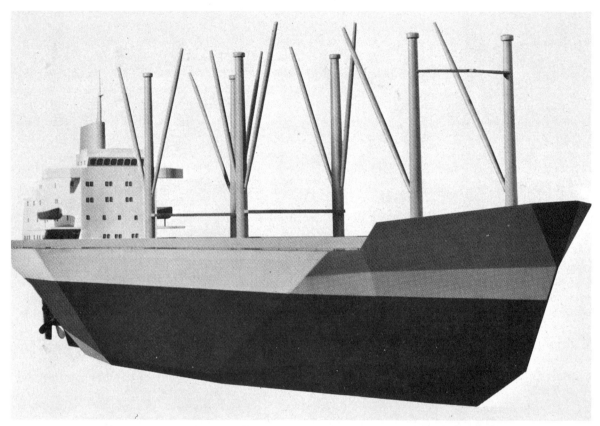

Courtesy of Blohm & Voss

Figure 10–8. A new construction technique is evident in these drawings depicting the flat surfaces of the hulls, which consist exclusively of flat, polygonal, and partly congruent plates set together at angles. This technique dispenses with the use of shaped plates with a curved profile and results in ships with no sheer, camber, or rise of floor.

Shipbuilding in the United States

At this point, the position of the United States in the modern shipbuilding picture is of interest. Undoubtedly, this is a source of concern in many ways; however, it is not a cause for despair. The labor skills and industrial know-how of America have shone as brightly in the world of shipbuilding as in any other industrial capacity. In recent years, U.S. shipyards have produced such great sea-going ship systems as the nuclear aircraft carrier *Enterprise* and the many complex and efficient nuclear submarines, particularly the fleet of *Polaris Missile* subs. These are shipbuilding achievements not even approached elsewhere. It is unnecessary to mention further examples to make the point that this is a nation of builders of especially complex ships, custom made, where series building is not economically advisable or demanded.

The shipyards of the United States, both government and privately owned, have essentially only one substantial customer—the government.

Figure 10–9. U.S. Navy Destroyer Escort Being Built Upside Down to Allow Downhand Welding. The hull takes shape (top), being formed with longitudinal hull members of structural carbon steel Ts. After assembly, the hull is rotated to an upright position in giant turning rings (bottom). Then prefabricated bow, stern, and superstructure sections are installed, along with most engineering machinery. This assembly line system allows a launch rate of one ship every seven weeks.

There is little question that such a situation does not promote a healthy, competitive, and diversified atmosphere in shipbuilding circles. In addition, the trend seems to be a continued decline in the number of U.S.-built merchant ships (only 13 in one recent year) and a continued rise in the number of U.S. naval vessels. This rise in naval vessels is principally a result of the normal replacement of World War II ships, and to reflect it quantitatively over the 10 years from 1957 to 1967, the number increased steadily from 275,000 tons per year to 750,000 tons per year, or about 60 ships per year to 150 per year.

It is considered noteworthy to mention these statistics because of the impact that naval shipbuilding has had upon the overall shipbuilding industry and shipbuilding methods.

The Navy, recognizing that its procurement practices (see chapter 13) directly affected both the nature of the producing shipyard's and the immediate costs of the ships built, has adopted techniques to encourage plant investment and develop the economies in construction that result from series production of single-design ships. The three techniques intended for shipbuilding stimulation—multi-year procurement, contract definition and total package procurement (discussed in chapter 13)—are providing stimulus to the conversion of shipbuilding yards and the establishment of completely new yards.

Courtesy of Hitachi Zosen

**Figure 10–10. Aerial View of Sakai Shipyard in Osaka. The large gantry cranes in this yard
are typical and indicate the use of block building techniques.**

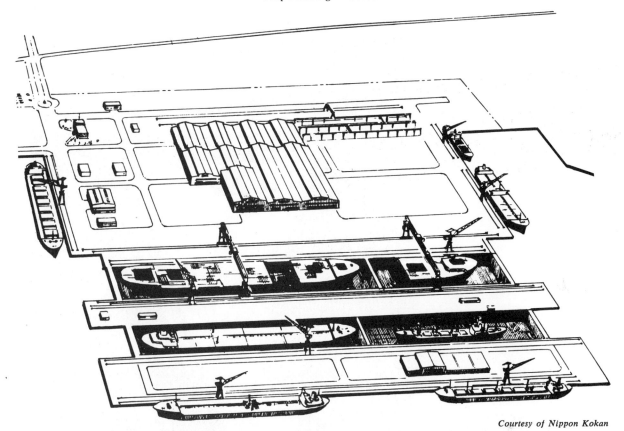

Courtesy of Nippon Kokan

Figure 10–11. The New Three-sided Building Dock Arrangement Developed in Japan

Courtesy of Newport News Shipbuilding & Dry Dock Company

**Figure 10–12. Newport News Shipbuilding Company's Steel Handling and Fabricating Facility.
This overhead photograph shows the progressive development of the largest and one of the
oldest U.S. yards. Note the automated plate-handling facilities from the plate storage yard in
the foreground. This is the first step in automated ship production.**

Courtesy of Newport News Shipbuilding & Dry Dock Company

Perhaps the largest and most versatile established shipyard in the United States is the Newport News Shipbuilding and Drydock Company at Newport News, Virginia. It is most natural that this yard is quick to respond to the progressive needs of the Navy as well as the shipbuilding industry. Recognizing the early need for maximum automation consistent with the flexibility of ship types, Newport News gave first attention in modernization to the steel flow process, from storage yard, through surface preparation, layout, cutting, and forming to the subassembly shop.

These early stages in the process of shipbuilding are much the same regardless of ship type. Up to the subassembly stage, the process is similar, with some variations in automation techniques, to those described in previous discussions of modern Swedish yards. Because of the required versatility and variations in design, no advantage can be taken of repetitive processes with forms, tooling, and personnel specialization beyond the simple subassemblies' modules. However, in the building of destroyer escorts and other particular types in the multi-year procurement plan, the

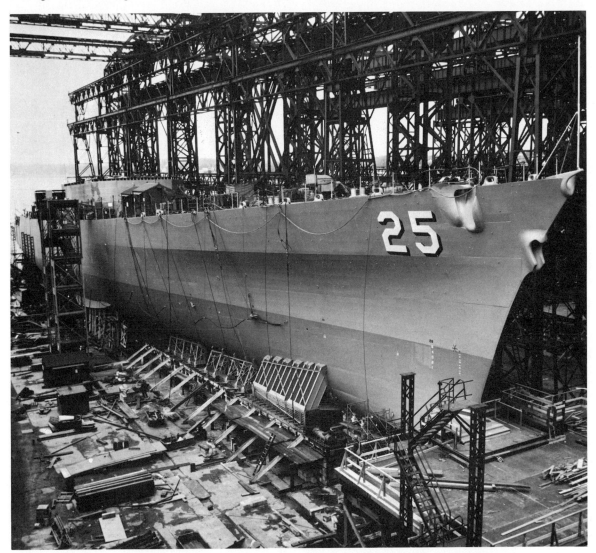

Courtesy of Newport News Shipbuilding & Dry Dock Company

Figure 10–13. USS Bainbridge (DLG-25) Undergoing Construction—Bow Subassembly (opposite page) and Nearly Ready for Launching (above). This type of vessel is custom built and does not lend itself to mass production. However, vessels such as this can be adapted to modular construction techniques.

maximum advantages of series production will be in the expanded bays of the new fabrication shops covering over six acres of land.

To fully exploit the advantages of assembly line techniques and series production, it is necessary to admit the necessity of a certain degree of specialization. Assembly line procedures become most difficult to adapt to established yards whose physical shape and dimensions are fixed. It is necessary, as it was by Götaverken in Arendal, Sweden, and by Litton Industries (owners of Ingalls Shipbuilding Corporation in Mississippi), to move to new and undeveloped real estate and construct entirely new shipyards.

The new shipyard facility undertaken by Litton Industries in Pascagoula, Mississippi, represents a typical example of the motivation toward shipyard modernization and renewal in the United

States inspired both by the procurement practices of the Navy Department and the developing techniques requiring optimum automation and assembly line processes. Although Litton's action represented a corporate decision independent of any contract commitment with the Navy, the layout suggests planning in terms of multi-year procurement.

The Litton yard is highly mechanized and, as can be seen in figure 10–14, is also unique in its layout. In scope of output, it surpasses all of the most modern foreign yards both in its capacity to build ships of virtually unlimited length and width as well as in the number of ships under construction.

There are a considerable number of other American shipyards that are undergoing or have undergone substantial modernization in response

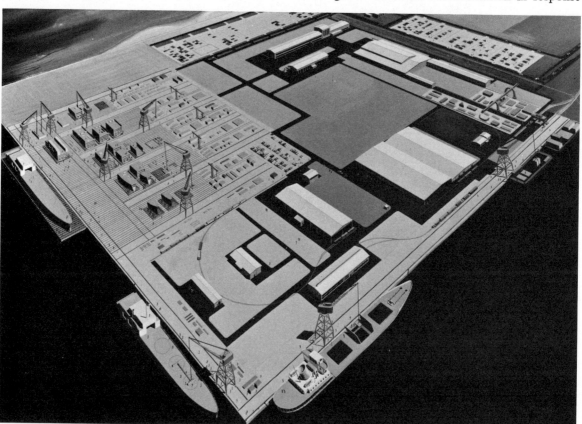

Courtesy of Ingalls Shipbuilding Division of Litton Industries

Figure 10–14. New Ingalls Shipyard. This drawing shows the subassembly, module assembly, and ship assembly areas of this modern shipyard. It is in these areas that the structurally complete panels and shell assemblies are brought together to form the nearly completed vessel. This method of ship assembly replaces the traditional method of fixed way erection and allows ships to be 90 percent completed prior to launching, compared to 68 percent completed with traditional methods.

Figure 10-15. "Production Line Destroyer." The new, high-performance destroyers (963 class)
are built near subassembly plattens and moved on sliding cradles to the launching pontoon,
as shown above at Ingalls Shipyard, Pascagoula, Miss.

to the developing techniques. In addition to those mentioned above, there is Avondale Shippards, Inc., of New Orleans, which is able to utilize production techniques in the series building of destroyer escort ships. Avondale's system is unique in that it is applying a technique formerly employed in building much smaller craft; it is essentially that of building the hull in an inverted position. By means of ingenious hydraulic mechanisms, the hull is rotated to its upright position for internal completion and launching. This method of construction requires a capital investment for the tooling of special jigs (construction forms) and other equipment for rotating the hull. Although welding downward seems the primary advantage, the builders are convinced that the economics of constructing a convoluted structure in an inverted position on a volume basis justifies such capital investment. Automated plate-cutting and handling have also been introduced by this company.

National Steel and Shipbuilding Company of San Diego is equipped for series production of LST-type ships and incorporates straight-line production together with improved steel handling and automated cutting.

It is not the intention here to review the modernization practices of all shipyards but only to mention in a few specific cases the efforts that have been undertaken necessarily to accommodate the new techniques available that have resulted from the economic pressures imposed.

In all of these efforts which blend a mix of the yard layouts and techniques devised by the individual yards and borrowed from earlier modernizations in Europe, the ideal shipbuilding yard has not yet been built and perhaps never will be built. In the first place, flexibility and diversification have been emphasized in some yards, while specialization has been made the primary factor in others. Some yards must retain the skills and facilities to build complex, one-of-a-kind ships. However, long-range planning, such as that stimulated by the Navy, can provide, within the framework of multi-year procurement, the advantages of series building even on such large and complex ships as nuclear carriers.

On the other hand, it is interesting to contemplate the so-called "ideal" shipyard plan. It would undoubtedly be a composite of the best features of the more advanced yards. In the most sketchy and simple diagrammatic plan it might have a sequential layout as shown in figure 10–16. Here the plate storage and handling of Arendal are used with their efficient mechanized gantry and roller movement into and through the plants for straightening, blasting, painting, and automatic marking. The second processing sequence is the automated cutting and forming and the small subassemblies adopted from Kockums in Sweden —also similar to Arendal. The third processing area is a composite, largely similar to Arendal, but because of the block extrusion used there (with its special and added complexity of stacking), it is suggested that advantages of large subassembly buildings such as those of Burmeister

and Wain be employed with their large traveling gantries. The lifting capacities of these gantries must be adapted to the yard's requirements, but for economical employment, they should be limited to something no greater than 600 tons in serving the building dock. A large outfitting plant with easy land transportation access should be adjacent to the building dock area and along the fitting-out pier area. It is advisable that ships built according to modern plans such as this

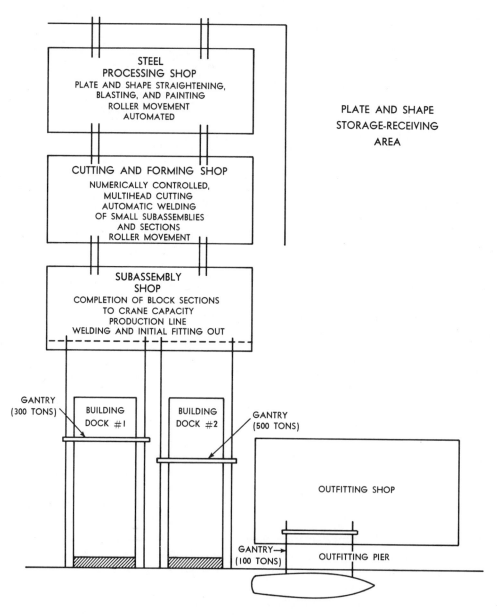

Figure 10–16. A Model Shipyard

Courtesy of General Dynamics

Figure 10–17. Automatic Plate Cutting. An operator sets up an automatic burning machine that cuts steel plates into desired shapes with much more speed and accuracy than hand torches. This machine can be operated by manual, optical, or computerized tape control. The cutting of plates is the initial major step in the fabrication of units.

should be launched when they are at least 90 to 95 percent complete, requiring the minimum of time at the fitting-out pier. (At the Arendal yard fitting out requires only about eight days.)

It is interesting to note that although sub-assembly techniques and production lines are a most important key to modern shipbuilding, they are not at all new to the ship construction process. The following is excerpted from the account of

and observer of the construction of Venetian war galleys by the Old Arsenal of Venice in 1436:

And as one enters the gate there is a great street on either hand with the sea in the middle, and on one side are windows opening out of the houses of the arsenal, and the same on the other side, and out came a galley towed by a boat, and from the windows they handed out to them from one the cordage, from another the bread, from

Figure 10–18. Double Welding. One of the latest developments in ship-welding equipment is this dual fillet welder, an improved adaptation of a Swedish original, which can weld both sides of longitudinal stiffeners to steel plate at a minimum rate of 1200 feet per day—four times the speed of hand welding.

another the arms, and from another the balistas and mortars, and so from all sides everything which was required, and when the galley had reached the end of the street all the men required were on board, together with the complement of oars, and she was equipped from end to end. In this manner there came out ten galleys, fully armed, between the hours of three and nine.*

In 1560, two new arsenals were added whereby the ships progressed from a multiple number of building dry docks, through rigging areas, armament shops, and fitting-out areas to completion in sail-away condition.

This was modern shipbuilding 500 years ago.

*Frederic C. Lane, *Venetian Ships and Shipbuilders of the Renaissance* (Baltimore: Johns Hopkins Press, 1934).

Courtesy of General Dynamics

Figure 10–19. Preoutfitting Construction Technique. In eight days' time, four keel sections, including the extensively pre-outfitted section in the foreground, were laid down for the Kansas City (AOR-3).

Courtesy of General Dynamics

Figure 10–20. The Kansas City Five Weeks After the Laying of the Keel. Several pre-outfitted and standard units have been put down.

Official U.S. Coast Guard Photograph

USCGC Taney Heading Seaward Over the San Francisco Bar

CHAPTER 11

Living with the Sea — The Strength and Structure of Ships

Strength

The structure of a ship must assume the configuration which is demanded by the physical requirements of hydrodynamics together with the man-made rules of measurements and dimensional limitations conforming to its purpose. In addition, and of such importance that it is the only phase of design not subject to compromise, the ship's structure must have sufficient built-in strength to withstand its anticipated loads. This inference of *no compromise* and *anticipated loads* is a design problem that admittedly must be treated with maximum rigor and seriousness, but at the same time is of an indeterminate nature.

The loads which are referred to are, of course, the static loads of the weights of cargo, machinery, and structure as well as the buoyant forces of the water. The loads further to be considered in design, because a ship is a free body and mobile unit, are the almost innumerable dynamic loads of the elementary sea that is the habitat of ships.

It is these loads, both internal and external, that result among other things in sudden impact forces, vibrations of propellers and machinery, fatigue from repeated bending, and many other phenomena that try ships' structures. It is largely these dynamic loads, as well as many static loads, that are the indeterminate factors—for who is able to say how large will be the waves encountered in some storm seas yet to happen?

At present, the approach to structural design is considerably enhanced by extended research into the effects of sea conditions together with the analytical facilities of electronic computers which are giving answers to complex questions heretofore not probed.

It will be well for the purpose of this treatment, as an introduction to the design problems in strength, to approach ship strength by the traditional route and methods that have long been used and are still the basis of structural design. The more recent applications of strength studies will be then considered as extensions of the processes described.

It will be most useful, before entering the discussions on ship strength, to review certain terms, nomenclature, and fundamental concepts that are a part of the study of strength of materials and that have applications to the strength of ships. The following are concepts in common use.

Stress. Stress is the force applied per unit area of material and is expressed in pounds or tons per square inch. Stresses are basically described under the following three categories:

1. *Tension* or tensile stress is the result of colinear forces acting in opposite directions tending to stretch the material.
2. *Compression* or compressive stress results when the colinear forces described immedi-

205

ately above move toward each other and tend to compact the material.

3. *Shear stress* results when two forces acting in opposite directions are not colinear but are resolved only in parallel lines.

Strain. Strain is the distortion (deformation per unit length) resulting from stress and is usually expressed in inches/inch. It includes distortion both up to the elastic limit and beyond through permanent distortion to the breaking point.

Load. Load, when applied to strength considerations, is the summation of all the forces acting on the member in question or the summation of these forces for any unit length.

Modulus of Elasticity. Modulus of elasticity refers to the stiffness or rigidity of a material and is defined as stress per unit of strain.

Bending Moment. A force acting at a distance from a designated location is, of course, a moment of force about that point. When acting on a bar or beam or other such member tending to produce a strain, it is said to be a *bending moment*. For example, the bending moment on a uniform cantilever beam would be the weight of the beam multiplied by its length from the point of support divided by two, or $M = \dfrac{WL}{2}$. In the case of such a beam supporting various weights, the total bending moment would be the summation of all the moments acting on the beam measured from the point of support. (This simplified example does not adequately describe the concept of the ship's *total* bending moment, but this variation will be developed later in the chapter.)

Neutral Axis. A beam of finite cross-section, when subjected to a bending moment, has a plane

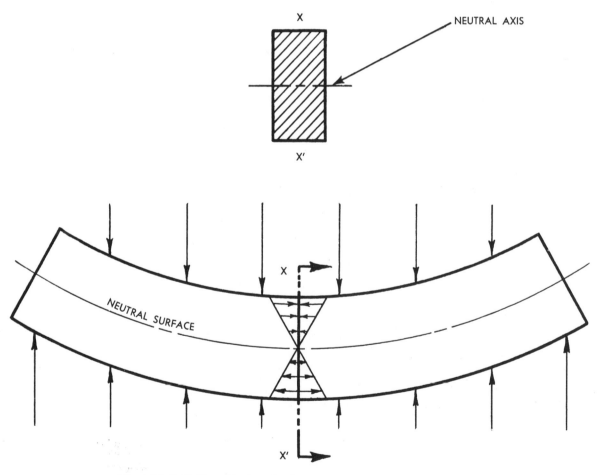

Figure 11-1. Uniform Rectangular Beam Under Simple Bending Moment

or surface of demarcation somewhere within it on one side of which the fibers are in tension and the other side of which they are in compression. At any transverse section through the beam, the line of this surface of demarcation is normally referred to as the *neutral axis*. Consider a beam of rectangular section supported horizontally in such a way that the supporting forces in the middle portion of the beam are less than the gravitational forces. It is thus subjected to a bending moment and will tend to assume the shape shown in figure 11–1. Under these circumstances, the neutral surface and neutral axis is halfway between the upper and lower surfaces of the beam above which the fibers are in compression and below which they are in tension. Upon further examination, the stresses of tension and compression increase in intensity with their distance from the neutral axis. (The actual variation of this intensity is the key to the primary problems of longitudinal ship strength and will be considered quantitatively in the subsequent discussion.)

From the example cited above, it would seem that in a beam subjected to this bending moment there will be a stress tending to elongate the material below the neutral axis where the fibers are in tension. Above the neutral axis, the compressive stresses will have a tendency to shorten the beam. Consequently, there is another stress to consider at the neutral axis. This stress, which is a *shear stress,* results from the parallel but opposite forces above and below. (See figure 11–2.) Where the area of the beam section is not uniform but is variable, the neutral axis will be proportionately closer to the portion of the beam with the greater sectional area. In any case, as noted above, the greater stresses occur farther

from the neutral axis. This would naturally suggest a beam section, such as an **I** beam, where the greater sectional area is concentrated farthest from the neutral axis. In the case of the **I** beam where the upper and lower flanges are identical to a uniform web (i.e., they are symmetrical), the neutral axis is still halfway between the top and bottom. However, where the upper flange is greater than the lower flange or vice versa, the neutral axis will, as noted above, be closer to the greater flange, the distance being inversely proportional to the distribution of area.

Section Modulus. It can be seen from the above that the stiffness of a beam or its resistance to bending is a function not only of its cross-sectional area but also of the distance that area is from the neutral axis. This characteristic, then, might be expressed as a resisting moment. It will be found that, for general purposes, the expression becomes a function of the moment of inertia of the section about its neutral axis. It is expressed as I/y, where I is the moment of inertia of the section about the neutral axis and y is the extreme distance from the neutral axis. This ratio is generally referred to as the *section modulus* and can be used as a reference criterion for beams or girders in comparing their resistance to bending.

BEAM STRENGTH

When a force or a system of forces is imposed upon a beam or girder resulting in a bending moment, the beam will bend or tend to bend an amount that depends upon the magnitude of the bending moment. The actual distortion or strain reaches its limit when the bending moment is opposed by a resisting moment of the same

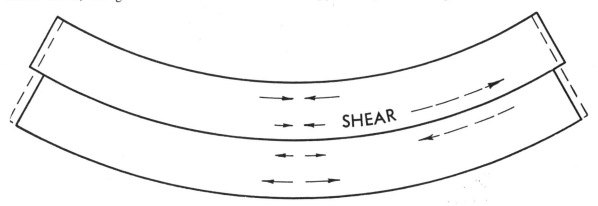

Figure 11–2. Stresses Above and Below Neutral Axis Producing Horizontal Shear

amount. In other words, the limit is reached when a condition of equilibrium has been established. In the foregoing section, the geometric relationship that expressed the resistance to bending was expressed as the section modulus, I/y.

This expression does not account for the physical properties of the material involved but only the geometrical distribution of the material. The complete expression for resistance to a bending moment, therefore, must include the unit fiber stress ($f = \text{lbs/in}^2$). Accordingly, then, we may state the classic equation for flexure used in every treatment of the strength of materials and applicable to the ship's structure as

$$M = \frac{I}{y} f$$

or in terms of stress intensity

$$f = \frac{M y}{I}$$

where f = stress intensity (compression or tension), stated by lbs/in²; lbs/ft²

  M = longitudinal bending moment at any section, stated by in.lbs.; ft.lbs.

  y = distance of f from the neutral axis, stated by in.; ft.

  I = moment of inertia of section about neutral axis, stated by in⁴; ft⁴.

SHIP STRENGTH AND THE BEAM THEORY

The *beam theory* assumes that a ship, for purposes of strength considerations, may be likened to a hollow, nearly rectangular girder. Basically, the comparison is correct. Assuming, first, a continuity of the material structure and, second, the known distribution of forces, it is possible to make calculations for the strength of such a beam of known cross-section regardless of size. However, because of the complexity of the ship's structure, the discontinuity of various members, the variations in fastenings (rivets and welding), the openings in the hull, the dynamic loads as well as complex static loads imposed, to cite but a few of the discrepancies, the simple beam theory becomes a rather general, instead of an exact, criterion. This is not to say, on the other hand, that it is of little value. The beam theory is a primary tool used in ship design, and, in all cases of structural damage, it should be the basic

relationship employed in analyzing any reduction in structural strength and should be the basic guide in considering restorative measures.

In spite of the details where discrepancies may be involved, the more important consideration is that the beam theory has produced a reliable basis from which an analysis may be made. It is a universally used approach and hence provides a standard from which strength calculations may be made, and the results may be analyzed and compared.

STRUCTURAL STRESSES WITHIN A SHIP

The foregoing section has emphasized the likeness of a ship to a single structural beam. This is, in fact, a basic premise in ship strength calculation; however, because of the complexity of structure and the forces imposed, all of the stresses of the ship's structure must be accounted for in the design in order to check the adequacy of the ship's strength. Therefore, the stresses, in order to differentiate their origin and effects, are ordinarily considered in two groups:

1. Hull girder stresses
2. Local stresses

HULL GIRDER STRESSES

A ship afloat is supported throughout by buoyant forces which vary longitudinally and transversely with the distribution of the ship's displacement or buoyant volume. These comprise the upward forces on the hull. The downward forces are the result of the distribution of all the various weights within the ship including the weight of the ship's structure. The difference between the upward and downward forces results in a load on the ship's girder which varies throughout its length and produces an overall bending moment with the associated shear stresses.

It should be noted that the stresses resulting from a transverse bending moment are less severe and less important than those due to a longitudinal bending moment. In general, the size of the structural members required to give the ship adequate longitudinal and local strength will keep the transverse bending within reasonable limits.

In calculating the longitudinal strength, the

simple beam theory becomes the basis of computations, and the relationship set forth previously is used. This relationship for any section in the ship's length is

$$f = \frac{M_x \, y}{I_x}.$$

The members included in the calculation for the moment of inertia of any section must be continuous longitudinally (fore-and-aft). The major longitudinal strength members of a destroyer are indicated in figure 11–25.

At any section, the severest stresses occur in that portion of the structure most remote from the neutral axis, i.e., in the deck and bottom plating. At any section, M_x and I_x are constant for that section; however, M_x and I_x will vary from section to section along the length of the ship. The stress will therefore be maximum in the deck or bottom plating of that section where $\frac{M_x}{I_x}$ is maximum (assuming that the maximum value of y will not vary appreciably), usually near the midship section in most ships. The superstructure and deck houses found on destroyers but not indicated in figure 11–25 are, of course, farther from the neutral axis than the deck or bottom plating. This upper structure is often designed to be noncontinuous at intervals along the length by expansion joints to prevent this structure from taking a portion of the longitudinal bending stresses.

From the discussion regarding the neutral axis of a beam, it was seen that a maximum horizontal shear developed along the plane of the neutral axis. This is true also in ships when subjected to a bending moment. Depending upon the longitudinal distribution of vertical forces (load), vertical shearing forces will develop also along the ship's length. Because of the essential similarity in ship's form and distribution of load, this vertical shear is maximum near the quarter-lengths from the forward and after ends.

A general corollary, then, is that the maximum shear stresses occur in the vicinity of the neutral axis at the quarter-lengths, and the magnitude of these shear stresses generally require local strengthening at these locations in and near the side of the ship.

It should also be further stated that because of *Newton's Law* (for every action there is an equal and opposite reaction) and the fact that equilibrium is maintained, an opposing force equal to the shearing force is set up. This means there is a force couple at 90 degrees to the shearing forces for both vertical and horizontal shear. In effect, the vertical shear and horizontal shear are interdependent near the neutral axis in the vicinity of the quarter-lengths.

LOCAL STRESSES

Local stresses are caused by hydrostatic pressure, concentrated loads of equipment, and dynamic loading.

Each unit area of the underwater body is subjected to a water pressure proportionate to its depth of immersion. The vertical component of the water pressure applied to the shell is transmitted through the internal framework and opposes the various loads of the ship. Although the horizontal components of the water pressure acting on each side cancel each other, preventing an athwartships movement of the ship, the force of the horizontal pressure components still acts on the shell. The hull and its internal framing must resist the tendency of the water to crush the hull. When the skin of the ship is ruptured and flooding follows, the hydrostatic pressure formerly exerted on the shell is now placed on the internal boundaries of the flooded space. These internal boundaries must be stiffened sufficiently to prevent their failure and hence to confine the flooding. Hydrostatic pressure is also imposed on the boundaries of intact fuel and water tanks.

The weight of each object rests at some point in the ship. These loads must be transmitted downward through the internal structure to the shell where they are opposed by the vertical component of the hydrostatic pressure. To prevent the excessive stress of concentrated loads, extensive foundation support is used to distribute the load over a large area.

In addition to the local stresses imposed by static loads, the ship's structure may be subjected to the buffeting action of the wind, waves, liquid load, and, on naval ships, the blasts of missiles.

Damage to the structure will impose greater stresses on undamaged members not only because of reduced effective cross section of the members but also because of the discontinuities in the structure that cause stress concentrations.

LONGITUDINAL BENDING MOMENTS AND
STRENGTH CURVES

If a body of constant cross section made up of homogeneous particles is floating in still water, there will be no bending moment because the body is in static equilibrium, and the uniformly distributed weight is balanced for each increment of length by the uniformly distributed buoyant force. A length of timber or a floating log is an example of this condition. If, however, a weight is added at some location along its length, the equilibrium between the weight and buoyancy distribution is disturbed, and a bending moment is introduced. Throughout part of the length of the body, the upward forces of buoyancy are exceeded by the downward forces of weight, while for the remainder of the length, the reverse will be true. The total buoyant force and weight must, however, remain equal for the body to remain floating in static equilibrium.

To illustrate this principle more thoroughly,

visualize a rectangularly shaped barge, such as the one in figure 11–3, whose length is *L*. Assume that the barge has a constant weight per unit length and that weightless bulkheads and ends divide it into four equal compartments. There are no concentrated local weights on board, and the barge is floating at the indicated waterline. As shown in figure 11–3, the weight and buoyancy per unit length must coincide. The total area under the weight curve equals both the total weight and the buoyancy, because the barge is floating in static equilibrium. There is no bending moment present, as the weight of the barge is supported equally throughout its length by the buoyancy.

Now, suppose the two inner compartments, numbered 2 and 3, are filled with a cargo such as a liquid. The barge will sink to a deeper draft, increasing the buoyant force until it equals the new displacement. The added weight, however, is concentrated in two compartments, 2 and 3 as indicated in figure 11–4. Compartments 1 and 4

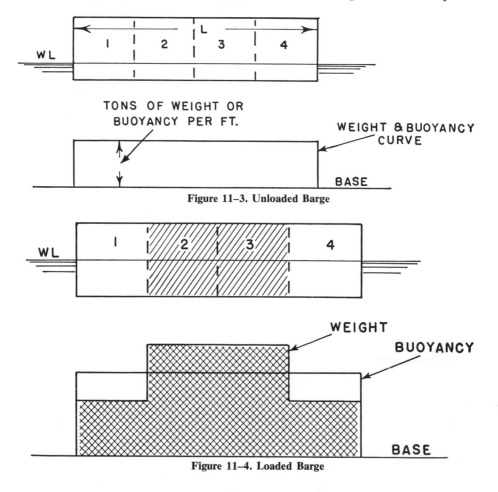

Figure 11–3. Unloaded Barge

Figure 11–4. Loaded Barge

retain the same weight per unit length as in the unloaded condition. In the two end compartments, the buoyancy will exceed the weight by the same amount that the weight will exceed the buoyancy in loaded compartments 2 and 3. The total weight must equal the total buoyancy in order to satisfy equilibrium conditions. Thus, the total area under each curve is the same.

The barge in this condition of loading is subjected to a bending moment throughout its length, due to the difference in weight and buoyancy distribution throughout the length. If this loading is then plotted as the difference between the weight and buoyancy for each increment of length, the result is a graphic representation of the loading over the entire length of the barge. The *load curve illustrates the net result of the difference between unit weight and unit buoyancy*. In figure 11–5, the negative values (below the base line) of the load curve refer to upward forces and the positive values (above the base line) to downward forces. Note that the area of the load curve above the axis of reference must equal the area of the load curve below the axis.

The load curve may be further used to determine the vertical shear force at any point in the length of the barge. By definition, the *vertical shear at any transverse section is the algebraic sum of vertical forces to the left of the section*. We may sum up the area under the load curve to the left of any section to give the shear at that section. Consequently, to represent the shear graphically, as in figure 11–5, we must plot these values of shear as ordinates on an appropriate scale at each designated section. The shear curve

is the integral of the load curve. The shear at any point, x_1, in the length, L, is

$$S_{x_1} = \int_0^{x_1} \bar{L}_x dx$$

where $\bar{L}$ = load at any point
dx = increment of length.

Notice that the maximum shear is exerted at the extremes of the loaded sections where the load curve passes through zero values at the base line. Also note that the total positive area under the shear curve will equal the total negative area and that shear at the ends is zero.

We may utilize the shearing force curve to obtain the bending moment curve. By definition, the *bending moment at any point in the length of the barge is the algebraic sum of the moments of forces to the left of that point*. Thus, since the area under the shearing force curve up to any section represents the moment of that section, the bending moment at various sections may be obtained by summing up the total area under the shear curve to the left of those sections, that is

$$M_{x_1} = \int_0^{x_1} S_x dx \quad \text{or} \quad \int_0^{x_1} \int_0^{x_1} \bar{L}_x dx dx$$

where M_{x_1} = bending moment at point x_1 in the length
S_x = shearing force at any point.

The bending moment curve is symmetrical in figure 11–5 because of the symmetrical loading. Note that the ordinate scales for the three curves differ. The units for the ordinate scale of the load, shearing force, and bending moment curves are tons per foot, tons, and foot-tons respectively.

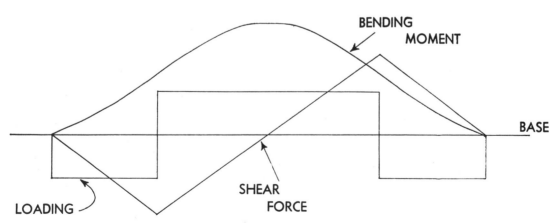

Figure 11–5. Barge Strength Curves

SIMPLIFIED CALCULATIONS FOR PLOTTING
STRENGTH CURVES (*Partially Loaded Barge*)

For the purposes of numerically illustrating the procedure outlined in general above, the following example is presented. Note that in this simplified case a barge form has been selected to eliminate the use of any approximate means or mechanical means of integration. In some of the situations below, the areas are computed by elementary geometry which would obviously not be possible in an actual ship form. However, it is the method involved and the relationship between the strength curves that are the important considerations rather than the mathematical technique employed.

For example, consider a box-shaped lighter $100 \times 25 \times 6$ feet that is floating empty at a draft of two feet. It is divided into four equal compartments by three transverse bulkheads similar to figure 11–4. The two center compartments are then filled with fresh water to 30 percent capacity. Assume that the weight per unit length of the barge before loading is constant.

The weight, buoyancy, load, shear, and bending moment curves are desired. The weight of the barge empty is

$$W_1 = \frac{100 \times 25 \times 2}{35} = 143 \text{ tons.}$$

The weight of the load per compartment is

$$W = \frac{25 \times 25 \times 6 \times .3}{36} = 31.25 \text{ tons.}$$

The weight of the loaded barge then is

$$W = 143 + 2 \times 31.25 = 205.5 \text{ tons.}$$

The buoyancy per foot length of the barge must be then

$$B = \frac{205.5}{100} = 2.055 \text{ tons/ft.}$$

The weight per unit length of the empty compartments is

$$\frac{143}{100} = 1.43 \text{ tons/ft.}$$

The weight per unit length of the loaded compartment is

$$\frac{143}{100} + \frac{31.25}{25} = 1.43 + 1.25 = 2.68 \text{ tons/ft.}$$

The loading in the empty sections is

$$1.43 - 2.055 = -.625 \text{ tons/ft.}$$

The loading in the loaded sections is

$$2.68 - 2.055 = +.625 \text{ tons/ft.}$$

The shear at the first bulkhead (25 feet from the left end) is

$$.625 \times 25 = 15.625 \text{ tons.}$$

The bending moment at the first bulkhead (25 feet from the left end) is

$$\frac{15.625 \times 25}{2} = 195.3 \text{ ft. tons.}$$

The bending moment at the second bulkhead (50 feet from the left end) is

$$2\left(\frac{15.625 \times 25}{2}\right) = 390.6 \text{ ft. tons.}$$

Figure 11–5 may be considered a plot of the curves for this example.

MEANS OF DETERMINING SHIP'S STRENGTH CURVES
(*Still Water*)

Weight calculations for use in strength curves, as well as displacement, stability, and other considerations, are begun in the early stages of design. For purposes of determining the strength curves, both the magnitude and the location of the weights must be accurately made. It will be advantageous to discuss the general practice followed in such weight calculations.

Weight Groups. To proceed with the weight calculations in an orderly fashion, the weights are classified and subdivided into logical groups. In naval designs, the current practice is to classify all of the component weights of the ship, its equipment, and its complement into seven primary weight groups as follows:

Group 1—hull structure
Group 2—propulsion
Group 3—electric plant
Group 4—communication and control
Group 5—auxiliary systems
Group 6—outfit and furnishings
Group 7—armament

The above weight groups are now standard in naval ship weight calculations and under each of these main groups are further detailed subdivisions. The complete description of the detailed subgroupings will be found in the Naval Ship

Systems Command publication, *Weight Classification for Ships of the U.S. Navy.*

Weight Calculations. In the preliminary design stage, weights are determined approximately. Main structural items are laid out, and the weight is calculated directly. Weights of other items are estimated by comparisons with corresponding items on similar existing ships. The weights are recalculated in much more detail in the contract design stage and in still more detail in the design made at the building yard.

The weights of such standard articles as guns, pumps, anchors, etc., are relatively easy to determine—either by reference to the manufacturer's records or the article's specifications. Other parts, such as frames, hull plating, and bulkheads, must be calculated inch by inch from the ship's plans. The weight of items such as turbines, boilers, and other large units must be broken down by component parts.

The first ship of a class to be built is frequently weighed. That is, each piece of material put aboard is actually placed on a scale and its weight recorded to be later totalled to give the final weight check.

The weights of the various groups are summarized along with their vertical and horizontal moment arms about the keel and midship section respectively. It is from this summarization that the weight data per unit length is determined and plotted as the *weight curve.* Figure 11–6 demonstrates that the weight curve is an extremely irregular curve, reflecting the concentrations and disuniformity of the ship's weight distribution.

Buoyancy Calculations. The calculations for buoyancy are relatively simple compared to those for weight. These values are determined by computing the sectional areas below the waterlines corresponding to the several loading conditions for which the weight calculations are made. For any given waterline or displacement condition, these sectional areas are plotted as ordinates to some convenient scale throughout the length of the ship. A smooth curve is faired through these ordinate points resulting in a curve that describes the buoyancy distribution longitudinally along the ship. Again, figure 11–6 shows that the buoyancy curve is fairly uniform with its maximum values near the midship section.

Load, Shear and Bending Moment Curves. After the weight and buoyancy curves have been determined, the subsequent procedure is straightforward. The load curve is obtained by merely subtracting the buoyancy values from the weight values at selected intervals along the length and plotting the resulting differences at each location. This curve is then integrated by approximate means to obtain the shear curve which, in turn, is integrated in a similar manner to obtain the bending moment curve. The principles involved in the actual procedure of obtaining the ship's strength curves are obviously identical to those for the simple loaded barge described previously. The meaning and analysis is also identical; however, because of the complexities of weight distribution and ship form, the process is tedious, and the irregular curves reveal a more complex strength problem. This becomes increasingly ap-

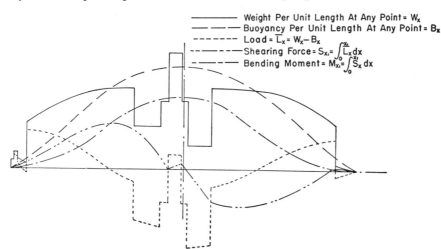

————— Weight Per Unit Length At Any Point = W_x
— — — Buoyancy Per Unit Length At Any Point = B_x
– – – – Load = $\bar{L}_x = W_x - B_x$
– · – · – Shearing Force = $S_{x_i} = \int_0^{x_i} \bar{L}_x dx$
— · · — Bending Moment = $M_{x_i} = \int_0^{x_i} S_x dx$

Figure 11–6. Strength Curves for Cargo Vessel

parent when we consider the condition of the ship no longer in still water but at sea among waves.

SHIP IN A SEAWAY

The foregoing discussion considered the vessel floating in still water. This condition provides a distribution of buoyancy along the length of the vessel that is similar to the distribution of displacement below the designer's waterline. A ship among waves is alternately supported by the wave crest at the midship region or the ends. That is, the buoyancy distribution varies with the position of the wave crests passing under it. For the purpose of studying the stresses on the ship's girder among waves, certain values of a wave's size must be assigned in order that the corresponding buoyancy distribution may be calculated. The general practice for such a study is to assume that the ship is supported by a wave whose length is equal to the length between the ship's perpendiculars and whose height is $1.1\sqrt{L}$. The evaluation of the buoyancy distributions, in one case where the wave crest is amidships with the wave hollows at the ends of the ship, and in another case where the wave hollow is amidships with the wave crests at the ends of the ship, will approximate the most severe stresses to which the ship normally will be exposed.

With a wave of these dimensions, curves showing the distribution of buoyancy are drawn. Figures 11–7 and 11–8 indicate the variation in the buoyancy curves for these conditions. When the bow and stern are riding on wave crests and the midship region is in the trough, the ship will bend with compression on the weather deck and tension in the bottom plating. The ship is said to be *sagging*. When the ship advances one-half a wave length from the sagging condition, so that the wave crest is amidships and the bow and stern are in the trough, the ship will bend with the weather deck in tension and the bottom plating in compression. In this condition the ship is said to be *hogging*.

Strength curves are normally developed for several displacements considering both the hogging and sagging condition at each displacement. To insure that the most severe condition is examined, the weight distribution curves for the hogging condition are constructed considering that the consumable load amidship is expended and for the sagging condition considering the consumable load at the ends is expended.

From the structural section plans, similar to, but in much more detail than in figure 11–25, the designer calculates the section modulus, (I_x/y), at various sections. Knowing the bending moment at each section for each loading condition, the

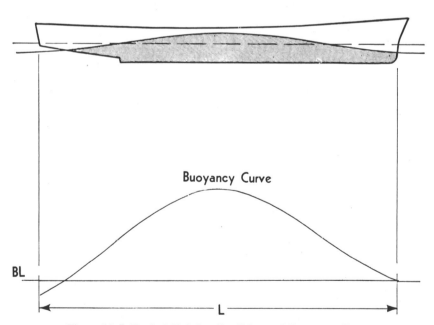

Buoyancy Curve

BL

L

Figure 11–7. Typical Hogging Condition and Buoyancy Curve

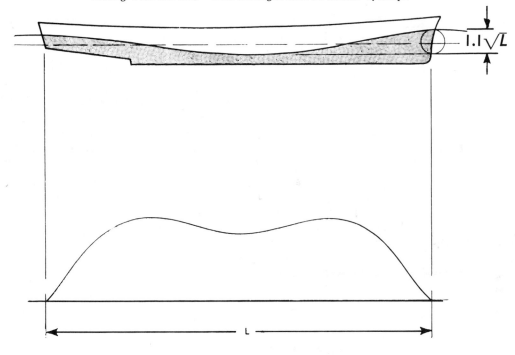

BUOYANCY CURVE

Figure 11–8. Typical Sagging Condition and Buoyancy Curve

maximum stress at each section can be determined from equation $f = \dfrac{M_x\, y}{I_x}$ to insure it is within allowable limits. The maximum longitudinal bending stress occurs normally in the deck or bottom plating in the vicinity of the midship section.

To resist longitudinal bending strains the hull girder of figure 11–25 is composed of the deck plating, sheer strakes, and deck girders at the top and the bottom plating, keel, and longitudinals below where the greatest stresses occur. These correspond to the flanges of an **I** beam. The relatively thin side plating in the vicinity of the neutral axis act together as the web of an **I** beam.

The size of each structural member must be proportionate to the stress it carries. It is important to avoid having any member of greater strength and weight than necessary. In such a case, the neutral axis is moved toward the stronger member, and the stress in the extreme fiber is proportionately increased. It is generally good design practice to reduce the size of structural members beyond the middle half-length of the ship. This reduction is made as gradually as possible, since the prefabricated members are each of constant cross section.

Where the continuity of the structure is interrupted by openings in the deck, bottom, or side, the structural continuity must be preserved by auxiliary strength members. When hatches, ports, lighting holes, smokepipes, etc. are present, this is usually accomplished by introducing doubling plates or stiffening rings about the openings.

There is, at present, inadequate and insufficient data on the real bending moments to which a ship is actually subjected under sea conditions. A number of alternative methods have been proposed for such calculations to take the place of the arbitrary $1.1\sqrt{L}$ wave and its static change of buoyancy distribution. There are undoubtedly important and unconsidered dynamic effects as well as random buoyancy distributions to vary the actual bending moments. Particularly in the case of very large ships (over 1,000 feet), there are few guidelines in estimating the stresses involved. The American Bureau of Shipping, which sets the rules for the structural specifications of merchant vessels, has recently reacted to a growing concern for more precise knowledge on which to base its rules. It has, accordingly, recently instrumented the very large tanker, *Universe Ireland* (312,000 deadweight tons), as well as other large ships with strain gauges, electronic recorders, and data processing equipment to determine the bending moments actually experienced in sea conditions along various ocean routes.

RELATION AMONG STRENGTH CURVES

In all strength curves the following general relations exist:

- The area under the buoyancy curves must equal the area under the weight curve.
- The centroids of the weight and buoyancy curves are vertically in line.
- The net area of the load curve must be equal to zero.
- Peak shear values will exist at those points in the length where the load curve crosses the axis. (The word *maximum* is not used, in that there are usually several peak values.)
- Maximum bending moment will occur where the ordinate of the shear curve is zero.
- Points of inflection occur in the bending moment curve where the ordinates of the shear curve have peak values (where the load curve intersects the base line).
- The shearing force and bending moment curves have zero values at their extremities.

CONTINUITY IN STRENGTH

The effectiveness of the ship's hull as a box girder and the effective application of the beam theory equation depend primarily on the longitudinal continuity of the strength members in the hull structure. Unfortunately, because of operational requirements, the hull structure must contain many openings in the vicinity of which it is impossible to maintain the continuity of some structural members or structural plating. To as great an extent as possible, these openings are located in such a way as to eliminate interference with principal structural members. For example, it is prohibited in any ship to cut, notch, or place an opening of any kind in the main deck stringer plates. Likewise, the keel and other key longitudinal members cannot be disrupted by an opening or any other part of the structure that might interfere with their continuous nature. (See figure 11–25.) However, because the deck, side, and bottom plating make up a considerable portion

of the longitudinal strength, it becomes a problem of design to maintain as much continuity as possible and still allow for necessary openings.

An opening in the shell of the hull will reduce the section modulus in that location because of the sectional area of plating lost by the opening. Therefore, this area must be reinforced around the periphery of the opening with additional plating called *doubler plates* or thicker insert plates. These doubler plates, as a general rule, are of such dimension that they are equivalent to the area of the opening. The shape of the opening is also of critical importance. Any sharp corners or square cuts around the hole must be avoided because of the concentration of stress at these points of abrupt change in direction. Not only are openings involved in this phenomena of stress concentration, but also any feature of design that might result in an abrupt change in curvature or direction of plating. This is noted in ships where superstructure decks or raised forecastle decks become a part of the strength deck. In such design, it is necessary to fair the side plating from one deck level to another in a gradual, smooth arc to eliminate the angle.

Recent investigations have been conducted by the U.S. Maritime Commission to determine adequate hatch corner design. Failure of deck plating in large merchant ships in the vicinity of hatch corners because of great stress concentration has resulted in new construction and alterations, which produce a rectangular hatch with rounded corners not only in the deck plating but also in the hatch framing. The framing and coaming around the hatch have become a much stronger structure in modern design, being an all-welded, integral unit.

Structure

Because of the varied types of ships and craft in naval and maritime service, it will be necessary to confine the discussion of a ship's structure to general terms. In the following development, no attempt will be made to examine all types of structure, but rather typical and common practices will be emphasized. It should be noted that, while the most common and well-known shipbuilding practices are concerned with merchant ships because of their greater numerical superiority, the objective of the student of this text is primarily familiarity with naval vessel structure. In general theory, there is little difference. However, because of the greater speed requirements of naval vessels, there are certain variations in hull form that require special considerations in construction. Also, the requirements for strength, resistance to battle damage and flooding, and flexibility in ship control all demand that a naval vessel be a more complex structure. Not only must the structural members be suited to greater stresses and be able to stand up when adjacent members have been damaged or destroyed, but also the entire vessel must be subdivided more extensively to restrict and contain flooding damage. These factors, together with the high-speed form requirements, produce structural digressions from the conventional shipbuilding practices that may be treated as extensions of the more simplified ship structure. With these elements in mind, it is best to use the more elemental ship structure that is conventional to all shipbuilding practices as a frame of reference and to extend beyond these limits whatever direction is called for by the particular structural requirements of naval vessels. Because of the scope of this text and the objective of the student, the material related here to the structure of ships must, in any event, be limited and elemental in nature. For the student or reader seeking more detailed information there are numerous shipbuilding texts and manuals available.

STEEL IN SHIPS

Since the development of the Bessemer and open-hearth processes of steel manufacture, the principal material for ship hulls has been steel in its various forms and alloys.

Steel is a homogeneous material with excellent strength characteristics; it may be cast, forged, or worked in plate form. It is susceptible to various welding processes, and the weldments are uniform and reliable.

The primary disadvantage of steel for shipbuilding use is its lack of resistance to corrosion. It is exceptionally vulnerable to corrosion in the presence of seawater, and this characteristic, therefore, demands careful attention to painting and constant vigilance in maintenance.

Mild steel is the standard and customary material for most economical ship construction; however, in modern naval vessels, particularly in the structural members, *high-tensile steel* (HTS) is consistently used. HTS has approximately 25 to 30 percent greater tensile strength than mild steel.

Where corrosion is a particular problem or where painted surfaces are undesirable, *corrosion-resisting steel* (CRS) is frequently used. This alloy, which contains chromium, is difficult to weld and, in addition, is quite expensive. Consequently, its use aboard ship is rather limited.

For ballistic decks and where protective bulkheads and shields are required, *special-treatment steel* (STS) is employed. This is a nickel-steel alloy which has excellent strength characteristics. The presence of nickel increases its hardness, toughness, and elasticity while decreasing its ductility only slightly.

Steel is manufactured in various forms and, in most cases for structural members and plating, may be obtained from the mills in the forms desired. Where special shapes or sizes are required (in naval construction the requirements are numerous) arrangements are made with the steel mill for supply if possible; otherwise, they are made from the standard sizes or shaped by the shipyard facilities. Common examples of this are the reduction of **I** beams to **T** bars, or channels to angles.

Steel comes from the mill generally in two basic forms—plates and shapes.

Plates are steel flat stock of a quarter inch or more in thickness (less than quarter-inch steel is termed *sheet* steel). They vary in width from approximately 60 inches to 110 inches. Plate is normally designated in size by its weight in lbs/ft^2 and varies normally from about 10 to 20 pounds plate, although the plate used in the pressure hull of a submarine is considerably heavier. The density of steel is approximately 490 lbs/ft^3, and on this basis, a plate one inch in thickness would be 40.8 pound plate, or quarter inch steel, 10.2 pound plate, etc. (Normally the decimals are omitted in referring to the plate sizes.) Below 10 pound plate, the sizes are given in gauges.

Shapes are normally supplied as plain angle bars, beveled angle bars, bulb angle, **T** bars, **T** bulb bars, channels, and **I** beams.

Until very recently, merchant ships have been built essentially of steels designated *American Bureau of Shipping* (*ABS*) *Types A, B,* and *C.* These are mild steel having a minimum-yield strength of 32,000 psi and ultimate tensile strengths ranging from 58,000 to 66,000 psi (see figure 11–11 for shipbuilding material properties). Structural loading of vessels has been limited by the physical properties of these steels. However, recent years have seen the development of specialized steels for shipbuilding. They are more expensive, and their use is limited and specialized in the ship's structure, but the savings in weight and volume are significant. Such new steels are:

1. High-strength steels with three times the strength of mild steels
2. Steels that retain strength at low temperatures
3. Corrosion-resistance steels for greater dependability under corrosive uses in salt water

Ultra high-strength steels of yield strengths to 100,000 psi and ultimate tensile strengths of 135,000 psi are used in the critical locations of the hull structure such as deck stringers and sheer strake plating (see figure 11–9). Less high-strength steels, but still greater strength than mild steel, are used in the bilge strake where their toughness properties eliminate the need for the conventional riveted crack-arrestor strake in this region.

The stability of ships built with variations in strength properties of steels is considerably improved by an overall weight reduction of 17 percent and a 50 percent weight reduction in topside steel. Reduction in propulsion machinery for lighter, high-strength steel vessels saves on initial costs and still allows the speed-power requirements to be met. With the correspondingly smaller power plants, which have lower fuel consumption, operating costs are reduced accordingly.

NON-FERROUS METALS IN SHIPS

With the exception of aluminum and its alloys as noted here, there is practically no structural use made in shipbuilding of any other non-ferrous metal.

An excellent selection of aluminum alloys is available for shipbuilding use, and the range of characteristic properties is, in many ways, more adaptable than steel. The primary advantage and special characteristics of aluminum is its light weight and its superiority under bending stresses and special structures applications. In addition, it is superior to other metals in its greater ductility,

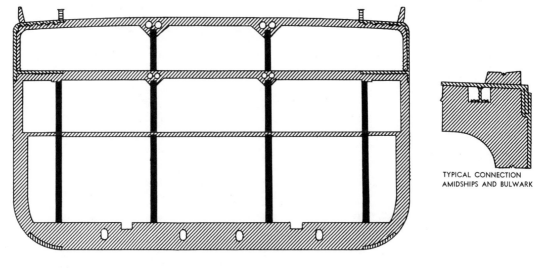

TYPICAL CONNECTION
AMIDSHIPS AND BULWARK

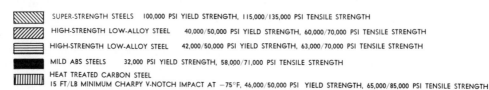

SUPER-STRENGTH STEELS   100,000 PSI YIELD STRENGTH, 115,000/135,000 PSI TENSILE STRENGTH

HIGH-STRENGTH LOW-ALLOY STEEL   40,000/50,000 PSI YIELD STRENGTH, 60,000/70,000 PSI TENSILE STRENGTH

HIGH-STRENGTH LOW-ALLOY STEEL   42,000/50,000 PSI YIELD STRENGTH, 63,000/70,000 PSI TENSILE STRENGTH

MILD ABS STEELS   32,000 PSI YIELD STRENGTH, 58,000/71,000 PSI TENSILE STRENGTH

HEAT TREATED CARBON STEEL
15 FT/LB MINIMUM CHARPY V-NOTCH IMPACT AT −75°F, 46,000/50,000 PSI YIELD STRENGTH, 65,000/85,000 PSI TENSILE STRENGTH

Figure 11–9. Section of Web Frame Showing Location of Various Steels Used in Modern Steel Vessels

distortion-strengthening, and impact resistance. It is nonsparking and nonmagnetic. Aluminum is, in certain of its alloys, highly resistant to corrosion. Unfortunately, it is more expensive than steel and more expensive to work. Welding techniques have continuously been improved, but it is still far more difficult to weld than steel.

With such attractive advantages, and being conscious of the several disadvantages, aluminum is a most interesting and, in some requirements, a most vital shipbuilding material.

While aluminum has been used in the superstructures of many large vessels, such as passenger liners and destroyer-type ships, its use for the

Courtesy of Selvage & Lee, Inc.

Figure 11–10. Technician Checks the Front Strut of the U.S. Navy's Tucumcari as It Nears Completion. Made from stainless steel, the front strut and foil assemblies are all ultrasonically inspected. In addition, all highly stressed joints are radiographed.

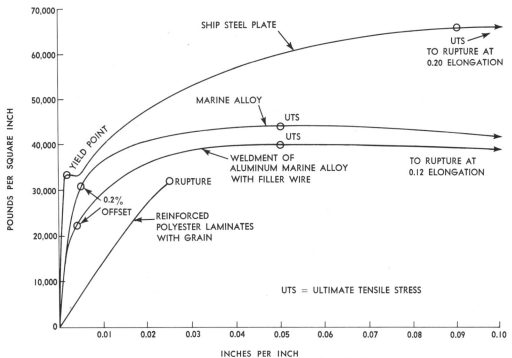

Figure 11–11. Typical Stress-Strain Diagrams for Hull Materials

entire hull structure has, to date, been confined to relatively small vessels where weight is critical. Such vessels are hydrofoil supported craft, high-speed coastal gunboats (see chapter 15), torpedo boats, tugboats for shallow waters, yachts, etc.

Aluminum would probably be in greater use for small craft had it not been surpassed in economy of fabrication by the ever-expanding use of reinforced polyester laminates. The relative strength properties of these primary shipbuilding materials are given in table 11–1.

In considering all of the types of materials in use for structural applications in ships, the focus is still essentially on steel for vessels of all sizes. For large vessels, because of steel's greater strength and relative economy, there is at present no other choice.

THE HULL STRUCTURE

The hull of a ship must be primarily, a buoyant, stable container for all of the machinery, living facilities, equipment, and storage spaces

Table 11–1. Comparative Strength Characteristics of Basic Shipbuilding Materials

| MATERIAL | Weight lb/cu in. | TYPICAL STRENGTH (psi) | | | Tensile Modulus of Elasticity ($\times 10^6$) | Ratio Strength-to-Weight Col. 3/Col. 2 ($\times 1000$) |
		Ultimate Tensile	Yield Tensile	Ultimate Shear		
(1) Aluminum alloy:						
5083-H113	0.096	46,000	33,000	27,000	10.3	480
5086-H34	0.096	47,000	37,000	27,000	10.3	490
6061-T6	0.098	45,000	40,000	30,000	10.0	460
Ship steel ASTM-A131	0.29	66,000	33,000		29.0	230
Mild steel ASTM-A100	0.28	56,000	30,000	42,000	29.0	200
Copper, hard sheet	0.32	46,000	40,000		17.0	140
(2) Reinforced polyester laminates:						
With grain	0.062	32,000		13,000	1.4	520
Across grain	0.062	21,000		14,000	1.1	340

(1) Aluminum alloys 5083 and 5086 have excellent corrosion resistance in seawater, hence are suitable for hulls under all conditions. Alloy 6061 has good corrosion resistance in seawater, hence is suitable for framing and superstructures under seawater conditions. This alloy is also much used for the hulls of small boats for seawater use that are generally hauled from the water when not in use, or for hulls of any type that are for freshwater operation principally.

(2) Values for polyester laminates depend upon composition and method of applying or forming. Those tabulated are typical short-term values under favorable conditions of application. Because of low ductility it is customary to design polyester laminates on basis of ultimate tensile strength after adjustment for factor of safety.

Courtesy of ALCOA

Figure 11–12. All-Aluminum 50-Foot Launches. These launches are constructed of an aluminum alloy that contains an extra-strength aluminum-magnesium combination exhibiting excellent corrosion resistance, a vital attribute for saltwater craft.

required for its functioning as an integral unit. It must also be of adequate strength and seaworthiness and must have an elongated shape of faired, smooth, underwater form for minimum resistance. The hull must have ample buoyancy combined with a form that provides stability. All in all, the operational requirements dictate a structural shape that is essentially similar in all surface ships.

It is possible, in describing the hull, to liken it to a box-shaped girder. The most significant modifications of this boxlike form are the tapered form of the sides and bottom at both ends and the sheer of the deck. Because of the rounding off at the bilges and the fairing in of the bottom toward the ends to provide a smooth underwater form, the boxlike form of the hull is further modified. Also, because the streamlined underwater form is symmetrical about the longitudinal center plane along with its departure from a boxlike form, it is necessary to provide a rigid center-plane girder from end to end. This girder, the *keel structure,* is one of the most important structural parts of the ship. Keeping in mind this centered structural member, the structural frame is further composed of longitudinal and transverse members integrally welded together, forming a framework to which the watertight skin or plating is attached. This framework will be referred to as the *structural frame* of the ship. Because it is made up of longitudinal and transverse members, that is, beams, girders, plates, bars, etc., that run in planes fore and aft and athwartships, the structural frame itself is given a finite thickness that is cellular in nature.

In addition to the structural frame, a considerable portion of the ship's overall strength and rigidity is provided by the watertight shell or plating. This plating is an integral part of the hull structure closing in the whole boxlike girder including the bottom, sides, and weather deck.

With the addition of bulkheads to provide transverse rigidity and support, the hull structure becomes the integral unit to meet the requirements set forth in the beginning.

It should be emphasized here, again, that the hull's strength depends upon a uniform and continuous structure. Any break or rupture in the structural frame or in a portion of the shell plating results in a discontinuity of the whole structure with a consequent overloading and concentrating of stresses in adjacent members.

THE STRUCTURAL FRAMING

Attached to the keel structure transversely are members called *frames*. The frames, in general, run continuously from the keel to the main deck edge. Distinguished from the frames, although actually a continuous part of them, are the *floors* in the ship's bottom. The floors are actually deeper frames that run from the keel out to the turn of the bilge or to a point where a transverse horizontal line from the top of the inner vertical keel meets the side of the ship. At the outer extremity of the floors, the frames are attached and run up the side to the deck line. The floors and frames together thus make up the major portion of the transverse structure of the ship's structural frame.

Longitudinal girders running parallel with the keel and intersecting the floors at right angles are known simply as *longitudinals*. The longitudinals and the floors divide the ship's bottom into relatively small rectangular tanks and voids collectively called the *double bottoms*. The bottom structure is thus an extensively subdivided portion of the ship and, in most ships by far, the strongest flange of the whole ship's girder. The longitudinals run throughout the length of the ship, continuing at regularly spaced intervals around the bilge and up the sides. The longitudinals along the sides, commonly called *stringers,* are proportionately lighter than those along the bottom as are the frames. The arrangement of these in a

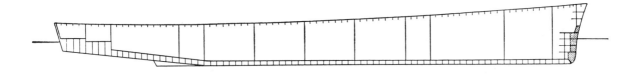

Figure 11–13. The Longitudinal Center Girder of a Naval Vessel

destroyer may be seen in figures 11–14 and 11–15.

The hull is closed in on the top by the deck structure, allowing for appropriate openings and portions of the ship that extend through the deck. The transverse members of the deck-framing structure are known as *deck beams*. The lighter

Figure 11–14. Sectional Model of Destroyer Showing Structure. (Note ends of longitudinals and stringers. Portions of floors and frames shown in lower right.)

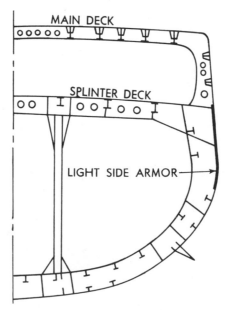

MAIN DECK

SPLINTER DECK

LIGHT SIDE ARMOR

Figure 11–15. Basic Frame Section (Longitudinal Framing)

deck beams are ordinarily, in naval vessels, interspaced at regular intervals with deep deck beams, particularly where there are openings and discontinuities in the deck. The longitudinal members of the deck-framing structure are called *deck girders* with the heaviest girders located, insofar as possible, at the center and near the outboard edges.

At appropriate locations, complete transverse bulkheads are placed which extend from keel to deck and side to side which provide considerable transverse stiffening. In addition to the frames and bulkheads as transverse strength members, the presence of deeper frames and built-up frames called *web frames* are found in modern ships. Web frames are most adaptable to combatant vessels in that they provide excellent compartmentation for protective layer tanks. Figure 11–16 shows the deep web frames adjacent to the machinery space in a destroyer. In this case, they provide the boundaries of the feedwater tanks and are part of the wing tank system.

There are two distinct systems of framing in common use that are distinguished from each other by the terms *transverse* and *longitudinal*. The transverse system consists of closely spaced, continuous frames with widely spaced, intercostal, deep longitudinals. The longitudinal system consists of frequently spaced, but shallower, longitudinals with widely spaced intercostal, web frames. In merchant shipbuilding practice, one or the other of these systems is used in nearly pure form, but modern naval surface ships use a combination of the two systems, which gives greater continuity of structure and less weight for a given strength. Figures 11–14 and 11–16 are examples of this combination system. Figure 11–14 shows the deep and shallow longitudinals, stringers, and deck girders piercing a main transverse bulkhead. The web frames in figure 11–16 are fitted every three or four frame spaces between lighter frames.

It should be emphasized at this point that, in combat naval vessels, the framing practices differ from noncombat and merchant vessels to an extent where it is difficult to identify the various types by a rigorous nomenclature. Primarily

Figure 11–16. Deep Frame Construction in a Modern Destroyer. Web frames such as this form wing tanks for the protection of machinery spaces and storage of fresh and feed water.

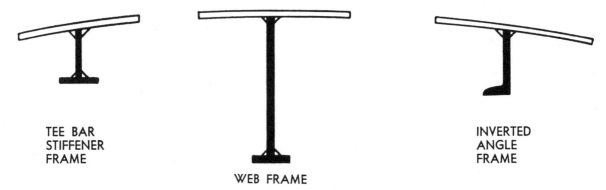

TEE BAR
STIFFENER
FRAME

WEB FRAME

INVERTED
ANGLE
FRAME

Figure 11–17. Types of Simple Frames (Sections)

because of the greater strength requirements and built-in resistance to damage, naval vessels have generally deeper frames. The primary frames in a destroyer, for example, could all be called web frames since the simple **T** bar frames are only used in the extreme bow sections for side stiffening. (See figure 11–17.) Here, they are spaced more closely than other frames. Adjacent to machinery spaces, the frames are so increased in depth that they might be called deep web-frames, bulkhead frames, or compartment frames. Some of these have large lightening holes, and others form a continuous ring inside a side compartment with stiffening flanges welded around their inner edges. Regardless of the shape and extent of the frames, their purpose is essentially the same in all vessels—to provide transverse stiffening, strength, and resistance to transverse forces. They supply a measure of overall longitudinal strength in their vertical and transverse support of the sides.

THE KEEL AND BOTTOM

The keel structure in most steel vessels consists of an *inner vertical keel* and an *outer flat keel*.

The inner vertical keel in small vessels is generally a welded assembly in the form of an **I** beam or **T** bar. In many large combat ships with a bottom protective layer, the inner vertical keel is a vertical assembly of two or more sections as would be formed by two **I** beams arranged one on top of the other. This structure is generally of welded construction composed of flat plate and angle bars. Figure 11–18 shows a typical example of a welded keel structure.

Longitudinally, the entire keel member is made up of a number of sections. These sections are seldom more than 100 feet in length.

The outer flat keel in small vessels often forms the lower flange of the inner vertical keel, but, in larger ships, it is an additional member attached to the lower flange of the inner vertical keel. This member is generally wider than either the upper or lower flange of the inner vertical keel. It is not generally flat but, where necessary, conforms to the shape of the hull. This is always necessary in the vicinity of sections that have any degree of deadrise. Although the outer flat keel is of heavier gauge plate than side and bottom plating, it, in reality, functions as the primary, centrally located strake of bottom plating. The line of separation between the top of this outer flat keel plate and the lower flange of the inner vertical keel is the base line defined in chapter 2.

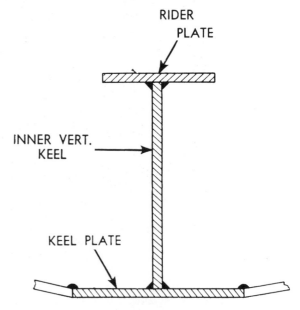

RIDER
PLATE

INNER VERT.
KEEL

KEEL PLATE

Figure 11–18. Typical Welded Keel Section

A cellular construction in a ship's bottom is the result of a large number of floors intersecting the longitudinals. (See figure 11–19.) These bottom compartments become liquid stowage tanks and voids, and, when covered over by plating, an inner and outer bottom is formed that constitutes the strongest portion of the ship. The greater strength of the ship's bottom keeps the neutral axis below the midpoint in the ship's depth. The double bottom should, on large ships, be considered as the integral part of the bottom strength of the ship.

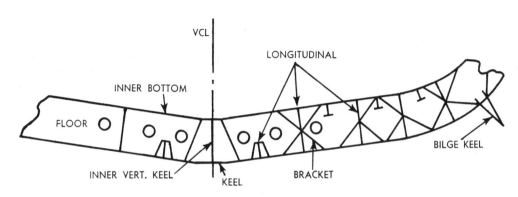

Figure 11–19. Floor with Longitudinals; Bottom Structure

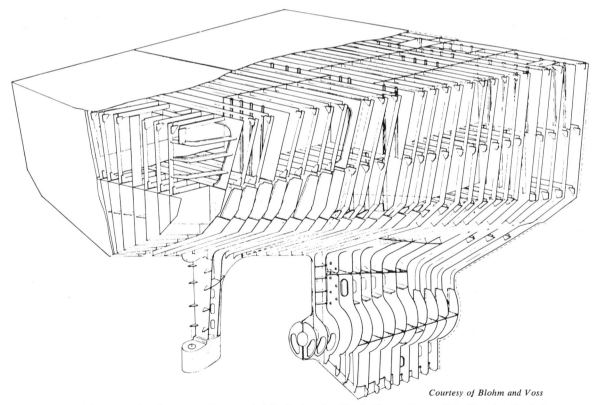

Courtesy of Blohm and Voss

Figure 11–20. Structural Frame of Afterbody of a Single Screw Cargo Ship Showing Typical Rudder Horn and Frames for Propeller Bossing

In considering the complete bottom structure, it should not be overlooked that bilge keels (see chapter 12) may contribute to the strength and structural continuity. An exception to this rule is the case wherein the bilge keels are not attached to the hull by a continuous weldment. However, the attachment is often continuous, and, in such cases, the bilge keels are similar to stringers or longitudinals. Ships' officers should remember that the bilge keels are particularly vulnerable to damage inasmuch as they are external structures.

STERN ASSEMBLY

At the after extremity of the keel is the *stern post assembly*. Because of the great variety of types and shapes of sterns, this assembly is

equally varied in its manner of construction. Generally speaking, for single screw vessels, the stern post is constructed to accommodate the propeller shaft and rudder stock bosses. It is generally made up of castings and forgings with the bosses and rudder gudgeons faired-in as an integral part of the form. The stern post, as such, is difficult to define in modern transom sterns and multiple screw warships, particularly those with twin rudders. Actually, the older type stern post in such ships has been replaced by an equivalent structure of deep framing, both longitudinal and transverse. This structure is extended throughout the width of the bottom in the vicinity of the stern and is so constructed to accommodate the necessary rudder posts. (See figure 11–21.) In the

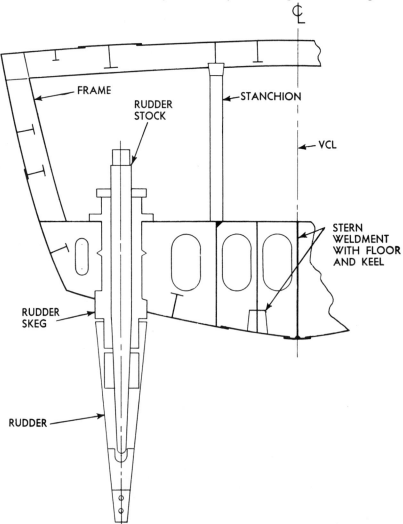

Figure 11–21. Floor and Frame Weldment in After Section at the Rudder Posts (Twin Rudder Mounts)

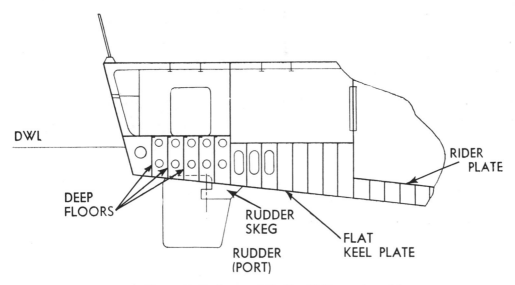

Figure 11–22. Stern and Rudder Weldment Assembly

vicinity of the rudder posts, the structure is additionally strengthened to withstand the additional static and dynamic loads imposed by the rudders. The structure there is commonly known as the rudder-post weldment. This is a particularly distinctive feature in naval vessel construction and is primarily the result of form dictated by speed requirements.

STEM AND BOW STRUCTURE

At the forward extremity of the keel, attached integrally, is the stem assembly. Ships' stems are also of varied forms; however, the requirements of resistance dictate a rather uniform shape that is similar below the waterline for most large ships. A form essentially bulbous at the forefoot (near the lower portion of the stem), tapering up to a sharp entrance near the waterline, and again widening above the waterline is the basic external shape of the stem structure. Internally this structure has a heavy centerline member which is the *stem post* itself. In modern vessels of large size, this member comprises the lower half of the stem. At various levels and regular intervals along the stem structure between keel and deck are horizontal members called *breast hooks*. Depending upon the shape of the bow at any level, these members are basically triangular in shape, made of heavy plate, and flanged. Deep transverse framing and transverse bulkheads complete the stem

assembly. The stem itself is fabricated from castings, forgings, and heavy, wrapped plate or, in the case of smaller ships, heavy, precut structural steel plate. The stem post may be a combination of two or more of the above fabrications, welded and scarfed together to form a rigid, central unit which maintains the continuity of keel strength up to the main deck.

A typical example of the stem assembly structure is shown in figure 11–23, which is representative of destroyer construction. Notice here that

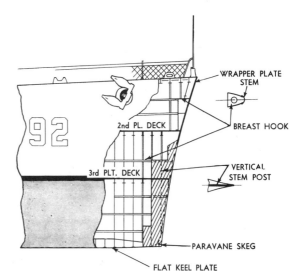

Figure 11–23. Bow and Stem Construction of a Destroyer

the lower portion consists of a flat plate stem lying in the longitudinal, vertical centerplane and attached to the keel structure at its base. At its upper end, the structure tapers in to a rolled steel plate which forms the upper portion of the stem and is actually a heavy wrapper plate. This type of upper stem construction is called a *soft nose* stem in opposition to the older sharp stem plate or casting that was continued up to the weather deck.

In larger vessels, of 10,000 tons and greater, in place of the vertical plate at the keel, several heavy forged plates are used with a greater number of breast hooks to tie in to the longitudinal members and to conform to the greater dimensions of the bulb. (See figure 11–24.)

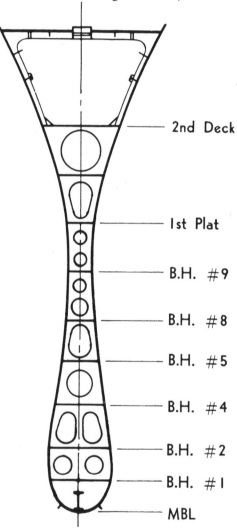

Figure 11–24. Forward Frame Structure of a Large Ship

Regardless of construction technique used, the stem and stern fabrication serve to extend the centerline continuity of the keel and tie the ends of the hull structure together in a faired, streamlined form.

BOTTOM AND SIDE PLATING

The bottom shell on most ships is formed by the outer bottom plating and the inner bottom plating or tank tops. The inner bottom plating here performs a double function on heavier warships. It completes the structure of the boxed-in bottom flange of the ship's girder and provides the ship with an inner watertight shell adding to the underwater protection. In the largest combatant ships, the bottom is subdivided into a double layer of bottom tanks by three layers of plating, the innermost of which is called the *third bottom*.

The shell plating on both the bottom and sides is worked in longitudinal rows called *strakes,* similar to the fore and aft planking on old wooden vessels. It is common practice to weld all connections but to rivet the seams of one or more strakes of shell and strength deck plating and, in some cases, the bilge strake to serve as crack arrestors. There are various plating systems in use, but the methods used are readily recognizable by inspection. Figure 11–25 indicates the

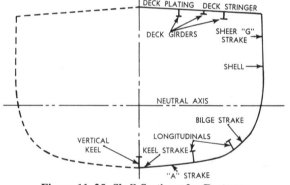

Figure 11–25. Shell Section of a Destroyer

arrangement of the rows of strakes. The number of strakes in the side of a ship depends, of course, on the size of the ship. Figure 11–25 is typical of a destroyer type. Figure 11–26 indicates the heavier structure of a larger ship. In any event, the shape of the individual plates that make up the strakes is roughly rectangular, but near the ends of the ship, where the greatest curvature is found, these plates will have to be tapered and formed, either hot or cold, in rolls and presses to conform to the ship's curvature. In any given strake, the adjoining plates join each other in a connection called a *butt*. These butts are generally, in naval vessels, welded flush. Where two adjoining plates in a strake are lapped, in the older practice, the projecting plate edges below the waterline and transverse to the flow of water are chamfered off to an angle of 45 degrees.

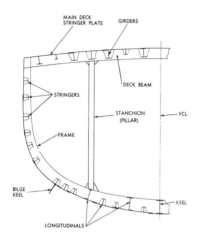

Figure 11–26. Shell Section Showing Deep Frames, Inner Bottom, and Heavy Deck Beams

The *General Specifications for Ships of the United States Navy* require that all welded connections of the plating below the waterline must be fitted flush. However, where the strakes adjoin each other longitudinally (along a *seam*), they are often lapped and riveted. Where the connection is riveted, they are not required to be flush.

Naval vessels are distinctive in their smooth underwater shell plating. While the lapped seams are in evidence, the lack of projecting butt-laps provides an exceptionally unobstructed line of flow to the water. Although the general specifications do not require it, most of the above-water shell plating is butted with flush joints as well.

Where penetrations through the shell plating are required, and in every naval vessel there are a great many, such as sea chests, evaporator blow downs, sanitary drains, and scores of others, the plating must be reinforced. When the opening is greater than 24 inches transversely, insert or doubler plates (making up for the area lost in the opening) and internal framing around the opening must be used. For smaller openings, in the case of sea chests, for example, the sea-chest

fitting itself may, in many cases, be considered as sufficient reinforcing material.

In general, the requirements regarding the locations of the butts and seams of the shell plating with respect to the adjacent structural frame are such that they must avoid interference with longitudinals, bulkheads, decks, and other structural members that fasten to the shell plating.

The plating is always greater in thickness amidships and decreases forward and aft gradually to preserve the structural continuity of the whole ship's girder.

DECK PLATING

The strength deck, forming the top flange of the ship's girder, rests on the main deck beams and main deck girders, the former being tied in with the frame heads by brackets. The deck plating is laid on similarly to the side plating in fore and aft rows. Wooden deck planking is often fitted on top of the steel deck plating on weather decks of large ships. This decking is bolted to the steel plating.

The lower decks, whose primary purpose is to divide the ship horizontally into various levels for work or other activities, are of similar but usually lighter weight than the main strength deck. The plating is carried on similar deck beams and fore and aft girders. The deck beams are connected to the frames with welded brackets. In all strength-deck plating, the outboard strake adjacent to the frames is of heavier plating than the others, and is known as the deck *stringer*. It is a continuous longitudinal stringer similar to all of the other longitudinals and stringers in the hull's structure.

The importance of stringer plates in relation to the ship's longitudinal strength cannot be overemphasized. Because there is no centerline strength member in the deck structure, and because there are many openings of irregular size, shape, and location causing stress concentration problems, the structure of the ship where the sides and main strength-deck meet becomes of extreme importance in the maintenance of longitudinal strength continuity. The sheer strake in the side and the main deck stringer plate along the deck edge form the upper corner of the ship's box girder. In some instances, the stringer plate has failed when its importance has been disregarded and adjacent strength members accordingly have deteriorated.

In naval vessels, it is a rigid building practice never to allow a penetration, an abrupt change in dimension, or, in any way, a limitation of the continuity of the deck stringer-plate. Any opening in the deck interrupts the continuity of the structural members of the deck. The openings caused by hatches, boiler uptakes, barbettes, etc., may cut through several deck beams and deck girders. Consequently, the material surrounding the opening must be reinforced to supplant the material eliminated, so that the section in the vicinity of the opening will not be weakened and the stress distribution will be uniform.

Along the sides of the openings are fitted short deck girders called *carlings* or *headers* running at right angles to the deck beams and welded to them. Figure 11–27 shows the cellular structure formed by the deck beams and girders. Intermediate deck beams are fitted where the opening does not extend fully between the primary deck beams. The plating about the opening is increased in thickness to compensate for the discontinuity of the regular plating.

THE STRENGTH DECK

The uppermost continuous deck is referred to as the strength deck and serves in most ships to complete the enclosure of the box girder and the continuity of the ship's structure. In most naval combat vessels (except aircraft carriers), the superstructure, deck houses, gun mount enclosures, etc., do not extend from rail to rail nor are they continuous throughout the length of the ship. They are, for the most part, nonwatertight spaces designed to house and shelter various ship's activities, in many ships, and contribute in no way to the structural strength of the ship. Consequently, they are made of light steel plate, except where armor is necessary. Where the length of deck houses or similar superstructure is considerable, expansion joints are customarily provided. On recent aircraft carriers of the largest type (*CVA*), it is the practice to utilize the flight deck as the strength deck. Other aircraft carriers are constructed with the main or hangar deck as the strength deck.

A good practice in modern ship design is to maintain a comparatively low profile in the superstructure, extend it to the full beam of the ship,

Figure 11–27. Deck Structure Looking Forward from Port Quarter Showing Cellular Construction Formed by Deck Beams and Girders

and thus carry the structural continuity into the uppermost deck. This concept was first introduced in the construction of the SS *United States* in the early 1950s. The superstructure not only must be made of the equivalent structural members ordinarily used in hull strength construction but also must be stressed accordingly for the increased distance from the neutral axis. Actually, the primary advantage of including the superstructure in the strength structure of the hull is that of greater overall strength with little increase in structural material. The theory is simply to increase the vertical dimension of the box girder form. The extensive use of aluminum instead of steel above the main deck in ships for structural considerations contributes substantially to improving stability and weight advantage.

Generally speaking, the strength deck in any ship should be as high as possible and yet compatible with stability considerations. Structural material high in the ship will have a pronounced effect on the center of gravity. Consequently, it is, like most other phases of the ship's design, a well-considered compromise.

BULKHEADS AND VERTICAL SUPPORT

Most bulkheads provide four important functions within the ship. First, they act as stiffeners for the entire hull structure; secondly, they distribute the vertical forces of weight and buoyancy through the hull's structure; thirdly, and most obviously, they serve to separate the ship's activities and functions; and, finally, they provide watertight subdivision. Some bulkheads, such as the main transverse bulkheads, are constructed to withstand severe hydrostatic pressure and the fluctuating stresses that might be imposed through flooding in free communication with the sea.

The first function (stiffening the hull's structure) is accomplished primarily by the *main transverse bulkheads* that extend continuously through the watertight volume of the ship from keel to main deck. Figure 11–28 shows a main transverse bulkhead at the forward end of the machinery spaces in a destroyer. These bulkheads resist the longitudinal twists and transverse stresses in the structure since they are stiffened both vertically and horizontally by stiffeners supported at the bottom, sides, and deck by brackets.

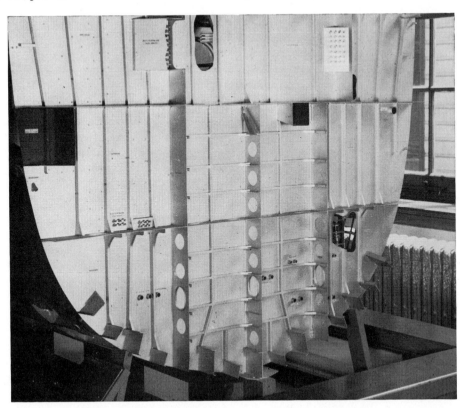

Figure 11–28. Main Transverse Bulkhead. (Note vertical and horizontal bulkhead stiffeners.)

They are joined to all structural members, plating, and longitudinal bulkheads which they contact. Where horizontal access or openings are required in bulkheads, the same means of preserving the strength continuity is used as in the decks. These transverse bulkheads perform all four of the above functions of bulkheads.

Longitudinal bulkheads are generally not continuous in the vertical direction unless they are side bulkheads providing space for liquid stowage and voids in the protective layer. In such case, they will extend continuously from the bottom to the second deck or just above the waterline.

Bulkheads, which are a structural part of the ship's girder, are called *structural* or *strength bulkheads*. Those which act strictly as partitions or divisions are called *nonstructural bulkheads*. There are, finally, special bulkheads which are a part of the protective system and are called *protective* or *splinter bulkheads*.

Nonstructural bulkheads are fabricated usually of light plate, often of stainless steel, aluminum, corrugated steel, or wire mesh. Usually, only light stiffeners are provided to prevent distortion. They are limited to the height of one deck and are not generally watertight.

Deck beams are supported at the sides by the frames to which they are attached. When away from the immediate vicinity of bulkheads, additional vertical support for deck beams is provided by stanchions. *Stanchions* are columns which are fitted in a vertical line from the highest deck down to the floors or frames to aid in carrying the vertical load.

The Basic Structure of Naval Submarines

The structure of a modern submarine consists of a watertight envelope, which is designed to resist the predetermined operational hydrostatic pressure. The principal elements are stiffened cylindrical sections, stiffened conical sections and the noncircular sections of the stiffened pressure hull, and closed end sections. Additionally, there is a secondary structure, which does not withstand the submerged sea pressure, called the nonpressure hull or outer hull.

The primary structural components, as in any ship, are the hull plating, hull stiffeners, and bulkheads. In the case of submarines, however, the thickness of the pressure hull plating is considerably greater than the hull plating for a surface ship, since it is designed to resist the hydrostatic loads of depths below 1000 feet. This heavy steel shell, well over one inch thick, is further strengthened by circular ring frames positioned externally and/or internally depending on location (see figure 11–29). These hull frames are of either **T** or **H** cross section and are either rolled or welded-up shapes. They are generally spaces at 0.1 to 0.2 diameters apart. Further wing bulkheads are placed to form tank boundaries, and additional stiffening with the shaped-end closure bulkheads complete the watertight hull.

To delineate the study of submarine structure, we will consider the structure in several main categories.

PRESSURE HULL

The pressure (strength) hull or the inner hull, as it is commonly referred to, must be comparatively strong and heavy to withstand hydrostatic pressures of deep submergence (test depth pressure). See figure 11–29. The principal structures associated with the pressure hull include the transverse bulkheads, which subdivide the submarine's length into watertight compartments, and circular transverse frames, both inside and out, which strengthen the hull and prevent collapsing when subject to test depth pressures. The pressure hull must form a watertight shell completely enclosing the operating spaces of the ship. Specifically, the pressure hull in nuclear submarines includes

- The main cylinder which extends for about 25 percent of the ship's amidship length. This is a single-hull section.
- A single-hull section comprising about 30 percent of the length, located aft.
- All boundaries of tanks subjected to full sea pressure.

OUTER HULL

The outer hull forms the external boundary of the submarine except for appendages such as the superstructure, conning tower, and fairwater (sail). See figure 11–29.

The principal outer hull structure includes a system of frames and bulkheads to subdivide the enclosed volume into tankage compartments. Certain portions of the outer hull, however, are subject to test depth pressures. These tanks (hard tanks) have heavily constructed frames and bulkheads which are almost a continuation of pressure

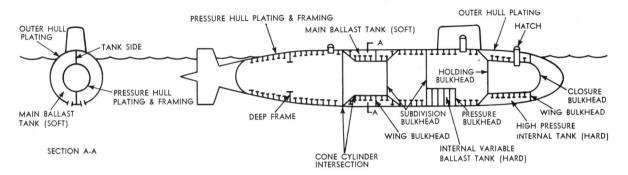

Figure 11–29. Structural Profile of a Submarine

hull framing rather than the lighter structure found in the portion of the outer hull forming external boundaries for tanks not subject to sea pressure. The outer hull structure also includes the vertical and flat plate keels.

APPENDAGES

Appendages are structural items, control surfaces, piping, and other gear external to the outer hull. It should be noted that the total volume displaced by a submerged ship equals the volume displaced by the outer hull plus the volume of the appendages.

SUPERSTRUCTURE AND FAIRWATER

The superstructure and fairwater are constructed of lightweight plating, as they are not subjected to any severe stresses and are not an integral part of the vessel's strength members. The form of the superstructure and fairwater provides an easy flow of water around blunt projections, thereby decreasing submerged resistance to forward motion. It is important to note that the void space enclosed by the superstructure and fairwater has nothing to do with the ship's submersible properties as it is completely vented and free flooding.

TANKAGE

Generally, submarine tankage can be separated into two main classes: high-pressure tanks and nonpressure tanks. High-pressure tanks are heavily constructed tanks built to withstand test depth pressures. During normal submerged operations these tanks may be full, partially full, or empty. Nonpressure tanks are of light construction and, though exposed to the sea, are not subject to hydrostatic pressures. During normal sub-

merged operations, these tanks are always completely full either with seawater, fuel oil, or a combination of both. Nonpressure tanks not directly connected to the sea, such as normal fuel oil tanks, are equipped with seawater compensating lines to admit seawater and maintain pressure equilibrium.

Another division of the principal tankage is by groups according to their function. The abbreviations *HP* and *NP* in the following list refer to the high pressure and nonpressure classification:

1. Diving ballast, *NP*, (soft)
   a. Main ballast tanks
   b. Fuel ballast tanks—used as such when converted to be a part of the main ballast system
2. Variable ballast, *HP*, (hard)
   a. Forward trim tank
   b. Auxiliary tanks
   c. After trim tank
   d. Variable fuel oil tanks

Safety and negative tanks can also be used in the variable ballast system.

3. Fuel tanks
   a. Normal fuel tanks, *NP*
   b. Fuel ballast tanks, *NP*—used as such when not part of the main ballast system
   c. Variable fuel oil tanks, *HP*
   d. Fuel oil collecting and expansion tanks, *NP*
4. Special purpose tanks
   a. Bow buoyancy tanks, *NP*
   b. Safety tank, *HP*
   c. Negative tank, *HP*

The functions of the above tanks are more fully considered in chapters 2 and 4.

Destroyer in a Rough Seaway

CHAPTER 12

The Ship in Motion with the Sea

During the design process, it is, perhaps, too easy and natural for the designer to think of the ship as a stationary structure or one that moves in equilibrium through a flat and motionless sea. Rationally and realistically, we know that this is not always true. However, because of necessity, many ship design concepts are based on quasi-static considerations. *Yet the ship's operational environment is the moving surface of the sea.*

This environment, together with the requirements of mobility, dictates a structure that is almost continuously in motion—a structure that must be so shaped and constructed that it can move safely, economically, and with some degree of comfort in the six degrees of freedom that it will encounter in the real sea.

Referring to figure 12–1, these six degrees of freedom (or motion) can be identified as:

Roll —rotation about the *XX'* axis.

Pitch —rotation about the *YY'* axis.

Yaw —rotation about the *ZZ'* axis.

Sway —lateral, linear motion (to port and starboard) along the *YY'* axis.

Surge —longitudinal motion, forward and astern, along the *XX'* axis. (Surge is, of course, superimposed on the ship's own velocity along its propelled track.)

All or any of these motions may coexist in a given short time period, one being superimposed on another, resulting in a most complex and confusing total movement. The underlying source of this random and complex motion is, of course, the motion of its supporting element, the sea. To better understand this motion and to admit it to its most important design consideration, we must break it down to its six components cited above. In this way, we can better understand and emphasize the more important elements of the motion as well as its more significant components.

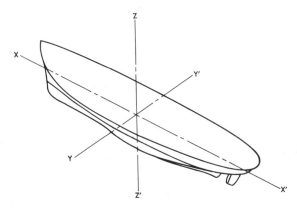

Figure 12–1. The Six Degrees of Freedom (or Motion)

Water in Motion

Before considering the motion of the ship, it is most necessary to have an understanding of the motion of the sea which is the basis for the random movement of the ship.

The wave motion of water at sea, or even in more restricted waters, is of a heterogeneous nature. To describe such motion analytically is extremely difficult and, in some phases, not possible, though theories based on geometrical and mathematical analysis have been advanced that follow closely certain actual wave phenomena.

Ocean waves generate some of the most powerful of all existing natural forces. Because of their tremendous power and their peculiar phenomena, they are also difficult to analyze, measure, and observe in a quantitative sense. However, it will be useful here to describe in a more qualitative way their source of origin, and the results of some observations about them.

WAVE ORIGIN

Sea waves are primarily the result of the transference of kinetic energy from the wind which, in turn, is the result of thermal energy transfer-

ence in weather phenomena. Wind passing over a broad, flat surface of water will set in motion small particles of water that accumulate along closely spaced, successive ridges at the surface and produce the small, rippled effect also commonly seen on sand dunes. As the wind force continues, the increased pressure on the windward side of each wavelet causes a further depression on the water, and the lower pressure on the leeward side causes a further elevation of the water in that area. The wave continues to grow with the persistence of the wind, and, under this distribution of pressures, the wind continually augments the size of the wave. The wind will continue to supply energy to the wave, and the wave will continue to grow in height and length until the excess energy supplied by the wind is entirely consumed by the internal friction of the water in the wave. In other words, energy will be supplied only as long as the wind velocity exceeds the velocity of the wave, and this, in general, limits the magnitude and the wavelength of the resulting wave.

The rate of increasing wave height is dependent on the difference in wind and wave velocities. A

Courtesy of Netherlands Ship Model Basin

Figure 12–2. A Ship Model in Irregular Waves

suddenly increasing wind in normal weather changes will cause a wave to increase in height at the rate of one or two feet per minute.

The increasing wavelength generally lags behind the increasing wave height, and, in land locked or restricted waters with a sudden squall, a maximum or limiting wave height is reached quickly. Further growth in wavelength becomes inhibited because surplus wind energy is absorbed in the turbulence of the water tumbled off the tops of the waves as *whitecaps*. This maximum wave height is a function of the ratio of wave height to length ratio is about 1/7 in deep water.

It is necessary here to use the oceanographer's term, *fetch*, to further amplify the discussion of wave height. This term refers to the distance that a wave has to run before it is destroyed by obstructing land. Depending upon the rate of build-up, the resulting height is also, of course, dependent upon the *life* or time the wave exists

before it is destroyed. So, if the rate of buildup is fast, the wave's height is restricted by the maximum wave height to wavelength ratio. If the rate of build-up is slow, the wave's height is restricted by the fetch.

Therefore, waves of great height cannot be built-up in restricted waters, such as bays and lakes, but winds gradually increasing to gale force over oceans where a fetch of 600 or 800 miles exists produce waves that carry enormous energy and reach the great heights peculiar only to ocean waves.

UNIFORMITY

A relationship of wave velocity, wavelength, and wave height is shown in figure 12–3. This curve is based on empirical data and is consistent with the best average observed data. One wave

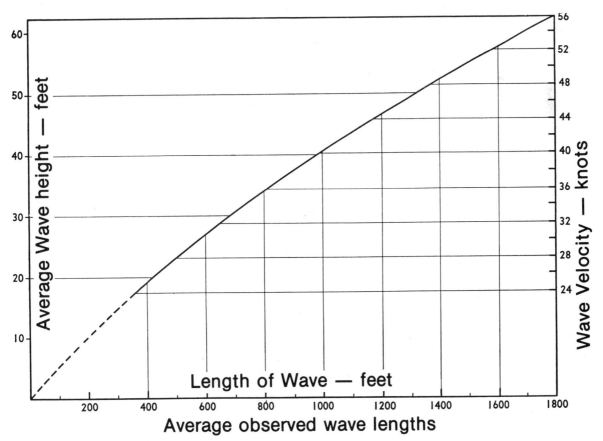

North Atlantic — Zimmerman's Report on wave observation

Figure 12–3. Wave Length, Height, and Velocity Relationship

train overriding another, wave trains crossing each other, waves moving against or with ocean currents, waves encountering shoal water, and waves interacting with island obstructions are only a few examples of the multiple causes that produce waves of irregular size and inconsistent variation in behavior. The pattern of actual waves in shape, magnitude, and behavior, then, can hardly be reduced to exact equations.

To an extent, however, an ideal condition can be constructed which adequately describes true ocean waves which are more or less uniform and are acting under a single influence. Such a theory will be presented later.

In recent years, a considerable amount of actual data has been amassed from extensive sea observations, and, with the help of electronic processing, it has been possible to isolate and identify the various components which produce the seemingly undescribable sea state. This concept of *superposition* of one wave train or system on another in a multitude of combinations is most helpful as will be seen later in analyzing the motion of a ship. At this particular point in the discussion, it will be more helpful to concentrate our attention on the nature of the isolated, regular wave or single, wave train.

Courtesy of the San Francisco Examiner

Figure 12–4. Long, Cresting Seas off the U.S. West Coast. The height of the breaking sea on this ship's bridge can be easily gauged, since the height of the ship's bridge deck is 33 feet above her waterline.

WAVE DURATION AND EXTENT

The maximum ratio of wave height to wave-length was given in the foregoing section as 1/7. This represents the limiting ratio where any increase beyond it results in an unstable (breaking) wave. If the wavelength is allowed to grow beyond 100 feet, there is little likelihood that such waves will ever encounter this limiting ratio. As a matter of fact, with increasing wavelength, actual observations show a continual decrease in the height-length ratio. For 500 to 600 foot wavelengths, the ratio is about 1/20; for the longest ocean waves (of about 1000 feet), the ratio drops to 1/50.

It was noted above that a multitude of factors influence the dynamics of water waves. We are primarily interested in the shape and motion of the longitudinal profile of a wave—specifically, the height, the length, the velocity, the period, the wave slope, etc. The mass of water involved, however, must necessarily involve the width dimension which is in a direction normal to the velocity. Theoretically, waves are considered to have an infinite width. Actually, the width of a wave is generally quite limited, seldom extending more than a few hundred yards. These are commonly known as *short-crested waves* and are the result of two longer crested waves of less height and nonparallel courses combining on a shorter front and increased height. It is possible, according to some authorities, that as such waves move farther away from an active storm area, they will separate again into their longer crested components. This theory would account for the long and extensively wide swells encountered hundreds of miles from low-pressure storm areas. Such ocean swells, sometimes misnamed *ground swells,* slowly diminish in height as they dissipate their original energy. This dissipation of energy may extend over more than a thousand miles of unobstructed ocean or over a few thousand feet of beach.

THE STRUCTURE OF A TROCHOIDAL WAVE

It is a matter of simple observation that a wave is a type of vertical change in the conformation of the water surface and *not* the horizontal movement of the water itself. This periodic and vertical oscillation of the water would suggest that the particles of water might be moving up and down linearly in harmonic motion. On further consideration, it will be seen that such vertical, linear motion cannot be possible. If the concept were true, there would be a compression in the water under a trough and a void under a crest at some depth in the water. Consequently, we must look for a more valid description of the motion of the water particles. It is an acceptable hypothesis that the particles of water in wave motion travel in vertical orbits which may be circular or elliptical. These orbits would diminish in size with increasing depth from the surface, until at some depth (depending upon the height and length of the surface wave), there is no further vertical motion. Presuming that this path of a water particle in a wave is circular and not elliptical, which appears to be the case from observed deep water waves under ideal conditions, it is possible to construct, in vertical cross section, the motion of water in a wave from trough to crest. A somewhat modified illustration of this structure is given in figure 12–5.

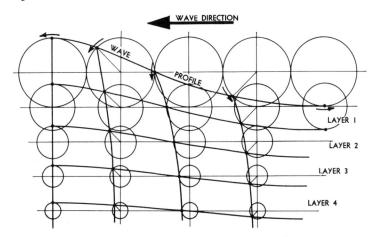

Figure 12–5. Vertical Structure of a Trochoidal Wave

In this diagram, a particle of water on the surface rotates in the largest circles. Such a particle will be at the top of its circular orbit when the crest of the wave is, at that instant, passing it. Likewise, the same particle will be at the bottom of its orbit when the trough of the wave is passing. It is in fact this uniform rotational velocity of each adjacent particle on the surface that produces the wave motion. At each successively deeper layer, the orbits of the particles become successively smaller in radii, thus producing waves in these layers of decreasing amplitude. The orbital radii approach in infinitesimal value as the depth is further increased, and the resulting wave disturbance at some finite depth below the surface becomes negligible.

Geometrically, a point on a circle rolling on a horizontal line describes a curve called a cycloid.

A point on a concentric circle of smaller radius within this first circle describes a trochoid. In figure 12–5, the points on adjacent orbits which show the relative position of the particles in the orbits are connected by a curve. This curve is a trochoid. The trochoidal wave generated may be steep or shallow, depending upon the ratio of the diameter of the generating circle to the wave-length. This trochoidal wave-form corresponds very closely to observed actual waves, and its exact geometrical structure allows analysis of the motion and the forces applied to a ship floating in waves. A typical example of its application has already been described in chapter 11, where hogging and sagging stresses of a ship were analyzed on a trochoidal wave of height $1.1 \sqrt{L_w}$. (See figures 11–7 and 11–8.)

Photograph by Bernard Benson

Figure 12–6. A Tanker's Bow Meets the Oncoming Sea. The sea's force is evident as the vessel fails to rise out of the trough adequately. The ship is the 50,000 ton tanker, Marita, of Ocean Oil Carriers, Inc.

WAVE ENERGY

The energy in a wave is the result of the transference of wind energy, and, as such energy continues to be imparted, the increasing wave height is a manifestation of the wave's accumulating energy.

It was shown in the foregoing section that in deep water each wave particle moved in a circular orbit at a constant angular velocity. Consequently, each particle of water will have a constant kinetic energy of

$$\frac{m}{2} (\omega r)^2$$

where m is the mass of the particle and ωr is the instantaneous velocity. For a whole wave stratum of a single wavelength, including one trough and one crest, the energy is half potential and half kinetic. By integration of the above, the total energy may be reduced to an expression which, when simplified, gives

$$E \approx \frac{\rho L_w a^2 g}{8}$$

ρg = density of the water (lbs/ft.³)
L_w = wave length (ft.)
a = wave height (ft.)
E = energy per ft. of wave breadth.

According to the above expression, a 600-foot wave whose height is $L/20$ would have an energy of 2000 foot-tons per foot of width.

Actual instrument tests have measured wave forces as large as 6000 pounds per square foot. Assuming that a wave of this magnitude were traveling at an instantaneous velocity of 30 knots, this would indicate an energy of 18 million foot-pounds per minute per square foot of frontal area. Ships that move in seas whose energy is of this magnitude obviously cannot counter or resist it. As much as possible, they must and do move with the motion of the water, and, in such a head sea, the speed must be reduced to a bare steerageway. Extraneous deck gear and superstructure outside the structural limits of the hull must be designed to withstand wave energies within reasonable limits. (See figures 12–4 and 12–6.)

By referring again to the equation above, it will be seen that the energy necessary to produce a wave varies approximately in proportion to the square of its height; thus, a wave twice as high as another of the same length and speed requires four times the energy to sustain it. This is an important and interesting facet of wave theory when applied to the wave-making resistance of a ship. It has undoubtedly been noticed by anyone who has observed ships moving close at hand that some vessels make a deeper and more pronounced wave system than others. This is in the direct relation as shown in the above equation where the amount of energy expended in producing a wave of a given length and speed varies in proportion to the square of its height. This visible, deep wave along the side of a tugboat or cargo vessel is evidence of a comparatively large amount of power expended at a fairly low speed. A destroyer or cruiser moving at the same low speed would have an almost imperceptible transverse wave of the same wavelength. Thus, ships with large displacement-length ratios or large beam-length ratios produce large wave systems which represent the energy required for moving larger masses of water per unit of time.

It should be reiterated that the *trochoidal theory* briefly described is based entirely on an assumed geometrical structure with the corresponding motion computed on such a structure. The theoretical structure, however, corresponds so closely to the actual observed wave that the theory for practical applications is in most cases useful and valid. It is helpful to itemize some of the theoretical assumptions with their limits below as a summary of the value of the trochoidal wave.

- The motion is assumed to be two-dimensional.
- The orbital paths of the particles are assumed to be circular and their velocity in these paths uniform.
- Particles whose orbit centers are at the same horizontal level move in successive phases differing by a constant amount.
- Particles whose orbit centers lie in the same vertical line all move in the same phase.
- Dimensional relationships for a trochoidal wave are

$$c = 1.34 \sqrt{L_w}$$
$$T = .442 \sqrt{L_w}$$
$$L_w = .557 c^2 = 5.118 T^2$$

where

c = velocity in knots
T = period in seconds
L_w = wavelength in feet.

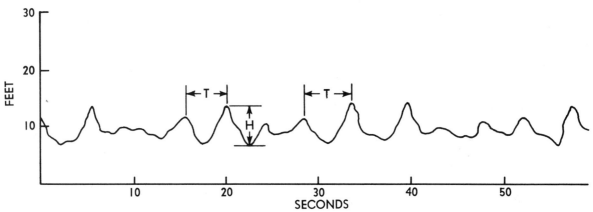

Figure 12–7a. Typical Record of Wave Heights and Periods with Resulting Wave (Profile) Spectrum

The trochoidal structure assumes that the water is infinitely deep and that the orbital motion of the particles becomes infinitely small, approaching zero at this infinite depth. However, for practical purposes, computations show that at a depth of water equal to the length of the wave itself, the orbital radius is so small that the motion of the water is virtually zero.

The naval architect finds it useful and practical to utilize the trochoidal wave model to guide him in many design problems involving ship motion and buoyant support in a seaway. As a pure geometric form, it can be easily constructed graphically and introduced mathematically into equations of motions. However, it must be reiterated that the surface of the sea seldom is characterized by a long-crested wave system of even approximate regularity. A two-dimensional profile of a typical ocean surface is indicated in figure 12–7a. The irregularity of the profile is the most common feature of this typical representation.

Notice, however, that throughout the length of this limited sampling, there is a tendency for a uniform period to predominate. Also notice a recurrent buildup of large amplitude waves as well as a recurrent subsidence. These phenomena are indications of the superposition of a dominant wave system of some regularity on one slightly less dominant but following with more or less similar regularity another frequency. There are, sometimes, indications of the presence of multiple subsystems (which is also typical). By statistical analysis of thousands of samplings, such as this, as well as total surface contours, such as in figure 12–8 over a standard block area, it is

possible, through computer analysis, to isolate the significant components. It is possible, therefore, to construct a typical sea by the superposition of the component waves, thus providing a satisfactory base to study and analyze ship motions as well as creating small-scale duplicate conditions in model tanks. A graphical description, plotting a function of the square of the wave height versus wave frequency, characterizes a specific sea condition and is generally referred to as a *sea spectrum*. (See figure 12–7b.)

The most troublesome aspects of ship's motion resulting from the motion of the sea are confined to those involving the greatest amounts of acceleration. Basically, aside from steering difficulties in yawing, the angular motions would appear of more concern than the linear movement. Roll and pitch will, in the following discussions, be given the greater attention, but again, like the

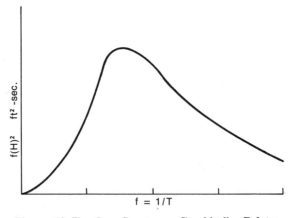

Figure 12–7b. *Sea Spectrum* Graphically Relates Functions of Wave Height and Period

Figure 12–8. Aerial View Showing Typical Random Wave Distribution of Confused Seas

surface of the sea, these motions must be thought of as the most predominant components of the total complex motion of the ship.

Before dealing separately with these components, a brief description of the combined motion may be appropriate at this point. A ship moving directly into a pure head sea will only undergo (when the sea is of sufficient wavelength) a pitching and heaving motion. However, as has been already noted, there is seldom if ever a sea motion that might be described as pure or regular. As the ship's bow drops into a wave trough and its stern rises on a crest, the water particles at the bow move against the ship in a direction opposed to those at the stern. Unless the ship encounters the wave directly head on this produces a yawing moment. As the ship responds to the pitching moment and the yawing moment, it finds itself astride a wave which produces a rolling moment. Here we have only noted the angular motion, but it takes little further imagination to appreciate the introduction of the vertical, lateral, and longitudinal components. We must, to bring some order from this confusing conglomerate, proceed to con-

sider the component motions singly and, from the design standpoint, to deal with them singly. Anti-roll devices have been developed and, when used, have all but eliminated the concern of roll. Anti-pitch devices have, however, shown little promise of providing a solution to the problem of pitch.

Rolling in a Seaway and Its Relation to Stability

NATURAL PERIOD OF ROLL

In a previous discussion of stability characteristics, a ship of comparatively large $\overline{GM}$ was found to be more uncomfortable in a seaway than a ship of a smaller $\overline{GM}$. This viewpoint, based on the consideration that a large $\overline{GM}$ results in a so-called "stiff" ship, reflects a comparatively short and rapid period of roll and a quick recovery at the limits of roll.

In still water, a stable ship can be made to roll by application and subsequent removal of an external heeling moment. In the inclined position, a righting moment exists equal and opposite in direction to the heeling moment. When the external moment is removed from the ship in this position, the righting moment produces rotation of the ship towards the upright position. The potential energy existing in the inclined position (neglecting friction of the water) is entirely converted to energy of motion, so that in the upright position, it is all kinetic energy. The ship will, therefore, continue its rotation to the other side until the kinetic energy has been reconverted to potential at the opposite limit of roll. Assuming no loss due to friction, the ship will continue to oscillate or roll indefinitely from side to side with constant amplitude. However, in practice, friction between the hull and water and radiating waves will dampen the oscillations as the original energy is gradually absorbed.

It may be assumed without appreciable error, that the axis of roll is longitudinal through G in most ships. Under this assumption and by keeping in mind the conception of rolling outlined above, the natural period of a ship rolling in still water without damping may be evaluated from the simple harmonic motion relationship for period as

$$T = \frac{1.108k}{\sqrt{\overline{GM}}},$$

where k is the transverse radius of gyration of the mass of the ship, and T is the period of a complete roll in seconds.

Subject to our condition that $\overline{GZ} = \overline{GM} \sin \phi$ for small angles, the period of roll will be independent of ϕ, the amplitude. Because it is a difficult and tedious job to determine the value of k for any ship, it is possible to assume that it is a function of the beam and that it varies directly with it, and further state the equation for roll empirically as:

$$T = \frac{CB}{\sqrt{\overline{GM}}},$$

where C is an empirical constant. (For large ships, C varies between .38 and .55, depending upon the ship and its loading.) B in this relationship is the extreme beam in feet.

A SHIP'S ROLL BY WAVE ACTION

The elements that cause a ship to roll in a sea are primarily the unbalanced moments resulting from a shifting center of buoyancy. As a wave approaches and passes under a ship, the waterplane is in a state of motion and is inclined at a rate depending upon the frequency, length, and amplitude of the wave. The center of buoyancy, whose position depends upon the slope of the waterplane at any given draft, will move out of a vertical line through the center of gravity if the waterline is inclined. The transverse component of this inclination results in an inclining arm being set up whereby the ship will heel and tend to align itself so that the center plane will be perpendicular to the wave surface. This action is, however, modified to some extent by the motion of the ship with the water itself.

It was developed earlier in this chapter that the water in a seaway involved in wave action moves in an orbital path. Halfway up on the upper slope of a wave, the water particles are moving vertically upward; at the crest, they are moving horizontally with the wave front; halfway down on the down-slope, they are moving vertically downward; and in the trough, they are moving horizontally against the wave front. Thus, a ship floating in large waves will be influenced by the orbital motion of the water itself. In so doing, there exists a centrifugal force that must be considered in addition to the forces of gravity and buoyancy. This centrifugal force is opposed by the dynamic force of the water which it produces, and consequently there are two distinct couples acting upon the ship and causing its rolling action—first, the familiar one between buoyancy and gravity and, secondly, the one between the centrifugal force of the ship moving in an orbital motion and the dynamic opposing force of the water. The periodic action of the first couple was described in the preceding article, where it was shown that the ship has a characteristic natural period of roll. The second couple is produced by forces which are entirely a function of the wave motion itself. The ship, and more specifically its center of gravity, moves in a circular orbit with a motion having the same period and orbital radius as the particles of water at the same level outside. The resulting centrifugal force, acting through the center of gravity and opposing the hydrodynamic force acting through the center of buoyancy, therefore, produces the new couple which has the periodic motion of the waves in which the ship rolls.

Consequently, the resulting period of roll is a function of both the ship's natural roll period and the period of the waves. Such a statement, how-

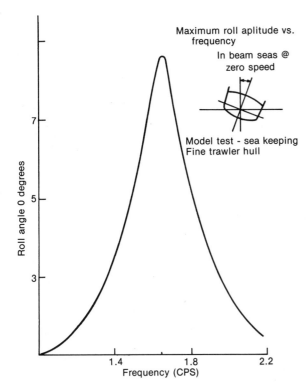

Maximum roll aplitude vs. frequency

In beam seas @ zero speed

Model test - sea keeping Fine trawler hull

Figure 12–9. The Roll Amplitude Related to the Period or Cyclic Frequency in Beam Seas shows the Sharp Tuning Phenomena of Synchronism

ever, is incomplete and inconclusive without taking note of another fundamental fact. In the preceding section, a ship rolling in still water in its own natural period was subjected to only a single initial impulse and allowed to roll freely until the energy from this initial impulse was entirely consumed by the resistance of the water. This motion is known as *free oscillation*. A ship rolling in waves, however, is subject to nearly periodic impulses, with the result known as *forced oscillation* or *forced rolling*. (See figure 12–9.)

It should be pointed out here that these periodic impulses are the predominant humps of the random, irregular sea, and that these waves tend toward regularity when they are the components of a predominant, underlying wave system.

Any suspended object, such as a pendulum, if free to oscillate when subjected to a series of forced impulses of regular frequency, will oscillate in the period of applied impulses. Thus the ship, if rolling in waves of exact uniformity and regular period, would assume eventually a period of roll identical to that of the waves. However, real sea waves are not constant in either period, ampli-

tude, or wavelength and will, therefore, produce a series of more or less non-uniform impulses. Under such conditions where the impulses producing the roll are not fairly regular, it is the ever-present tendency of the ship to revert to its own natural period of roll—a period which is the result of an independent impulse. Consequently, the overall result is a period of roll for the ship that is a combination of its own natural period and the period of the waves producing the rolling moment, where the *latter* is generally the more predominant *period*.

SYNCHRONOUS ROLL

When the apparent period (i.e., the interval at which the wave impulse strikes the ship) is the same or nearly the same as the natural period of the ship, a superposition of periodic inclining energies exists, and the result is an unduly heavy roll.

Such heavy rolling is not uncommon, nor is it difficult to distinguish from rolling or heeling caused by inadequate stability. However, synchronous rolling has frequently been mistaken, or misunderstood, and wrongly attributed to lack of stability. In most cases, nothing could be farther from the facts. As will be seen immediately below, ships of large $\overline{GM}$ or large static righting moments, are those which are more apt to encounter serious synchronous rolling. Ships of very low $\overline{GM}$ are much less frequently subject to such rolling.

It will be recalled from the equation for a ship's natural period of roll,

$$T = \frac{CB}{\sqrt{\overline{GM}}},$$

that the period varies inversely as the square root of the metacentric height. Therefore, the greater the metacentric height for the same beam, the shorter is the natural period of roll. At the same time, for larger vessels, the shorter the period of roll (12 seconds and below), the greater is the probability of synchronism among large sea waves. For example, large Atlantic storm waves are about 500 to 600 feet between crests (wave length) and have a period of 10 to 11 seconds. Under such conditions, a large ship of moderate or low metacentric height would have a period in excess of the period of these waves and would be comparatively steady in such a seaway. On the other hand, a similar ship of fairly large $\overline{GM}$, with a period of approximately 10 to 11 seconds, would be an extremely bad roller in this situation.

Furthermore, the factors determining the period of roll are the metacentric height and the beam as a function of the radius of gyration. It may be noted that approximate typical periods of a carrier and a destroyer in normal conditions are 17.0 and 8.0 seconds respectively. This would indicate that the destroyer of smaller $\overline{GM}$ might increase her natural period to be in synchronism with a heavy sea with a *decrease* in metacentric height. This is a more likely situation than the carrier which, in the case cited, would have to increase her $\overline{GM}$ to approximately 16 feet before the period would decrease to a synchronous value. Consequently, with the existing variety of ship sizes, shapes, and consequent variable values of $\overline{GM}$, it would be wiser to analyze any situation as a separate problem, noting only in general that for most large ocean-going vessels, is relatively high $\overline{GM}$ may result in a period producing synchronism in a heavy sea.

It should be noted also that naval vessels are designed with metacentric heights dictated by the requirements of stability in probable damaged conditions, beam winds, high-speed turning, etc. The metacentric heights of such ships are therefore maintained at relatively high values. Ocean-going passenger vessels have a much lower range of values of $\overline{GM}$, and thereby fulfill a requirement based essentially upon the comfort of passengers.

Pitching

With regard to the nature and causes of pitching, it may be considered as a phenomenon identically analogous to rolling except that the axis of rotation is at 90 degrees to the rolling axis in the same plane.

The natural period of pitch does not lend itself to an empirical expression as easily as the period of roll, primarily because of the lack of longitudinal symmetry of a ship. However, pitch period is related in a similar way to the longitudinal metacentric height, $\overline{GM'}$, as rolling period is to

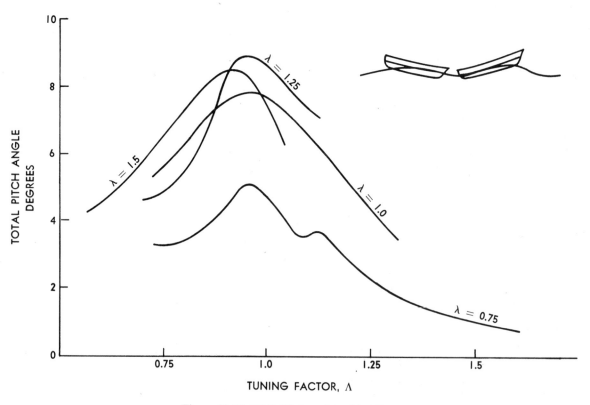

Figure 12–10. Pitch Motions from Test Results

$\overline{GM}$, and an expression, $T_p = 1.108\ k_{yy}'/\sqrt{GM'}$, is valid, however much its practical value may be limited. The natural period of pitch is usually between one-third and two-thirds of the natural period of roll.

Where pitch, yaw, and heave are concerned, it is more difficult to describe ship motion as a single phenomenon as in the case of roll. Particularly interrelated are pitch and heave, which are together influenced by roll, yaw, sway, and surge. To describe these predominant motions mathematically requires certain linearized theories, such as "strip" theory, together with the development of coupled differential equations. The entire theoretical study of ship motion is introduced in the more advanced courses of naval architecture.

It is more helpful in this discussion for the new student of ship design to consider the actual observed motions in model tests or those recorded in ships in a seaway in terms of two-dimensional movement.

Model tests in tanks producing predictable waves under programmed control are excellent analytical aids in investigating ship responses to the seaway. They permit a great number of variables to be explored quickly and efficiently and

provide a reliable prediction of any particular ship design's seakeeping character. (See figures 12–2, 12–10 and 12–11.)

In comparing responses that appear to be common for most ships and that are obtained from many model tests of a great variety of ship forms, it will be helpful to introduce two new parameters. One of these, *tuning factor,* has been mentioned before but not specifically defined. The ratio of the natural period of ship oscillation to the period of encounter of the wave action is referred to as the *tuning factor,* Λ, or

$$\Lambda = \frac{T}{T_e}.$$

In terms of pitch, then, the tuning factor would be the pitch period, T_p, divided by the apparent period of the wave component producing a pitching moment. If a ship in its usual circumstance is moving ahead at a constant velocity into a head sea or on the bow sea, this period of encounter of the wave action would be shorter than if the ship were stopped or going astern in the same wave system. The value may be obtained by actual observation or by computation using the equations

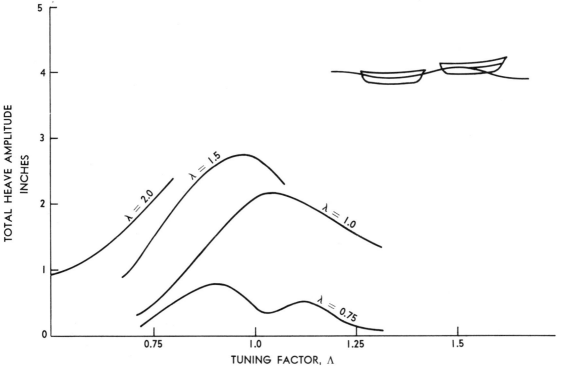

Figure 12–11. Heave Motions from Test Results

given earlier in this chapter for velocity and period of waves.

Another important ratio or parameter used in analyzing pitching and heaving characteristics is the ratio of the apparent wavelength to the waterline length of the ship, or

$$\lambda = L_w/L_{pp}$$

In referring again to actual ship observations and model test observations, typical ship response curves are given in figures 12–10 and 12–11 in terms of tuning factor and apparent wavelength ratio for both pitch and heave motions. The quantitative values for amplitudes in these curves are, of course, for particular model size but should be read *only* in a comparative way. The significant phenomenon in these curves, however, is the indication that peak values for both pitch and heave occur very near a tuning factor of 1.0 or close to pitch synchronism.

Not shown on these two plots but revealed in model tests is that the maximum acceleration values as well as the maximum amount of forefoot emergence also occur at or near synchronism. It is also interesting to note that the bow seems to be prone to plunge down into the crests and up at every hollow when in synchronism. (See figure 12–6.)

Pitch-heave motion acting as a coupled motion, as it does in a real sea, produces several objectionable conditions of ship operation, the most undesirable of which are reduction of speed, slamming, and wet decks as well as the related interference with human functions and machinery.

Apparently, moderate variation in hull form contributes relatively little to the reduction of synchronous pitch phenomena. There are certain damping factors, however, that can partially eliminate or noticeably reduce some of the objectionable conditions noted. In hull form design, a sharp or fine entrance combined with hollow, flaring sections produce an early and easily excited pitching motion. This condition may be offset by more convexity in the forward and after sections. There has also been some laboratory scale success with fixed fins installed horizontally and laterally on the forefoot. Full-scale experiments have generally failed because of structural failure of the fins. However, bulbous bows (described in chapter 5) appear to have a damp-

ing effect on pitching which is largely dependent on the volume, shape, and location of the bulb.

Heaving

When considered separately, heaving motion has several interesting aspects that must be considered. They are peculiar to only the heaving component of the coupled motion. (See figure 12–11.)

If a ship could be forced down vertically in still water and then have the force suddenly released, it would bob up and down vertically in a natural period of oscillation. This sort of oscillation is called *dipping*, and the natural period for such motion may be expressed as

$$T_d = \frac{2\pi}{\sqrt{\dfrac{12gTPI}{\Delta}}}$$

where *TPI* is tons per inch and Δ is displacement.

When the dipping motion is produced periodically by the vertical rise and fall of a wave, the resulting motion is *heaving,* and the resulting period is a combination of its dipping period and the apparent period of the waves. The wave period generally becomes the predominant factor but is subject to dampening factors in the hull form.

The primary significance of heaving motion alone is the effect of acceleration on the apparent mass of the ship. Recalling that transverse stability is expressed as the product of the ship's displacement and the righting arm, it is apparent that in a seaway, where the ship is subjected to heaving motion, the stability is both increased and decreased periodically as the acceleration becomes maximum in the positive and negative sense. A ship lifted upwards by a wave would, at the topmost position in this movement, have the minimum apparent gravity and consequently, at this instant, have the *least resistance to inclining moments.* The opposite would be true at the deepest point in the ship's downward movement.

Yawing

Yawing is the angular motion about a vertical axis through the ship's center of gravity. The motion may be generally said to be the result of three factors other than poor steering: (a) inequality of static pressures on the hull, (b) orbital motion of the water in a seaway, and (c) gyroscopic action.

Generally in a seaway, the wave profile on the port and starboard sides of the ship is not the same, and, as a result, the longitudinal position of the center of pressure on one side of the submerged portion of the ship is offset both longitudinally and vertically from that on the other side. This produces a rotating couple about the vertical axis or a yawing tendency, as well as a heeling moment. As the wave profile changes with the passing seas, this yawing couple changes in magnitude and alternates in direction, producing an oscillation. This oscillation will occur in the apparent period of the waves passing the ship. It is best corrected by anticipating the motion and meeting it with compensating rudder action.

In addition to the aforementioned quasi-static forces producing yawing, a dynamic yawing action is produced by the orbital rotation of the water in a wave. It will be recalled that the particles at the crest of the wave are moving at the top of a circular orbit in the direction of wave advance; in the trough of the wave, they are at the bottom of their orbit and moving in a direction opposite to the wave advance. Thus a ship moving in a quartering sea or with the sea at an angle on the bow is subjected to a yawing couple. (See figure 12–12.)

As the wave passes the ship, changing from the crest to the trough at the bow and from the trough to the crest in the after portions of the ship, this couple is reversed. The net result is a yawing oscillation with the same period as the period of encounter of the waves.

Rudder compensation for yaw from this dynamic and orbital motion of water is more difficult. This is because every half wavelength, the water in the vicinity of the rudder will be moving in the same direction as the ship, and a severely reduced turning couple can be developed by the rudder. This loss of control is especially critical if the rudder is not located in the propeller race. If

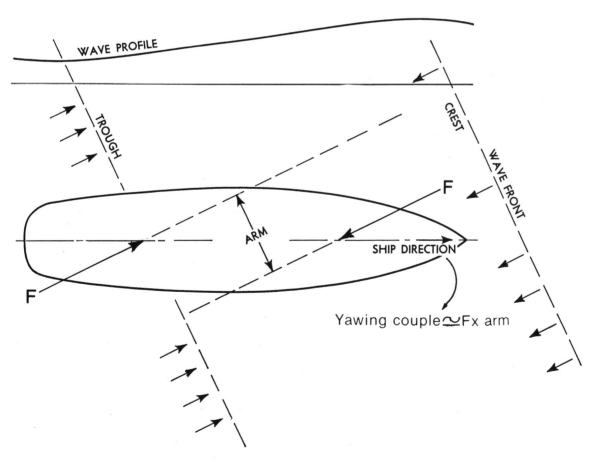

Figure 12–12. Yawing Couple in a Seaway

the seas are large and this dynamic yaw develops to serious proportions, the best resource with which to combat it on a multiple-screw ship is the opposed variation of propeller speed. In some cases, loading to trim by the stern may be helpful.

When a ship is pitching in a seaway and is also subjected to rolling action, the rolling motion is taking place about the *moving axis* caused by pitch. This angular motion occurring in two planes simultaneously results in a gyroscopic action which develops motion in the third plane, which is yaw.

Fortunately, the gyroscopic couple developing this yawing motion is seldom very large because of the relatively low velocities involved, and less rudder angle is required to control it than the yawing motion resulting from other causes.

Motion Damping Devices

It has been the ship designer's unhappy lot through the centuries to cope with the difficult movement of the ship in a seaway and to try to devise means to damp or reduce the more objectionable components of ship motions, primarily roll and pitch. The reduction of these motions as well as yaw has been the object of extensive research and many odd inventions. Most of the many devices of the past, as, for example, the passengers' salon of an early nineteenth century English Channel ferryboat which was suspended in gimbals, have been for one reason or another only partially successful. There have been in recent years several notable exceptions, and successful reduction and damping of excessive rolling to almost negligible proportions has been (where economically justified) accomplished. The mechanical problems have not been entirely solved nor indeed has any single device emerged as being more successful than any of the others.

In general, all stabilization systems depend on the motion of mass and may be classified properly as follows:

- Type of Force Utilized
  a. Counterweight. Gravitational force
  b. Acceleration. Inertial force
- Location of System
  a. Internal
  b. External
- Type of Mass
  a. Solid
  b. Liquid.

Not all of the above types will be described as examples of applications here—only those which are most successful and more frequently used. In the case of anti-roll devices, these include

- Bilge keels
- Controllable fins
- Anti-rolling tanks
- Gyrostabilizer (active type).

BILGE KEELS

The long fin-like projections attached to most ships along the turn of the bilge and extending from one-half to two-thirds of the ship's length are normally referred to as bilge keels or anti-rolling keels. These attachments are undoubtedly the simplest, probably the oldest, and one of the most successful and economical means of reducing the rolling motion of a ship.

The bilge keel is generally a continuous attachment of a single, heavy steel plate structure on large ships that projects from two to four feet from the hull and is approximately normal (perpendicular) to the hull surface. On larger ships, the bilge keel is of a **V**-shaped cross section and is generally filled solidly with wood to prevent crushing when docking or grounding. (See figure 12–13.)

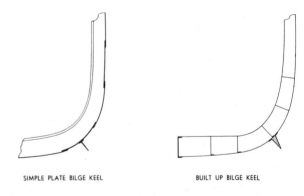

SIMPLE PLATE BILGE KEEL   BUILT UP BILGE KEEL

Figure 12–13. Bilge Keels

On some smaller craft, the bilge keel may be of light steel plate and may be attached by welding at regular short intervals and undercutting in between the welded attachments.

Regardless of the specific structural shape and details, bilge keels operate on a very simple and effective theory. Recalling the equation where

$$T = \frac{1.108\ k}{\sqrt{GM}},$$ it was pointed out that k was the

radius of mass gyration of the ship in roll. With

bilge keels projecting from the sides of the ship causing a somewhat increased mass of water to roll with the ship, the dimension, *k,* in the above equation is increased, thus increasing the period of roll. Under forced rolling conditions encountered in a seaway, with the increased natural period, the amplitude of roll is consequently decreased. The major effect of bilge keels, however, is the increased resistance to roll due to the viscous-eddy effect (see chapter 5).

From both test results and observed results, it is indicated that bilge keels are more effective on a ship when moving ahead through waves than when stopped. Such observations suggest that there is a hydrodynamic lift in the forward sections of the bilge keels. This hydrodynamic lift resists the lateral forces of roll and adds to the steadiness of the ship. In this sense, bilge keels are essentially elongated fins acting as hydrofoils and are a special application of fixed stabilizing fins. Fins and hydrofoils will be more fully explored in subsequent sections, but, in relation to bilge keels, further tests have shown that their dynamic effect could be improved by constructing them in shorter sections rather than in the conventional single continuous section commonly used. However, where dynamically suppressed roll is desirable, it is more effective to use controlled stabilizing fins. It should be pointed out that bilge keels must be considered as a means of reducing roll with no attempt toward nearly complete elimination. There must be a rolling action

Official U.S. Coast Guard Photograph

Figure 12–14. USCGC Dallas, a Modern Ship Fitted with Anti-Rolling Tanks. She is also equipped with the most advanced type of ship control system and propulsive equipment including CODAG—combined twin gas turbine engines (36,000 SHP) and twin diesels (7000 HP). She has controllable pitch propellers and bow thruster.

of some magnitude for them to be effective. They are essentially roll damping devices of a static type, requiring no energy supply.

That bilge keels are used on almost every ship regardless of size or type attests to their adaptability. Their simplicity, economy, and effectiveness make them universally attractive.

CONTROLLABLE FINS

Controllable fins are discussed in chapter 8 under *Other Control Surfaces*.

ANTI-ROLLING TANKS

There have been many types of internal tanks designed to produce counter-rolling moments, and they have been tried with varied degrees of success. No attempt will be made here to describe all these various systems. Rather, it would be more pertinent to single out one of the most successful of this type of anti-rolling device.

One such device is the *Frahm* anti-rolling tank which consists basically of a **U**-shaped tank system transversely arranged from side to side. Actually, the system contains two vertical legs (one to port and one to starboard) connected by a horizontal leg. The horizontal leg is of a smaller sectional area than the vertical legs, and when the system is approximately half filled with water, it is so designed that the natural period of oscillation of the water is approximately equal to that of the ship—actually slightly less. The vertical legs are connected across the top by an air line whose dimensions are also critical in affecting the period of the water in the system. This air line is equipped with valves which, upon adjustment, can control the amount of water transferred between legs and the phase relation between the roll of the ship and the transfer of the water. The phase lag is adjusted to about 90 degrees so that the water in the horizontal leg is always running downhill to the low tank thus creating a damping moment and resisting the roll of the ship.

It is customary to locate the tanks above the center of gravity of the ship. This is primarily because the moment of force due to the horizontal acceleration of the water should be in the same direction as the static moment of the water in the vertical legs.

Figure 12–15 is a schematic sectional sketch showing the arrangement of Frahm tanks with a record of the ship's oscillation with the system not operating and then operating.

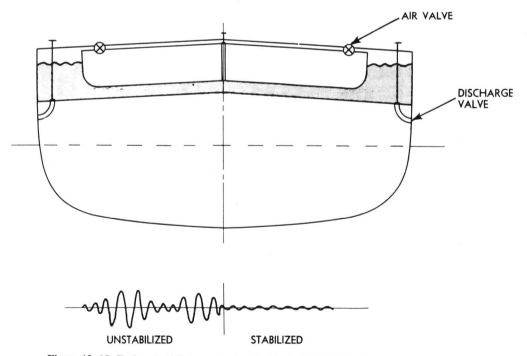

Figure 12–15. Frahm Anti-Rolling Tank with Typical Stabilizing Record

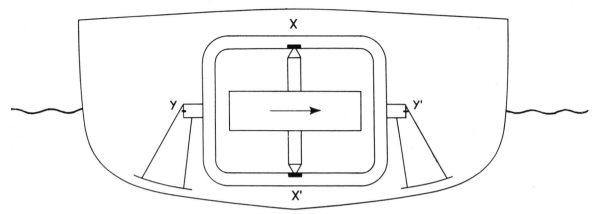

Figure 12–16. Simple Gyroscope Stabilization

GYROSTABILIZERS

The action of a gyrostabilizer is based on the elementary theory of a gyroscope. Assume a gyroscope spinning in its frame with its axis, *XX'*, vertical as in figure 12–16. The frame is attached through bearings to the structure of the ship along axis *YY'*. Now suppose the ship is subjected to a rolling moment, i.e., motion about its longitudinal axis. This will result in a precession of the gyroscope's axis and a resisting couple set up to the initial rolling moment. Such a simple arrangement as described above is the basic gyro which could be classified as the passive or responsive type. However, in application, it has been improved by the Sperry Gyroscope Co. wherein it becomes classified as an active type. In this development as it is applied in ships, there is a pilot gyro. The pilot gyro serves to actuate the primary gyro so as to cause it to precess in a direction opposite to that which would result from the rolling of the ship. Gyrostabilizers of this type have been used successfully for many years, particularly in smaller ships such as pilot vessels and yachts. The largest vessel in which the gyro system has been used was the passenger liner of the pre-World War II period, *Conte di Savoia,* an Italian luxury liner of more than 40,000 tons displacement. This ship contained three gyrostabilizers with rotors 13 feet in diameter, whose aggregate weight when installed was 690 tons or about 1.72 percent of the displacement. In operation, this installation accomplished about 60 percent stabilization (reduction of roll). While this is a fair amount of stabilization, it by no means represents the best performances of gyrostabilizers which have shown the ability to reduce roll up to 80 percent.

Gyrostabilizers are better installed on small- or moderate-size ships because of the structural limitations of size and mass. Larger vessels today depend almost exclusively on controllable fins or anti-roll tanks for effective roll stabilization.

PITCH STABILIZATION

With nearly completely effective roll stabilization, the motion of pitch takes on increased importance, and the awareness becomes acute where roll was previously the predominant problem. Unfortunately, pitch damping or control has not been as successful by any criteria primarily because of the greater moments to be overcome.

It has been mentioned previously in this chapter that fixed, horizontal, bow fins have been tried experimentally with disappointing results. Model tank experiments indicate that such fins, which are attached on each side of the forefoot, can be most effective. However, their impracticality to date has been the result primarily of side effects. Because of the fluctuation and variation of pressures on each side of the bow, these fins become subject to severe vibration. These racking vibratory forces, together with the impact forces of slamming and the reversal of hydrodynamic lift in normal pitch damping, make fins a major problem for structural strength. They are often lost in seas where they could be most helpful. This is an area offering stimulating opportunities for further research.

DYNAMIC STABILITY

The term *dynamic* pertains to energy and forces involving motion rather than static forces and forces in equilibrium. It is essential that this basic term be understood. The term *dynamic stability,* then, when related to a ship, is defined as the energy available, by virtue of the ship's righting moments, to resist any external heeling energy from the position of equilibrium to any inclined position.

A ship's total dynamic stability, likewise, is the total energy available to resist inclining energy from the position of equilibrium through its range of stability.

To understand some basic applications of dynamic stability, the following concepts will be of assistance. Let us take, for example, a coil spring suspended vertically from which a weight might be hung and supported by hand. If, after the weight has been attached, the supporting force is suddenly released and the weight is allowed to exert its full gravitational force at the instant of its release, the spring will extend to some extreme position. The work done in this downward motion is simply the gravitational pull on the weight multiplied by the distance the spring extends. Plotted on coordinates of force exerted on the spring against distance through which the spring is extended, the energy or work would result in a rectangular area as shown in figure 12–17(a).

Now, on the other hand, if the weight were allowed to extend the spring by a *gradual* removal of the supporting force, the work done on the spring is $E = \int_{0}^{L} FdL$. F is the force exerted on the spring, and L is the distance through which the spring is extended. If this measure of work is plotted on the same coordinates as above, the result would be a triangular area as shown in figure 12–17.

The forces involved in inclining a ship from its position of equilibrium are not unlike the examples of the spring described above in that they may be gradually or suddenly applied. The work necessary to incline a ship from its position of equilibrium to

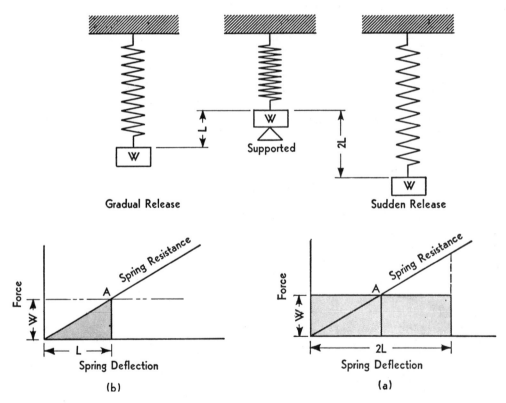

Figure 12–17. Energies on a Spring Released Suddenly (a) and Gradually (b)

some angle, ϕ_1 (i.e., the dynamic stability at angle ϕ_1), is

$$E_{\phi_1} = \int_0^{\phi_1} M_\phi d\phi$$

where E_{ϕ_1} = work required to incline the ship to angle ϕ_1.

M_ϕ = righting moment of the ship at any angle.

$d\phi$ = increment of angle of inclination, expressed in radians.

But $M_\phi = \Delta \overline{GZ}$

$$E_{\phi_1} = \int_0^{\phi_1} \Delta \overline{GZ} d\phi.$$

Since the displacement, Δ, is constant, then,

$$E_{\phi_1} = \Delta \int_0^{\phi_1} \overline{GZ} d\phi.$$

If the inclining moment were gradually applied, the ship would incline to an angle where the inclining and righting moments are equal. The work required to incline the ship is indicated by the above equation. This work must be supplied by the gradually applied inclining moment. This case is analogous to the gradual release of the spring weight shown in figure 12–17, where the spring is extended until its resistance is equal to the force applied.

The concepts of dynamic stability, while not only of concern for ship motion in a seaway, involve ship motion and energy. The student is referred for further and more detailed treatment of these problems involving dynamic stability to Appendix C in the back of the book.

Courtesy of Avondale Shipyards, Inc.

**USS Connole (DE-1056) Slides Down the Ways in a Side Launching. Side launching
conserves valuable shipyard property and restricted water.**

CHAPTER 13

Design Processes: Inception, Planning and Contracting

The design of a ship, like the design of anything, suggests a creative concept and the furtherance and implementation of that concept to its realization.

Design has many meanings and interpretations. Even within the engineering profession, design and design activity has a great many connotations. For instance, a research and development engineer most often thinks of his work as designing. The mathematical models worked out by mathematicians and theoreticians are really concepts in design. Systems analysts compose their diagrammatic flow charts in terms of functional systems design. In fact, most technological specialties contribute at least something to design, and in most engineering practices, the use of design concepts ultimately produces a better end product. However, in a more traditional sense, designing must still be thought of as a total creative process that progresses from an original concept to its final reality. It can involve one person or an entire community of individuals with diverse talents. Design must always be a unified procedure with the sole purpose of interpreting and communicating the basic concept, however simple or complex to the builder.

Involving ourselves in ship design and confining further discussion to this subject, we are confronted with the term *naval architecture*. This term will be used, hopefully with minimum controversy, interchangably with ship design. The naval architect, whether he works as an individual, with a group, or at the head of a firm, is the ultimate practitioner of this type of design—the interpretation and communication of creative concepts pertaining to mobile watercraft. Historically and traditionally, his means for this purpose are engineering drawings and precisely expressed specifications. Both mediums are universally recognized and are stylized tools of expression. They also achieve, in the contract with the builder, the stature of legal documents, accepted and upheld in courts of law. It becomes important, then, when hearing of some activity concerned with ship concepts and described as design, to inquire whether there is an effective description of the concept and its communication to the builder.

The process of ship design, whether for a privately or publicly owned vessel, must begin with a *concept*. This inception process may be as simple as a conference or discussion between the prospective owner and the designer, or, as in the case of a modern naval vessel, it may involve the entire naval bureaucracy whose systematic but complex planning procedures completely overshadow the ultimate process of engineering design. Planning is intimately associated with design, making it necessary for planners and designers to become involved with each other, and with the ensuing preliminary and feasibility studies where design must consequently be used. It must be understood also that the actual procedures described are necessarily the *current mode* of a flexible process that continually adapts to developing politico-economic patterns.

A ship concept in the Navy Department begins at the top level, most logically, the Office of the Chief of Naval Operations, having had its origin even higher in the Department of Defense. However, such origin is generally of little concern to the designers. After involved strategic studies and determination of needs and requirements at these higher levels, the project reaches the Naval Ship Engineering Center.

The Naval Ship Engineering Center is the Navy's principal design agency and an important part of the Naval Ship Systems Command. The actual ship design process begins here with a logically named and well-defined step or stage called *concept formulation*. This is part of the ship acquisition procedure and begins with the ship's mission only broadly defined and the ship system capable of fulfilling the mission largely remaining to be discovered. This concept formulation, consequently, is the determinative stage of the design requiring the optimum in creativity. The design office must employ its technical knowledge, judgment, experience, and even intuition to create a tentative solution. This early phase of the process begins with an examination and analysis of associated or competing configurations and a weapons and sensor analysis. It then proceeds to an early, detailed evaluation of all pertinent criteria that will lead ultimately to the preparation of a preliminary design.

Within the boundaries of this more closely circumscribed procedure of concept formulation, it is still most difficult to identify the *true ship designer* among all the personalities and skilled individuals involved.

Procurement Practices

We will provide a better perspective of ship planning and location of the true design processes if we digress briefly to sketch the general procurement procedure.

It is not possible (for obvious reasons), as in the case of aircraft procurement, to design and build a prototype ship and then proceed to test, evaluate, and "de-bug" it before proceeding with building and production contracts. Ship construction and production, whether for one-of-a-kind or for multi-units, begins after detailed design is completed.

Immediately after World War II, the Navy evolved a procedure of procurement that was applicable to its needs, practical, and comparatively straightforward. This older and conventional procurement procedure is not entirely outmoded, but its use is progressively decreasing. This procedure,

somewhat refined to present practices, is outlined diagrammatically in figure 13–1. It progresses from the original initiation by the Office of the Chief of Naval Operations through the Ships' Characteristics Board and after approvals, compromises, and feasibility studies, to the design division of what was then known as the Bureau of Ships (now the Naval Ship Systems Command). The first stage of design is called *preliminary design* and is an in-house (Navy) design process that includes the results of model testing and that is based on previous feasibility studies and performance specifications. This stage of design determines the ship's basic configuration, both hull and deck structures, as well as the broad com-

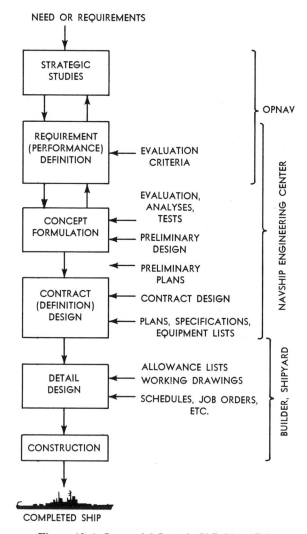

Figure 13–1. Sequential Steps in U.S. Navy Ship Acquisition Showing Customary Agencies of Cognizance

partmentation and subsystems requirements. The process proceeds to *contract design,* where the design (plans and specifications) is developed to the point at which the building contract can be extended. The design function after the contract is signed continues to the *detailed design* stage which is largely assumed by the contractor or builder under Navy supervision.

The other routes to ship construction followed by the U.S. Navy are indicated in figure 13–2. The procedure described above is on the first level and is identified as *conventional.* The second level, the *no contract definition* route, is a completely in-house or Navy developed design. This might be considered a variation of the conventional route and is reserved for ships of certain specialized types where there is no more than one available builder (or a very limited number of builders). The next level indicates the same form or process using an *alternate terminology* and phase identification. The fourth level, called the *contract definition* route, is perhaps the most significant and will receive further amplification later.

New Procurement Concepts

The Navy has recognized for many years that it is the primary customer of American shipyards, and that consequently its procurement practices affect not only the cost of producing ships but the nature of the shipyards. It has sought, therefore, to adopt procurement techniques that might encourage plant investment as well as cause economies in construction through series production of single-class ships. As a part of this approach shipyards and industry are offered more involvement and early participation in the design cycle.

Concept formulation, contract definition, total package, and *multi-year procurement* are significant of these techniques. Because the concern of this book is only with design, the discussion here will deal primarily with concept formulation and contract definition.

CONCEPT FORMULATION

Concept formulation is the in-house phase preceding contract definition—an implement to involve contractors in competitive study. This first phase is a type of design investigation wherein

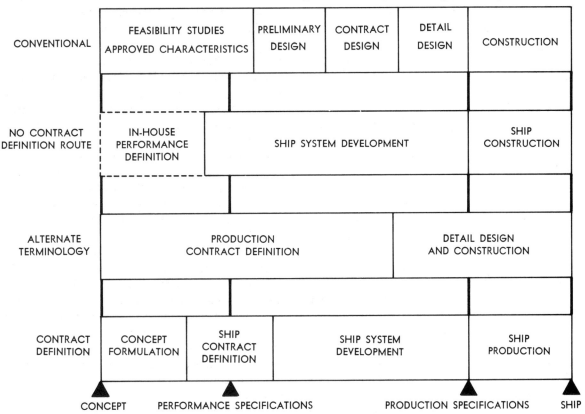

Figure 13–2. Current Routes to Construction

several alternative technical proposals are studied for feasibility with the objective of developing a system (in terms of a ship) that is most economical in meeting the operational mission requirements. In pursuing this objective, the following means are employed:

1. Refinement of mission and performance envelopes (limits or boundaries)
2. Preparation of conceptual design
3. Development of life cycle costs and system effectiveness

The concept formulation is considered to be complete when the following work and development categories have each been satisfied or met:

1. Engineering work rather than experimental work is required, and the technology is sufficiently in hand.
2. The mission and performance envelopes are defined.
3. A thorough trade-off analysis has been made.
4. The best technical approaches have been selected.
5. The cost effectiveness has been determined to be favorable in relationship to the cost effectiveness of competing vehicles on a Defense Department-wide basis.
6. Cost and schedule estimates are creditable and acceptable.

CONTRACT DEFINITION

The central thrust or objective of the design effort in *contract definition* is the determination of the best ship design from an operational standpoint. It is an analytical approach and makes use of all the computerized techniques available. According to the Ship Acquisition Branch of the Naval Ship Systems Command, the objective of contract definition is to produce a set of plans and specifications from which the most cost-effective ship system can be constructed. This system must meet the minimum operational requirements established in the concept formulation phase.

Actually, the Government purchases more than two or three sets of ship plans from the definition contractors. An impression of the scope and results of their effort may be had by a closer view of this phase of procurement.

The prime contractors involved in definition contracts generally represent multidisciplinary

teams or consortia of large industrial complexes, i.e., General Dynamics, Litton Industries, etc. In this process, they independently make optimum determinations based on hundreds of detailed trade-off analyses. These studies on every phase of the ship's systems are most frequently completed by the most qualified subcontractors or specialists. The subcontractors often employ the individual knowledge and skills of experts in the complex technical studies required. It is paradoxical that some of these experts are frequently found in the scientific branches of government research programs. This is an example of an undesirable but unavoidable stretching of national scientific resources where so large an industrial effort as procurement of ships exists.

The end product of a completed ship design and price proposal includes the detailed studies for the ship's life-cycle cost, as well as program plans for project management, standardization studies, "make-or-buy" considerations, manning requirements, provisioning and outfitting studies, reliability and maintainability assurance, and many additional benefits. In addition, competing shipyards frequently plan modernization of their facilities to accommodate new production in anticipation of a contract. Thus, what the Government is actually buying is two or three fully structured and competitive programs which enable the Navy to choose the best design in terms of military effectiveness, minimum production cost, and lowest lifetime operating costs.

Because the procurement programs for design and series production of a large warship or auxiliary naval vessel based on the formalized process described above frequently involve the relatively few capable shipbuilding concerns working in competitive concert, industrial capacity is consequently strained, and it is difficult to impose further procurement programs on it when required. Such programs are also expensive, and there is naturally a redundancy of effort. As a consequence of such difficulties, a modified or simplified contract definition plan has been devised for certain contingencies, such as when the ship is intended to be a replacement or is relatively uninvolved in advanced concepts. The features of modified contract definition can be briefly summarized:

1. Uses the same analytical procedures as the full regular program.

2. Uses only *one* prime contractor for the contract definition phase.
   a. Subcontracts to industry for "best brains" in special areas.
   b. May use full contract definition for selected subsystems.
3. Produces a fully developed competitive bid package to produce cost effectiveness.

This modified system has the obvious advantages of efficiency and expediency. It also has the possible disadvantages of being less competitive and reducing the number of alternatives for a new design.

Design Involvement

While the above procurement practices with their associated studies contribute to the final design and, in effect, control and direct the design, it is important for the purpose of this discussion to isolate the actual design functions. With the emphasis on optimization of design, satisfying performance requirements, and military effectiveness, it is necessary to examine a multitude of source data and analyze a great amount of detail.

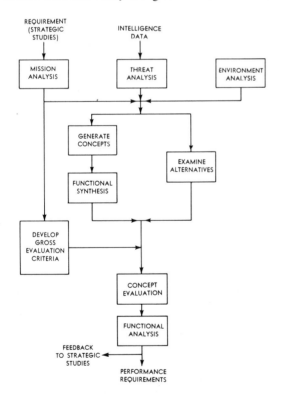

Figure 13–3. The Beginning Process— Definition of Requirements

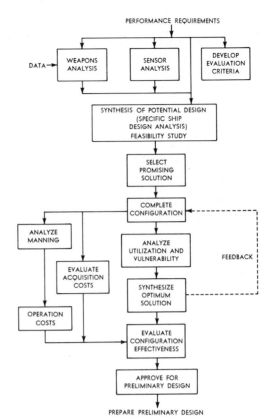

Figure 13–4. Concept Formulation

In this effort, the use of computerized techniques becomes a paramount consideration. It is of some interest, then, to refer to figures 13–3 to 13–6 where the design processes through the phases of procurement described in the foregoing are outlined in block diagrams. These are displayed to reflect the guidance of computer programming through the design processes.

Beginning with figure 13–3, this flow chart indicates the early inception studies occurring prior to concept formulation wherein the performance requirements are determined. This determination is perhaps the beginning point of every rational design, whether performed by either organizational analysis or the simple and traditional dialogue between the designer and prospective owner. These performance requirements enable the designer to proceed toward a preliminary design. For naval ships, this takes place through the concept formulation phase, and the various steps and detailed studies are indicated in figure 13–4. The end product of this phase is the *preliminary design*.

CONTRACT AND DETAIL DESIGN

The next phase of design, regardless of the type of procurement practice used, is the expansion of the preliminary design through the various subsystems determinations to contract design. This phase may be worked out through the conventional routes to construction or by the contract definition method. The block flow-diagram in figure 13–5 indicates the accumulation and expansion of detail required and shows four typical but not necessarily all of the subsystems examined for naval ships.

This phase is the fixed design which becomes, in all shipbuilding programs whether government or civilian, large ships or small boats, the agreed upon, contracted for, ship. The extent to which this design may be modified or changes may be made to the ship is determined in the contract to the mutual agreement of owner, builder, and designer.

Further design work is frequently necessary, particularly for large, complex ships and naval vessels, before and during the construction process. Such design work, because of its nature, is called *detail design*. A typical set of design programs and calculations are shown in the block diagram of figure 13–6.

Ship Design—A Process

Regardless of the type of design organization followed, the actual process of engineering design is a natural evolvement. Whether for a U.S. Naval vessel, a merchant ship, an ocean research ship, a yacht, or other craft, the naval architect builds his design in a manner that has universal similarity. While the design approach is an individual matter, the objectives are common and the requirements and criteria are similar and related. On the other hand there are various approaches taken in conceptual ship design and no clear-cut or established procedure can be set forth giving step-by-step guidelines. This is true mainly because of the creative nature of the process, the variations in working personalities, and the infinite types and requirements of seagoing craft. For most designs, there is generally an exploratory phase leading to a basic concept followed by a preliminary design. In this stage more than any other, the designer's *art* dominates far more than his *science*. The success of the

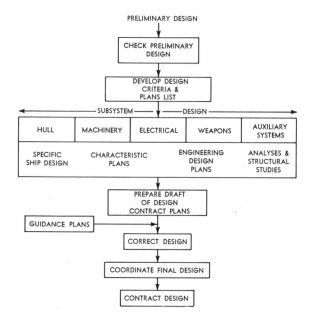

Figure 13–5. Contract Design

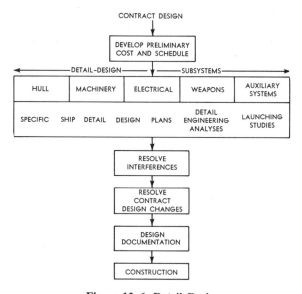

Figure 13–6. Detail Design

design depends largely upon the scope and depth of experience that the designer or design office can command. The direction of the design procedure frequently depends on the similarity between the ship-to-be and existing ships of similar design. There is so much useful data, normally the result of lengthy and laborious calculations, that can be used for estimates. The experienced designer working with coefficients, knowledge of similarities and dissimilarities between designs, and a well developed sense of modification can very successfully work up early preliminary concepts containing necessary and surprisingly accurate dimensional and performance characteristics. In fact, from these early preliminary and, to an extent, rough drafts, the design procedure becomes one of progressive and repetitive refinement. Indeed, this refining process is often described as a *design spiral,* and most naval architects agree that their work proceeds according to this path. Although the actual sequence of some work in the process may vary depending on ship type or individual choice, a typical sequence in the design spiral is shown in figure 13–7.

FEASIBILITY DESIGN

Feasibility design is an amorphous process in ship design consisting mostly of studies in comparison and analysis to satisfy the basic mission.

At the beginning of a feasibility design program, there is generally (for a naval vessel) an adequate synthesis of potential designs with available computer analyses. These are, of course, in the form of qualitative reports, dimensional comparisons, cost studies, etc. As yet, there is no definitive configuration or element of real engineering design. This stage follows directly and leads ultimately into the preliminary design. (This can be located on the flow diagram in figure 13–4.)

The designer most frequently steps into the design spiral with rough profile and general arrangement sketches. These are accompanied by estimates of volumetric and machinery space requirements which must precede the basic dimensional determinations. These studies are, of course, guiding the development at this point of a first draft general arrangement drawing wherein the profile configuration and basic width dimen-

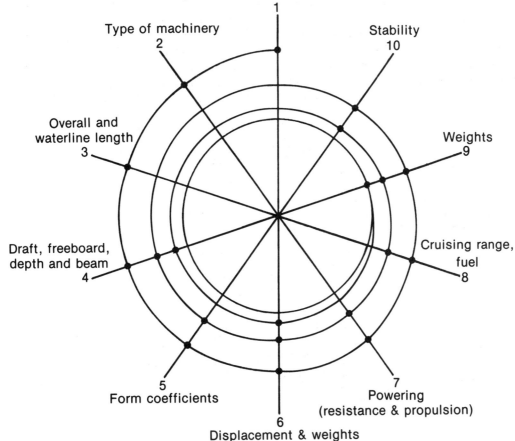

Figure 13–7. The Design Spiral

sions are beginning to determine configuration. As soon as the hull form coefficients (see chapter 2) can be decided upon, the displacement can be closely estimated and, following this, a powering determination can be made. With power determined, the fuel necessary for endurance requirements is calculated and, following this, the weights of both machinery and fuel are worked out. Knowing these major weights, a stability analysis can be started. The stability study will quickly reveal the adequacy or inadequacy of certain of the originally conceived dimensions and volumes. Since these dimensions, especially beam and draft as well as general volumetric arrangements, contribute heavily to stability, the second loop of the spiral begins with refinements to the basic configuration and additions to the three-dimensional concept. The circuit continues with additions and adjustments until all of the basic features of the design are in balance.

Somewhere early in this design spiral, probably in the early stage of the second circuit, a more complete hull configuration must be determined. The hull lines drawing, a very important design consideration, must ultimately be worked out. (A more detailed description and its origination are described in chapter 2.) However, in arriving at some of the more important decisions in hull form,

the designer must, at this stage, answer many questions concerning speed, power, wave-making resistance, seakeeping, stability, etc. Discussions of these factors in more detail follow elsewhere in this book, but it should be mentioned here that early determinations for purposes of the preliminary design are most frequently made on the basis of previously collected data, statistical analysis, tabular references of "series" model tests, curves of ship type performance, etc.

PRELIMINARY DESIGN

This phase of design is, in the minds of professional naval architects, the most significant of the whole design involvement process. It is this stage of design where the major characteristics and the "personality" of the ship are fixed. The dimensions have become firm, the requirements and the mission have come into clear focus and the primary tasks have been separated from the contingent tasks. The concepts of the design in hand and approximate hull character envisioned with its special features, its propulsion machinery, and the major sub systems determined and agreed upon, the designer now cleans off his drawing board and proceeds with the most basic of the drawings. Using the conceptual studies, either sketchy or scaled out together with numerical guide lines, he

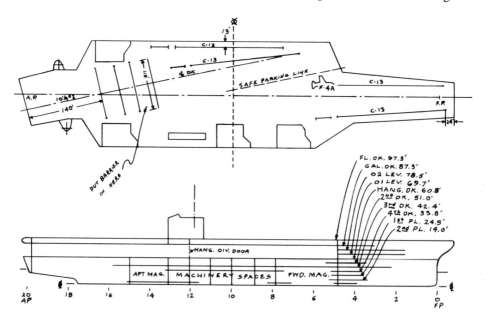

Courtesy of SNAME

Figure 13–8. Typical Study and Characteristics Sketches for a CVA

proceeds to lay out the hull delineation. He works mainly, here, from a conceptual arrangement plan which he will later refine when the hull *lines drawing* is complete. These two plans are developed parallel and together but the lines drawing is generally (particularly underwater configuration) given the dominant position. Together with the lines drawing all of the hull appendages that are to be structurally integrated are designed. These features must be worked out generally with the expertise of the structural designers who are now integrating their work with the hull designers. The hull designers must now move on in the spiral to the hydrostatic and weight studies. The speed-power estimates and analysis are simultaneously proceeding in the hydromechanics laboratories, (in the towing tank test), where the seakeeping and maneuvering studies are also underway.

Next, the stability criteria is applied and the safety and protection plans are worked out.

This uniform procedure is a fairly comprehensive statement of the activities that comprise *preliminary design*. It must be apparent to the reader that after this stage the basic character configuration and capabilities of the ship have been essentially established. Also it is apparent that there is much still left to be done—much, much more in *detail* and *time* involvement. There is, at the *preliminary design* completion, for example, nothing prepared to establish the shape of the steel plates that make up the skin of the ship. While the weights have been studied and estimated, the sub-system equipment designs which amount to staggering numbers of detailed plans have not yet been developed or detailed. No one has decided on the ship's bakery ovens, for example, nor has anyone specified the types and manufacture of the auxiliary generators nor the anchor windlass, nor the furniture for the crew's quarters. There are electro-magnetic compatability studies (which may have already been complex electronic systems), communications systems, piping and electrical systems, and perhaps a thousand others to be detailed. These must be part of the further detail and refinement phase next in order of procedure, but they are not of the basic design.

From here the professional naval architects must assume a more supervisory role. The sub-system specialists move in and the *contract design phase* with its seemingly endless outpouring of blue prints begins.

CONTRACT DESIGN

The contract design stage is the preparation of a complete set of plans and specifications for the guidance and use of the *contractor*. Understandably these plans must be far more detailed than those of either of the preceding stages. The process can only be considered now as one of further refinement and detailed definitions preparatory to bidding and construction. The resultant design not only must follow identically the product of the preliminary design but also must be in final form. To illustrate the comparative refinement through the progression of design stages and cycles, the following design working times for a moderate size ship might be revealing:

1. *Feasibility design*—10 to 80 man-days
2. *Preliminary design*—100 to 2000 man-days
3. *Contract design*—3000 to 20,000 man-days

From the naval architectural standpoint, the design work is essentially completed with the end of contract design. However, the builder's detailed construction plans continue to be developed prior to and through the construction stage.

The process of ship design described in the foregoing paragraphs is essentially that used in the U.S. Navy, together with its methods of acquisition of ships. It is difficult to say whether it is the best of procedures for its purpose for there are many disgruntled opponents. There is no question that the procedure is, as are many government activities, plagued by gross inefficiency. There is no point in trying to disguise the facts that are continually appearing in the public press concerning cost over-runs and petty or serious scandals pertaining to naval ship acquisition. There is certainly justification for serious concern as well as a need for reexamination of the whole unwieldy procedure.

Before closing the discussion of naval ship design and acquisition, it is necessary to add that the processes as described are anything but static and this alone may or could be the saving factor. Indeed, there are some details in the above discussion that some individuals closely related to the various tasks will dismiss as relatively unimportant or in fact obsolete and there are yet other details given little or no notice here that have grown to disproportionate import, particularly in the minds of those directly involved. In fact, if there is a particular cause for the delays, the excessive costs, and the gross inefficiencies where ship acquisition is concerned, whether it is naval or civilian, it could well be the predominance of sub-administrators intent on building small empires of their own special interests. In fairness, to further comment, the process of naval ship acquisition is continually subject to self-examination. In recent months new concerns have moved to reduce costs and inefficiencies. The process as described in the foregoing (figure 13–2) has most recently been restated as the *Current Design Sequence.* (See figure 13–9.) Together with this a commendable attempt toward clarification of terms has been made in the following series of redefinitions, which have not as yet, however, been universally accepted.

Ship design is the orderly, iterative process of defining physical characteristics and systems to provide a ship with capability specified by the user, "accomplished in phases which are identified with their purposes."

Feasibility Studies determine potential ship vehicles or major systems which will meet requirements and criteria established by the user. "A review of prepared alternatives establishes that a ship solution is feasible. Normally, (feasibility design) is the basis for setting the design-to-cost goal."

Preliminary Design establishes and delineates the naval architectural and system characteristics of the best or most suitable result of feasibility studies. This is carried to the necessary degree to permit preparation of contract design. Preliminary design "provides the engineering basis for establishing appropriate budget estimates and the completion of the Functional Base Line. Tradeoffs and reductions to remain within the cost restraints are the essence of this design phase."

Contract Design develops the preliminary design into plans and specifications suitable for bid by a knowledgeable shipbuilder. It "is the engineering process which develops the ship's Specification, Contract Drawings and the Contract Guidance Drawings. Its end product is the Allocated Base Line."

Detail Design is "the preparation of the working drawings which serve to build and define the product base line."

Top Level Requirements (TLR) is "a document promulgated and approved by the Chief of Naval Operations which defines the operational requirements of a ship to be produced and stipulates the maximum cost, and all other program constraints affecting the design and utilization of the ship. As a minimum, the Top Level Requirements will state the ship's mission, operational re-

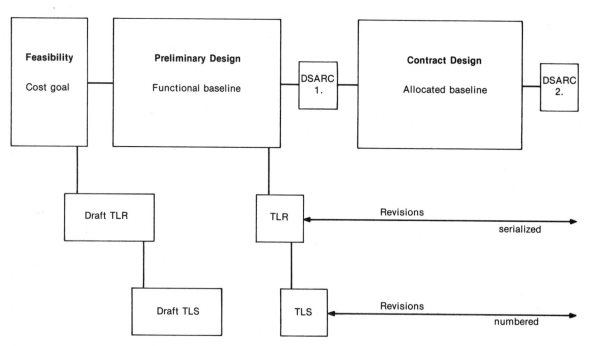

Figure 13–9. U.S. Navy–Current Design Sequence, June 1974

quirements, major configuration constraints, the plan for use, the maintenance concepts, the supply support concepts, manning limitations, minimum operational standards, and maximum allowable cost."

Top Level Specifications (TLS) is "a document promulgated by the Naval Ship Systems Command which translates the Top Level Requirements into a physical ship description thus providing a bridge between the Top Level Requirements and the ship procurement specification."

"*Base Lines* are defined in accordance with DOD Directive 5010.21. For the ship design process, the *Functional Base Line* (FBL) is comprised of the Top Level Requirements document and the Top Level Specification document and such other referenced drawings as are deemed appropriate to maintain under formal configuration management within the government.

"The *Allocated Base Line* (ABL) consists of the specifications and drawings incident to contract award and maintained thereafter under configuration management between the government and the shipbuilder.

"The *Product Base Line* (PBL) is such documentation as is required by the government at the time of ship delivery."

—From ASNE paper, June 1974,
Rear Admiral Randolf King, Jr., USN

In the "Private Sector," a civilian naval architectural firm or a professional ship designer in private practice is perhaps understandably confused or bemused by the rigorously structured procedures of design described herewith and in the forgoing paragraphs. The labyrinths of compartmentalized, step-by-step procedures, sub-system design and sub-sub system analysis; all these, often with indifferent and inefficient results, are not impressive to the practicing civilian designer or design firm. Many are by choice (and/or economic attraction) involved in naval contractual design, either wholly from the beginning or only in part as a sub-contractor. In these cases they must be attentive to the processes, the compartmentalization, and the translations of ever-blooming new jargon.

Yet there are other designers who still produce ideally, following a pattern of procedure surprisingly familiar to the sequences described for the naval ship design process. This is not, when reflected upon, so unusual. The processes when stated and adhered to directly are a logical and orderly procedure kept in a uniform sequence of developing refinement. A professional designer in a non-military or non-government organization is not as likely to be diverted because he is propelled by the basic needs for both productivity and high-quality practice. This designer also is less likely to think in terms of identifiable phases of procedure, those that we have isolated with lines and boxes. He can think of it and does in the most ideal examples as a smooth and orderly progression of delineation of concept from the initial proposal to the final contract specifications and detailed drawings.

If this process of idealized design *could* be outlined, boxed in and "compartmentalized" for the ideal ship designer, it would appear very much as shown in figure 13–10.

These procedures, both naval and civilian, are involved, of course, with comparatively large ships of at least several thousand tons displacement, or of the more complex specially powered or equipped small naval craft. Generally as the vessel to be designed becomes smaller, receding from the thousand-ton category to less costly commercial craft or the luxury pleasure craft, the design processes become accordingly less complex. The feasibility studies and preliminary design phases usually merge into one and may consist of only a few rather simplified drawings and numerical analysis. There are outlined performance schedules and operational requirement statements that are agreed upon with the owner/client and then the detailed or contract design is prepared consisting of (in normal or conventional vessels) from twenty to perhaps one hundred separate sheets of drawings, depending upon the size and complexity of the design.

There is a notable exception to all of the above, however, which is less frequently employed in this country. This procedure, if indeed it is a procedure, is used by some shipyards that produce their own designs. This situation exists in countries competing in the world shipbuilding market such as Japan, Sweden, Germany and others. The process of design involved here can be dealt with briefly, primarily because the design concepts are so strongly subordinated to building economics and practices. The design office of a shipbuilder, because of the structure of the corporation, must be dominated by the corporate concern of the prod-

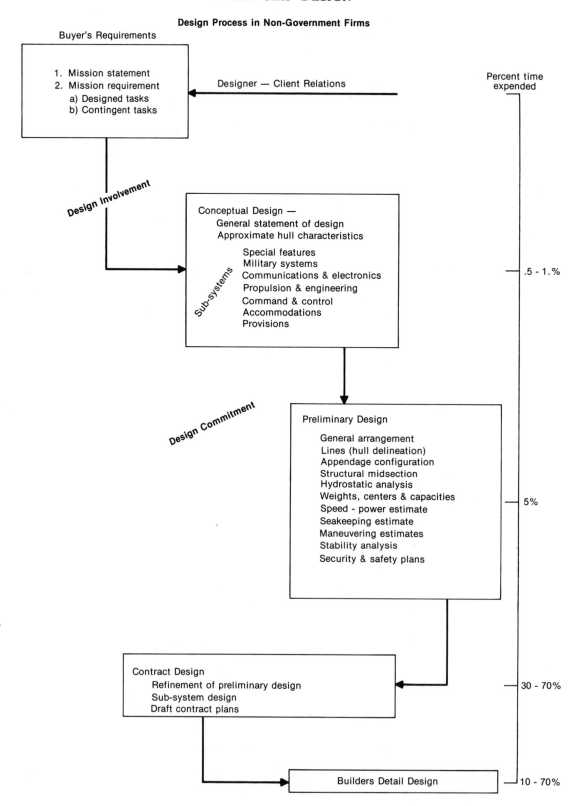

Figure 13–10. The Flow Sequence of Design Procedures as Followed in Nongovernment Organizations

uct's cost in a very competitive market. Such close control of design tends toward "frozen," stylized concepts. While it is felt that there should be definite, independent, and separate design organizations in the shipbuilding industry, it is also considered necessary that they develop a consciousness and sensitivity toward the problems of the builder. Such awareness in this country has frequently been neglected by designers in their independent zeal to produce "progressive" designs, many of which, in the final analysis, prove only to be unrealistic and very expensive.

A Computer Prints Out Design Data for a Modern Ship

CHAPTER 14

The Computer in Ship Design and Construction

Computer Facilities and the Naval Architect

The modern ship designer must recognize the electronic computer as an ever-growing and developing adjunct to design methods. To use a computer in engineering simply as a sophisticated calculator to perform routine tasks of repetitive computations is basically an underestimation of its capacities.

The naval architect who has attained some familiarity with computer operation and application soon realizes that he must continually keep abreast of developments or rapidly fall behind, both in programming skills as well as terminology. This effort to keep-up produces a frustrating conflict between computer technology and the ever-expanding professional knowledge of naval architecture—a conflict that will ultimately require resolution and decision. The decision, of course, must be made in favor of one's profession; in the case of the naval architect, it will be to employ the computer to his advantages without becoming involved in the technology of operation. The primary advantage, of course, is the release from time-consuming calculations. While this has been mentioned as an underemployment of computers, it need not necessarily be so in the practice of an imaginative designer. The designer, through this very time release, can employ such time to increased advantage by (1) producing a more

thorough and complete design, (2) increasing his input to the computer for analytical purposes, and finally (3) integrating and optimizing all of the ship's systems to provide the most efficient unit.

There *are* limits to the use of the computer, as there are for any tool. However, due to the versatility and the constant advances of computer technology, its applications have been probed only slightly. The imaginative designer who uses the computer wisely will be constantly alert for new applications. From the early advent of computers in engineering, there has been considerable concern with *computer design*. Unfortunately, these words have been rather loosely used and have been picked up by popular media sources and beginners and students alike to indicate some sort of push-button world where mechanisms can be designed wholly through the electronic wizardry of a computer. Alas, this is not, nor should it be, the case.

The misunderstanding of computer design probably stems from the poor understanding or loose application of the term *design* itself. As stated in chapter 13, design involves a form of *creative* process. There are aspects of this total process that require analysis, computations, dimensional determinations, and ultimately communication of the results to the builder. These aspects can in many ways profit from the aid of a computer. The Navy, in identifying its very important development plan and activity involving this subject, has very carefully called it *Computer-Aided Ship Design and Construction.*

Computer-aided design is a most important element in the education of a naval architect, but his first realistic awareness should include emphasis on the word *aided.*

Before discussing the availability of computer processes and employment, it will be helpful to note that it is not the purpose here to develop specific programming techniques but rather to cite and describe briefly the areas commonly served by computers where programs have been successfully developed and are in use.

Modern Computer Systems

The modern digital computer is capable of performing millions of computations per second and moving large volumes of data rapidly between its memory elements and printers, plotters, card readers, and other input and output devices, allowing people to communicate with computers efficiently and rapidly in terms familiar to people.

The digital computer is indeed a very impressive and useful tool. One needs only to go into a large department store after withdrawing the necessary funds at an automated bank to realize the extent to which the computer has taken over virtually all of the repetitive tasks involved in doing business such as making change, accepting deposits, and verifying credit requests.

Virtually every industry is feeling the impact of computers in every facet of their operations and the shipbuilding industry is no exception. For many years shipyards have employed computers to automate the standard accounting functions:

- payroll calculations and check printing
- accounts receivable
- accounts payable
- project cost control
- general ledger

Beginning in the late 1950s, designers and engineers found they could use the same computers to perform many of the tedious, repetitive calculations necessary during the design process. Since then, the use of computers in shipyards and design offices has escalated steadily to the point where all of the standard design calculations are routinely performed on computers.

In 1963, following the development of the automatic flame cutter which could be controlled by a punched paper tape to cut arbitrary shapes out of steel plate, the first version of the Autokon system was put into production. Autokon and other systems which have followed are collections of programs which enable shipyard workers to describe parts to be cut in a way somewhat familiar to them. These descriptions or "parts programs" are then used as input data for a program which translates the parts program into punched paper tapes that the automatic flame cutter can read.

With these three application areas the shipbuilding industry has a strong foundation on which are growing integrated design, production, and management systems. These promise to have major impacts on the entire ship design and construction process and will rely heavily on the following developments in computer technology:

- Economical random-access mass memory devices
- Improved man-machine interfaces
- Microcomputers
- Minicomputer systems
- Low-cost telecommunications

The availability of very large capacity memory systems at low cost will enable the shipyard to keep large data bases which can be accessed almost instantaneously to retrieve or update single data items. These large data bases can contain current and historical design information, the detailed status of every project, libraries of details and engineering drawings, detailed equipment specifications, and descriptions of standard parts. Large random access memory systems also make it possible to write computer programs of almost unlimited size, greatly reducing software development costs.

The man-machine interface is one of the most important keys to utilization of computers in the marine industry. The traditional method of talking to a computer consists of writing a program in a high-level language such as FORTRAN, BASIC, PL-1, or COBOL, punching it on cards, and submitting it to the computer center for execution. Hopefully, the computer interprets the coded program and produces the correct results within a few hours. In recent years, the development of the time-shared computer has made it possible for many users to talk to a single computer at virtually the same time via remote terminals. This allows the user to carry on a dialogue and interact with the computer. This type of man-machine interface is very important when using the computer to help with design work since it allows the designer (if his programs are properly written) to change design parameters at will and immediately see the results of the changes on the design calculations. However, to use even a time-shared computer effectively, it is necessary to become familiar with at least the BASIC language.

Needless to say, it is difficult for a naval architect or marine engineer to keep current both his or her programming skills and engineering knowledge. If, then, the computer is to further the science of ship design and construction, tools must be continually developed to make it easier for the designer and shipbuilder to carry on meaningful dialogue with the computer in familiar and convenient languages.

Parts programming languages such as ALKON are a step in this direction but even more important are hardware devices such as electronic digitizers, plotters and CRT displays which, if properly implemented, allow designers and builders to communicate in the language they usually know best —pictures. An important adjunct to these graphical input and output devices are special purpose keyboards. This class of communication devices can be designed for practically any application. With the proper arrangement of push buttons, display lights, and thumbwheel switches, the computer can be programmed to carry out the most complex of calculations and procedures by people completely untrained in the use of computers.

These hardware-based man-machine interfaces which make computers potentially so easy to use have only become practical with the development of the relatively inexpensive minicomputer and the minicomputer's grandchild, the microcomputer. The small, inexpensive, minicomputer can do, on a limited scale, virtually anything many large, gen-

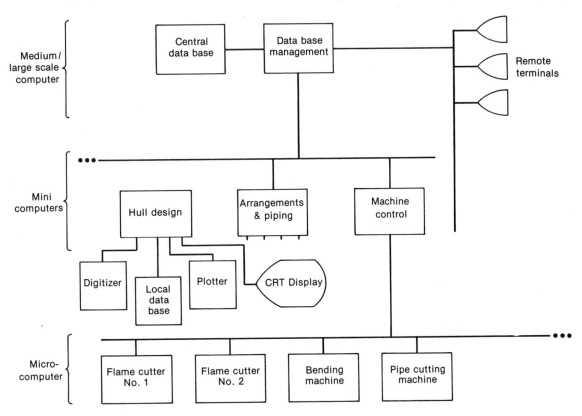

Figure 14–1. Typical Shipyard Computer System Illustrating a Hierarchical Organization. The shipyard machinery at the base of the hierarchy could be controlled by dedicated microcomputers.

eral purpose computers can do for a fraction of the cost. They can run fairly large FORTRAN and BASIC programs, they can be time-shared by up to 60 users, and, most importantly, they can be interfaced very easily to digitizers, cathode ray tube displays (CRTs), plotters, flame cutters, control panels, and other devices which people find easy and comfortable to use.

Although less than three years old, microprocessors are already finding their way into a host of new industrial equipment—factory-automation systems, machine-tool control, data-acquisition systems for such jobs as monitoring apportionment of meat for hamburgers, electronic scales, control of conveyor lines, numerical control, robot manipulation of piece parts, data-sensing, and component-insertion. They are also being used for environmental monitoring and phototypesetting.

These microprocessor-based systems offer the flexibility to adapt manufacturing systems to changing demands and upgrade them as production expands. All that is necessary is for integrated circuits containing new instructions to be inserted when peripherals are changed, equipment is added, or the system itself is modified.

These small computers that are now finding their way into shipyards and design offices in increasing numbers have to be able to talk to each other if the goal of integrating the management, design, engineering, and production functions is ever to be realized. Traditionally, the telephone company has provided all necessary data communication services. However, the demand for data has induced several other independent companies to develop data transmission capabilities using microwave, laser, and satellite techniques which will be of great help in speeding up the flow of data between design offices, governmental agencies, and the shipyards.

According to most experts, the modern shipyard will employ a hierarchy of computers similar to that shown in figure 14-1. A large central computer will manage the central data base. Several minicomputers will perform engineering and interactive design functions and communicate data to the central data base. Another minicomputer will have the responsibility of monitoring and sending data to the microcomputers whose task it is to control flame cutters, milling machines, welding machinery, bending machines, pipe cutters, and other shipyard machinery. With such a hierarchal system the engineers and production workers can always interact with the computer system at a level they can understand to ensure that ships are designed and built as men know they should be and not as the computer dictates.

The Computer as an Aid to Design

GENERAL

As stated in Chapter 13, design is a creative process. There are aspects of this process that require analysis, computations, dimensional determinations, and ultimately communication of the results to the builder. These tasks can be made much simpler with the aid of a computer. Certain applications of computers in the design process have found wide acceptance. These programs have enabled the designer to design a ship in a shorter time with greater accuracy and thoroughness than before.

Many standard design calculations have been computerized for many years. These traditional calculations are being constantly improved through the employment of new algorithms and the applications of graphic input and output devices.

The development of reliable numerical optimization methods and algorithms is resulting in a slow but steady change in the traditional preliminary design process. The new philosophy involves the use of numerical optimization in the design loop. The introduction of an optimization algorithm forces the designer to specify a measure of superiority between alternatives and by this means the computer is able to choose an optimum value for a given design problem.

This approach to design is a systematic approach to the explicit formulation of the design model. It is now possible to formulate many practical problems in optimization terms, but the practicing designer must be given enough familiarity and confidence in computer-aided optimal design to prompt him to use these methods in everyday design work.

The computer has enabled the structural designer to formulate ship structures problems in terms of small "finite elements" and accurately predict detailed stresses and deformations in complicated structures that would be virtually impossible to analyze using traditional methods.

Small computers are finding their way into the towing tank and making it easier to generate reliable test data in formats that the naval architect can readily interpret. In addition, the computer is being used to great advantage to realistically simulate the maneuvering and seakeeping behavior of ships early in the design phase while the design is still fluid enough that corrective changes can be made economically. Ideally, these simulations are based on towing tank data as well as theoretical hydrodynamic calculations in order to increase their validity.

In the following sections several existing representative applications of computers to design are briefly presented.

TRADITIONAL APPLICATIONS

Individual programs and integrated systems for carrying out standard naval architectural calculations are fairly common. Most shipyards and many naval architecture firms have programs for making one or more of the following calculations:

- Intact stability calculations
- Damaged stability and flooding calculations
- Longitudinal strength calculations
- Floodable length calculations
- Power and speed prediction
- Tank capacities
- Seakeeping and ship motions analysis
- Lines fairing

The U.S. Navy and the U.S. Maritime Administration have a complete library of well-documented programs for performing these and other computations. These programs were developed or purchased at government expense and the documentation as well as program decks are willingly distributed to interested parties. Several private firms offer complete design services to shipyards and naval architects. Some computer-aided design firms in private or commercial service will perform all standard calculations and provide tabular and graphical output similar to that shown in figure 14–2. Such applications can be performed on a low-cost, real-time, computing system configured for ship design and construction. For example, the CADSHIP system is modular in design and can be easily tailored to specific needs of the design office, small shipyard, classification society, or for dedicated applications in the large shipyard. To facilitate input to and output from the system, a coordinate digitizer and graphics display are standard equipment. One of the standard software packages offered with the system allows the user to automatically digitize a rough sketch or preliminary lines drawing and interactively develop a hull form definition (table of offsets) suitable as input for design calculations and lines fairing. Figure 14–3 is a picture of the display screen showing a body plan in the process of being faired.

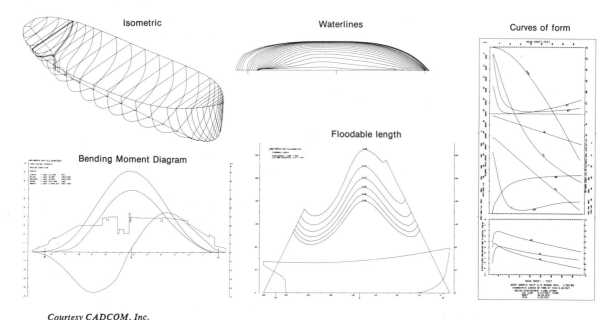

Courtesy CADCOM, Inc.

Figure 14–2. Machine-Generated Graphical Output from Hull Form Calculations

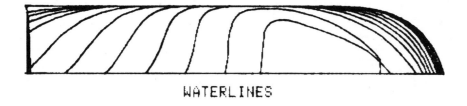

WATERLINES

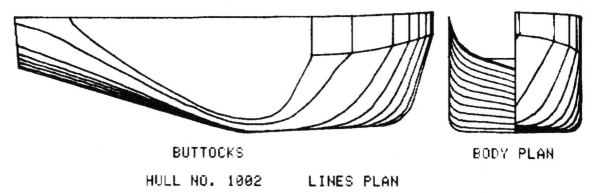

BUTTOCKS

BODY PLAN

HULL NO. 1002   LINES PLAN

Courtesy CADCOM, Inc.

Figure 14–3. Graphic Display of a Ship Hull Form in the process of being faired on the CADSHIP system

Several other major ship design systems exist or are now in wider development. Space does not permit the description of these systems in any detail here.

OPTIMIZATION

The goal of the naval architect when designing a ship is to calculate a large number of feasible design alternatives and pick the best of the lot, i.e., optimize. However, seldom are naval architects afforded the luxury of enough time and money to exhaustively examine enough alternatives to be confident that an optimum design has indeed been achieved. The concept of optimization is certainly not new to ship designers. For example, bulbous bows are designed to minimize wave resistance; the midship section is designed to minimize weight or cost; propellers are normally designed to maximize efficiency. Traditionally, however, this type of design problem has been solved by the application of special purpose techniques designed to facilitate manual methods of solution. Propeller design charts are good examples of this type of approach. The computer's

high-speed computational and decision-making ability have made general purpose optimization methods applicable to a wide range of design problems. These methods require that the ship design process be defined in a mathematical sense so that a design algorithm can be developed which the computer can process. To most designers this task seems impossible. They argue that no successful comprehensive "design equation" has ever been developed for ship design, and there is no hope of ever getting even two naval architects to agree on a standard procedure for performing their work. In fact, they continue, any one designer probably never approaches a project the same way twice. Their concluding argument asserts that the creative process of designing a ship just does not lend itself to mathematical treatment.

Professor H. Nowacki of the Technical University of Berlin challenges these arguments by defining the role of the computer in design as follows:

1. Create a balanced man-computer interaction where the designer maintains the prerogative of feeding in new concepts and passing critical judgment.

2. Refrain from seeking anything like a "design formula." Rather, seek a mathematical format (or general problem type) which represents the common denominator of the class of design problems of interest.
3. Do not require a consensus as to standard design assumptions or techniques since a sufficiently general design logic will be compatible with a broad variety of design applications and styles.

With this definition of the computer's role some typical ship design algorithms and techniques can be discussed.

Stated succinctly, the objectives of preliminary ship design are:

Given the functional requirements for a ship to be designed for given service or mission, and *given* the well-known environmental technical, and regulatory constraints of ship design;

Find the principal characteristics (dimensions, proportion, etc.) of the design that will result in a competitive ship.

Given these objectives, in fact, any design problem can be restated as an optimization problem:

Find a set of design variables, $X_1, X_2, X_3 \ldots X_n$, that will maximize or minimize the *objective function* $F(X_1, X_2, X_3 \ldots X_n)$ subject to a set of *constraints*

$$G_1(X_1, X_2, X_3 \ldots X_n) \geqslant O$$

$$G_2(X_1, X_2, X_3 \ldots X_n) \geqslant O$$

.

.

.

$$G_m(X_1, X_2, X_3 \ldots X_n) \geqslant O$$

Where the *design variables* are the quantities under the designer's control such as length, beam, draft, and prismatic coefficient. The *objective function* or "measure of merit" is a single valued function of the design variables and the constraints which is developed by the designer in a fashion consistent with his design objectives. The constraints are the influences not under the designer's control which enter the problem, such as required stability, allowable stress, harbor depth, etc.

This formulation of the design problem is consistent with the formulation of a non-linear programming problem. By stating design problems in this way a great variety of existing non-linear pro-

gramming solution techniques can be applied as general purpose design algorithms.

Nowacki, Brusis, and Swift, in a paper given before the Society of Naval Architects and Engineers in 1970, describe the application of these techniques to a problem in tanker design. They attempted to select the principal characteristics and operating speed of tankers on the basis of economic measures of merit by using non-linear programming techniques.

Figure 14–4 shows a block diagram of the approach used. By using two different optimization techniques, they were able to confirm the trend to larger, fuller tankers on economic grounds. Figure 14–5 shows the results of the optimization for a speed-length ratio of 0.45 which is near the optimum. The practical optimum design (minimum R) lies in the corner governed by the L/D and $C_B \leqslant .88$ restrictions (constraints). The trends suggest still better results in the regions of the decision space arbitrarily declared illegal. They used a roll period constraint ($T > 15$ seconds) to illustrate the bad effect a relatively arbitrary constraint can have on the economic success of a design. The formulation of ship design processes as dynamic programming problems so they may be solved on a computer using standard optimization techniques is becoming more and more widespread in the marine industry.

Such techniques, if used wisely, enable designers to judge their designs on a more rational basis and hence, allow their true creativity to manifest itself in better ships.

Structural Analysis and Design

Many organizations in the marine industry are now using advanced computer-based analysis techniques to determine the stress and deformations to be expected in any given ship design. The leaders of this effort to date have been the U.S. Navy and various classification societies, whose primary job is to evaluate and approve proposed designs for the purposes of obtaining insurance. The American Bureau of Shipping, Det Norski Veritas (Norway), Bureau Veritas (France), and Lloyd's Register (Britain) are the leaders in this area. Also, working in close association with ABS, Professor Hussein A. Kamel, of the College of Engineering, University of Arizona, has developed some interesting approaches for structural analysis using minicomputers.

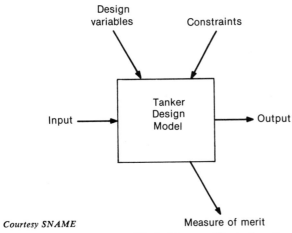

Figure 14–4. System Block Diagram Illustrating Optimization Techniques as Applied to Tanker Design

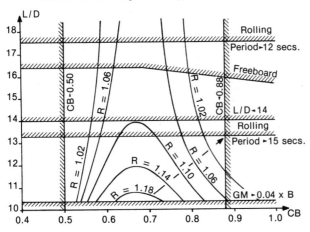

Figure 14–5. Contours of the Measure of Merit Function (R = actual/optimal required freight rate) and Design Constraints; $V/\sqrt{L} = 0.45$; $B/T = 2.91$; $L/B = 6.88$

The classification societies are continually faced with the problem of accurately predicting the stresses in new ship designs which are more complex than those which were being designed when the traditional design methods were developed.

Classical structural mechanics, despite its ever-increasing sophistication, is severely limited to solving severely idealized problems. Modern computers and the finite element method allow designers to analyze real engineering structures relatively easily and accurately. The concept of finite elements, originally introduced by M. J. Turner and others in 1956, assumes that real structures can be represented by a collection of structural elements interconnected only at a finite number of nodes at which some fictitious forces, representative of the distributed stresses actually acting on the element boundaries, act. The structural elements, of which the idealized model is constructed, are selected in such a way that their structural behavior under the loading conditions encountered when inserted into a finite element model can be precisely determined by classical methods. Beams, triangular plates, columns, and rectangular plates are examples of such elements.

The American Bureau of Shipping co-sponsored the development of DAISY (*D*isplacement *A*utomated *I*ntegrated *SY*stem) at the University of Arizona. DAISY is a series of programs which, taken together, comprise a general-purpose finite element structural analysis program. ABS is now using DAISY in three ways:

- To analyze ship structures for day-to-day plan approval
- For studying the structural integrity of novel and unique vessels
- To assist naval architects with their structural design problems

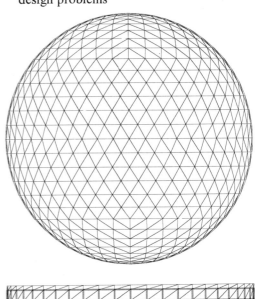

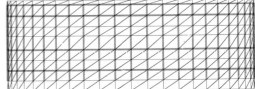

Figure 14–6. Computer Plot of Finite Element Mesh for a Spherical Liquified Natural Gas Tank and Supporting Skirt

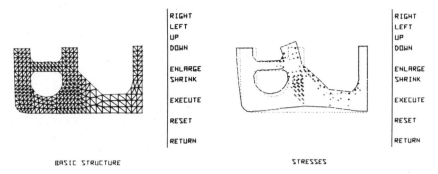

BASIC STRUCTURE

STRESSES

Courtesy University of Arizona

Figure 14–7. CRT Display of Finite Element Mesh, Stresses, and Deformation of Tanker Webframe

Figure 14–6 shows a computer-generated plot of the finite element representation of a spherical liquified natural gas tank and its supporting skirt.

Professor Kamel has developed an interactive structural analysis system which is implemented on a minicomputer with disk storage and refreshed cathode ray tube display. Two dimensional and axisymetric structures can be analyzed using the finite element method. A mesh generation program module produces a geometric model in terms of nodes and elements. The model is then used as input to one of many two-dimensional analysis programs which operate in an interactive design cycle. During each pass the user of the system may edit his model or alter loads and boundary conditions until his design requirements are satisfied. The capacity of the system is currently 350 nodes and 700 elements. Figure 14–7 shows the basic finite element structure, the deflections, and the stress distributions of a typical tanker webframe as displayed on the CRT display.

Figure 14–8 is a flow chart of the operation of the system.

Simulations and Model Testing

The ship model towing tank, discussed in Chapter 9, has long been the standard tool of the naval architect for simulating the performance of new designs. Models can be tested in the towing tank in an idealized but realistic environment and performance parameters such as resistance, seakeeping qualities, and maneuvering capability can be accurately estimated. However, the normal towing tank facility is not a convenient or relatively economical tool for simulating real-life situations in-

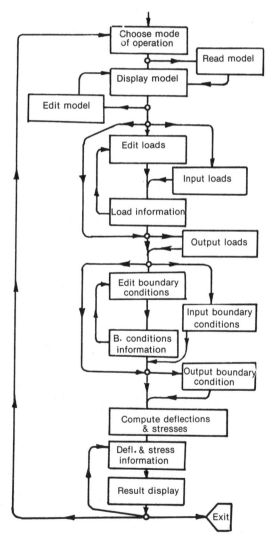

Courtesy University of Arizona

Figure 14–8. Flow Chart of Interactive Finite Element System

volving the operation of a ship, a fleet of ships, or for examining the performance of a design as a function of several design parameters.

The computer is rapidly becoming a standard tool in the towing tank for quickly and accurately acquiring test data and generating final full-scale predictions. In some cases it is even being called on to control the experiment, for example, by starting and stopping the towing carriage, and controlling the wavemaker. In addition, as simulation techniques proliferate, the computer is becoming a virtual extension of the towing tank. Problems involving operation of the completed ship or system which are affected by random factors not under the designer's control can be studied effectively by simulating the system on the computer, using towing tank data in conjunction with real-life operational parameters. The results of such simulations are valuable in determining how the random factors, over which the designer has no control, interact with the design parameters, which can be controlled. An example of a typical computer simulation and a computer system for automating towing tank operation are described in the following paragraphs.

SARSIM (Search and Rescue Simulation)

SARSIM is a package of computer programs prepared for the Coast Guard by the National Bureau of Standards for analysis of the Coast Guard's complex search and rescue function. SARSIM is described in great detail in a six-volume documentation published by the U.S. Coast Guard in 1971. Excerpts from several of these volumes are paraphrased to give an idea of the capabilities and structure of this simulation package:

> SARSIM is comprised of three major program packages, one or more of which may be employed to explore a particular set of conditions. The first major component in the sequence is the PREPROCESSOR, or PREPRO, founded on a historical accounting of cases served by Coast Guard stations. PREPRO is used to generate the timing of case arrivals and the specification of requirements for service. In other words, PREPRO supplies a scenario, or a preliminary "event list" which may, if desired, be used for many different computer runs.
>
> The heart of SARSIM, the OPERATIONAL SIMULATOR (or OPSIM), is essentially a bookkeeping system which logs in arrivals, registers their needs, investigates the availability of

service facilities, assigns resources for servicing, and generally keeps track of simulated time spent in the several possible activities represented within the model.

> The third major component is the POST-PROCESSOR (or POSTPRO). This program module permits the calculation of a variety of statistics of interest to the user, either as a supplement to the output from OPSIM or to enhance the usability and comprehensibility of the program's output.

A comparison of the real-life search and rescue (SAR) and SARSIM processes may be useful to the reader:

(a) Actual search and rescue cases occur at random times; each case has a specificable location and a particular set of needs for service. SARSIM reproduces typical cases and randomizes their injection into the simulation within the PREPROCESSOR.

(b) When the Coast Guard receives notice of a case requiring service, a suitable resource is dispatched, if available. SARSIM similarly reviews available resources for suitability in assignment. Both the real and the simulated systems keep track of cases waiting for service if facilities are not available. The OPSIM portion of the model makes resource assignments, as well as maintaining statistics of interest.

(c) The Coast Guard periodically assesses SAR performance, including collation of data on individual stations, districts, resource types, and classes of cases. Similar statistics are provided as the output of OPSIM. In addition, POSTPRO permits specialized sorting and analysis of data of particular interest.

AUTOTANK

The towing tank has been, for more than a century, the classical tool used for determining, experimentally, full-scale ship performance characteristics from tests on scale models. Typically in such a test, the model vessel is towed through the water by a carriage to which the model is attached by various force and/or motion sensing devices and mechanical linkages. The carriage, in turn, may be either self-propelled or pulled by a cable attached to a falling weight or some other drive mechanism.

The force and/or motion sensing devices, or dynamometers, generate electrical signals describing the behavior of the model during a test run. These signals are then recorded for later correlation with other characteristics of the run and extrapolation to full-scale results.

A flexible, user-oriented computer software system called AUTOTANK, capable of automating virtually all types of ship model towing tests, was developed for the United States Naval Academy's Hydromechanics Laboratory in Annapolis. (See chapter 12.)

The AUTOTANK system is capable of accepting multiple channels of analog data, scaling that data, performing various naval architectural and time series calculations on the data and interactively displaying, in either tabular or graphical output format, the results of these calculations. In addition, the system contains an interactive test setup capability, to allow the operator to describe a test scenario and to perform other pre-test functions, such as calibrating the dynamometers.

The system accommodates input and output in the MKS, CGS, English, or any other system of units. Units may be mixed within a given variable on input as all input values are converted to the MKS system for computations.

The system itself is highly modular consisting of some 60 individual program modules. These routines may be broken down into several categories:

- executive
- I/O utility
- computational utility, time series analysis
- data acquisition
- graphic output
- tabular output
- test setup

The system was developed for implementation on minicomputers with at least 32K words of memory and a random-access disk storage system.

The software is virtually all written in FORTRAN IV and all AUTOTANK plotting routines are standardized.

The software package is, hence, quite transferable and machine independent. Figure 14–9 shows a block diagram of AUTOTANK. Interactive commands are listed in the adjacent column.

The Computer's Role in the Shipyard

As has been previously described, computers are now being extensively utilized in the design of ships with the result that designs are more quickly generated at lower cost. However, design costs are invariably less than 10% of the total

Operator-Interactive
Command Summary

COMMAND	FUNCTON
FT	Fourier Transform of a specified time series
AQUIR	Allows user to acquire analog data
COF	Creates a named output file
PLOT	Interactive plotting
PRINT	Interactive printing
NAME	Enter test heading
NUMB	Enter run number
TNUM	Enter test number
FRAME	Enter frame rate to be used
HEADER	Write current header information on file
CAL	Interactive calibration of channels
ASSIGN	Assign channels interactively
AVE	Average a specified variable's values
REZERO	Interactive channel rezeroing
CIF	Create a named input file
DISP	Displays header of a named file
RAO	Computes response amplitude operator of two spectra
STATS	Computes 5 statistical parameters of named variable
RESP	Computes the response amplitude spectrum of an RAO and excitation spectrum
DELETE	Deletes a file
NORMAL	Normalizes a spectrum
STOP	Stops execution of the O/I mode

shipbuilding budget, with more than 90% devoted to construction cost. Therefore, even large reductions in design costs are relatively insignificant in terms of economic impact when compared to relatively minor improvements in construction techniques.

For this basic reason the major thrust today in the shipbuilding industry is to find ways to use computers effectively to reduce construction costs.

To date, the introduction of numerically controlled flame cutters into the shipyard has made the largest impact on construction costs. Most large yards and some small yards are now using numerical controlled cutters to cut shell plates,

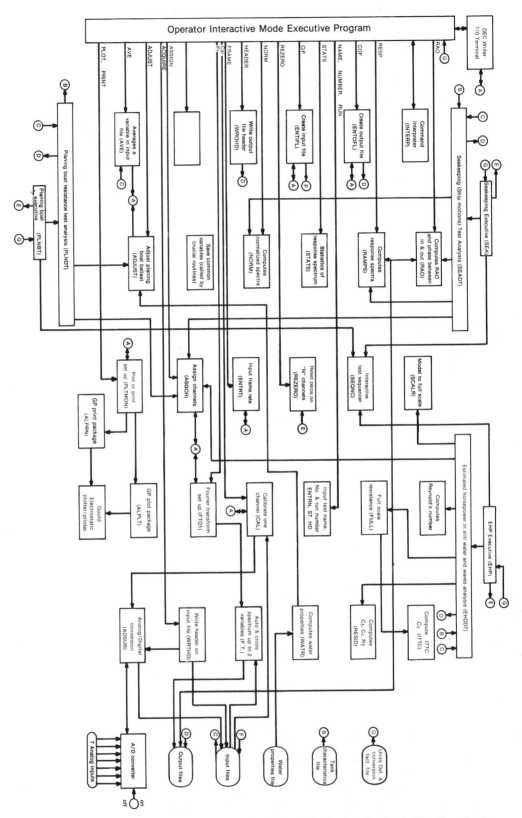

Figure 14–9. Systems such as AUTOTANK will enable Towing Tanks to Significantly Decrease Setup Time and Improve Throughput

frames, brackets, and all other parts that can be cut from steel plate. Because generating the necessary punched paper or mylar tapes containing instructions for the flame cutter is an unreasonably tedious task, all of these yards are using one of the many integrated production software systems developed specifically for that purpose. These systems are different in detail but all of them, in one fashion or another, allow shipyard production personnel to efficiently and quickly generate punched tapes for controlling flame cutters which cut out the pieces of the ship. A typical system consists of the following programs or program modules:

• Hull Definition

This program uses as input data a preliminary table of offsets. The output is a fair, full scale table of offsets which define the molded hull surface at every frame location.

• Shell Plate Development

This module accepts the fair hull form as well as the user-specified location of the butts and seams of the hull shell plating. It develops the flat outline of each plate and stores the offsets in a form suitable for punching a tape.

• Parts Programming

This module is used to generate the numerical description of each piece of the ship. It usually is implemented as a problem-oriented language in which two-dimensional geometrics (circles, straight lines, etc.) can be easily and simply described. Details such as cutouts, snipes, brackets, etc., can be described once and then used over and over by calling them out by name. The curvature of the hull at any location can be obtained automatically from the original hull form definition. The outputs of this module are numerical descriptions of parts suitable for punching tapes.

• Nesting

This program is used to arrange individual parts on a large plate with a minimum of waste. The input for the program consists of the numerical descriptions of the parts to be nested,

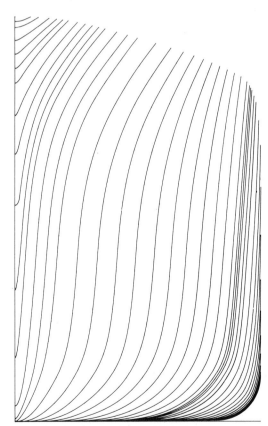

Courtesy of Swedish Shipbuilder's Computer Center

Figure 14–10. Bow Sections (right) and Stern Sections (left) of a Body Plan Drawn and Faired by a Typical Hull Definition Program

the position and orientation of each part relative to the plate, and the location of "cutting bridges" which tie the pieces together during the cutting operation. The output of the nesting program is a master tape which is used to cut all the parts on the plate in one continuous operation.

• Design Programs

Many of the systems also have a suite of design programs which accept as input the hull definition and perform the standard naval architectural calculations described earlier in this chapter.

A typical faired body plan as generated by a hull definition program and drawn on a numerically controlled drafting machine is shown in figure 14–10. A computer-generated drawing of a shell plate as developed by the shell expansion module of the FORAN system is shown in figure 14–11.

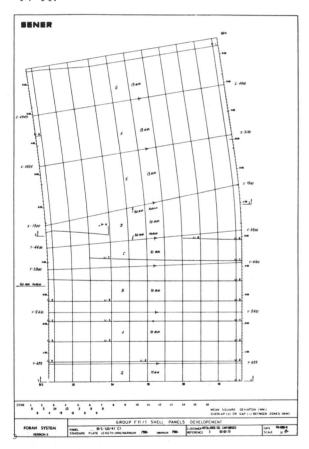

Courtesy SENER Technica Industrial & Naval S. A.

Figure 14–11. Shell Plate Development Drawing Generated by FORAN

A typical drawing representing the output of the nesting modules is shown in figure 14–13.

Although all of the existing systems are similar in concept, they each have special features which make them unique. In the following paragraphs the unique characteristics of several existing systems will be described.

AUTOKON '71

AUTOKON '71 has been purchased by the U.S. Maritime Administration and is the most widely used system in the United States. Developed in Norway, it was the first of the integrated production systems. In addition to the basic capabilities it generates bills of materials and workshop documentation.

SPADES

Being developed and marketed by Cali and Associates, New Orleans, Louisiana, SPADES utilizes a sophisticated disk-based data base and features excellent user-oriented reports and supporting documentation as output together with the usual paper tapes. The data base can handle up to 15 hull configurations simultaneously and has good built-in protection against accidental data base accesses and destruction.

CASDOS

CASDOS is an acronym for Computer-Aided Structural Detailing of Ships. It is a U.S. Navy system meant to be implemented in the design office instead of the production shop where the users are structural designers and naval architects. Outputs, in addition to tapes, include complete shop drawings, bills of materials, welding reports, alignment reports, stiffener fabrication reports, and weight reports. CASDOS is directed toward the ultimate in process automation from design through production. Parts programming is largely eliminated. Tapes are generated automatically.

STEERBEAR 2

Developed by KOCKUMS in Sweden and in use by Sun Shipbuilding and Dry Dock Company, STEERBEAR 2 has some limited capability for automatic generation of NC tapes for such items as brackets, etc. The system generates both production and administrative information, including time and piecework rates.

FORAN

Developed initially as a design system in Spain by SENER, FORAN emphasizes efficient and rapid design. It has as a major goal complete inte-

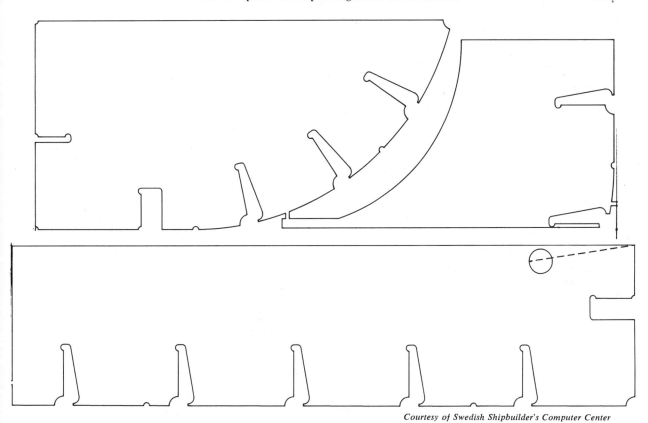

Courtesy of Swedish Shipbuilder's Computer Center

Figure 14–12. Plate-cutting Patterns for Deep Frames and Double Botton Tanks Drawn by Computer. This is a typical output of the parts programming module.

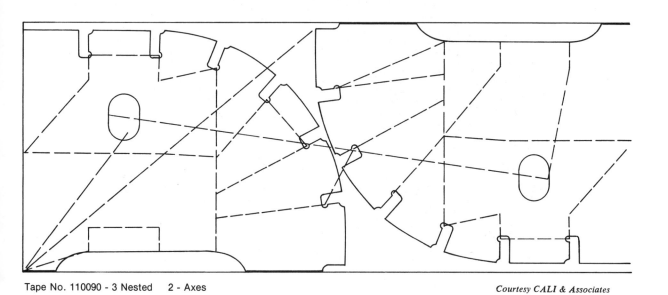

Tape No. 110090 - 3 Nested   2 - Axes   *Courtesy CALI & Associates*

Figure 14–13. Computer-Drawn Output of the Nesting Module of the SPADES System

gration of design and production. It has a lines generation module for creating new hull forms from form parameters.

Information Systems

For a shipyard to function smoothly, great quantities of information must move rapidly between management, production, design, maintenance, and procurement personnel. Hence, computer based information systems are becoming important tools for shipyard management. But because of large variations in management techniques, organizations, and personnel, information systems must necessarily be generalized to such an extent that they can be tailored to each shipyard's needs.

Some of the functions provided by existing information systems are summarized below:

- Production planning and control
- Materials and inventory control
- Scheduling and project management
- Accounting

The ultimate goal is to integrate these individual systems into a single system that can almost instantaneously report the detailed status of the shipyard to management and generate accurate schedules for the future.

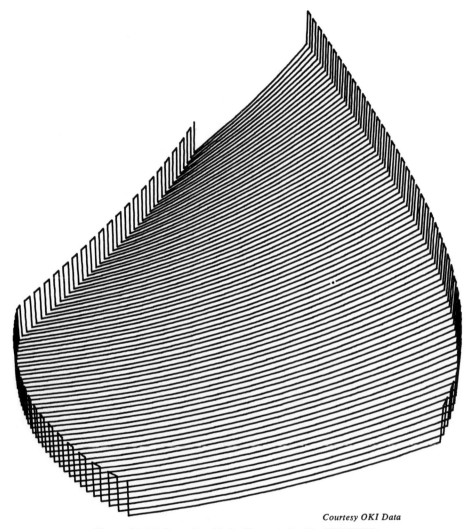

Courtesy OKI Data

Figure 14–14. Propeller Blade Generated with OKI-SURF

Miscellaneous Applications

Numerically controlled machinery is becoming available for automating many manual processes in the shipyard. To support these sophisticated machines, extensive computer software is necessary. For example, the OKI-SURF system developed in Japan makes possible the automatic preparation of control information necessary for the machining of complex three-dimensional shapes. This software system has successfully been used to machine marine propeller blades. Figure 14–14 shows a computer plot of a propeller blade surface generated with the OKI-SURF system.

Also in Japan, Kawasaki Heavy Industries are experimentally using a numerically controlled universal press connected to a minicomputer to gen-erate curved plates as shown in figure 14–15.

A fruitful area for automation in the shipyard is piping design and fabrication. Both the U.S. and Japan are progressing rapidly in this area. Mitsui Shipbuilding, Ltd., has developed a complete numerically controlled pipe shop system which consists of the following automated processes:

- feeding and cutting of pipe
- feeding, fitting and welding the flange
- finishing
- bending

The data for the system is generated from the piping specifications and pipe arrangement drawings. A schematic of the process is shown in figure 14–16.

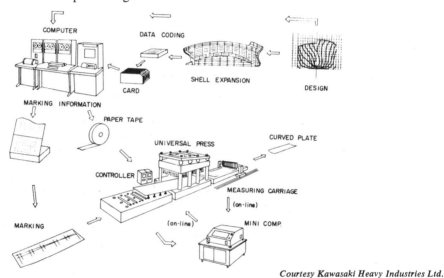

Courtesy Kawasaki Heavy Industries Ltd.

Figure 14–15. Plate-Forming System developed by Kawasaki Heavy Industries

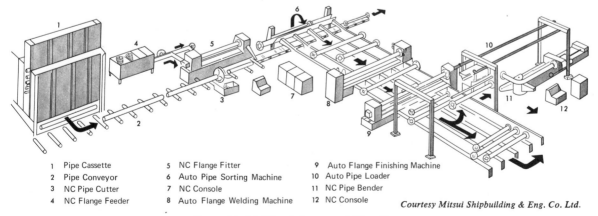

1 Pipe Cassette	5 NC Flange Fitter	9 Auto Flange Finishing Machine
2 Pipe Conveyor	6 Auto Pipe Sorting Machine	10 Auto Pipe Loader
3 NC Pipe Cutter	7 NC Console	11 NC Pipe Bender
4 NC Flange Feeder	8 Auto Flange Welding Machine	12 NC Console

Courtesy Mitsui Shipbuilding & Eng. Co. Ltd.

Figure 14–16. Mitsui Automated Pipe Shop

Boeing Aerospace Company

Jetfoil One, a Commercial Hyrofoil, Flies Above the Water on Her Maiden Voyage

CHAPTER 15

Present and Future On and Beneath the Sea

Increasing attention has been focused on special seagoing craft since the conflicts of the Pacific and Southeast Asia have emphasized the extent and importance of the oceans. Domination of the oceans, not necessarily as a sea power but rather as the domination of a difficult element about which relatively little has been known is essential.

That most of the seagoing tonnage of the world consists of what is called *displacement craft* reflects our inability to effectively solve the problem of speed in ocean transport. This has spurred research and development of many and various design concepts to conquer or override the resistance-drag of ships' wave-making phenomena. Also, the difficulty of coping with the problems of the deep ocean has brought forth special-purpose craft designed to operate at greater depths and to assist in deeper salvage operations. This chapter will concern itself with discussions and descriptions of such craft as these and the general state of the art of their design and development.

Greater Speed

The improvement of the speed of waterborne craft involves, of course, the reduction of any or all of the forces of resistance. (Much of the theory of this was discussed in chapter 5.) While some success has been indicated in the research toward reducing the *frictional resistance* in the boundary layer, there has been little indication of practical methods for applying this research. There is little evidence of the use of such theories that suggest boundary layer ingestion, polymerization of the boundary layer, or other means of boundary layer control.

The most successful approaches to the reduction of resistance are almost exclusively in the reduction or near elimination of *wave-making resistance*. Very simply, these approaches have provided means of either rising above the static flotation level or out of the water entirely to reduce the amount of displacement volume at the interface of the water and air, or, on the other hand, submerging beneath the water's surface to reduce or eliminate the energy absorbed in wave formation.

To review the theories and the associated types of craft that resort to lifting the hull to or above the surface, we must consider first *hydrodynamic support* briefly in theory.

Every ship, when moving at a reasonably high speed, is supported to a greater or lesser degree by hydrodynamic forces acting on her lower surfaces. In most ships of conventional, deep hulls, the amount of this type of support within the range of speeds actually employed is neglig-

Figure 15–1. Two Navy Hydrofoil Ships Underway at More Than 40 Knots on Submerged Foils. These craft were the first two advanced hydrofoil vessels in operation with the Navy. At the right is the 110-ton patrol craft High Point which became operational in 1963. At the left is the 57-ton gunboat Tucumcari which went into Navy service in 1968. The Tucumcari is powered by a water jet propulsion system, and the High Point is driven by two pairs of tandem propellers.

ible. On the other hand, where high speed in smaller ships is involved, such as destroyers, patrol craft, etc., there is often an appreciable dynamic support.

Considering $V/\sqrt{L}$ for a moment, we may recall from chapter 8 that wave-making phenomena are such that when the value for this ratio exceeds about 1.4, an excessive amount of power is required for a further increase in speed. In other words, for normally designed displacement hulls, excessively increasing resistance is encountered in speed-length ratios above this value. In terms of speed-length ratio, then, we may qualify and define the limitation of *displacement hulls*.

In order to exceed speed-length ratios of 1.4, the hull must have some features which provide a measure of hydrodynamic support. And to go further into speed-length ratios above 2.0, it is necessary that the hull form be designed primarily to take advantage of hydrodynamic support. It is obvious, then, that there must be some hull forms that are of a transition type—that at higher speeds they will obtain partial dynamic support

and at lower speeds they will react with the same facility of other slow-speed displacement hulls. Such ships, however (among which modern destroyers could be classified), require extremely large power plants; they have an engineering and machinery space volume that would be totally impracticable in other displacement hulls where requirements other than high speed are more important. The discussion which follows will *not* be devoted, however, to these transitory types inasmuch as they normally, at moderate operating speeds, behave as all displacement hulls, and at their maximum speeds, the effective dynamic support is a similar dynamic action to that discussed subsequently.

The positive dynamic lift on the undersurface of an inclined, flat plate moving in contact with a fluid surface constitutes dynamic support. This is essentially the vertical component of the forward-acting pressures on the inclined surface in the moving stream of fluid. It is the same dynamic lift, either on an aircraft's wing or on the bottom surfaces of a high-speed boat.

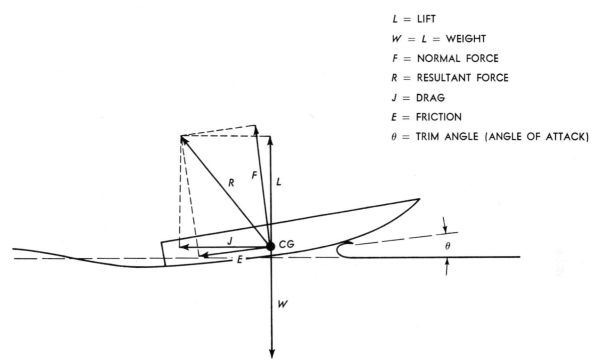

L = LIFT
W = L = WEIGHT
F = NORMAL FORCE
R = RESULTANT FORCE
J = DRAG
E = FRICTION
θ = TRIM ANGLE (ANGLE OF ATTACK)

Figure 15–2. Vector Forces on a Simple Planing Craft

Where this dynamic lifting force exists, there also exists a rearward retarding force known as *induced drag* or *pressure drag*. This lift and drag are the vertical and horizontal components of the resultant force, R, which is the reaction to the dynamic impact force of the fluid on the surface. These forces may be considered to be acting at a point called the center of pressure, P, of the immersed or wetted portion of the surface. In figure 15–2, the forces are resolved on a simple planing craft through the center of gravity. The lift, L, when the surface is in dynamic equilibrium, is balanced by the gravitational force or weight of the boat in the case of waterborne craft. L will vary directly with the amount of wetted surface, with speed, and with the angle of attack.* However, because of the necessity for dynamic equilibrium, L must, in this ideal case, be balanced by the weight, W. Hence, in a surface craft or planing hull, as speed is increased, the wetted surface decreases (assuming a constant angle of attack) and equilibrium is maintained. This reduction in wetted surface means, therefore,

a consequent reduction in frictional resistance which is the major portion of the total resistance in dynamically supported surfaces.

The above analysis constitutes the essential theory of dynamically supported or planing surfaces without introducing the many operating variables and complex form and scale factors. When this analysis is applied to waterborne craft, we may make the following generalizations.

Assuming that the craft is so designed that it has a broad, flat undersurface and that the power plant is capable of driving it above speed-length ratios of 1.8, we see that it will assume a finite angle of attack (i.e., its static waterline becomes inclined to the surface). The speed continues to increase and the wetted surface decreases as the hull is lifted further out of the water. This action, as speed increases further, will (in some planing hulls) almost completely eliminate the formation of waves and the resulting wave resistance. When such a point is reached, a noticeable leveling off in resistance occurs. It is often possible to throttle back on the engines and continue at a constant

---

*There is a small component of L which is essentially a buoyant force but which becomes negligible when full planing is achieved.

speed, or continue to apply the power to reach a higher speed where dynamic equilibrium is imposed by increased frictional resistance and induced drag. A typical resistance curve for this sort of planing hull performance is shown in figure 15–3 and is compared with that for a comparable displacement hull of similar dimensions and power. While different types of planing hulls have their own individual characteristics, figure 15–3 provides a very typical comparison.

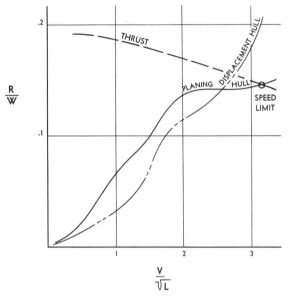

Figure 15–3. Typical Resistance Curves of Comparable Displacement and Planing Hulls

It will be noticed from this curve of the planing hull that there is some speed, in this case at a $V/\sqrt{L}$ of about 2.5 to 3, at which the resistance is substantially constant with increasing speed. When this condition has been reached, it may be said that fully developed planing exists. As speeds continue to increase beyond this range, the resistance will again increase because of the increasing frictional resistance and the induced drag with speed.

In actual planing form hulls, it must be kept in mind that pure dynamic support is approached only at the highest speeds and that the term *planing* is a broad and relative reference. In using these terms, it is understood that the buoyant force is, relatively, a very small portion of the vertical supporting forces of the ship or craft. The weight of the ship is supported almost entirely by the dynamic lift. The horizontal component, drag, along with the frictional resistance on the wetted

surface is opposed by the propeller thrust. The increase in resistance after planing conditions have been achieved is due primarily to the increased frictional resistance, induced drag, and air resistance. It will be recalled from chapter 5 that these latter types of resistances do not increase at the extreme rate that is characteristic of wave resistance.

To make an overall comparative statement, it may be said that a planing hull encounters greater resistances than a similar displacement hull at low speeds before planing is reached, but after planing, it is capable of greater speeds with a lesser and more linear increase in power beyond that required to achieve planing.

The above discussion confines itself to the considerations of dynamic support of an integral

Official U.S. Navy Photograph by PH1 Jean C. Cote

Figure 15–4. The Swift Boat with a 50-foot Planing Hull Capable of Speeds in Excess of 25 Knots.

hull form of characteristic shape—a type of hull with the supporting surface integral and one that operates on the surface of the water. There is, however, an important application of dynamic support involving the use of supporting surfaces carried on surface craft as appendages that project below the surface. These appendages are known as *hydrofoils.*

A hydrofoil operating completely immersed produces a greater lift per square foot than a planing surface because, similar to an airfoil, it derives the greatest amount of its lift from the upper surface. The total lift on such a foil is derived from the sum of the dynamic pressure on the lower surface and the negative pressure induced by the increased rate of flow over the upper surface.

The familiar lift equation,

$$L = C_L \frac{\rho}{2} Sv^2,$$

from aerodynamics is applicable in water as well as air, and it may be immediately appreciated that by substituting the density value of water for that of air (which is some 800 times as great), we may maintain the same order of lift with a much lower velocity. By taking advantage of this fact, the designer can use a proportionately smaller foil surface for hydrofoils to be able to attain reasonably high speeds. To illustrate this principle, the following simple example may be useful.

Suppose that it is desired to support a boat weighing 1200 pounds at a speed of 30 knots with a hydrofoil system whose section characteristics at a small angle of attack and minimum drag have a lift coefficient of 0.5. The mass density of water under standard conditions being 1.990 lb sec²/ft⁴.

Then using the lift equation, we have

$$S = \frac{2L}{\rho \, C_L \, v^2}$$
$$= \frac{2 \times 1200}{1.990 \times 0.5 \, (30 \times 1.689)^2}$$
$$= 0.94 \text{ ft}^2,$$

or, a total foil surface of less than one square foot would be necessary (assuming negligible frictional and eddy resistance) to support this craft at 30 knots.

The above example is an oversimplification but is given merely to illustrate the advantage of the use of hydrofoils and is in no sense intended to reflect all the actual variables.

Like airfoils and planing surfaces, immersed hydrofoils have an accompanying induced drag. Also like airfoils, there is some advantageous angle of attack for a given hydrofoil where there will be a high value of lift with a corresponding low value of drag. This is usually expressed as a ratio called the *maximum L/D ratio,* and it varies with speed. Many simple hydrofoil-supported craft have fixed or rigid hydrofoils, and the angle of attack is therefore built in at some value close to this maximum *L/D* over the range of speeds expected.

In addition to the induced drag above, there is also frictional and eddy resistance on the hydrofoil surfaces and the connecting fins as well as air resistance on the hull structure. Consequently, it may be seen that the example above reflects a more optimistic situation than is actually encountered. However, because there is such a relatively small amount of hydrofoil area and immersed surfaces, there is also a relatively small amount of frictional and eddy resistance (the hull of the supported craft being entirely out of the water).

Planing Hulls

Planing hulls must, because of their dynamic requirement, be all of a basically similar, characteristic form. The requirements dictate a broad, flat supporting surface to bear and distribute the dynamic supporting pressure. A shallow **V**-shaped section or dihedral angle in this surface is necessary to provide adequate directional stability. In general, the major requirements both of high-speed dynamic support and water conditions at high speed have resulted in a form commonly referred to as a *hard chine* form (the chine being the edge formed at the juncture of side and bottom surfaces). The chine is well above the waterline at the bow and curves down to the waterline at about one-third of the waterline length and thence to a very flat angle running out to the lower corners of a broad, flat transom stern (see figure 15–5). Because planing is, to a great extent, dependent upon trim, the longitudinal position of the center of gravity is extremely important. A planing craft operates most efficiently at a planing angle of approximately 3.5 degrees. A small shift in the longitudinal position of *G* might easily change the trim by this amount.

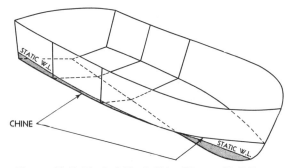

Figure 15–5. Typical Hard Chine Planing Hull Form

Trim by the bow or by the stern in amounts of this magnitude or sometimes less will result generally in a failure to reach planing speed.

The description of the hull form indicated above was intentionally brief and undefinitive. Like displacement hulls, planing hulls must be designed specifically for the requirements demanded of them. The speed range, the gross weight, the length limitations, and the water conditions are the major variables that affect the form of a planing hull. The most satisfactory form of hull to fit any given combination of these variables is determined best by model experiments.

One of the most successful high-speed planing forms incorporates a constant **V**-section dihedral from the transom to amidships (or slightly aft of it). Horizontal, longitudinal surface ridges are often built into the hull's planing bottom surface. These ridges are spaced closely and run essentially parallel to straight buttock lines along the bottom.

SINGLE CHINE FORM

The most common and frequently used planing form is the single hard chine described in the preceding section. This form has the advantages of (1) being a substantially good planing surface form, (2) being simple and economical to produce, and (3) having excellent accommodation space for machinery, armament, and crew.

As a planing form, it has the disadvantage of having greater wetted surface when planing than the types outlined below with consequent greater resistance. Its characteristics in a seaway compared to other planing hulls are only fair, but it must be remembered that all planing hulls are poor in rough water. Altogether, however, this form is probably the most satisfactory type of

Official U.S. Navy Photograph

Figure 15–6. PT-809 From Aft (Note Dry Transom). These planing craft are of welded aluminum construction.

planing hull for general utility work and military applications when moderately high speeds are required.

The stepped chine form, in which the bottom is made up of two or more planing surfaces in successive steps, is a modification of the hard chine form. In most such stepped forms, only one step is used, but three and four steps have been used experimentally and in racing hulls.

The single stepped form has been used in water-based aircraft hulls and has the advantage of quickly reducing wetted surface when accelerating as well as restricting the position of the center of pressure. This form of hull is important where rapid acceleration to maximum speed is desirable. Disadvantageously, the stepped hull form has even worse rough-water characteristics than the simple chine form because of the disproportionate distribution of buoyant volume toward the bow. In general, it is capable of higher speeds than other comparable planing forms primarily because of the decreased aspect ratio and decreased wetted surface with consequent decreased induced and frictional drag.

INVERTED V FORM

Planing hulls of the inverted **V** form have a characteristic bottom surface, while the normal **V** bottom surface is inverted with the apex at the top instead of the bottom. This produces sections which form a peaked tunnel longitudinally along the bottom. The apex of the sections flattens as it approaches the stern and the aftermost sections are essentially flat across the bottom.

The primary advantage of this type of hull is the improved rough water characteristics caused by the cushioning action of the water in the inverted **V** section. There may be slightly improved resistance characteristics produced by a greater aerodynamic lift caused by the tunneling effect under the bottom.

It must be pointed out in summarizing that, while planing hulls have the attractive advantage of high speed with a relatively moderate power expenditure, there are specific disadvantages that limit their usefulness in naval service. Principal among these are

1. *Limited variation in operating displacements.*

This limitation places a premium on the amount of fuel capacity (which means cruising range) or the amount of payload.

2. *Poor rough-water characteristics.* This limitation results in limited time of operation or, if operation is undertaken in rough water, uneconomical powering characteristics at necessarily lower speeds. Modifications in the planing hull form are frequently made to adapt them, to some extent, to rough water. These modifications, while improving the hull's rough water ability, invariably decrease its effectiveness as a high-speed planing hull in flat water. Such modifications, however, will often preserve the high-speed characteristics to an extent where partial planing is possible.

Hydrofoil Craft

The hydrofoil craft is described as a hull supported, when operating, clear of the water surface by the hydrodynamic lift of underwater wings or hydrofoils. This type of dynamic support provides a greater reduction in resistance and basically superior rough-water performance when compared to both planing and displacement hulls in the same speed range.

The development of hydrofoil craft is still somewhere between research and practical design. Hydrofoils are available in small pleasure craft but more serious adaptation and primary current use is in high-speed passenger ferries, naval patrol craft, small premium cargo carriers, or military-naval applications requiring dependable high-speed water transportation.

TYPES OF FOILS

The two basic types of foil arrangements (with design variations) in extensive use are surface-piercing foils—**V**- or **U**-shaped foils—and submerged foils in several orientations (see figure 15–7). The surface-piercing foils, regardless of their individual design and shape, have the advantageous feature of compensating automatically for speed. The active surface area decreases as speed increases (and conversely) which maintains equilibrium between weight and lift at any speed with a fixed angle of attack. Such foils have the ability to *profile,* which is to follow in forward movement the profile of the water's surface, i.e. to move ahead up and down the waves.

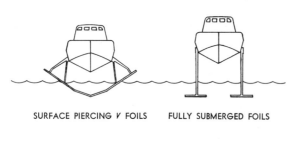

SURFACE PIERCING V FOILS   FULLY SUBMERGED FOILS

NONSPLIT   SPLIT

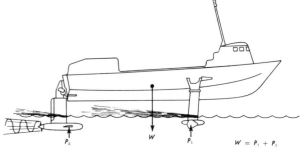

Figure 15–8. Vector Forces on Hydrofoil Craft

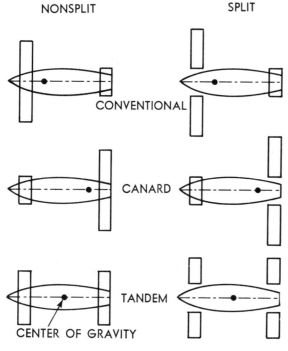

CONVENTIONAL

CANARD

TANDEM

CENTER OF GRAVITY

LATERAL CONFIGURATION

Figure 15–7. Standard Hydrofoil Configurations and Arrangements in Modern Use

While the surface-piercing foils appear to be the simplest and most rugged, they unfortunately are the least efficient of the two types, providing a rougher ride and becoming cumbersome in larger sized craft. The greatest effort in present hydrofoil development is being put forth on controlling devices, particularly for rough-water response and recovery, for the submerged type of foil.

OPERATION

Regardless of the type of foil, the basic action is essentially the same. The boat starts from rest in a displacement condition and is accelerated, generally through a conventional marine propul-

sion drive, to a "take-off" speed where the weight of the boat is finally and completely transferred to the foils. The lift on the foils brings the hull clear of the water, leaving only the propelling equipment and the effective foil surfaces submerged. The very close analogy of this action to that of aircraft is immediately apparent, and the terms such as "take-off," "flying," and "touch down" are used with their obvious analogous meaning. In fact, since much of the data required in determining powering and design characteristics is derived from tests of airfoils and aircraft components, aeronautical terminology is used as a matter of convenience. Unlike the resistances of either the displacement or planing hulls, the characteristics of a hydrofoil show a distinct hump or peak resistance. Figure 15–9 shows typical resistance curves for two types of hydrofoils with that of a comparable planing hull. Take-off occurs in both types of foils after the peak resistance is passed. Depending upon the lift coefficient for the particular foil configuration used, the take-off speed will determine the minimum foil

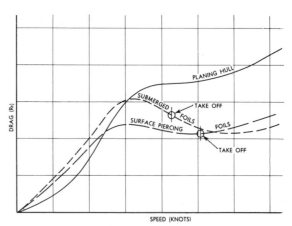

Figure 15–9. Comparative Resistance versus Speed Curves of Dynamically Supported Craft

area required in submerged types of hydrofoils. It should be noted in the above figure that the typical submerged foil craft has a higher peak resistance and a lower take-off speed than the surface-piercing foil. This greater *hump drag,* as it is called, occurs with the submerged foil by the necessity to produce the required lift for take-off by increasing the angle of attack, thus inducing at the same time a higher drag. It is interesting to note that at the lower speeds before the hump both hydrofoils show greater resistances than the planing hull. At such low speeds it should be remembered, also, a displacement hull in the same category will have the *least* resistance.

In representing resistance characteristics graphically for the purpose of comparing performance for all hydrofoil craft, the absolute ordinates of drag and speed are, of course, as inadequate as would be resistance versus speed for all types of displacement hulls. However, the speed coefficient, $V/\sqrt{L}$ is hardly more useful since there is little significance to the L dimension. This is also true, to a degree, for any planing hull. Consequently, it becomes necessary to find some more adaptable coefficient that retains the significance of Froude's law of similitude, i.e., one that contains the essential dimensions and relationships in either Froude's Number or the speed-length ratio. One such coefficient that is very useful and seems to satisfy the necessary restrictions is the relationship, k, which is expressed as the Froude speed-displacement coefficient:

$$k = \frac{v}{\sqrt{\nabla^{1/3}}}\ C$$

where

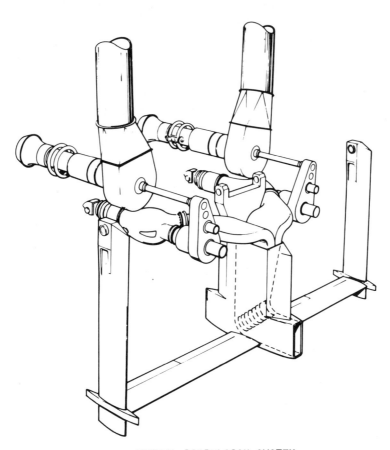

JETFOIL PROPULSION SYSTEM

Figure 15–10. This Propulsion System was first used successfully on the USS Tucumcari and is now in use on the large passenger-carrying JETFOIL ONE capable of carrying 280 passengers at 45 knots in a 12-foot sea.

Figure 15–11. USS Plainview, the World's Largest Hydrofoil Vessel (220 feet, 320 tons). The ship is driven at speeds in excess of 40 knots when foilborne by titanium propellers powered by marinized jet engines at 28,000 HP

C = constant $\left(\text{derived from } \dfrac{1}{\sqrt{g/4\pi}} = 1.056\right)$

v = velocity in ft/sec

∇ = volume of displacement or equivalent sea-water volume corresponding to the total weight, W.

Strictly for the use of hydrofoil craft the factor of ∇ (volume) in its relationship to W might be expressed more usefully in terms of lift, making the speed coefficient,

$$\textcircled{H} = \frac{v}{\sqrt{\dfrac{L_i^{1/3}}{\rho}}} \, C$$

where L_i = Lift = total weight of craft.

Such coefficients, either $\textcircled{k}$ or $\textcircled{H}$, have the advantage over the speed-length ratio in that they are based on the determinate factor of displacement or weight and make possible the comparison of performance of planing and hydrofoil craft, regardless of their overall size or gross weight. This is to say that the true significance of size and weight is considered rather than only the linear function of length, L.

SPEED AND POWER FOR HYDROFOIL CRAFT

It was noted previously that hydrofoils have an advantageously low value of resistance for a limited range of speed-length ratios. Above or below this range, they will either have poor resistance characteristics or else their adaptation will be entirely impossible. Referring to the lift equation and the example cited in illustrating it, it must be pointed out here that the dimensions of the craft and the speed selected were deliberately chosen in an advantageous range. As another example here, let us increase the size of the craft and reduce the speed to the dimensions of a low-speed merchant ship. Using a displacement of 6000 tons and a speed of 15 knots we find that

$$S = \frac{2L}{\rho\, C_L\, v^2}$$
$$= \frac{2 \times 6000 \times 2240}{1.99 \times 0.5 \times (14 \times 1.689)^2}$$
$$= 42{,}000 \text{ ft}^2.$$

Assuming two hydrofoils of this total projected area, they would each have a span of 700 feet. This, of course, would be ridiculously impractical. It would be found equally ridiculous in terms of drag or thrust required, considering that even when the most optimistic L/D ratio is approximately 15, the induced drag would be 896,000 pounds.

In considering the adaptation of hydrofoils to large vessels, it must be remembered that *weight increases as the cube of the linear dimensions and lift as the square*. This fundamental rationalization is often referred to as the *cube-square law* for hydrofoils. The hydrofoil surface area must be increased to a greater proportionate size therefore to maintain the equilibrium between weight and lift.

The above example may seem an unreasonable selection of values but it serves to emphasize the upper limitations. A more reasonable comparison might be cited on destroyer dimensions where the following tabular comparison may be made.

	Conventional Ship	*Hydrofoil Ship*
Speed (knots)	35	35
Length (feet)	400	400
Displacement (tons)	3,000	3,000
Wetted surface (or foil surface)	19,000 ft²	8,500 ft²
EHP_t	37,500	41,300
EHP_f	12,000	7,000
EHP_r	25,500	34,300
Total shaft horsepower	60,000	66,000

Using rather high values of L/D and lift coefficient, this remains, on the basis of power, definitely disadvantageous for the hydrofoil.

In terms of smaller hulls and immediately realistic possibilities a more meaningful comparison may be made with large planing hulls as follows:

	Planing hull	*Hydrofoil*
Weight (displ.)	50,000 lbs	50,000 lbs
Speed	50 knots	50 knots
Shaft horsepower	4,000	1,200

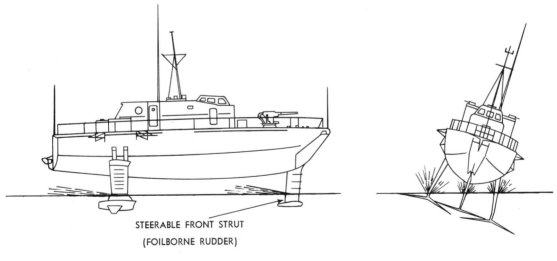

STEERABLE FRONT STRUT

(FOILBORNE RUDDER)

NORMAL FOILBORNE

TURNING

Courtesy of Boeing

Figure 15–12. Tucumcari in Foilborne Operation. The turning view shows how the anhedral or drooped design of the aft foils allows the craft to make high-speed banked turns without the foil tips coming out of the water. The gunboat is designed for speeds in excess of 40 knots.

Figure 15–13. Two Japanese-Built Hydrofoil Craft. These passenger-carrying craft are basically of the popular Italian Supramar class. Boats with this type of V foils are used extensively in Western Europe and Scandinavia for rapid transportation on lakes, sounds, fjords, and other protected waters.

The rather large number of variables involved makes it difficult to fix an exact range of practical applications for hydrofoils, although it is apparent that limitations must be in some terms of speed and weight which govern in turn the relative size of the hydrofoil involved. The amount of weight being supported also directly affects the induced drag. For large, heavy hulls, the power required to overcome this accompanying drag is beyond all reasonable considerations.

In general, it might be said that for practical applications, a lower limit of speed in terms of Froude's Number would be in the range of 0.6 to 0.7. An upper limit, in terms of weight, using the most efficient type of power plant currently available, could not be more than 1000 tons and then only with a particularly efficient type of submerged foil. A more realistic estimate considering actual performance experience, transmission and propulsion difficulties, strut losses, etc., would be approximately 300 tons. In terms of power available, it would seem that a ratio of shaft horsepower per ton of displacement of at least 75 would be required for all craft with other suitable hydrofoil characteristics to reach a flying condition.

SPECIAL FOIL AUGMENTATION

In order to improve performance and exceed some of the restrictive limits indicated above, hydrodynamic research has shown the effectiveness of ventilated submerged foils and the superior high-speed performance of special foils called *supercavitating foils.*

Recalling first the phenomena of cavitation described in chapter 6, the same phenomena are encountered on hydrofoils when speeds above approximately 40 knots are reached. This cavitation on the upper surface of the foil is not widespread at these speeds, but occurs in small critical areas. The lift is partially and locally reduced, and this results in an unstable lift-drag situation producing an unsteady force system. The resulting situation in operation is referred to as *buffeting.* Such cavitation, even though it produces in addition a progressive erosion on the metal surfaces above 45 to 50 knots, can be endured. However, at about 55 to 60 knots (depending on the effectiveness of foil design, size of craft, etc.) cavitation spreads over most of the foil surface and becomes an intolerable deterrent to further speed. A transient solution in this speed range has been developed by injecting air down the supporting strut to the base of the foil surface. The type of foil used is essentially designed to produce uniform and controlled cavitation. It has a sharp leading edge with gradual taper back to a blunt or axe-head base or trailing edge. The air injection controls and improves the fluid flow, reduces the tendency toward buffeting and erosion, and increases the efficiency of the foil in transition to full cavitation.

The same foil shape described above with a slightly sharper leading edge with increased camber (earlier developed for propeller blade sections) is a *supercavitating foil.* Such foils are most effective in speed ranges above 80 knots and hold much promise for development of larger, higher speed hydrofoil craft. However, improvement and development are particularly needed in combination foil systems which will further ease the transition between lower and intermediate speeds to high speeds. There is a basic stand-off in operating characteristics between subcavitating foils and supercavitating foils. Where one is poor the other is good. At low speed, the supercavitating

foil develops very little lift and requires a high angle of attack giving large drag. At high speed, the subcavitating foil loses lift due to cavitation and is subject to eventual destruction by erosion.

There are other basic problems, such as propulsion, in higher speed hydrofoil craft. Supercavitating propellers are being extensively used with some success. However, their efficiency peak can be exceeded when the foil speed is not reached and their lower speed operation is inefficient. One solution is reflected in the increased attention being given to water jet propulsion. An excellent example of this adaptation is in the Navy's PGH–2. Her basic installation and configuration is shown in figure 15–12.

A most successful adaptation of commercial hydrofoil craft design is the Grumman *Dolphin* (see figure 15–10). This design has been adopted by a number of foreign countries and has been franchised to foreign builders. The *Dolphin's* excellent rough-water characteristics and dependable operation indicate replacement of an older and very stylized foreign design in use for so many years in Europe and the Orient.

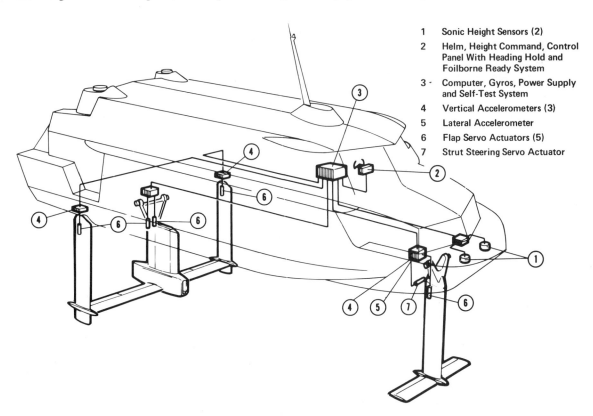

1　Sonic Height Sensors (2)
2　Helm, Height Command, Control Panel With Heading Hold and Foilborne Ready System
3　Computer, Gyros, Power Supply and Self-Test System
4　Vertical Accelerometers (3)
5　Lateral Accelerometer
6　Flap Servo Actuators (5)
7　Strut Steering Servo Actuator

Figure 15–14. The Foil Control System on the passenger-carrying JETFOIL ONE. This craft is capable of operating with this automatic system in 12-foot waves.

APPLICATIONS OF DYNAMICALLY
SUPPORTED CRAFT

In the field of water transport, dynamic support represents a new concept—new and perhaps radical when projected again a background of the development of displacement vessels over a period of three thousand years. It is easy to be impressed by demonstrated performances, yet at the same time it is risky to think in generalizations by extrapolating possible performances based on limited demonstrations.

We have seen from the foregoing paragraphs that where the basic and natural desire to improve speed and resistance characteristics of waterborne craft has led to various types of hydrodynamic support, there have also been introduced, naturally, some new and troublesome limitations. Basic among these limitations is weight. Secondly are the hydrodynamic speed phenomena—minimum supporting speed and maximum limiting speed that produce excessive resistance and cavitation. Particularly for hydrofoil craft, there is the critical lift-drag relationship; the L/D ratio must always be considered as a critical and limiting factor. Finally there is the power requirement—not only high powers for high speeds but also high powers in small compact engines with reasonable fuel requirements. These power requirements are directly associated with weight as is speed with weight.

It would be reasonable to combine these factors together in a single expression of efficiency, calling it, as one authority has, *transport efficiency*. With such a parameter, then, it might be possible to compare and relate the operating capabilities or possibilities of conventional displacement hulls, planing hulls, and hydrofoil craft. The factor called *transport efficiency* is an expression of the net weight of the hull in tons, speed in knots, and actual shaft horsepower in the form of

$$T.E. = \frac{WV}{SHP}.$$

This variable, when plotted against the most common, significant dependent variable, $V/\sqrt{L}$ or, in more universal and dimensionless form, the Froude Number, provides a related area of comparison as shown in figure 15–15.

Reference to such a graphical comparison will

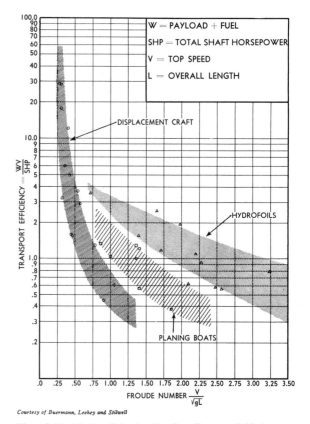

Courtesy of Buermann, Leehey and Stilwell

Figure 15–15. Possible Application Range of Hydrofoils and Planing Hulls versus Displacement Hulls.

quickly reveal the practicability or impracticability of the three related types of waterborne hulls. The shaded areas are intended to show in a comparative sense only the limiting boundaries of application. They are based on present and past experience and, in the case of hydrofoil craft, future possibilities within the realm of engineering and industrial capabilities.

Air Support Craft

In the further search for more efficient speed in larger water-based craft beyond the realm of planing hulls and hydrofoils, we must consider briefly the use and adaptation of craft whose structures are separated or partially separated from the water by a differential pressure of air.

During the development period of such craft, there have been many experimental configurations, and there are several categories and applications that are operationally successful or hold considerable promise of future success. Of these, it will be of interest to examine generally air cushion vehicles and captured air bubble (CAB) craft.

Air cushion craft have assumed many experimental configurations and operational sizes, the first and most successful having been developed in England in 1958 by Hovercraft Development, Ltd. Like the hydrofoil, the concept is not entirely new, but lack of adequate power and structural material has delayed its realization.

The principle of the air cushion craft is quite simple. A flow of ducted air through a comparatively low-pressure fan or blower is directed down through the enclosed rigid canopy-like structure creating a lifting force over the broad base of the craft. The air then escapes or leaks out around the base periphery. The craft is thus lifted off the surface, and the height is a function of the power available in the blowers to increase the air pressure. The forward velocity of the craft is provided by separate engines driving air propellers. The directional control is accomplished by vertical fin stablilizers and rudders mounted in the airstream aft of the propellers.

Greater efficiency in lift is attained in the design where the air is directed down from the blower duct through annular jets. Instead of going into the center of the chamber, air is channeled to ring slots around the inside periphery and thence down to outlets that are angled inward at the base. Thus the air provides its own seal and holds about 60 percent of the cushion beneath the craft. The addition of a peripheral skirt around the base adds to the craft's further efficiency in maintaining an air seal and a flexible base which materially improves its capacity to negotiate moderately rough water.

The very great and impressive advantage of this craft over hydrofoil craft is that there is no limiting size or load-carrying barrier. The hydrofoil is confronted by the so-called *cube-square law*. To the contrary for air cushion vehicles (ACV), an increase in the linear dimensions of the craft (such as length and beam) increases the lift capacity exponentially (by the square). Thus, in doubling the dimensions of an ACV we quadruple its load carrying area; consequently, the larger the craft the more efficient is its use of power.

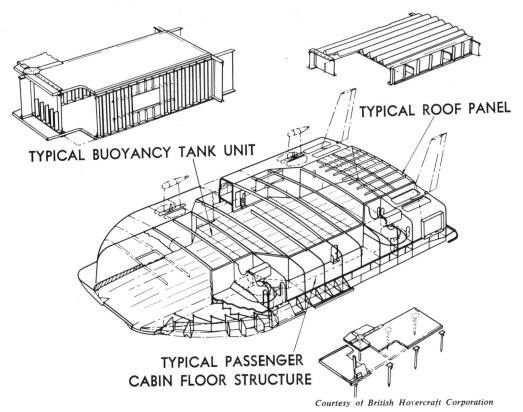

TYPICAL ROOF PANEL

TYPICAL BUOYANCY TANK UNIT

TYPICAL PASSENGER CABIN FLOOR STRUCTURE

Courtesy of British Hovercraft Corporation

Figure 15–16. Typical Large Passenger-Type Aircushion Vehicle Structure

Figure 15–17. The U.S. Navy's 100-ton High-speed Surface Effect Ship with Admiral Elmo Zumwalt, USN, then Chief of Naval Operations, at the Controls. The ship achieved a speed of over 55 knots in the choppy waters of the Gulf of Mexico during its test and evaluation mission.

The ACV is essentially an amphibious vehicle, but its ability to negotiate uneven surface obstacles is a function of its power to elevate itself above the surface. The tough flexible skirt at present improves this ability and in sea waves nearly eliminates the interference of choppy water and in heavy seas permits *profiling,* or following the wave contour, as does a hydrofoil craft.

Because an air cushion vehicle has no direct contact with the water, there is scarcely any frictional resistance to overcome.* The vehicle is actually a low-flying aircraft, and the air drag problem is identical to that of an aircraft. The speed of such a craft is presently in the order of 75 to 100 knots.

These craft have been operational in passenger ferry service for some years, with regular runs across the English Channel, San Francisco Bay, and locations in Scotland, Germany and Norway. Vessels with capacities to 500 passengers have been built.

In naval service they have found unparalleled success where military operations require speed and mobility in difficult marshy and swampy terrain. (See figure 15–17.)

---

*At some speeds a substantial wave drag is encountered, however.

For other commercial service there is great promise for development. The Maritime Commission has projected large ACVs with capacities to deliver containerized cargoes in lots of 1000 to 1500 tons on regular and frequent schedules at speeds of 100 knots in proper surface weather.

However, there are no vessels that have no disadvantages or limitations. The air cushion vehicle is very weather sensitive and its response to increasing wave height is unhappily negative. As wave heights build up over a few feet and their lengths increase beyond several lengths of the vehicle, the craft is forced to a slow-speed mode. In a storm, it must inconveniently ride it out at only a few knots or uncomfortably accommodate to wave slopes in profiling at reduced speed and increased vertical accelerations.

Captured air bubble (CAB) craft are a variation and extension of the air cushion vehicle. The primary difference is in the structure and configuration. CAB craft are rigid, elongated structures (as are ships) with parallel sides which actually penetrate the water surface. There is a forward and an after flap covering the opposite ends of the long central air chamber. The air cushion or bubble supporting the craft is supplied by ducted air fans in the craft's upper portion. Water jet propulsion is the most ideal propulsive force for these large CAB craft. The air leakage in these craft is out of the stern flap and is designed to be of a lower percentage than that of the air cushion vehicles.

These hulls are essentially designed for seagoing use and are generally heavy and fast transport vessels—hence their rigid structure. The drag of the side panels in the water produces some fluid friction which, of course, requires greater installed horsepower per ton than the simpler air cushion craft. Taking advantage of the lifting potential with increased size, these vessels are projected in the largest practical sizes.

Figure 15–19 shows the profile of a projected large assault transport of the captured air bubble type.

Courtesy of British Hovercraft Corporation

Figure 15–18. Mountbatten Class Hovercraft (SR.N4) in Operation

CHARACTERISTICS

Length overall	130 ft.
Beam overall	77 ft.
Height overall	42 ft.
Vehicle headroom	11 ft.
Cushion area	7342 sq. ft.
Cushion loading (165 tons AUW)	50 lbs./sq. ft.
Cushion length	112 ft.
Cushion beam	68 ft.
Skirt depth below buoyancy tank	8 ft.
Clearance height (calm water)	4 in. approx.
Finger length	4 ft.
Maximum speed (calm conditions)	165 tons-65 knots
	140 tons-70 knots

Multihull Vessels

Multihull vessels, more often called catamarans for those with two hulls and trimarans for those with three, have been used or experimented with periodically for centuries. The obvious gain in stability when two hulls are arranged in the same direction, separated from each other yet attached by a common deck, proves an interesting attraction to further investigation. Because of the greater stability than a single hull, and without increasing their weight or outside ballast, they have a much greater sail-carrying power per pound of displacement. This factor alone has made them most popular among some sailing enthusiasts.

Aside from sailing craft, multihulls find their greatest justification is specialized uses such as ocean research vessels, submarine rescue ships, etc., where the protected space between the hulls, at the location of minimum motion in a seaway, is advantageous for working in the water.

The distribution of displacement between two or three hulls instead of one allows the individual hulls to operate with an appreciably less wave-making resistance at the higher speed-length ratios; however, the increased wetted area increases the frictional resistance to the order that there is no total reduction in the *EHP*. Actually an increase in *EHP* results. The normal or customary arrangement of the hulls relative to each other is parallel and abreast.

Very frequently, hull form is such that the outboard surfaces of the hulls are vertical planes. This is the result of the so-called *split hull configuration*. A single hull form of the desired shape is in theory split longitudinally along its longitudinal centerline, and the resulting halves are reversed port for starboard to make the two supporting catamaran hulls. The curved surfaces are then inboard and opposite each other. The principal advantage of this arrangement is to further reduce the wave-making component of resistance on both outboard sides of the assemblage. A further extension of this reasoning is a staggered arrangement of the hulls in their longitudinal placement, allowing one hull to overlap or lead the other by a distance that is preconceived to produce a wave cancellation on the

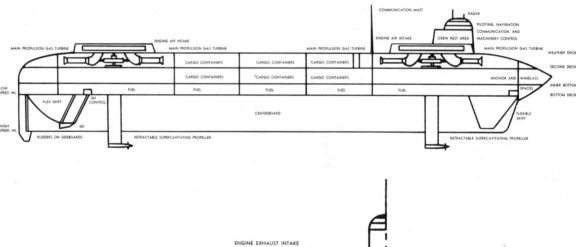

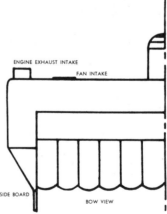

Figure 15–19. General Arrangement of a Captured Air Bubble Ship

lagging hull. Recalling that the bow wave pattern of a displacement hull emanates at an angle from the bow as it moves through the water, we find that the hulls can be so separated that this wave moving out from the leading hull falls on the trough formed at the inboard side of the lagging hull's bow, thus producing a partial wave cancellation.

The immediately apparent design fault in the staggered hull arrangement described above is the lack of transverse symmetrical support and stability caused by the resulting imbalance of heeling moments. The rolling action would produce motion about an unsymmetrical or angled axis in catamaran vessels with staggered hulls. However, for trimarans there can be and is a symmetrical arrangement for staggered hulls. In addition, together with the advantage of wave cancellation, the center hull is not split but is a fully contoured symmetrical hull and is generally so arranged as to be the leading hull. The port and starboard hulls are often split to present a straight, flat surface on the outside.

It would appear then that to take the most advantage of wave cancellation, the trimaran is more adaptable than the catamaran. However, the trimaran has considerably more wetted surface than either the catamaran or a single hull of

Courtesy of Bell Aerosystems

Figure 15–20. Proposed Air Cushion Merchant Ship. The 420-foot vessel would have a beam of 140 feet and could cruise at 80 knots. Lift and propulsion would be provided by 140,000 SHP engines. The ship would weigh 4,000 gross tons.

comparable total displacement, and consequently any advantages in powering do not exist except at very high or overdriven speeds where wave-making resistance is predominant in single hulls. The poor performance of trimarans at lower speeds certainly resistricts the application of this type of craft; the most likely uses are for higher speed, short haul passenger ferries, special short haul, light cargo, roll on/roll off vessels where unencumbered deck space is important, etc.

The research on multihull craft performed by naval researchers, specifically Mr. Herbert Meier of the Naval Ship Systems Command (an expert on multihull vessels), has presented some very objective and interesting results based both on tank tests and Taylor series analysis. Figure 15–22 shows the results of this analysis and is based essentially on the investigation of catamaran hulls for use in the Navy's ASR vessel, a 210 foot, 16 knot ship for submarine rescue work. The dimensions of this multihull (catamaran) vessel are as follows:

LWL (LBP)	— 210 feet
Beam (each hull)	— 24 feet
Draft	— 18 feet
Displacement (each hull)	—1400 tons
Speed (designed)	— 16 knots
Cp	— .55

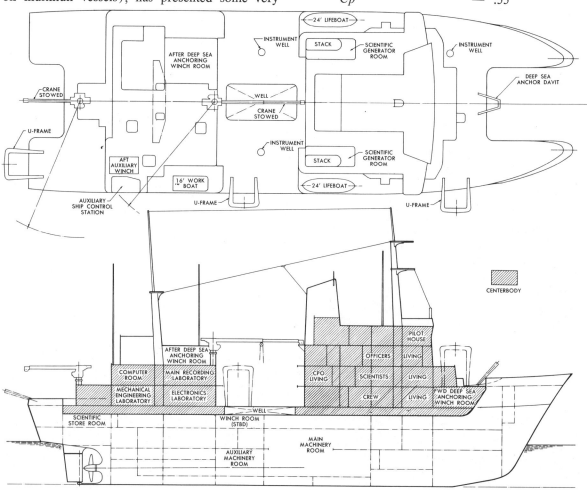

Figure 15–21. Hull Configuration and Characteristics of New Multi-hull Navy AGOR

CHARACTERISTICS

LOA	234 ft. 6 in.	Draft	19 ft. 0 in.
LBP	210 ft. 0 in.	Light Displ.	2575 tons
BEAM (Max.)	86 ft. 0 in.	Full Load Δ	3200 tons
BEAM (Each Hull)	26 ft. 0 in.	Speed, Sustained	16 kts.
MAIN DK.ABV.W.L.	16 ft. 0 in.	Endurance/13 KTS	10,000

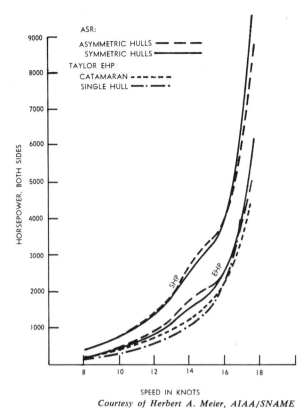

SPEED IN KNOTS

Courtesy of Herbert A. Meier, AIAA/SNAME

**Figure 15–22. Comparative Powering Characteristics
of Catamaran Hulls versus Single Hull**

The body plans of the combined asymmetric and symmetric hull forms are shown in figure 15–23. The asymmetric hulls, in this case, are asymmetric only in the portion forward of amidships.

The comparison using Taylor's series for both the catamaran and single hull were for hulls of the same length, draft, displacement, and coeffi-

cients. It has been pointed out in the report that because of the extreme beam/draft ratio required for the catamaran hull, some extrapolation was necessary in the tables.

It can be seen from the plotted curves that, again, any favorable situation for the catamaran hulls is not evident until the higher speeds are reached. In this case, 16 knots corresponds to $V/\sqrt{L} = 1.1$. It would seem that the asymmetric hulls are superior at speed-length ratios in excess of 1.2, in the hull configurations used.

In the case of this Navy ASR, it would also seem that the asymmetrical model is not affected adversely as much as the symmetrical model by variations in hull spacing. There is obviously a critical minimum spacing in catamaran hulls as shown in figure 15–24. However, there has been so little objective research or tank tests of series hulls and arrangements of multihull craft that it is not possible to generalize too far.

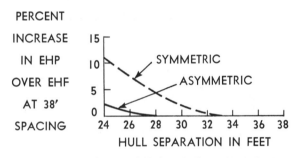

Courtesy of Herbert A. Meier, AIAA/SNAME

Figure 15–24. Effect of Hull Spacing on Power

The advantages of multihull craft that have been objectively established and demonstrated are relatively few. For a narrow speed range in the high Froude Number values, staggered, split (or asymmetric) hulls on both catamarans and trimarans show a small improvement in powering characteristics over the conventional and comparable displacement hull; they are unquestionably more stable initially; they offer a platform for special working and rescue craft that presents a protected water surface at the point of minimum motion. No attempt will be made to categorize their disadvantages, but it should be apparent to the student that the configuration of multihull craft presents a multitude of structural problems. There is little analytical data available to guide the designer in his solutions to multihull structural problems.

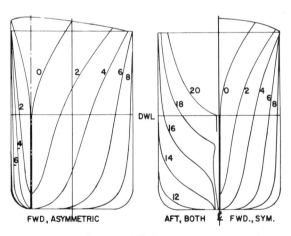

Courtesy of Herbert A. Meier, AIAA/SNAME

Figure 15–23. ASR Body Plans

Deep Submergence Craft

RECENT TRENDS

For many years, man's curiosity about the ocean depths has led him toward the development of deep ocean vehicles that were capable of entering this most mysterious and almost unknown world. At this writing, only a little more than five percent of the earth's surface under the sea has been explored. Prior to 1960, there were few submersibles capable of going deeper than the relatively shallow depths considered operational by naval combat submarines.

In 1960 the *Trieste*, a manned Navy bathyscaphe, dove to the bottom of the Marianas Trench in the Pacific, a depth of nearly 36,000 feet. While this dive in itself was successful and set a depth record that would appear to be the ultimate limit, the operation of the *Trieste* left much to be desired and pointed up the need for craft of greater mobility and operational capacity even at much lesser depths.

It is difficult to classify the *Trieste* as an undersea vehicle; having a minimum of mobility and no self-contained pressure hull, this craft was simply an observation gondola suspended from a large variable buoyant chamber. She was a sort of underwater free balloon capable of sinking to the desired depth with negative buoyancy, discharging ballast, and rising to the surface. The buoyant hull-like (figure 15–25) chamber contained, as the buoyant fluid, gasoline with two ballast tanks in each end containing water. The dischargeable ballast and the ballast controlling the negative-positive attitude was metallic pellets contained in two hoppers in the base of the buoyant structure. The observation gondola was fitted, in addition to the instruments and basic controls, with a heavy glass circular observation port and an access hatch leading to the vertical access tunnel through the upper structure. This craft was abandoned shortly after her record dive in favor of the new and improved *Trieste II*.

The *Trieste* is only significant historically and served perhaps to stimulate further deep ocean research. Her inadequacy, reflected by the somewhat less limited capacities of the improved *Trieste II*, was forcefully revealed in the search for the lost submarine, *Thresher*, in 1963. This tragic event produced an impact which changed

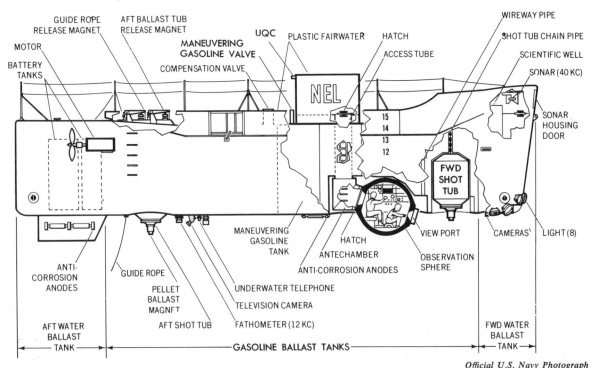

Official U.S. Navy Photograph

Figure 15–25. Trieste II. A bathyscaph such as this submersible differs from submersible workboats primarily in its greater depth capability and reduced mobility. This craft and others like it are capable of limited search operations at the greatest ocean depths.

the national outlook on deep-diving search and rescue capabilities. It was apparent to all that there were no techniques available for such an operation, even if the *Thresher* had been in shallower water short of hull collapse pressure.

At this time, a newer design (among several) was being evolved which was to be a more capable craft, however at lesser depths. The construction of the *Aluminaut* had been started in 1961 under an Office of Naval Research contract by the Reynolds Aluminum Co. but was not yet operational. (She has since become a capable craft but less sophisticated than modern deep submersibles.)

Primarily because of the *Thresher* tragedy, the Navy launched a five-year development program originally funded by a budget of about $200 million. To this was added the stimulant of underwater working requirements, such as mineral deposit searches, off-shore oil service facilities, and other activities, until in a few years (by 1965) a veritable fleet of undersea craft were either nearing completion or in operation. The most distinguished feature to date in all of the various deepwater submersibles is their lack of conformity or similarity. This is due partly to their development by various independent contractors, their differing operational requirements, and a variety of individual development budgets. It is not the purpose here to describe or even illustrate these vehicles. They are a profusion of evolving types. It will better serve the purpose of this text to indicate a few of their major design requirements and to describe briefly the construction of several of the more representative and successful craft.

WEIGHT VERSUS STRENGTH

The obvious and most difficult requirement for designers to confront is that of deepwater environment and the attendant pressures. It is of primary interest in this respect to examine the environment and note that the operational employment may quite likely control the maximum depth and hence, structural weight. Figure 15–26 indicates the ocean depth percentages of the world. It can at once be seen that a deep ocean vehicle designed for 20,000 feet is capable of operating in about 96 percent of the waters of the world. It would be a ridiculous waste to use such a craft in waters of the continental shelves which comprise perhaps 15 percent of the oceans. It is in such water that

mineral deposits are most attractive and biological research can be most productive. Submarines of less than 5,000 foot depth capacity would be most capable in this environment and to date comprise the majority of the small, deep submersibles.

The design problem imposed primarily by great pressure is reflected in the compressive strength of the structure and the strength of the material used. Where conventionally available steel is used, as in the *Trieste*, the pressure-proof gondola is so thick and heavy that an overly large and buoyant canopy must be used. Such a buoyant support becomes most awkward. Consequently, for the deeper depths, a search for stronger materials is most urgent. Referring to figure 15–26, it will be seen that the materials suggested for the depths of 12,000 feet or greater are the several titanium alloys, and for the greatest depths beyond 18,000 and 20,000 feet of water, combinations of glass-reinforced plastics or glass and ceramics are recommended. The techniques of fabrication of these latter materials are such that the cost factors become most critical.

The common factor which relates the strength-weight characteristics for hulls of various materials and configurations for given design depths is the ratio of the weight of the hull to the weight of the seawater displaced by the total submerged volume of the hull. The ratio is called the weight-displacement ratio, W/Δ. The ratios are calculated as a function of depth for the various hulls and based on the failure criteria and assumed material properties. The required W/Δ ratios, assuming factors of safety of 1.5 (based on static collapse depths), are limited to approximately 0.5 to 0.7 and reflect the necessity of lighter and stronger materials for deeper water capabilities as indicated in figure 15–26.

Because of the varied requirements and mission-related applications as well as the slowly evolving design knowledge, there are no well developed guidelines to design processes for these deepsea submarines beyond the usual systems engineering approach.

GENERAL DESIGN FEATURES

While there may be considerable divergence in external configuration, instrumentation, articulation, and other dependent features, there are essentially some basic features common to the

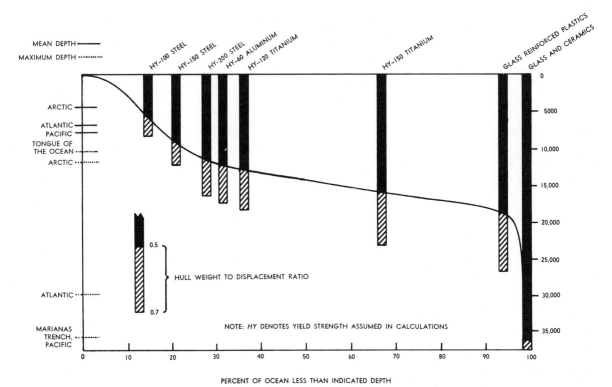

Figure 15–26. Relative Ocean Depths and Necessary Structural Material Chart

great majority of deep submergence craft. These essential components are discussed below.

The *pressure hull* is a spherical or cylindrical chamber which houses the operating personnel. It is constructed to withstand the designed operational pressure, is fabricated in high-stress steel, aluminum or titanium, and is generally dependent on the strength-weight ratio requirement. Sometimes the pressure hulls are several connected spherical chambers or two spheres with an interconnecting tunnel.

The *ballast system* consists, as in most submarines, of diving or main ballast tanks or weights and variable ballast systems. These systems are either reversible or nonreversible, preferably the former. The dropping of shot pellet ballast or lead weights is a nonreversible system. Most deep-diving submarines maintain very little reserve buoyancy for surface diving trim, hence these ballast systems are generally of minimum volume. The variable ballast system used for fine hovering control is generally a small, hard tank with seawater flooding and compressed air blowing.

Propulsion systems vary in design and may include such elements as single stern propellers

with controllable side propellers, inverted **Y** side-mount propellers capable of being swiveled on their axes in any required direction, cycloidal propellers, and shrouded and tunneled propellers. In nearly all cases, the driving motor is self-contained in or near the hub of the propeller in a free-flooding mount. The driving motor is usually electrical, deriving its power from an internal battery.

The *trim control system* generally consists of reservoirs built into external hull ends interconnected for transferring heavy fluid, generally mercury. Trim control (in this sense, pitch angle) is also maintained actively by controlled axis propellers in many types. Active fins are of little or no help in deep submersible design because of the very low speeds and the necessity for attitude control when hovering or backing.

The *power system* employs electrical storage batteries, most frequently lead-acid in oil-scaled containers in the free-flooding chamber of the outer hull. They are of such capacity as required for main propulsors, auxiliary pumps, lighting instruments, control systems, etc. They are generally of 64 volt and 30 volt for main propulsors and auxiliary use in the commonly used systems.

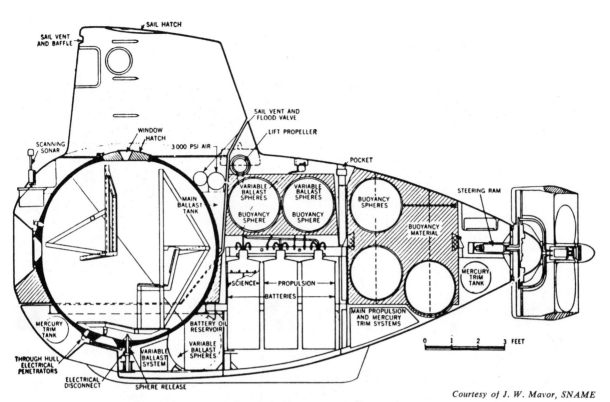

SAIL HATCH

SAIL VENT
AND BAFFLE

SAIL VENT AND
FLOOD VALVE

WINDOW
HATCH

LIFT PROPELLER

SCANNING
SONAR

3 000 PSI AIR

POCKET

STEERING RAM

MAIN
BALLAST
TANK

VARIABLE
BALLAST
SPHERES

VARIABLE
BALLAST
SPHERES

BUOYANCY
SPHERES

BUOYANCY
SPHERE

BUOYANCY
SPHERE

BUOYANCY
MATERIAL

MERCURY
TRIM
TANK

SCIENCE

PROPULSION

BATTERIES

MAIN PROPULSION
AND MERCURY
TRIM SYSTEMS

MERCURY
TRIM
TANK

BATTERY OIL
RESERVOIR

VARIABLE
BALLAST
SPHERES

THROUGH HULL
ELECTRICAL
PENETRATORS

VARIABLE
BALLAST
SYSTEM

ELECTRICAL
DISCONNECT

SPHERE RELEASE

0   1   2   3 FEET

Courtesy of J. W. Mavor, SNAME

Figure 15-27. Deep Submersible Alvin (6000 + foot capability). This early and most successful deep submersible workboat was responsible for the recovery of a lost hydrogen bomb off the coast of Spain in 1965. More recent and improved submersibles have been designed on her basic concept and as the result of her experience. This craft was lost by dropping in 8000 feet of water in the North Atlantic in 1968 but was successfully recovered one year later.

An emergency power supply in a separated battery system is provided. Batteries exceed no more than 10 percent of the total submersible weight.

The *safety system* in most deep submersibles provides a built-in ability for the craft to rise to the surface in situations involving entanglement or damage to the basic buoyancy or propulsion system. These vary in design but an example is droppable weights, such as the batteries, solid-fixed ballast bars, or other operational weight. In the case of *Alvin* I (figure 15–27), the very successful oceanographic submarine and retriever of the lost hydrogen bomb in the Mediterranean, the submarine was designed to release its pressure sphere and conning tower assembly from the entire afterbody. Such extreme safety measures are not commonly design features, however.

The *external hull* is simply a container for the various systems, providing a streamlined and protective configuration, yet free-flooding and thus nonpressurized. Its configuration must be so designed to provide the whole system with stable, directional control both statically and dynamically. This often requires a tail fin stabilizer surface, a faired sail surrounding the surface conning tower, and an access hatch. Structural mountings for propeller pods, shrouds, rudder, manipulator arms, etc. must be built into this structure as well as provisions for solid mountings for all internal systems. Bottom skids or skis are often built into this external hull. The construction material is most frequently fiberglass.

BASIC DESIGN

It is of some importance to consider the most critical design feature in the preliminary planning of deep submergence craft, which is that of weight and strength of the pressure hull. Most craft use either high-stress steels or aluminum for these pressure hulls (see figure 15–26). Because of the low density-strength factor of aluminum, it is desirable for submarines of the intermediate depth range that comprises two-thirds of the world's oceans. The Aluminum Company of America has conveniently provided a very usable chart for determining the design parameters and weights of an aluminum pressure sphere. Refer to figure 15–31.

Courtesy of North American Rockwell Co.

Figure 15–28. Submarine Workboat Beaver IV.

CHARACTERISTICS

Length .... 24 ft.
Operating Depth .... 2000 ft.
Payload .... 2000 lbs.
Pressure Hull .... HY-100 Steel
Structural Hull .... Aluminum and Fiberglass
Personnel .... 2 crew, 3 passengers
Submerged Speed .... 5 knots, max.
Weight .... 12.5 Tons

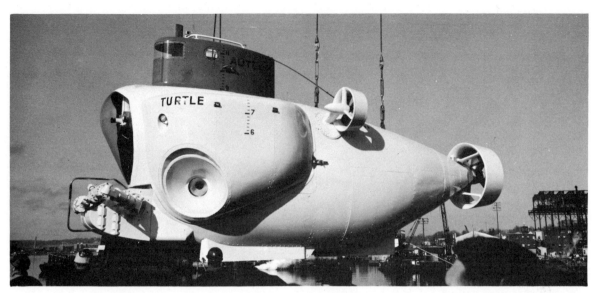

Courtesy of General Dynamics Corp.

Figure 15–29. Submarine Workboat Autec II

CHARACTERISTICS

Length .... **26 ft.**
Operating Depth .... **5,000 ft.**
Payload .... **1,200 lbs.**
Pressure Hull .... **HY-100 Steel**
Personnel .... **2 crew**
Operating Speed .... **2.5 knots**
Weight .... **21 tons**

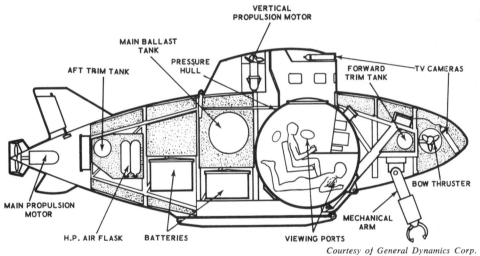

Courtesy of General Dynamics Corp.

Figure 15–30. Submarine Workboat Star III

CHARACTERISTICS

Length .... **24.5 ft.**
Operating Depth .... **2,000 ft.**
Payload .... **1,000 lbs.**
Pressure Hull .... **HY-100 Steel**
Personnel .... **2 crew**
Operating Speed .... **5 knots**
Weight .... **10 tons**

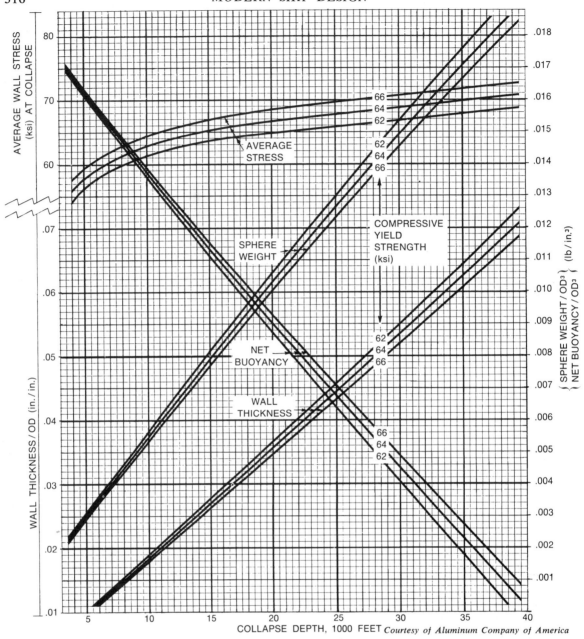

Figure 15–31. Design Chart for Approximation of 7079-T6 Aluminum Alloy Undersea Spheres

How to Use the Design Chart*

An example of the use of the Design Chart is as follows... Assume sphere OD is 96″ and it needs to operate at 10,000 ft. depth with 1.5 safety factor.

1. Each sphere feature is determined by intersection of its curve with vertical line at required collapse depth which is 15,000 ft. in this case. Exact curve depends on CYS (Compressive Yield Strength).

2. To determine proper CYS value, refer first to wall thickness curves (see scale at lower LH side of chart); wall thickness/OD at 15,000 ft. is about 0.027, so finished wall

---

* Aluminum Company of America, "Design Chart for Approximation of 7079-T6 Aluminum Alloy Undersea Spheres."

thickness is approximately 2.6 inches. Suggested rough machined wall (heat treat thickness) is 3.1 inches. From table of CYS vs. heat treat thickness, CYS is 64 ksi.

3. Corresponding sphere features are:

Wall thickness	=	0.0270×96
	=	2.59
Net buoyancy	=	$0.013 \times \overline{96}^3$
	=	10,000. pounds
Sphere weight	=	$0.0079 \times \overline{96}^3$
	=	7,000. pounds
Av. stress @ collapse	=	65 ksi

Because of the excessive weight developed in the strength requirements of the pressure hull, all other systems are forced into undesirable limitations on performance to accommodate the low weight components. The life support systems are reduced to approximately 45 to 50 hours. The propulsive motors in the two or three men craft can be no more than 1.5 to 2 horsepower, limiting speed and maneuverability. All systems served by electrical energy are severely limited because of battery weight.

Depth, then, becomes the basic limitation. The deeper the operational requirement, the more limited the mission must be in endurance and performance.

These are no doubt transitory limitations. Advanced metallurgy, more efficient energy sources, and greater knowledge of the environment will continue to advance the state of the art outlined above for deepsea vehicles.

It is conceivable that, not too far in the future, propulsion energy will be supplied by small nuclear reactors as in the larger subsurface craft. Such designs are already in the planning stage.

The Future

In the absence of an adequate crystal ball or some other reliable supernatural device for viewing the future, we can only be guided by existing trends. It is sometimes difficult to keep from being thrown off by salesmen of the spectacular or the overenthusiastic promotions of new devices that suddenly break upon the scene. However, throughout history, technological progress was made by day to day, step by step conservative investment in new ideas, trial and research, and often much error. The trends are generally clearly established. They are at this time, or any point in time, existing and pointing, waxing or waning. The only problem is reading them correctly.

Dynamically supported craft, while developing still with improved propulsion and better materials and structure, have become fairly stabilized in application. Planing hulls, because of the relatively poor rough-water capability, should not be looked to for any expansion in employment or growth in volume (except in pleasure boat use). Hydrofoil vessels, on the other hand, are continuing to grow in size but are confronted with the physical limitation of the cube-square law, and future seagoing craft of this type should not be expected to exceed much more than 1000 tons. This limit could perhaps be exceeded with the development of a more efficient foil configuration and improved cavitation control. The research trends with base-ventilated foils and supercavitating foils operating with smooth transition from subcavitation foils have pointed the way toward speeds of 100 knots.

Air cushion craft appear to hold the greatest promise for high-speed, oceangoing transport in larger vessels. Concepts of 400 to 500 foot ships capable of cruising at 80 knots have been worked out. The Navy has contemplated high-speed assault ships of the captured air bubble type for some time, and considerable research in towing tanks and laboratories is going forward on them. The Maritime Commission has projected the possibility of a fleet of 5000 ton ships of the air cushion type capable of 100 knots in calm water (40 to 50 knots in storm waves of 30 foot height) with a sustained speed adequate to cruise around predicted storm centers and deliver 1500 tons of cargo in transatlantic runs several times a week. The cost per ton-mile could possibly be nearly as low as the conventional cargo ship.

There undoubtedly will be, because of the urgency, an increased undersea craft development, with vessels descending to much greater depths and becoming capable of far more mobility and ability to work at great depths. It is in this area that the greatest effort and money is being expended in watercraft research and development.

The visible, existing indications remain, however. The world still moves on heavy commerce; iron ore, oil, fertilizers, and automobiles must be transported together with great quantities of an infinite variety of other merchandise and bulk cargoes. The key to profitable and economical transport is a flow of large quantities. The lowest costs per ton-mile for the greatest part of the world's commerce continues persistently with the large displacement ships. Oil will continue to travel in supertankers, dry and selective cargoes in faster container ships. And as long as warships are required, mobile aircraft bases will be the most complex of all displacement vessels. The ubiquitous destroyers, guided missile ships, communication ships, light draft gunboats, and evolving special purpose ships will be required. The day is not foreseeable when man will be able to do without ships—and ships as we conventionally and traditionally know them. The technology of building them, propelling them, and servicing them will change and improve—they will still be very recognizable, floating buoyant or submersible mobile vessels carrying people and their commerce.

APPENDIX A

Symbols, Abbreviations, and Terms

The following symbols are considered the most applicable and convenient notations for use by a student of naval architecture. In most cases, they conform to the standard usages approved by the Society of Naval Architects and Marine Engineers and the International Towing Tank Conferences. In certain instances, minor deviations are considered more advantageous for use in this text,

resulting in less confusion because of duplication of meaning. Where more than one use exists for a given symbol, the most frequent usage is listed first. Standard mathematical symbols are always used where applicable and are not defined in this table. Numerical subscripts following a symbol denote successive locations, progressions, or values of the basic symbol.

General Symbols

A—Area (generally in square feet)

A_{dwl}—Area of designer's waterline

A_m—Area of midship section up to any waterline

A_w—Area of a waterline

A_x—Area of maximum section if not amidships

a—Area (generally a small area within a system)

a—Linear acceleration

AP—After perpendicular

B or CB—Center of buoyancy

B—Beam or breadth (molded) of ship

B_x—Buoyancy per unit length of ship

b—Breadth of a tank or space; center of buoyancy of added buoyant layer; span of hydrofoil

$\overline{BL}$—Molded baseline

$\overline{BM}$—Transverse metacentric radius

$\overline{BM'}$—Longitudinal metacentric radius or $\overline{BM}_L$

bm—Metacentric radius of free liquid

C_a—Resistance coefficient for model-ship correlation

C_b—Block coefficient

C_f—Frictional resistance coefficient

C_m—Midship section coefficient

C_p—Prismatic coefficient

C_r—Residual resistance coefficient

C_t—Total resistance coefficient

C_w—Coefficient of wave resistance

$C.G.$—Center of gravity of a system of weights

$c.g.$—Center of gravity of a weight within a system

CL—Centerline

D—Molded depth of ship hull; drag, force

D—Drag, a force

d—Change in draft (usually inches)

d_a—Change in draft aft due to change in trim

d_f—Change in draft forward due to change in trim

dx—Increment of length of ship

dz—Increment of length of tank

$DTWL$—Diving trim waterline

$\overline{DWL}$—Designer's waterline

$\overline{DWT}$—Deadweight tonnage

E_ϕ—Dynamic stability at any angle; energy

EHP—Effective horsepower

EHP_f—Frictional effective horsepower

EHP_t—Total effective horsepower

EHP_r—Residual effective horsepower

f—Stress intensity; coefficient of friction; function of area, volume, and moment in Trapezoidal Rule

F—Center of flotation (center of gravity of waterplane)

F—Freeboard

F_n—Froude Number

FP—Forward perpendicular

G—Center of gravity of the ship

g—Center of gravity of added or movable weight on a ship; acceleration of gravity

$\overline{GG}_1$—Distance through which ship's center of gravity moves

$\overline{GG}_{(long.)}$—Distance through which ship's center of gravity moves longitudinally

$\overline{GG}_{(trans.)}$—Distance through which ship's center of gravity moves transversely

$\overline{GG}_{(vert.)}$—Distance through which ship's center of gravity moves vertically

$\overline{GM}$—Transverse metacentric height

$\overline{GM}'$—Longitudinal metacentric height or GM_L

$\overline{GZ}$—Righting arm

h—Common interval; half breadth of tank; depth of water

I—Moment of inertia generally

I_T—Transverse moment of inertia of waterplane about longitudinal axis through c.g.

I'—Longitudinal moment of inertia of waterplane or I_L

I_x—Moment of inertia of section about neutral axis

i—Moment of inertia of free surface of loose liquid

K—Point at bottom of keel (amidships) or on any horizontal plane through the baseline

K_q—Torque coefficient

k—Mass radius of gyration

$\overline{KB}$—Height of center of buoyancy above keel or baseline

$\overline{KG}$—Height of center of gravity above keel or baseline

$\overline{Kg}$—Height of center of gravity of added or shifted weight above keel or baseline

$\overline{KM}$—Height of transverse metacenter above keel or baseline

$\overline{KM}'$—Height of longitudinal metacenter above keel or baseline

L—Length in general; lift

L_{oa}—Length overall

L_{pp}—Length between perpendiculars

L_{wl}—Waterline length

L_w—Length of wave

L_x—Load at any point in length of ship

LCB—Longitudinal position of center of buoyancy

LCG—Longitudinal position of center of gravity

l—Length of internal compartment or tank; prismatic coefficient; longitudinal distance through which weight is moved

M—Transverse metacenter; moment of area or volume in Trapezoidal Rule

M_l—Longitudinal metacenter

M_x—Bending moment at any section in ship's length

M_T—Trimming moment

M_ϕ—Righting moment at any angle

MTI—Moment to trim one inch

m—Pro metacenter; metacenter of free liquid; midship section coefficient; mass

n—Any integer; revolutions per minute, or rate of revolutions

O—Center; origin

P—Pitch of propeller; waterline coefficient

P_d—Delivered power at propeller

P_s—Shaft power

PHP—Propeller horsepower

Q—Torque

R_a—Model-ship correlation allowance

R_f—Frictional resistance of ship

R_n—Reynolds' Number

R_r—Residual resistance of ship

R_t—Total resistance of ship

r—Half-breadth of ship; ratio defining shape

S—Wetted surface; true slip ratio

S_x—Shearing force at any section in ship's length

s_a—Apparent slip ratio

s_r—True slip ratio

SHP—Shaft horsepower

T—Draft

T—Period of oscillation

T_a—Draft aft

T_f—Draft forward

δT—Change in draft

TPI—Tons per inch immersion; period of roll; propeller thrust

TPI_{fw}—Tons per inch immersion for fresh water

t—Thrust deduction coefficient; transverse distance through which weight is moved

V—Speed in knots; linear velocity

v—Volume of flooding or free liquid; speed over ground (ft/sec or ft/min); vertical distance through which weight is moved

v_a—Ship's speed relative to wake

v_r—Resultant velocity

W—Weight of ship; weight in general

$\overline{W}_x$—Weight per unit length of ship

w—Weight in pounds or tons, usually of a movable or added weight aboard ship; wake fraction

WL—Any waterline

X—Height of bottom of damaged compartment above keel

y—Transverse distance from ship's centerline to center of gravity of floodwater in free communication with the sea; any ordinate; distance of point to neutral axis

Special Symbols For Naval Architecture

α—Angle of attack

θ—Angle of longitudinal inclination; angle of attack

δ—Specific gravity; small increment

ϕ—Transverse angle of inclination; any function; potential function

λ—Ratio of linear dimensions of ship and model (scale ratio); wave length to ship's length

μ—Volume permeability factor

μ_s—Surface permeability factor

ν—Kinematic viscosity

ρ—Mass density; weight per unit volume/g

Σ—Summation

ϕ—Any function; potential function

$\unicode{x2BE1}$—Midship section designation

$\unicode{x2BE1}_{pp}$—Midlength between perpendiculars

Δ—Displacement weight

$\mathcal{C}$—Centerline or center plane axis

$\mathbb{B}$—Baseline

Λ—Tuning factor, relative to synchronism

ω—Angular velocity (or circular frequency)

∇—Volume of displacement, 35 Δ

η—Efficiency in general

η_d—Propulsive coefficient (delivered)

η_h—Hull efficiency

η_o—Propeller efficiency (open water)

η_b—Propulsive efficiency

η_r—Relative rotative efficiency

η_s—Transmission efficiency (shaft)

APPENDIX B

Numerical Solutions for Designers

Computation of an Area by the Trapezoidal Rule

An integration rule frequently used in ship calculations is known as the *Trapezoidal Rule*. To find the area under a curve such as *ABCD* in figure B–1, we divide *AB* into any number of equal parts and at the points of division erect perpendiculars.

The area of a trapezoid is equal to one-half of the sum of the bases multiplied by the altitude. The area of the trapezoid, *ADGH*, is therefore

$$A = h\left(\frac{1}{2}y_0 + \frac{1}{2}y_1\right)$$

where *h* is the distance between ordinates.

If the ordinates are sufficiently close together, the curve will not vary appreciably from the chord, and the small area between *D* and *G* bounded by the straight line and the curve will be negligible. It is upon this assumption that the Trapezoidal Rule is based. The area of the second trapezoid then is $h\left(\frac{1}{2}y_1 + \frac{1}{2}y_2\right)$, the third is $h\left(\frac{1}{2}y_2 + \frac{1}{2}y_3\right)$, and so on. It thus appears that in computing an area, every ordinate appears twice except *the end ordinates*. Summing up, we obtain

$$A = h\left(\frac{1}{2}y_0 + y_1 + y_2 + y_3 + y_4 + y_5 + y_6 + y_7 + \frac{1}{2}y_8\right)$$

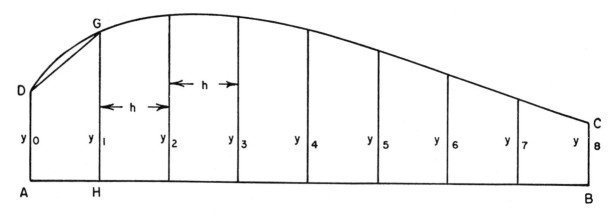

Figure B–1. Ordinates for an Area

322

or in general

$$A = h\left(\frac{1}{2}y_0 + y_1 + y_2 \ldots y_{n-1} + \frac{1}{2}y_n\right)$$

where n is any integer. This expression is the Trapezoidal Rule.

To illustrate the use of this rule in the calculation of an area, assume the ordinates of area $ABCD$ of figure B–1 are listed in table B–1 with an ordinate spacing of 10 feet. The solution of the area in table B–1 is self-explanatory.

Table B-1

Station	Ordinate, feet	Multiplier	Function of Area $f(A)$
Y_0	12	1/2	6
Y_1	14	1	14
Y_2	16	1	16
Y_3	16.5	1	16.5
Y_4	17	1	17
Y_5	16	1	16
Y_6	15	1	15
Y_7	13	1	13
Y_8	10	1/2	5

$$\Sigma f(A) = 118.5$$
$$h = 10 \text{ feet}$$
$$A = h \times \Sigma f(A) = 10 \times 118.5$$
$$= 1185 \text{ square feet}$$

Location of the Centroid of an Area

To find the location of the geometric center of an area (or its center of gravity), we must first find its moment about some reference axis. This overall moment must then be divided by the total area in order to find the arm or perpendicular distance of the center of gravity from the reference axis.

It must be pointed out before explaining an example that the use of the Trapezoidal Rule is less accurate in solving for centers of geometric figures

than it is for solving for areas and volumes. Note that this rule was derived in the preceding section on the basis of trapezoidal areas. However, it may be applied to the solution of centers of areas as an approximate means of obtaining a mean moment from moments of incremental areas.

To illustrate, we will consider figure B–2 and the ordinate values listed in table B–2. For the reference axis, let us assume in this case one of the mid-ordinates, say y_4, which obviously will be fairly near the centroid. (This selection is purely arbitrary.)

Table B-2

Station	Ordinates (feet)	Multiplier	$f(A)$ Function of Area	Moment Arm about y_4	$f(M)$ Function of Moment
0	0	1/2	0	+4	0
1	5	1	5.0	+3	15
2	10	1	10.0	+2	20
3	14	1	14.0	+1	14
					+49
4	16.5	1	16.5	0	0
5	17.8	1	17.8	−1	17.8
6	17.1	1	17.1	−2	34.2
7	15.3	1	15.3	−3	45.9
8	11.4	1/2	5.7	−4	22.8

$$\Sigma f(A)\ 101.4 \qquad -120.7$$
$$+49$$
$$\Sigma f(M) -71.7$$

$$h = 10$$
$$A = h\,\Sigma f(A) = 10 \times 101.4$$
$$= 1014$$
$$My_4 = h^2\,\Sigma f(M) = 100 \times (-71.7) = 7170$$
$$CG_{y4} = \frac{7170}{1014} = 7.05 \text{ feet to right of } y_4$$

Also let us establish, arbitrarily, that values to the left of this ordinate will be positive and to the right, negative. In this case, we shall use the ordinate as a function of the area, and for each ordinate multiply

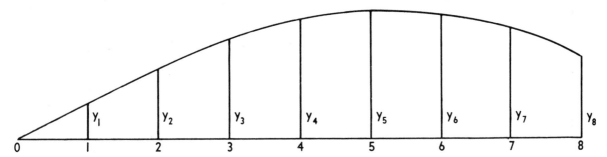

Figure B–2. Ordinates for an Area and its *CG*

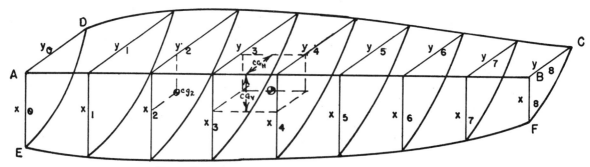

Figure B–3. Ordinates for Center of Gravity of a Volume

it by the moment arm (distance of the ordinate from the reference axis). It will be noticed that in each case the moment arm has a common factor, i.e., the spacing between ordinates. This factor can conveniently be omitted until the end and then be multiplied by the summation of the function of moments. Remember also, that since we used linear ordinates as functions of area, we must multiply the summation of the functions of moments again by the ordinate spacing to account for the fact that we are summing up the moments of small sectional areas. This will make our summation of the moment about the line y_4 take the form of

$$M_{AD} = h^2 \, \Sigma f(M).$$

The distance of the CG from y_4 is the net moment of the area divided by the area.

$$CG_{AD} = \frac{h^2 \, \Sigma f(M)}{h \, \Sigma f(A)} = \frac{M y_4}{A}.$$

Table B–2 gives the solution for the distance of the center of gravity from line y_4.

The centroid of waterplane areas, i.e., centers of flotation, are computed according to the example discussed above. Since waterplanes are symmetrical areas, centers of flotation are located on the centerline axis, and only one reference axis need be used in defining them.

For unsymmetrical areas, a second reference axis must be used to define the point, just as two systems of coordinates are needed for the location of any point in a plane area.

Computation of a Volume

The calculation of an area as shown in the foregoing section is the first step in the computation for a volume. Because ships are irregularly shaped volumes, it is most convenient to pass reference planes, generally the waterlines or sections, and compute

their areas. Those areas, which are at equally spaced intervals, may now be used as *ordinates* in computing the volume of the space through which they are passed. Suppose, for example, a tank such as the one shown in figure B–3 in a bottom compartment or double bottom of a ship is bounded on one side and the bottom by the shell plating of the hull, on the ends by transverse bulkheads, on the top by a flat deck, and on the inboard side by a longitudinal bulkhead. Transverse sections are passed equal distances apart giving areas such as BCF and ADE of figure B–3. The areas of each of these sections may be computed in the same manner as that of $ABCD$ in figure B–1. These areas will now be used as ordinates for the computation of the volume.

To illustrate this, assume the transverse areas of figure B–2 are as listed in table B–3 with the sections spaced 10 feet apart. The computation is as indicated in table B–3.

Table B–3

Station	Ordinates, sq. ft.	Multiplier	Function of Volume, $f(V)$
0	22	1/2	11
1	38	1	38
2	60	1	60
3	68	1	68
4	72	1	72
5	62	1	62
6	50	1	50
7	32	1	32
8	16	1/2	8

$$\Sigma f(V) = 401$$
$$V = h \times \Sigma f(V) = 10 \times 401 = 4010 \text{ cubic feet}$$

To express this volume in tons of water if the tank were filled, the volume would be divided by the appropriate density factor.

Computation of the Displacement of a Ship

The preceding sections indicate the two basic steps in calculating the displacement of a ship. In actual practice, however, the areas of each half-section up to the designer's waterline are obtained mechanically by use of a planimeter. The naval architect uses these values as ordinates and calculates the volume as in table B–3 or by some equally useful approximate integration method. The displacement of the ship at the designed draft in salt-water is obtained by dividing the volume in cubic feet by $35 \; \dfrac{\text{ft}^3}{\text{ton s.w.}}$. In fresh water, the volume of displacement would be divided by $36 \; \dfrac{\text{ft}^3}{\text{ton f.w.}}$.

The displacement may also be calculated by obtaining the areas of equally spaced waterlines and using these as ordinates between the keel and the designed waterline. This method is not as accurate, however, as the use of section areas for ordinates. On the equivalent spacing, waterlines change shape much more rapidly than do sections, making a greater error in the approximate integration. Also, waterlines are too extensive in area to be convenient for mechanical measurement of the area by a planimeter.

Displacements are calculated over a range of drafts through which the ship is expected to operate. From these, curves of displacements against drafts are drawn for both fresh and salt water.

Location of the Center of a Volume

Locating the center of gravity of a volume of uniform density is simply a further development and application of the foregoing discussion. Since we will work now in three dimensions instead of two, the distances of the center of gravity from three reference axes or planes will be required in order to completely define the point.

First, it will be necessary to pass equally spaced transverse sections through the volume giving plane areas such as ADE and BCF of figure B–3. In order to obtain the moment arms of each plane surface, the location of the centroids of each area must be computed as outlined above. Using the areas of these planes as ordinates, the volume is computed. The moment of the volume about each of the three reference axes divided by the volume will give the distance of the center of gravity from that axis. It can be readily seen that the process briefly outlined here is a long and tedious exercise.

To illustrate as simply as possible, let us assume that we know the areas of the transverse sections and have determined the location of the centroid of each by the method outlined just previously. This will reduce the numerical work in this example to the minimum necessary to illustrate the method of locating the center of gravity of a volume. Also, let us work from some centrally located ordinate for one reference axis as indicated above. The volume for this illustration will have the values listed in table B–3 for the computation of a volume. The reference axes or planes are arbitrarily selected as

1. The transverse vertical plane through y_4, parallel to $\overline{ADE}$
2. The horizontal plane, $\overline{ABCD}$
3. The longitudinal vertical plane, $\overline{ABFE}$.

We shall assume that the center of gravity of each area has been located as listed in table B–4.

These distances from the reference axis to the centers of gravity will now be the moment arms which, when multiplied by the functions of volume, will become the functions of moment from their respective reference planes.

Summarizing the procedure for the problem, we must, first, locate the center of gravity longitudinally in reference to some plane, in this case the plane containing x_4 and y_4; secondly, locate G in reference to a horizontal plane, in this case, plane $ABCD$; and finally, locate G in reference to a vertical plane, in this case, plane $ABFE$.

Table B-4

Station	Centroid from ABCD, ft.	Centroid from ABFE, ft.
0	7.2	4.2
1	7.0	5.6
2	6.8	7.7
3	6.3	7.9
4	6.2	8.2
5	6.5	7.6
6	6.6	6.8
7	6.8	5.7
8	7.1	4.1

Before tabulating in the form, let us point out with reference to one ordinate what the moments will be. If a vertical plane through y_4 is taken as our central reference plane, then taking station 2 as the example:

Moment about $y_4 = y_2 \times 2h$, where y_2 is the area of station 2

Moment about $ABCD = y_2 \times 6.8$

Moment about $ABFE = y_2 \times 7.7$.

(The values, 6.8 and 7.7, are obtained from table B–4.)

The complete tabulation and solution is given in table B–5.

$$M_{y4} = h^2 \times \Sigma f(M)_{y4} = 100 \times 56 = 5600$$
$$M_{ABCD} = h \times \Sigma f(M)_{ABCD} = 10 \times 2635 = 26{,}350$$
$$M_{ABFE} = h \times \Sigma f(M)_{ABFE} = 10 \times 2874 = 28{,}740$$

$$\therefore\ CG_{y4} = \frac{M_{y4}}{V} = \frac{5600}{4010} = 1.40 \text{ feet to left of } y_4,$$

$$CG_{ABCD} = \frac{M_{ABCD}}{V} = \frac{26{,}350}{4010}$$

$$= 6.57 \text{ feet below horizontal reference plane,}$$

$$CG_{ABFE} = \frac{M_{ABFE}}{V} = \frac{28{,}740}{4010}$$

$$= 7.17 \text{ feet outboard of } ABFE.$$

The center of gravity of a volume is used in many ship computations. The most frequent usage is in determining the location of the *center of buoyancy*. The *center of buoyancy is the center of gravity of the immersed volume of the ship* and is located by giving its vertical distance from the keel and its horizontal distance from the midship section. Because the ship's hull is always symmetrical, the center of buoyancy must lie on the longitudinal vertical center

plane, and a third reference axis is unnecessary. Curves of vertical and longitudinal positions of centers of buoyancy are plotted against drafts in feet.

The method outlined in table B–5 is frequently used to locate the centers of irregularly shaped tanks. It should be realized that the term *center of gravity* of a volume as used in this discussion refers actually to the geometric center and is in no way related to the actual center of gravity of the ship or any system of weights.

Other Rules for Approximate Integration

The Trapezoidal Rule, as illustrated in the foregoing sections of this appendix, is used more frequently perhaps because it requires no specific number of sections and is adaptable to the gradual curvature in most ship waterlines. There are other rules having their own particular limitations and advantages that are also used in the same basic manner as the illustrations with the Trapezoidal Rule.

Simpson's First Rule, commonly called Simpson's Rule, requires, in contrast to the Trapezoidal Rule, that the figure or volume be divided into an even number (n) of parts. The area (or volume) is then considered to contain $n/2$ elements, each with a length of base equal to twice the common interval, h, between ordinates.

The basic assumption of Simpson's Rule is that the curved side of the figure in an elementary seg-

Table B-5

Station	Ordinate (square feet)	Multiplier	Function of Volume, $f(V)$	Arm about y_4	$f(M)$, Function of Moment about y_4	Arm about $ABCD$	$f(M)$, Function of Moment about $ABCD$	Arm about $ABFE$	$f(M)$, Function of Moment about $ABFE$
0	22	1/2	11	+4	+ 44	7.2	79	4.2	46
1	38	1	38	+3	+114	7.0	266	5.6	213
2	60	1	60	+2	+120	6.8	408	7.7	462
3	68	1	68	+1	+ 68	6.3	428	7.9	537
					$+\overline{346}$				
4	72	1	72	0	0	6.2	446	8.2	590
5	62	1	62	−1	62	6.5	403	7.6	471
6	50	1	50	−2	100	6.6	330	6.8	340
7	32	1	32	−3	96	6.8	218	5.7	182
8	16	1/2	8	−4	32	7.1	57	4.1	33
		$\Sigma f(V) = 401$			−290	$\Sigma f(M)_{ABCD} = 2635$		$\Sigma f(M)_{ABFE} = 2874$	
					+346				
				$\Sigma f(M)_{y4} =$	+56				

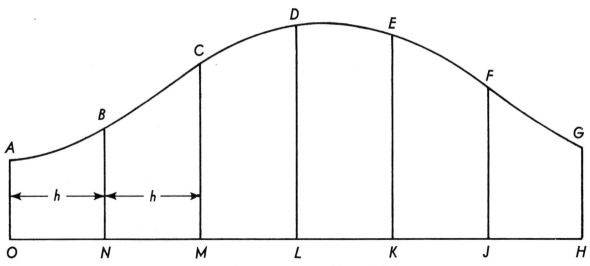

Figure B–4. Ordinates for Simpson's Rule

ment (such as *ABC* of figure B–4) conforms to the equation of a second-order parabola, thus

$$Y = ax^2 + bx + c.$$

The areas under the curved portion may therefore be expressed mathematically, and from figure B-4

$$\text{Area } \overline{OABCM} = \tfrac{1}{3}h(OA + 4BN + MC),$$

$$\text{Area } \overline{MCDEK} = \tfrac{1}{3}h(MC + 4LD + KE),$$

$$\text{Area } \overline{KEFGH} = \tfrac{1}{3}h(KE + 4JF + HG).$$

By addition, the total area of the figure is

$$\text{Area } \overline{OAGH} \text{ (total)} = A = \tfrac{1}{3}h(OA + 4BN$$
$$+ 2MC + 4LD + 2KE + 4JF + HG).$$

The trapezoidal multipliers are therefore of the sequence 1, 4, 2, 4, 2, 4, 1. The alternate multipliers—4 and 2—are used sequentially as many times as there are intermediate ordinates with unity as the multiplier for end ordinates.

As mentioned, this rule is accurate for areas bounded by parabolic curves and is approximate to the extent that the basic curvature approximates the parabola.

Simpson's Second Rule is developed from a third-order equation and can be reduced to the expression for an area (referring to the area in figure B–4) as

$$A = \tfrac{3}{8}h(OA + 3BN + 3MC + 2LD$$
$$+ 3KE + 3JF + HG).$$

In the case of this rule, the basic area or volume must be divided into a number of parts that is a multiple of 3. The multipliers are apparent from the preceding equation.

There are other rules for approximate integration, such as the *Five-Eight Rule*, *Tchebycheff's Rule*, etc., that are useful in specific cases but are not as generally applicable as those cited. In any case, all these rules for approximate integration are useful basic tools and are most adaptable to computer programming and applications described in chapter 14.

Approximation for the Vertical Position of B

Because the various rules for approximation of integration (as have been described previously with the uses of the Trapezoidal Rule) do not lend themselves conveniently to ship forms in vertical layer integration, an empirical method has been developed for locating the centers of volume in typical ships' forms. Mr. S. W. F. Moorish developed such an equation in 1892 that remains very useful in most modern ship forms and provides a very close approximation for the vertical position of the center of buoyancy of a ship throughout a reasonable change of drafts. This formula is generally acceptable to designers, but the position of *B* should be checked by a method using one of the rules of integration for at least two waterlines before plotting the values on the hydrostatic curves.

The formula, as first presented by Moorish, is

Distance of B below waterline $= \dfrac{1}{3}\left(\dfrac{T}{2} + \dfrac{\nabla}{A_{WL}}\right)$

where T = molded draft (mean)
   ∇ = volume of displacement at T
   A_{WL} = area of corresponding waterplane.

The above equation may be modified to give the height of the center of buoyancy above the base line and is more convenient in this form, thus

$$\overline{KB} = \dfrac{1}{3}\left(\dfrac{5T}{2} - \dfrac{\nabla}{A_{WL}}\right)$$

Another approximate formula of similar scope, but in some cases giving values closer to the more precisely calculated values by computer-based integration, is

$$\overline{KB} = T\left(\dfrac{A_{WL}}{A_{WL} + \nabla/D_M}\right).$$

It is recommended that the above equation be adopted for design work by students.

APPENDIX C

Parameters, Solutions, and Dimensional Analysis

Weight, Volume, and Draft Definitions

W—weight of ship

Δ—ship's displacement

Δ—W

∇—submerged volume = Δ 35 (salt water)

Trim by stern—$T_a - T_f$

Trim by bow—$T_f - T_a$

Mean draft—$T = \dfrac{T_a + T_f}{2}$

Tonnage and Weight

1 *ton*—2240 pounds $\approx$ 1000 kilograms (so-called long ton)

Displacement—actual weight of ship (naval usage)

Deadweight — carrying capacity in tons (merchant usage)

Registered tons—
volume (1 ton considered 100 ft^3)

$\left. \begin{array}{l} \textit{Legal usage,} \\ \textit{canal fees, etc.} \end{array} \right\{ \begin{array}{l} \text{Gross Tons} \approx \text{cargo + ma-} \\ \quad \text{chinery + quarters volume} \\ \text{Net Tons} \approx \text{cargo volume} \end{array}$

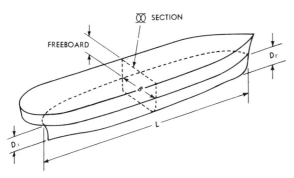

Figure C–1. Weight, Volume, and Draft Definitions

Flotation and Archimedes' Principle

A floating ship displaces a volume of water equal in weight to the weight of the ship (Δ). Consider the box-shaped lighter in figure C–2.

For vertical equilibrium, verticle force = ship's displacement,

Verticle force = $P(A_b) = (T\delta)(BL) = \nabla \delta$,

Buoyancy = $\nabla \delta$—equal and opposite to displacement.

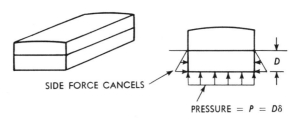

Figure C–2. Archimedes' Principle

RESERVE BUOYANCY (*see figure C–3*)

Reserve buoyancy = (reserve volume) δ

DENSITY FACTORS

35 ft^3 of seawater = 1 ton (2240 lbs.)

36 ft^3 of fresh water = 1 ton (2240 lbs.)

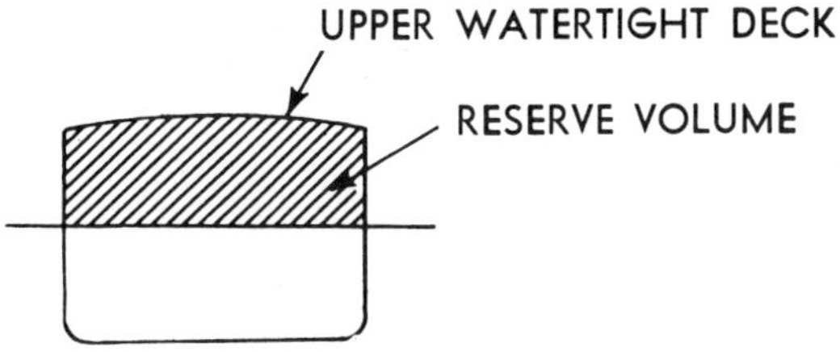

Figure C–3. Reserve Buoyancy

CENTERS

Center of gravity (G)—point where all gravitational (mass) forces are acting (where the sum of gravitational moments are zero)—"balance point."

Center of buoyancy (B)—geometric center of immersed ship's volume. (*CG* of "hole in water.")

WATERPLANE (*see figure C–4*)

The waterplane is the plane of the waterline at which the ship actually floats.

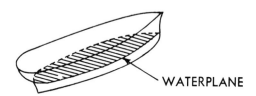

Figure C–4. Waterplane

Initial Stability—Parameters and Terms

K—keel

M—metacenter = point through which buoyancy acts as ship inclines through small angle = center of rotation of buoyancy vector.

$\overline{KB}$, $\overline{KG}$, $\overline{KM}$—distance of points *B*, *G*, *M* above *K*—note that they do *not* equal $(K)(B)$, $(K)(G)$, $(K)(M)$.

$\overline{BM}$—distance from point *B* to point *M* = metacentric radius

Righting movement—couple (Δ) $(\overline{GZ})$

$\overline{GZ}$—righting arm

$$\boxed{\overline{GZ} = \overline{GM} \sin \phi} = \overline{GM} \, \phi \text{ (radians), where}$$

$\phi < 7°$

INITIAL STABILITY: $(\theta < 7°)$

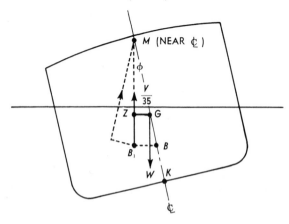

Figure C–5. Initial Stability

$$\therefore \boxed{\text{Moment} = \Delta \, \overline{GM} \sin \phi} = \overline{GM} \, \phi \text{ (radians)}, \phi < 7°$$

$\overline{GM}$—metacentric height, an index of initial stability.

DETERMINATION OF STABILITY PARAMETERS

$$\boxed{\overline{GM} = \overline{KB} + \overline{BM} - \overline{KG}}$$

$\therefore$ Find $\overline{KB}$, $\overline{BM}$, & $\overline{KG}$ (determined as follows).

$\overline{KB}$ is the center of buoyancy, determined by integration for centroid of hull form. (See appendix B for methods.)

$\overline{BM}$ measures the righting effect of asymetric buoyancy. It is a function of the triangular volumes and their arms. (See figure C–6.)

$\overline{BM}$:

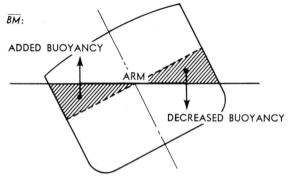

Figure C–6. Stability

$\therefore \overline{BM} = \phi \, (B^n \, \& \, L)/\text{Volume}$

By geometric coincidence (see chapter 5),

$$\boxed{\overline{BM} = \frac{I}{\nabla}} = \frac{B^3 L}{12 \nabla}, \text{ for box-shaped lighter only,}$$

where I = moment of intertia of the waterplane about the fore and aft centerline

Δ = submerged volume

(note that I is not really an inertial property, rather it is a geometric coincidence.)

SOURCE DATA—CURVES OF FORM

(*Displacement and other Curves*)

The source data are calculated by the designer, who tabulates $\overline{KB}$, $\overline{KM}$, Δ, etc. versus mean draft.

FINDING KG FOR SHIP IN DESIGN

By detailed weight estimate by the designer,

$$\overline{KG} = \frac{\Sigma \text{ vertical moments}}{\Sigma \text{ individual weights}}$$

for every item on the ship. (See figure C–7.)

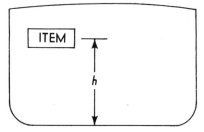

ITEM HAS WEIGHT, *w*

VERTICAL MOMENT IS *wh*

$$KG = \frac{\Sigma wh}{\Sigma w}$$

Figure C–7. Finding *KG*

FINDING KG FOR A SHIP IN SERVICE

$\overline{KG}$ is found by using the *inclining experiment* (see chapter 5). In practice, the damage control assistant will account for the ship's *KG* daily by considering the effects of any weights added or subtracted. The primary variables are

- Fuel
- Water
- Ballast
- Ammunition
- Alterations

Computations for Effective Horsepower and Propulsion Theory*

For the purpose of clarifying the propulsion calculation procedure outlined in chapter 10, consider a model of a ship having the following dimensions and tank-tested in fresh water at 61 degrees Fahrenheit:

$$L = 20.76 \text{ ft.}$$
$$S = 66.19 \text{ ft.}^2$$
$$W = 2027 \text{ pounds}$$

The load waterline length of the prototype is 519 feet.

Hence, linear ratio of dimensions, $\lambda = \dfrac{519}{20.76} = 25$

Speed ratio, $\sqrt{\lambda} = \sqrt{25} = 5$
Wetted surface ratio, $\lambda^2 = 25^2 = 625$
Displacement ratio,

$$\frac{\text{Density of salt water at } 59°F}{\text{Density of fresh water at } 61°F}$$
$$\times \lambda^3 = \frac{1.991}{1.938} \times 25^3 = 16,050.$$

For the ship,

$$S = 66.19 \times 625 = 41,370 \text{ square feet}$$
$$\Delta = 2027 \times \frac{16,050}{2240} = 14,520 \text{ tons.}$$

---

* Data taken from Taylor Model Basin Report #576.

The data recorded on the model resistance tests are indicated in table C–1.

Table C-1

Model Speed, Knots	Total Resistance of Model, Pounds	Model Speed, Knots	Total Resistance of Model, Pounds
0.995	.75	4.100	12.15
1.990	2.70	4.210	13.26
2.400	3.83	4.300	14.10
2.795	5.15	4.400	15.10
3.000	6.05	4.500	16.02
3.195	7.00	4.600	16.90
3.400	8.00	4.705	17.75
3.495	8.45	4.800	18.60
3.595	8.95	4.900	19.55
3.700	9.45	5.010	21.00
3.800	9.90	5.110	22.55
3.995	11.30		

For a model speed $V = 4.600$ knots taken at random, the total model resistance $R_t = 16.90$ pounds.

$$C_t = \frac{R_t}{\frac{\rho v^2 S}{2}} = \frac{16.90}{\frac{1.938}{2} \times (4.600 \times 1.689)^2 \times 66.19}$$
$$= 4.367 \times 10^{-3},$$

where 1.938 is the mass density of fresh water at a temperature of 61 degrees Fahrenheit, and 1.689 is the conversion factor from knots to feet per second.

$$R_n = \frac{vL}{v} = \frac{4.600 \times 1.689 \times 20.76}{1.194 \times 10^{-5}} = 1.351 \times 10^7,$$

where 1.194×10^{-5} is the kinematic viscosity of fresh water at a temperature of 61 degrees Fahrenheit. The frictional resistance coefficient is obtained from a table of C_f versus R_n, using the calculated Reynolds Number as the entering argument and for this run is 2.796×10^{-3}.

$$C_r = C_t - C_f = 4.367 \times 10^{-3} - 2.796 \times 10^{-3}$$
$$= 1.571 \times 10^{-3}.$$

The speed-length ratio is

$$\frac{V}{\sqrt{L}} = \frac{4.600}{20.76} = 1.010.$$

The calculated value of C_r is then plotted against the speed-length ratio and faired along with the values calculated for the data from the other model test runs to give the curve of figure C–8.

For a ship speed of 24 knots taken at random, the speed-length ratio, $V/\sqrt{L}$, equals 1.054. From figure C–8 at this speed-length ratio, the residual resistance coefficient is 1.632×10^{-3}.

$$R_n = \frac{vL}{v} = \frac{24 \times 1.689 \times 519}{1.282 \times 10^{-5}} = 1.644 \times 10^9,$$

where 1.282×10^{-5} is the kinematic viscosity of seawater at a temperature of 59 degrees Fahrenheit. By international agreement, effective horsepower requirements of ships are given for standard seawater at 15 degrees Centigrade or 59 degrees Fahrenheit. At this Reynolds Number,

$$C_f = 1.442 \times 10^{-3}.$$

The correlation allowance, C_a, is assumed as $.400 \times 10^{-3}$. The total resistance coefficient of the ship is

$$C_t = C_r + C_f + C_a$$
$$= 1.632 \times 10^{-3} + 1.442 \times 10^{-3} + .400 \times 10^{-3}$$
$$= 3.474 \times 10^{-3}.$$

From chapter 10, the total effective horsepower,

$$EHP_t = \frac{C_t \dfrac{\rho v^3}{2} S}{550}$$

$$= \frac{3.474 \times 10^{-3} \times \dfrac{1.991}{2}}{550}$$

$$\times \frac{(24 \times 1.689)^3 \times 41,370}{550}$$

$$= 17,330,$$

where 1.991 is the mass density of seawater at a temperature of 59 degrees Fahrenheit. The frictional horsepower at this speed is

$$EHP_f = \frac{(C_f + C_a) \dfrac{\rho v^3}{2} S}{550}$$

$$= \frac{1.842 \times 10^{-3} \times \dfrac{1.991}{2}}{550}$$

$$\times \frac{(24 \times 1.689)^3 \times 41,370}{550}$$

$$= 9187.$$

The calculations for the frictional and total effective horsepower are made for the various speeds over the anticipated range of ship speeds and are plotted against these speeds to give the final curves of *EHP* versus speed (knots).

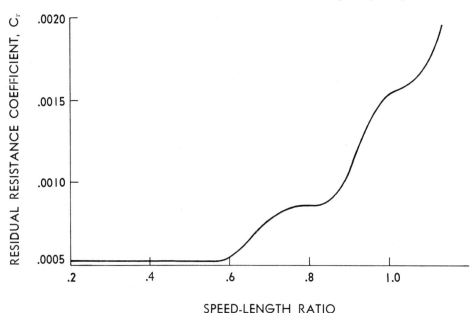

Figure C–8. Curve of Residual Resistance Coefficient versus Speed-Length Ratio

The Resistance Equation—Development of Dimensional Analysis for Surface Bodies

Assuming that the resistance of an object moving horizontally through the surface boundaries of a liquid is the product of several unrelated variables, the most significant of which may be expressed as

ρ—mass density (lb sec^2/ft^4)
L—length (ft)
S—surface (L^2)
v—velocity (ft/sec)
μ—absolute viscosity (lb sec/ft^2), or v = kinematic viscosity = μ/ρ, ft^2/sec
g—acceleration of gravity (ft/sec^2)
r_1, r_2—ratios of linear dimensions defining form.

Therefore, in the foot/pound/second system, the total resistance, R_t, in pounds may be expressed in terms of these variables as

$$R_t = \phi(\rho, L, v, \mu, g, r_1, r_2 \ldots),$$

and also

$$R_t = \Sigma\, C\, \rho^a L^b v^c \mu^d g^e,$$

or by the fundamental dimensions of mass, M, length, L, and time, T.

$$MLT^{-2} = (ML^{-3})^a(L)^b(LT^{-1})^c(ML^{-1}T^{-1})^d(LT^{-2})^e.$$

The exponents of the above functions may be evaluated for

$(M),\ 1 = a + d$
$(L),\ 1 = -3a+b+c-d+e$
$(T),\ -2 = -c - d - 2e$

where

$a = 1 - d$
$b = 2 - d + e$
$c = 2 - d - 2e$

(*d* and *e* cannot be determined).

Now

$$R_t = \Sigma C\rho^{1-d}L^{2-d+e}v^{2-d-2e}\mu^d g^e$$

or

$$R_t = \rho L^2 v^2 \cdot \Sigma C\left(\frac{vL}{\mu}\right)^{-d}\left(\frac{v^2}{gL}\right)^{-e}$$

Thus

$$R_t = \rho S v^2 \phi\left(\frac{vL}{v}, \frac{v^2}{gL}, r_1, r_2 \ldots\right)$$

$$\left(\text{where } \frac{vL}{v} = R_n, \frac{v^2}{gL} = F_n\right)$$

or

$$R_t = \rho S v^2\, \phi(R_n, F_n, r_1, r_2 \ldots).$$

Determination of Dynamic Stability

From the equation as developed in Chapter 12, i.e.,

$$E_{\phi 1} = \Delta \int_0^{\phi 1} \overline{GZ}d\phi$$

it may be said that the dynamic stability at any angle is the integral of the righting moment up to that angle. With such a basic relationship, it is possible to evaluate the dynamic stability at any angle, or at regular intervals of inclination throughout the range of stability. A curve through the various values of dynamic stability plotted as ordinates against angle of inclination as abscissa throughout the range of stability is called the *dynamic stability curve.*

It may be of value to follow through a typical example, determining the dynamic stability for several angles of inclinations at regular intervals. Assuming that the static stability curve for the ship is at hand and shows ordinate values in righting moments instead of the usual righting arms, let us take values at intervals of 10° of inclination.

The righting moments from the static stability curve are measured as 600 ft. tons at 10°, 1275 ft. tons at 20°, and 1940 ft. tons at 30°.

Using the trapezoidal rule as an approximate means of integration, and using 10° as the common interval, h, with the righting moments as the variable ordinates, we have

At 10°

$$E = \frac{10}{57.3} \times \frac{600}{2} = 52.4 \text{ ft. tons}$$

At 20°

Ord	Mult.	$f(A)$
0	1/2	0
600	1	600
1275	1/2	637
	$\Sigma f(A)$	1237

$$E = h \times \Sigma f(A)$$
$$= \frac{10 \times 1237}{57.3} = 215.5 \text{ ft. tons}$$

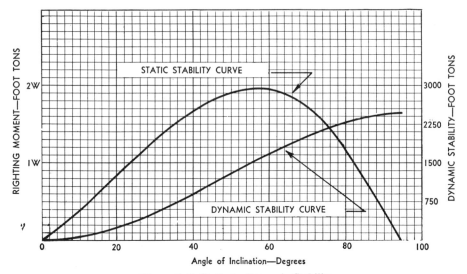

Figure C–9. Static to Dynamic Stability

At 30°

Ord	Mult.	$f(A)$
0	1/2	0
600	1	600
1275	1	1275
1940	1/2	970
	$\Sigma f(A)$	2845

$$E = h \times \Sigma f(A)$$
$$= \frac{10 \times 2845}{57.3} = 497 \text{ ft. tons.}$$

This process may be continued for angles of 40°, 50°, 60°, etc., throughout the range of stability, or up to any prescribed angle. If it is continued throughout the range of stability, and the dynamic stability plotted as a linear ordinate for every 10°, the dynamic stability curve will be as shown in figure C–9. Note that this curve is plotted with its corresponding static stability curve, using the righthand ordinate scale as ft. tons of energy (dynamic stability), as opposed to the lefthand ordinate for the static stability as ft. tons of righting moment.

At this time, it might be of further value to point out what may have already become obvious to the student. The relation between dynamic and static stability as indicated in equation shows that, for analytical purposes, and for a more easily visualized concept, the dynamic stability may be represented as the area under the static stability curve up to any desired angle of inclination. The advantages of this concept will be brought out in subsequent paragraphs.

Dynamic Stability vs. Dynamic Heeling Moments

DYNAMIC HEELING MOMENTS

In the foregoing articles of this chapter, it was shown by inference and example that the dynamic stability of a ship was, in effect, the ship's energy available to resist an external heeling moment. The situations producing external heeling moments on a ship are infinite in variety. Likewise, the resulting heeling moments are infinite in both nature and magnitude. It will be of value to discuss the nature of a few of the more commonly encountered heeling moments.

Primarily, like stability, there are both *static and dynamic heeling moments*. Static heeling moments have been already discussed in connection with static stability in the foregoing chapters, so with dynamic stability, we are concerned primarily with dynamic heeling moments.

By definition, the terms *heel* or *heeling* describe a temporary or semipermanent inclination, generally involving motion. This definition, in the use of the words "temporary or semipermanent," indicates the presence of an external inclining moment, and the statement "generally involving motion," would indicate that the moment is in some degree a dynamic one. For our consideration here, however, we must more explicitly define *dynamic moment*.

These moments, which will be considered in this discussion in their relationship to the ship's dynamic stability, will be those consisting of a heeling arm and a force *instantaneously* applied when the ship is in equilibrium. They will also be considered to be made up of a force or forces that act in a straight line, causing the moment to vary according to the cosine of the angle of heel. The force will be of a constant nature, and will be considered to persist after the dynamic reaction has subsided. Such moments as these described are common and would include occurrences such as wind suddenly striking the sails of a sailboat, or the dropping of a weight on the side of the dock. A most significant example, from the standpoint of damage control, would be the case of the sudden flooding of an off-center compartment caused by a large hole suddenly torn open by underwater damage.

In each of the briefly cited examples mentioned above, the forces involved are of a semipermanent, or persisting, nature. If these forces were applied gradually, the ship would gradually heel to the new position of equilibrium where the final inclining moment would be equal to the righting moment at that angle. If the sailboat were not to heel past her equilibrium angle, the wind would have to increase very slowly from calm air. If the ship with an off-center weight were not to roll beyond her equilibrium angle, the weight would have to be settled gently with a gradually decreasing vertical support. The case of flooding an off-center compartment would have to be a slow gradual filling through a small hole. In any of the cases, if there were to be no dynamic considerations involved, the heeling moment would increase at an equal rate with the righting moment as the angle of inclination increased.

DETERMINATION OF HEELING ENERGY VS. RIGHTING ENERGY

In order to describe the pure dynamic moment, we must describe the case where the moment suddenly is released in its maximum magnitude on the ship in a position of equilibrium. At this position, where the heeling moment is maximum, the righting moment has not yet developed any magnitude. At the equilibrium, or normally the up-

right position, there is, of course, a zero righting arm, and it develops only as the angle of inclination becomes finite.

It will be of value at this point to return briefly to the original example of the spring in Chapter 12. Consider figure 12–17. Here the weight with gravitational force, W, has been suddenly released, expending energy equal to $W \times 2L$. The force resisting W, the spring's resistance, is originally zero, but increases at a *uniform rate* of force per unit length as indicated. The area under the spring resistance curve up to the extreme deflection of $2L$ is $2W \times 2L/2$. This area is the work required to extend the spring through a distance of $2L$. Note that this work is equal to the work done by the spring weight in moving this distance. This equality of energy available to deflect the spring and energy required to deflect the spring establishes the maximum deflection.

At the extreme limit of spring extension, $2L$, the downward force on the spring is still the gravitational force W, but the upward force of spring resistance has increased to $2W$. This means that the motion must reverse; the potential energy in the spring will be returned to the weight at the original position (neglecting friction), where the motion is again reversed, and the transferral of energies repeated. The oscillation will continue about the position of equilibrium A, where the resistance of the spring and the force of the weight, W, are equal.

The similarity of this example of the spring will be seen in the following discussion of the action of a dynamic heeling moment upon the dynamic stability of the ship.

The heeling moment curve, when plotted on the same coordinates as the static stability curve, is a function of the cosine of the angle of heel as was brought out in Chapter 3. It may also be referred to as a curve of static heeling moments, or a static heeling curve, as indicated in figure C–10. Now, if this heeling moment acts instantaneously at $0°$ in the magnitude indicated against the ship whose static stability curve is shown, it may be considered a dynamic moment. It is therefore possible to integrate it in the same manner as the static stability curve to obtain a curve of dynamic heeling energy.

Since $\int_0^{\theta_1} \cos \theta d\theta = \sin \theta_1 + C$, we will obtain a sine curve of the same amplitude as the cosine curve.

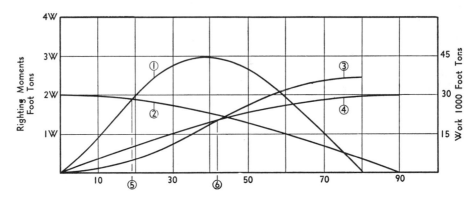

1 Static Stability Curve
2 Heeling Moment
3 Dynamic Stability Curve
4 Dynamic Heeling Energy
5 Angle of Permanent List
6 Angle of Maximum Roll

Figure C–10. Dynamic Stability and Heeling Moment Curves

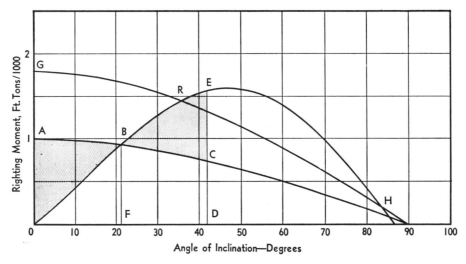

Angle of Inclination—Degrees

Figure C-11. Curves of Righting and Inclining Moments

The vertical ordinate of such a curve at any angle, is the heeling work done on the ship up to that angle. Where this curve of dynamic heeling moments intersects the curve of dynamic stability, as in figure C–10, it is significant that the heeling energy and the righting energy are equal. This point is at the angle representing the maximum limit to which the ship will roll. There can be no further inclination of the ship, because, beyond this point, the righting energy exceeds the heeling energy. It may be seen also from figure C–10, that at the angle of maximum roll, the static righting moment exceeds the static heeling moment. This means that there can be no static equilibrium at this angle, and the ship, because of this unbalance of static moments, will roll back towards the upright where a similar but opposite unbalance exists. The oscillation would continue indefinitely, if it were not for the friction between the hull's surface and the water, which finally absorbs the original excess heeling energy.

Should the original heeling moment be so great that the resulting dynamic heeling moment curve will always be above, and never intersect the dynamic stability curve of the ship, then the ship will capsize.

GRAPHICAL COMPARISON OF DYNAMIC STABILITY
AND HEELING ENERGY

An alternate approach to the problem of dynamic stability may be accomplished by using the static stability curve with the static heeling moment curve only. This may also give a clearer picture of the relationship between the static and dynamic stability.

If we may regard dynamic stability as the area under the static stability curve, which is an acceptable conception as was brought out in Chapter 12, then let us consider figure C–11.

Let us say that the heeling moment is suddenly applied in the amount *OA* at 0° inclination. The heeling energy then up to *F*, the angle of static equilibrium, is the area under the inclining moment curve, *ABFO*.

The energy resisting this inclining energy is the dynamic stability at the angle *F*, which is the area under the static stability curve, *OBF*. In comparing these two areas, *ABFO* and *OBF*, it is apparent that the inclining energy is greater in the amount of the area *OAB*. This means that there is an excess of inclining energy by this amount at the static equilibrium angle. Hence, the ship thus inclined will not stop heeling until it reaches some point where there is a balance of inclining energy with dynamic stability. Such a point would be at angle *D*, where the area of triangle *BEC* is equal to that of *OAB*. Between the angles *F* and *D*, there is an excess of resisting energy of the ship (i.e. dynamic stability) which at angle *D* is represented by the area *BEC*. Therefore at angle *D*, the difference between the dynamic stability and the heeling energy is zero. This balance determines the limit of roll at *D*, but because the static righting moment of the ship exceeds the static heeling moment at this position, the ship will not be at rest, but will return and oscillate about point *B*, as was pointed out in the previous paragraph, finally coming to rest at the position of static equilibrium.

Suppose now, that the original inclining moment was of greater magnitude, such as indicated by *OG*. Following the same reasoning as above, it will be seen that there is insufficient reserve dynamic stability beyond the equilibrium angle at *R* to balance the excess inclining energy. That is, the area *OGR* is greater than the area *REH*. This being the case, the ship will continue to heel through the range of stability and capsize.

In reference to figure C–11, which is typical, it may be seen that for relatively small heeling moments and small angles of heel, the evaluation of energies by comparative areas may be reduced to a simple geometric analysis. In other words, for small ranges of inclination, the slight amount of curvature in the stability curve and inclining moment curve may be considered negligible, and the areas computed approximately on the basis of triangles and trapezoids.

In order to emphasize the practicability of such approximate methods of solution it will be of value to cite the following examples.

Let us take a ship at a displacement of 1900 tons with no trim or list. Suppose that in this condition a weight of 100 tons is released suddenly on deck 10 feet to starboard of the centerline so that the resulting *KG* will be 12.9 feet. What will be the extreme angle of roll and the dynamic stability at this angle? A solution by approximate means is as follows:

From the cross curves of stability, plot the righting arms for the final displacement of 2000 tons and correct this curve in the usual manner for a *KG* of 12.9 feet (figure C–12). Convert the righting arm ordinate scale to righting moments by multiplying by the displacement (2000 tons).

Now plot the heeling moment curve which is $w \times t \cos \theta$. The zero degree ordinate for this curve is 1000 ft. tons. Now, by inspection of this particular stability curve (and this is fairly representative in shape for all destroyers and destroyer escorts), it may be seen that the slope of righting arms is practically constant up to 25°.

The intersection of the heeling moment curve with the stability curve at the position of static equilibrium, point *B* in figure C–12, appears to be at an angle of inclination of about 11°.

Draw a horizontal line through point *B* to *A* forming triangle *OAB*.

OAB is approximately the area of the excess heeling energy that must be balanced by the dynamic stability as was noted in the earlier discussion in this article.

Consequently, with a practically constant slope of the stability curve, it is only necessary to duplicate the right triangle *OAB* with another of identical form from point *B* to point *C* where *BD* = *AB* and *CD* = *OA*.

Thus the angle of maximum roll is, 2 × 11° or 22°, and the dynamic stability at this angle is:

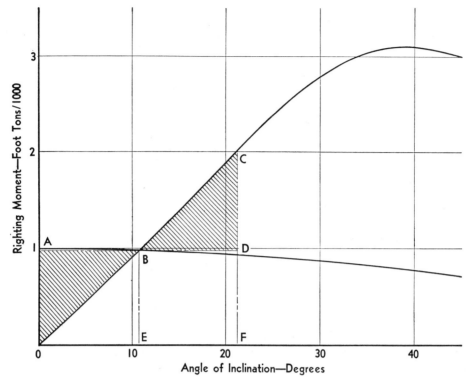

Figure C–12. Approximate Solution for DD

$$4 \times \frac{1000 \times 11}{2 \times 57.3} = 384 \text{ ft. tons.}$$

This final statement is based on the close approximation here that the dynamic stability *OCF* is composed of four equal triangular areas, *OBE*, *BDE*, *EDF* and *BCD*.

Now consider a type ship whose stability curve is of a materially different form than the destroyer's above. Figure C–13 is a good example. In this figure, the curves represent an escort carrier at a displacement of 20,000 tons, *KG* = 29 feet under a heeling moment of 20,000 ft. tons.

In this case, the best approach to evaluating areas would seem to be a breakdown to component trapezoids and triangles as follows.

Area of *OAB* in figure C–13 is composed of trapezoids *AabO* and *abdc* and triangle *cdB*. In order to establish the extreme angle of heel, it will be perhaps simpler to use a system of dimensionless units for establishing equality of areas, thus 10° = 1 unit and 20,000 ft. tons = 1 unit.

So area $\quad AabO = \dfrac{1 + .8}{2} \times 1 = .9$ sq units

Area $\quad abcd = \dfrac{.8 + .3}{2} \times 1 = .55$ sq units

Area $\quad cdB = \dfrac{.3 \times .3}{2} = \dfrac{.045}{1.495}$ sq. units

Now, by estimate establish area *FCD* to equal *OAB*. Assume *CD* = 2.0 and *FD* = 1.5

then area $\quad FCD = \dfrac{2.0 \times 1.5}{2} = 1.5$ sq units.

This, within reasonable limits, establishes the angle of max. roll to be approximately 1.5 × 10 or 15° beyond the angle of static equilibrium at approximately 38°. A similar breakdown, but using the actual dimensions for moment and angle would establish the area *OCE* as the dynamic stability up to the angle of max. roll.

From the analysis outlined in the foregoing article, we may draw the following general conclusions regarding dynamic stability and external heeling energy:

(1) When a dynamic force capable of producing an inclination acts on a ship, the inclination reached by the ship, before starting to return, is not determined by an equality of moments, but by an equality of energies.

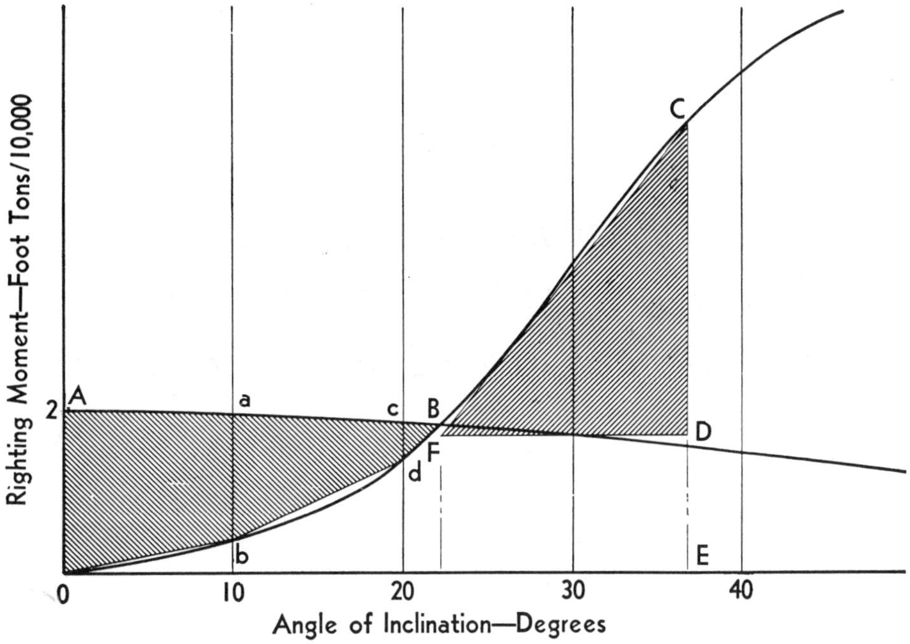

Figure C–13. Approximate Solution for CVE

(2) The maximum angle of inclination reached by the ship will be that for which the righting energy of the ship (dynamic stability) is equal to the energy expanded on the ship by the inclining moment.

(3) If a dynamic inclining moment expends energy upon the ship greater than the dynamic stability of the ship, she will capsize even though the maximum static inclining moment may be less than maximum righting moment of the ship.

Dynamic Stability in a Seaway

The assumptions made in the foregoing were necessarily hypothetical ones based upon ideal as well as mathematically pure situations. The instantaneous application of a heeling moment, and its conformation to a cosine function over the heeling range do not necessarily follow situations actually encountered. They do, however, describe the extreme conditions and in assuming them therefore a margin of safety between the actual and assumed becomes a factor in the problem.

The dynamic rolling moment of a wave is never applied instantaneously nor does it persist. A finite time function in its growth and subsidence is always present. Although it is not possible to evaluate this function with a satisfactory degree of accuracy or simplicity it is of definite importance that its nature be recognized. Let us assume that

the rolling moment of a wave acts as described in Chapter 12, *Ship's Roll by Wave Action,* as a function of transverse shift of the center of buoyancy and a centrifugal force at the center of gravity. If it can also be assumed that these combined moments will at any instant be a cosine function it would follow that the time interval involved will cause the cosine or heeling moment curve to grow from zero to its maximum and then collapse. This is to say that the heeling moment begins in such a way that it is greater than the righting moment and continues to increase at the same time that the ship has begun to respond to the earlier and smaller heeling moments rather than in the earlier assumption where the ship was not allowed to respond until the full maximum value of heeling moment had been applied. The ship therefore has absorbed some finite amount of heeling energy by virtue of its dynamic stability before the maximum heeling moment has been impressed. When the maximum heeling moment is reached a materially reduced excess heeling energy remains to be absorbed and hence a lesser angle of maximum roll may be expected.

This modifying influence of time interval in a seaway may as a rule be anticipated and as was mentioned in the preceding paragraph provides a safety factor when analyzing the effect of a heeling moment in its most restrictive sense.

Additional Examples of Computer Programs for Solutions to Ship Design Problems and Computer-Aided Data Compilations

Hydrostatic Data

METHOD DESCRIPTION

The program calculates hydrostatic data at an even keel and displacement for different trims.

Input data can be used as either manually recorded section coordinates or analytically calculated hull form data from the program for fairing of ship hulls.

The results are obtained in tabular form in such a way that scanning can be made at very small intervals, which means that the *drawing* of hydrostatic data is not necessary for purposes of interpolation.

The calculations are made for a number of waterlines given as input data. Longitudinal integration is made with Simpson's Rule. Calculated hydrostatic data are stored on magnetic tape as functions of the height of the calculation waterlines above the baseline (*BL*). Hydrostatic data are printed on lineprinter for desired waterlines.

INPUT DATA

Input data consists of two groups—one referring to instructions of calculation, the other referring to instructions of wanted result.

The following input data are required:

- Data for waterlines for which calculations are to be made. Since waterline division determines the accuracy of the master tabulation, values between calculated waterlines are retrieved by rectilinear interpolation.

- Trims for which displacement is desired. The trim is defined as the difference between draft fore and draft aft at the perpendiculars.
- Numering of frame
- Thickness of keel plate (displacement addition for shell plating can be calculated for different plate thicknesses)
- Appendix addition necessary in case of larger volume parts (for example rudder)
- Waterlines for which hydrostatic data are to be printed.

RESULTS

All calculated hydrostatic data are stored on magnetic tape. Results can be printed on lineprinter for given waterlines as follows:

- Draft measured from underside of keel in feet and inches
- Total displacement in tons in saltwater. *Total* means here the whole underwater body, including shell plating and appendices.
- The same as above but in fresh water
- Moulded displacement volume
- Tons per one-inch immersion in saltwater. (Information is calculated from total water planes, i.e. including shell plating.)
- The same as above but in fresh water
- Distance of centroid of water planes from midship section

- Longitudinal center of buoyancy from midship section. Calculation is made on total displacement.
- Center of buoyancy above base line
- Moment to alter trim one inch in saltwater
- The same as above in fresh water
- Transverse height of the metacenter above base line
- Longitudinal height of the metacenter above base line
- Transverse moment of inertia (molded)
- Longitudinal moment of inertia (molded)
- Block coefficient (molded)
- Prismatic coefficient (molded)
- Water planes coefficient (molded)
- Midship section coefficient (molded)
- Area of water planes (molded)
- Wetted surface of ship calculated from curve lines of frames
- Total displacement of aft body
- Total displacement of fore body
- Moment of aft body around $L/2$
- Moment of fore body around $L/2$.

Stability Data

METHOD DESCRIPTION

The program calculates stability data for arbitrary displacements, trims, and heeling angles.

The calculations begin with the definition of Simpson coefficients for frames which are to be included in the calculation. Then sectional areas and sectional area moments around the keel are calculated. These calculations are made for each heeling angle and displacement stated as input data. By interpolation in tables of area and moments, data for each trim position are received also.

INPUT DATA

Input data are given in two groups—one for calculation instructions and the other for printing instructions. Calculation instructions include:
- Stations which are to be lever-arm calculated
- Frame number according to the frame building program. (Lever-arm calculations can usually be made with satisfying accuracy with a smaller number of frames than those required, for instance, in calculations of displacement.)
- Heeling angles desired
- Data for waterlines
- Data for trim.

The second group gives information about desired results. Thus, results can be obtained in meters or in feet. Division can be given for displacement or for draft. If the center of gravity, KG, is given, GZ is obtained for actual displacements, trims, and heeling angles.

RESULTS

Calculated lever-arm data are stored to be used in printing results and for future use in calculations of damage stability. Stored data are displacement and moment of displacement around the keel.

Results are printed on a lineprinter. Output condition is stated by displacement and draft. For each trim position, a table is printed where the following results are obtained for each heeling angle:
- Draft at $Lbp/2$, which is the vertical distance from keel point to actual waterline
- Position of center of buoyancy from $Lpp/2$ (minus aft, plus fore).
- Lever arm, KN, which is the perpendicular distance from keel point to force line of the resultant upward buoyancy force
- Lever arm, $MS = KN - \overline{KM} \sin \phi$
- $\overline{GZ} = KN - KG \sin \phi$ is obtained for three different positions of the center of gravity of weight.

Calculation of Damage Stability

METHOD DESCRIPTION

Damage stability calculation is made by treating leakage water as an additional weight.

The calculation is made by stages in separate programs. Damage stability calculations are based on existing facts of the damage case, i.e. approximate corrections are not to be found. Thus, static righting moment for each trim position of the hull occurring after the actual damage case is calculated. Real heeling moments of inflow and liquids in the ship are calculated for actual heeling angles.

Since the input data supplied depend upon the specific damage involved, no explicit input instructions are given.

RESULTS

For each damage case, output is obtained showing:
- Identification of damage as well as certain constants
- Lever arm at certain displacements for various heeling angles

- Trim, which is the difference between draft fore and draft aft
- $\overline{GM}$ value before and after damage.

The information is written for the initial condition and for intermediate inflow periods. The number is decided in the input data, and finally for the balanced position after ended water inflow.

Calculation of Longitudinal Strength

METHOD DESCRIPTION

The program calculates moments and shear curves for the ship hull at still water at different weight conditions.

The ship is divided into a number of calculation parts. Within each of these parts, both cargo and resultant upward buoyancy force are supposed to be of constant intensity.

INPUT DATA

The hull form is described in the same way as for the calculation of hydrostatic data. Within each calculation part, light weight and load are given by the superposition of an arbitrary number of trapeziform loads. The size of the loads is given for an arbitrary number of weight conditions.

RESULTS

Either the whole moment or shear curve, or merely the maximum moment and the shear and their positions can be obtained as the result.

Expansion of Shell Plates

METHOD DESCRIPTION

The program for shell plate expansion replaces the manual work now being done for designing the plane shell plate when the bending shape is known. The possibilities of facilitating the shell plate expansion are utilized when the hull surface is mathematically faired and the joints have been defined by this hull description.

Besides producing a drawing tape and a cutting tape with appropriate coordinate tables, the plate weight, scrap percentage, cut length, etc. are calculated.

The program does not develop the most complicated plates of the hull. The most complex ones must be specially dealt with.

INPUT DATA

The program requires that complete information is given about the location of the plate joints in the hull. The ship hull is to be described by having the frames coded on punched cards. This means that the hull need not be mathematically faired; the offsets can be measured from a body plan and can be transferred to a numerical code by a drawing program. It is also possible to make a mathematical fairing of the hull. Then the directrices can be used as input at the calculation of the shell plate expansion, and the result will be greater accuracy in the expansion and shorter running times in the computer.

The routine generally will be a mathematical fairing of the hull at first. A body plan will be given as a result on which the seams will be drawn. These seams will then be described mathematically and used as input to the shell plate expansion program.

Some other information must also be given as input, for example

- Identification number of plate
- Tolerances of raw plate
- Starting point of expansion.
- Longitudinals
- Decks, etc. for which markings are desired on the plate
- Rolling and bending templates which are desired drawn.

RESULTS

The result of the shell plate expansion can be roughly divided into:
- Cutting tape
- Coordinate tables.

Tapes are obtained for:
- Contour of plate, points of intersection between plate edge and the rolling line (midship section, decks, stringers, and longitudinals will be marked).
- Inner marking lines
- Three rolling templates
- Two bending templates and the position of transversed joints will be marked.

Coordinate and measuring tables for:
- Points of contour (corner points specially marked), points of intersection as above
- Points of marking lines (two on the shell and one in the middle of the plate).

Miscellaneous:
- Weight, surface, and circumference of plate
- Dimensions and surface of the circumscribed rectangle
- Weight, dimensions, and surface of raw plate.

Calculation of Ship Tanks

METHOD DESCRIPTION

The program calculates volumes and coordinates of the center of gravity and transverse moments of inertia of the free liquid surface for arbitrary compartments and tanks at different filling degrees.

Results are stored on magnetic tape to be used at calculations of sounding and ullage. Forms of frames and bulkheads, which are stored, can be used for calculations of limitation curves for a number of cross-sections which are the basis for calculations of area and moment. Areas and moments of volume cross-sections around the baseline and centerline are calculated as functions of height above the baseline. Integration over ship length is made by Simpson coefficients. Then volumes are corrected with regard to area reductions, corrugated bulkheads, etc.

A center of gravity table containing the volume of the tank, position of the center of gravity, and the transverse moment of inertia with regard to the centerline is obtained as a result. On the basis of stored calculation results from the volume program, sounding and ullage tables can be obtained.

INPUT DATA

Required input data for the calculation are hull form and other surfaces limiting the tank. The program is based on data for hull form obtained from the hull fairing. Another requirement is the description of bulkhead forms (corrugated bulkheads, etc.) limiting the tank and the reductions which are possible to make.

If soundings and ullage tables are desired, input data describing length and position of the sounding tube and possible trim positions are required.

RESULTS

Tables of the center of gravity are printed on a lineprinter. It is possible to get these on paper-tape for a typewritten transcript. Results from calculations of sounding and ullage tables are printed on paper-tape for typewritten transcript.

The following result is obtained:

- Height above the baseline
- Volume
- Center of gravity·
- Transverse moment of inertia.

Hydrodynamic Computations

In addition to the preceding computations based on geometric forms and static considerations, the computer, both digital and analog, is extremely useful in such dynamic problems as resistance and propulsion, propeller calculations, seakeeping, etc.

Since most of these calculations fall in the area of research and are not normally a part of the design process except in special instances (as propeller design), they will be noted only briefly.

Propeller Calculations

These programs are based on the methods developed by Van Manen, Morgan, Kerwin, and others using their design chart data and theories.

Input data include engine power, ship speed, wake fraction, rpm, propeller diameter, cavitation limit, immersion depth, material, and blade pitch. (Not all this data is required for any single problem but it can be used, depending upon desired results.) The results may include efficiencies, reduction factors, pitch, weights, blade area, and inertia values.

GLOSSARY

FOR COMPUTER DESIGN

ACCESS, RANDOM—Obtaining data from or placing data into storage where time required is independent of location of information most recently obtained or stored.

ACCURACY—Degree of exactness of an approximation or measurement. Accuracy normally denotes absolute quality of computed results; precision refers to the amount of detail used in representing those results.

ADP—Automatic Data Processing.

ALGORITHMIC—Constructive calculating process usually assumed to lead to solution of problem in finite number of steps.

ALPHAMERIC—Contraction of alphanumeric and alphabetic-numeric. Characters which include letters of the alphabet, numerals, and other such symbols as punctuation or mathematical symbols.

ANALOG—Representation of numerical quantities by means of physical variables: translation, rotation, voltage, or resistance. Contrasted with digital.

ANALYSIS, NUMERICAL—Study of methods of obtaining useful quantitative solutions to mathematical problems, regardless of whether an analytic solution exists, and study of errors and bounds on errors in obtaining such solutions.

APPLICATION—System or problem to which a computer is applied. Reference is often made to an application as being either computational type, wherein arithmetic computations predominate, or data processing type, wherein data handling operations predominate.

AUTOMATION—(1) Implementation of processes by automatic means; (2) theory, art, or technique of making a process more automatic; (3) investiga-tion, design, development, application of methods of rendering processes automatic, self-moving, or self-controlling.

BINARY—Characteristic, property, or condition in which there are but two possible alternatives: binary number system using 2 as its base and using only digits zero and one.

CAPACITY, STORAGE—Number of elementary pieces of data that can be contained in storage device. Frequently defined in terms of characters in a particular code or words of fixed size.

CARD, PUNCH—Heavy stiff paper of constant size and shape, suitable for punching in a pattern that has meaning and that can be handled mechanically. Punched holes are sensed electrically by wire brushes, mechanically by metal fingers, or photo-electrically by photocells.

CHARACTER—(1) One symbol of a set of elementary symbols such as those corresponding to typewriter keys. Symbols usually include decimal digits 0 through 9, letters A through Z, punctuation marks, operation symbols, and any other single symbols which computer may read, store, or write: (2) electrical, magnetic, or mechanical profile used to represent character in a computer, and its various storage and peripheral devices. Character may be represented by a group of other elementary marks, such as bits or pulses.

CHART, FLOW—Graphic representation of the major steps of work in process. Illustrative symbols may represent documents, machines, or actions taken during process. The area of concentration is on where or who does what rather than how it is to be done.

COBOL—Common Business Oriented Language.

CODE—(1) System of symbols for meaningful communication; (2) system of symbols for representing data or instructions in a computer or tabulating machine; (3) to translate program for the solution of a problem on a given computer into a sequence of machine language or psuedo instructions and addresses acceptable to that computer; (4) machine language program.

COMPATIBILITY, EQUIPMENT—Characteristic of computers by which one computer may accept and process data prepared by another computer without conversion or code modification.

COMPILER—Computer program more powerful than an assembler. In addition to its translating function which is generally the same process as that used in an assembler, it is able to replace items of input with series of instructions (subroutines). Thus, where an assembler translates item for item, and produces as output the same number of instructions or constants which were put into it, a compiler will do more. Program which results from compiling is a translated and expanded version of the original.

COMPUTER—Device capable of accepting information, applying prescribed processes to that information, and supplying the results of these processes. It usually consists of input and output devices, storage, arithmetic, and logical units, and a control unit.

COMPUTER, ANALOG—Computer which represents variables by physical analogies. Any computer which solves problems by translating physical conditions such as flow, temperature, pressure, angular position, or voltage into related mechanical or electrical quantities and uses mechanical or electrical equivalent circuits as an analog for the physical phenomenon being investigated. Computer which generally uses an analog for each variable and procedures analogs as output. Thus an analog computer measures continuously whereas a digital computer counts discretely.

COMPUTER, DIGITAL—Computer which processes information represented by combinations of discrete or discontinuous data as compared with an analog computer for continuous data. A device for performing sequences of arithmetic and logical operations, not only on data but its own program. A stored program digital computer capable of performing sequences of internally stored instructions, as opposed to such calculators as card-programmed calculators, on which the sequence is impressed manually.

COMPUTER, GENERAL PURPOSE—Computer designed to solve a large variety of problems; a stored program computer which may be adapted to any of a very large class of applications.

COMPUTER, SPECIAL PURPOSE—Computer designed to solve a specific class or narrow range of problems.

CONFIGURATION—Group of machines which are interconnected and are programmed to operate as a system.

CONTROL, NUMERICAL—Descriptive of systems in which digital computers are used for the control of operations, particularly of automatic machines wherein the operation control is applied at discrete points in the operation or process.

CONVERSION—(1) Process of changing information from one form of representation to another, such as from the language of one type of machine to that of another or from tape to print; (2) process of changing from one data processing method to another, or from one type of equipment to another; conversion from punch card equipment to magnetic tape equipment.

DATA BASE—Storage, usually on magnetic tape or disk which is arranged to facilitate convenient access and update of individual data items. Data bases are usually designed for specific applications.

DIGITIZER—Electronic instrument for converting graphical coordinates to computer compatible numbers. Normally a special pen or cursor is touched to point on a drawing. The coordinates of the point are generated and transferred directly to the computer.

EDP—Electronic Data Processing.

EXECUTE—To interpret a machine instruction and perform the indicated operation(s) on the operand(s).

FORTRAN—FORmula TRANslator. Programming language designed for problems which can be expressed in algebraic notation allowing for exponentation up to three subscripts. The FORTRAN compiler is a routine for a given machine which accepts a program written in FORTRAN source language and produces a machine language routine object program. FORTRAN II added considerably to the power of the original language by giving it the ability to define and use almost unlimited hierarchies of subroutines, all sharing a common storage region if desired. Later improvements have added the use of Boolean expressions, and some capabilities for inserting symbolic machine language sequences within a source program.

GENERATOR, RANDOM NUMBER—Machine routine or hardware designed to produce a random number or series of random numbers to specified limitations.

GRAPHIC CRT DISPLAY—Device on which a computer can draw pictures, display graphics, and output text; some displays need to be refreshed much like a television, some actually store the created image directly on the screen.

IMAGE, CARD—Representation in storage of the holes punched in a card, so that the holes are represented by one binary digit and the unpunched spaces are represented by the other binary digit.

INPUT—(1) Information or data transferred or to be transferred from an external storage medium into internal storage of the computer; (2) describing the routines which direct input as defined in (1) or the devices from which such information is available to the computer; (3) device or collective set of devices necessary for input as defined in (1).

INPUT-OUTPUT—General term for the equipment used to communicate with a computer and the data involed in the communication.

INSTRUCTION—(1) Set of characters which defines as operation together with one or more addresses, or no address, and which, as a unit, causes the computer to perform the operation on the indicated quantities. "Instruction" is preferable to the terms "command" and "order"; "command" is reserved for a specific portion of the instruction word: the part which specifies the operation which is to be performed. Order is reserved for the ordering of the characters, implying sequence, or the order of the interpolation, or the order of the differential equation; (2) the operation or command to be executed by a computer, together with associated addresses, tags, and indices.

INTERFACE—Common boundary between automatic data processing systems or parts of a single system.

ITERATIVE—Procedure or process which repeatedly executes a series of operations until some condition is satisfied. Can be implemented by a loop in routine.

KEYPUNCH—(1) A special device to record information in cards or tape by punching holes in the cards or tape to represent letters, digits, and special characters; (2) to operate a device for punching holes in cards or tape.

LANGUAGE—System for representing and communicating information or data between people, or between people and machines. A system consists of a carefully defined set of characters and rules for combining them into larger units, such as words or expressions, and rules for word arrangement or usage to achieve specific meanings.

LANGUAGE, ALGORITHMIC—Arithmetic language by which numerical procedures may be precisely presented to a computer in a standard form. Language is intended as a means of directly presenting any numerical procedure to any suitable computer for which a compiler exists, and also to communicate numerical procedures among individuals. The language itself results from international cooperation to obtain a standardized algorithmic language.

LANGUAGE, PROBLEM ORIENTED—(1) Language designed for convenience of program specification in a general problem area rather than for easy conversion to machine instruction code. (Components of such language may bear little resemblance to machine instructions); (2) machine-independent language where one need only state the problem, not the how of solution.

MICROCOMPUTER—Small minicomputer with the processor usually contained on a single integrated circuit.

MINICOMPUTER—Inexpensive digital computer which utilizes 8–22 bit data and instruction words.

MULTIPROGRAMMING—Technique for handling numerous routines or programs simultaneously by an interweaving process.

OPERATION, PARALLEL—The performance of several actions, usually of a similar nature, simultaneously through provision of individual similar or identical devices for each such action. Particularly flow or processing of information. Parallel operation is performed to save time over serial operation. Parallel operation usually requires more equipment.

OPERATION, SEQUENTIAL—Performance of actions one after the other in time. The actions referred to are of a large scale as opposed to the smaller scale operations referred to by the term serial operation. For an example of sequential operation consider $A \times (B \times C)$. The two multiplications indicated follow each other sequentially. However, the processing of the individual digits in each multiplication may be either parallel or serial.

OPTIMIZATION—The process of finding the maximum or minimum of an objective function by examining the value of the function at various points according to a specific strategy.

OUTPUT—(1) Information transferred from internal storage of a computer to secondary or external storage, or to any device outside of the computer; (2) to transfer from internal storage on to external media.

PLOTTER—Visual display or board in which a dependent variable is graphed by an automatically controlled marker as a function of one or more variables.

PROCESS—General term covering such terms as assemble, compile, generate, interpret, and compute.

PROCESSING, REAL TIME—Processing of information or data in a sufficiently rapid manner so that the results of the processing are available in time to influence the process being monitored or controlled.

PROGRAM—Complete plan for the solution of a problem, more specifically the complete sequence of machine instructions and routines necessary to solve a problem.

RANDOM ACCESS—See *Access, random.*

READER, PAPER TAPE—Device capable of sensing information punched on a paper tape in the form of a series of holes.

SIMULATION—The representation of physical systems and phenomena by computers, models or other equipment; an imitative type of data processing in which an automatic computer is used as a model of some entity; a chemical process. Information enters the computer to represent the factors entering the real process, the computer produces information that represents the results of the process, and the processing done by the computer represents the process itself.

SOFTWARE—The totality of programs and routines used to extend the capabilities of computers, such as compilers, assemblers, narrators, routines, and subroutines; contrasted with hardware.

STORAGE—(1) The term preferred to memory; (2) pertaining to a device in which data can be stored and from which it can be obtained at a later time. The means of storing data may be chemical, electrical or mechanical; (3) a device consisting of electronic, electrostatic, electrical, hardware or other elements into which data may be entered, and from which data may be obtained as desired; (4) the erasable storage in any given computer.

STORAGE, MAGNETIC DISK—Storage system consisting of magnetically coated disks, on the surface of which information is stored in the form of magnetic spots arranged to represent binary data. These data are arranged in circular tracks around the disks and are accessible to reading and writing heads on an arm which can be moved mechanically to the desired disk and then to the desired track on that disk. Data from a given track are read or written sequentially as the disk rotates.

SUBROUTINE—(1) Set of instructions necessary to direct the computer to carry out a well-defined mathematical or logical operation; (2) subunit of a routine. A subroutine is often written in relative or symbolic coding even when the routine to which it belongs is not; (3) portion of a routine that causes a computer to carry out a well-defined mathematical or logical operation; (4) routine arranged so that control may be transferred to it from a master routine and so that, at the conclusion of the subroutine, control reverts to the master routine (usually called closed subroutine); (5) single routine may simultaneously be both a subroutine with respect to another routine and a master routine with respect to a third. Control is usually transferred to a single subroutine from more than one place in the master routine; the reason for using the subroutine is to avoid having to repeat the same sequence of instructions in different places in the master routine.

SYSTEM, INFORMATION—System for locating and selecting, on demand, certain documents or other graphic records relevant to a given information requirement from a file. Examples of information retrieval systems are classification, indexing, and machine searching systems.

SYSTEM, OPERATING—Integrated collection of service routines for supervising the sequencing of programs by a computer. Operating systems may perform debugging, input-output, accounting, compilation, and storage assignment tasks.

TAPE, PAPER—Strip of paper capable of storing or recording information. Storage may be in the form of punched holes, partially punched holes, carbonization or chemical change of impregnated material, or imprinting. Some paper tapes, such as punched paper tapes, are capable of being read by the input device of a computer or a transmitting device by sensing the pattern of holes which represent coded information.

TAPE, PUNCH—Tape, usually paper, upon which data may be stored in the form of punched holes. Hole locations are arranged in columns across the width of the tape. There are usually 5 to 8 positions (channels) per column, with data represented by a binary coded decimal system. All holes in a column are sensed simultaneously in a manner similar to that for punch cards.

TIME-SHARING—Use of a device for two or more purposes during the same overall time, accomplished by interspersing component actions in time.

Index

References to illustrations are in **boldface** type.